Essays on Old Testament Hermeneutics

Essays on
Old Testament
Hermeneutics

Edited by CLAUS WESTERMANN
English translation edited by
James Luther Mays

JOHN KNOX PRESS
Richmond, Virginia

Originally published as *Probleme alttestamentlicher Hermeneutik* by Chr. Kaiser Verlag, München, 1960.

Published in Great Britain under the title
Essays on Old Testament Interpretation.

Fourth printing 1969

The translations of the essays by von Rad, Noth, and Zimmerli, and Wolff's "The Hermeneutics of the Old Testament" first appeared in *Interpretation* and are used by permission of the editors of *Interpretation.*

The translation of the essay by Bultmann first appeared in the book *Essays Philosophical and Theological,* by Rudolf Bultmann, published by SCM Press and is used by permission.

Unless otherwise indicated, Scripture quotations are translated from the German. Those given in the Revised Standard Version are copyright 1946 and 1952 by the Division of Christian Education of the National Council of the Churches of Christ in the United States of America.

Standard Book Number: 8042-0108-X
Library of Congress Catalog Card Number: 63-10637
© M. E. Bratcher 1963
Printed in the United States of America

CONTENTS

LIST OF ABBREVIATIONS

ANET	*Ancient Near Eastern Texts*, ed. by J. B. Pritchard, Princeton, 1955[2]
AOT	*Altorientalische Texte zum AT*, hrsg. H. Gressmann
ATD	*Das Alte Testament Deutsch*, Neues Göttinger Bibelwerk
BEvTh	*Beiträge zur Evangelischen Theologie·*
BK	*Biblischer Kommentar*, Altes Testament, Neukirchen
BWANT	*Beiträge zur Wissenschaft vom Alten und Neuen Testament*
BZAW	*Beihefte zur Zeitschrift für alttestamentliche Wissenschaft*
cT	*Textconjecture*
EKL	*Evangelisches Kirchenlexikon*
ELKZ	*Evangelisch-Lutherische Kirchenzeitung*
EvTh	*Evangelische Theologie*
JBL	*Journal of Biblical Literature*, Philadelphia
JThSt	*The Journal of Theological Studies*, Oxford
KD	*Kirchliche Dogmatik*, Karl Barth
KuD	*Kerygma und Dogma*
NTD	*Das Neue Testament Deutsch*, Neues Göttinger Bibelwerk
RGG	*Die Religion in Geschichte und Gegenwart*
Schw. ThU	*Schweizer Theologische Umschau*
TGI	*Textbuch zur Geschichte Israels*, K. Galling, 1950
ThEx(h)	*Theologische Existenz heute*
ThLZ	*Theologische Literaturzeitung*
ThSt	*Theologische Studien*, hrsg. Karl Barth
ThZ	*Theologische Zeitschrift*, Basel
VuF	*Verkündigung und Forschung*
WA	*Weimarer Ausgabe der Werke Luthers*
ZAW	*Zeitschrift für die alttestamentliche Wissenschaft*
ZDPV	*Zeitschrift des deutschen Palästina-Vereins*
ZdZ	*Die Zeichen der Zeit*, Berlin
ZSTh	*Zeitschrift für systematische Theologie*
ZThK	*Zeitschrift für Theologie und Kirche*

PREFACE
by Claus Westermann

This collection of essays on understanding the Old Testament is occasioned in part by the fact that a number of them are no longer easily available. The wish has been expressed in many quarters that at least some voices which in the last decade have spoken concerning this matter, so important not only for the interpretation of the Old Testament but also for theology in general, might be heard again by means of a published collection. This book can be no more than the presentation of such a collection, and it is intended to serve no other purpose. It is offered as a workbook to furnish a basis for discussion about the recent investigation of the question concerning the understanding of the Old Testament. The essays which are included represent only the smallest selection from the many available. Only articles from journals have been used; portions from the numerous books which have dealt in significant fashion with the subject had to be omitted. A look at the bibliography at the end of this volume will give some indication of the scope of the publications which have dealt with this problem. Because of the limits of space, it has been impossible to include the important contributions which have been made in other lands outside Germany. The editor hopes that this collection will serve the ecumenical conversation about the understanding of the Old Testament. The bibliography is hardly, however, complete enough for this concern, especially in relationship to the long series of Catholic works on this theme.

The basic core of the collection is made up of essays which were published in the two issues of *Evangelische Theologie* of 1952, 1/2, in 1956, 8/9. The authors are co-workers on the *Biblischer Kommentar,* which is currently appearing. The sharpest opposing answer to the thesis of this circle, itself character-

ized by a rich variety, appeared in a series of works by F. Baumgärtel. The work of F. Hesse has been added in order to give
the viewpoint of Baumgärtel further support by one who follows
essentially the same line. The conversation between these various
positions about the question of the proper understanding of the
Old Testament is vitally important, as many of the essays clearly
demonstrate. The conversation reaches beyond the limits of Old
Testament science. The essays by R. Bultmann and W. Pannenberg show that precisely in the discussion of our problem a promising exchange between the practitioners of all theological disciplines has begun.

The question concerning *understanding* as such in theology
has moved to the center of its various disciplines and has become
the focus of theological work in many lands and churches during the last two decades This has its basis, not only in theological and ecclesiastical presuppositions, but also in a deep and
broad intellectual environment characteristic of our period in
history. In a certain sense, the question about *understanding* as
such is an expression of the situation of the churches in a sec-
ularized world. They begin to see that they do not work and
exist for themselves alone and in terms of themselves, but must
engage in a confrontation with others and turn to men as they
are—men who do not live in terms of religious structures, nor
speak a religious language. It is a very hopeful sign that in thinking about this question of understanding, i.e., the hermeneutical
question, all theological disciplines are concerned and at work,
and that in this work after a long interval biblical and systematic
theology once again attend and converse with each other. It is
something new, at least as seen from within Germany, that in
journals which serve the field of dogmatics one reads exegetical
investigations of the Old and New Testaments, and that in con-
ferences devoted to one particular theological discipline themes
are handled which are concerned with bringing exegesis and
dogmatics once again nearer to each other.

It is to this larger context that the discussion concerning the
understanding of the Old Testament belongs. The essays in this
volume often make it apparent that the question must be put

within the perspectives of a comprehensive horizon spanning all of theology. We can recognize here the changed form of a question which concerned intensively the past generation of Old Testament scholars: How is the historical philological exegesis of the writings of the Old Testament related to biblical theology or, more particularly, a theology of the Old Testament? The new way of putting the question is more precise, but that has had the effect of making the disagreements about answering the question even more pronounced. Probably the disagreements between those who describe their positions in this collection are stronger than their agreements. As a common point of departure, all affirm that "the Old Testament must be allowed to tell its own story." Every one of the contributors emphasizes that all means of historical philological explanation of the text must be used, but this common assumption by no means indicates a fundamental agreement. The story which the Old Testament itself requires one to tell looks very different to different investigators. The current debate within the Old Testament research appears to concentrate particularly on two questions: What is the relationship between the story of the acts of God as testified to by the people of God, on the one hand, and the history of Israel as the historical research of our time sees it, on the other? And the second question: Can the interpretation of the Old Testament, in presupposing a unity of Old and New Testaments as the Bible of Christianity, presuppose some one concept which will guide and determine interpretation as a whole—some one concept, for instance, such as typological exposition? Is the relationship of the Old Testament to the New Testament essentially simple or is it complex?

An agreement has been reached that the relationship of Old Testament and New Testament research to each other is not to be seen from only one side. Those who are working in the field of the Old Testament view their work in relationship to the New Testament, and vice versa. How the Old Testament is heard, appropriated, and interpreted in the New can no longer be a matter of indifference to the Old Testament scholar, nor can the New Testament interpreter any longer be unconcerned about whence come the concepts, images, forms of speech, and names which are met in almost every text of the New Testament. It is commonly said today that in order to understand the Old Testament we have to listen to the New, and that in order to be able to interpret the New Testament we must know the Old. In this matter a fundamental and broad agreement has been reached. But to see how various are the conclusions which one draws from this recognition, one has only to compare the contrasting theses of Zimmerli and Bultmann in their reviews of the relationship of both Testaments to each other.

Just at this point a very crucial distinction between German and English theological traditions appears. A separation of New Testament study from Old Testament exegesis and theology has existed longer in Germany and has created sharper differences in theological thinking and conceptions than in English-language theological tradition. An intensive confrontation of both traditions, which this translation is meant to serve, may produce both clarifications and demands for both. For the present, however, it is a fact that in German theological work concepts and thought in the fields of Old Testament and New Testament theology are widely separated (I know, for instance, of no German work which treats the history of Old Testament and New Testament research in one presentation, as the last two chapters of J. D. Smart's *The Interpretation of Scripture* do). It appears to me that a point of particular difficulty here is the understanding of history. Today's leading New Testament scholars understand history in a punctual manner, as is indicated by their concepts of historicity, decision, understanding of the self, and so forth. In contrast, Old Testament research can understand history only as a line, as an extension which can in no wise be reduced to a punctual event. In this matter there are deeply rooted disagreements to be overcome which have their inevitable effect on the understanding of God's Word and action, on the interpretation of tradition and worship.

Finally, there are certainly the great difficulties which have to be surmounted in bringing the exegesis of the Old and New Testaments into a clear and well-based and consistent relationship to systematic theology. In an earlier time one could describe this relationship in the following fashion: the exegete of the Old and the New Testament had the responsibility simply of placing his results at the disposal of dogmatics, somewhat in the fashion of hewn stones, which the systematician could then incorporate in the structure of doctrine. This definition of the relationship is no longer possible for us; the problem has become much more complex. And we are still far from a fundamental clarification. One thing can now be said for certain: those who work on the text of the Bible can no longer ignore the fact that the *traditionsgeschichtliche* aspect of their work points them inevitably to the church, its doctrine, its confessions, and its worship. They find in the Bible formulated confessions, a fullness of liturgical forms and developments, doctrine, and preaching; and it can be said on the other side that contemporary doctrine of the church can no more ignore the way which has led to contemporary worship, confession, preaching, and dogma. It can no longer be disregarded that this is not presented in the Bible in the form of a timeless doctrine or an unhistorical dogma, or in the form of a definition fixed once for all. Rather, in the Old as in the New Testament, it appears as a history, with changes and contradictions, with heights and depths, the history of God with his people which continues in the history of the church until it comes to that consummation toward which the Bible points.

CLAUS WESTERMANN

PREFACE
by James Luther Mays

Four of the articles in this collection appeared first in English translation in the 1961 issues of *Interpretation*. The interest and appreciation which their publication evoked is one of the reasons for the preparation of an English translation of the entire volume. Another is the scarcity of writing in English on Old Testament hermeneutics. The translators and publisher hope that the availability of these essays will give a fresh stimulus to work on the problems with which the book is concerned, and they believe that it is a valuable source book for reading in the area.

The English edition is not completely identical with the original. Whereas G. von Rad's article was published in abridged form, it has been reproduced here in its entirety because of its relative inaccessibility to most English readers. The final essay in the German edition ("Das Prophetische," by S. Herrmann) has been omitted since it dealt in detail with problems peculiar to the Continental situation. The bibliography at the end of the book has been revised to include some of the relevant literature in English, and some of the items included in the original have been omitted to bring the whole within reasonable limits. Professor Westermann has written the above Preface especially for this edition; the editor of the English version is responsible for its translation.

Since the articles of Stamm and Vriezen review a work not available in English (A. A. van Ruler's *Die christliche Kirche und das Alte Testament*), there is a certain awkwardness in retaining them in this edition. But van Ruler's book is significant, not only because of the position it describes, but because it approaches the problem from the side of dogmatics. Neglect of his proposal would have meant a serious lacuna in the book, and the reviews describe his position fairly as well as criticize it.

James Luther Mays

15

1.

TYPOLOGICAL INTERPRETATION
OF THE OLD TESTAMENT*
by Gerhard von Rad

translated by John Bright

1. It might be well to make it clear at the outset that what we are accustomed to understand under the heading of typology is, in the broad sense, by no means a specifically theological concern or, indeed, a peculiarity of ancient Oriental thought. Rather, typological thinking is an elementary function of all human thought and interpretation. It is, for example, employed in a certain respect in our proverbs, which continually relate a not immediately controllable multiplicity of things to something relatively or absolutely normative, and thus enable us to discern the order that is nevertheless immanent in them. And, above all, without this interpretive, analogical sort of thinking there would be no poetry. The poet goes ceaselessly to and fro; he sees the often insignificant, obvious things and recognizes in them ultimate value. In the movements of the elements, the passing of the years and the days, in the most elementary relationships of man with man, in simple mechanical performances—in everything regularity "reveals" itself, and hints at an order that dwells deep within things, in which the smallest as well as the greatest things participate. Schiller's "Song of the Bell" is an especially beautiful example of this most elementary poetic procedure. It is the world of the mechanical, of the unspiritual, of performances bound by rigid law—yet all of this to the highest degree charged and symbolically powerful and, in any case, re-

* For a later and fuller treatment of the matters covered in this paper, cf. Professor von Rad's *Theologie des Alten Testaments*, Band II, Chr. Kaiser Verlag, München (1960), pp. 329-424. This article appeared originally in *Evangelische Theologie* (Jahrgang 12, 1952, Juli/August), Heft 1/2, pp. 6 ff.

lated through and through to a Higher, to a final order in the
spiritual, which, as has been said, can be seen everywhere delineated, by him who has the vision, in the very mechanical performances which are, in themselves, so difficult to invest with
meaning. The theological or pseudotheological presuppositions
of this poetic mode of interpretation ought to be of interest to
theologians too, for concern here is continually with revelations,
and with the belief that the world that immediately surrounds
man possesses transparence. The spiritual heritage of the Platonic
doctrine of ideas is ever and again to be recognized in this form
of interpretation which has become so familiar to us: The soul
before its entry into the realm of the corporeal has beheld the
ideas—that which is immutable and alone truly exists—and so
is able to remember them once more on viewing their images.

2. We encounter quite another form of this analogical thinking in the ancient Orient. There we find the mythological conception of an all-embracing correspondence between the heavenly
on the one hand, and the earthly on the other. This "is so of
the notion that, in conformity with the law of the correspondence
of macrocosm and microcosm, the prototypes of all countries,
rivers, cities, and temples exist in heaven in the form of certain
astral figures, while those on earth are only copies of them."[1]
This notion of correspondence, according to which what is below
is only a copy of what is above, perhaps appears in the building
inscriptions of the Sidonian kings Bodashtart and Eshmunazar,
where *shmm rmm* ("high heaven") and *shmm 'drm* ("mag-
nificent heaven") are used to designate parts of the city. Earthly
Sidon is only the copy of its heavenly prototype.[2] So too, the
sixth tablet of the Babylonian Epic of Creation points out how
the city of Babylon and its sanctuary had first been founded in
the world above. The city of Berytos (Beirut) is still called in a

---

[1] B. Meissner, *Babylonien und Assyrien*, I, p. 110.
[2] Lidzbarski, *Altsemitische Texte*, I, pp. 16 ff., 19 f. O. Eissfeldt, *Ras
Schamra und Sanchunjaton*, pp. 62 ff. My colleague Herr Falkenstein calls
my attention to a Sumerian text according to which an earthly temple, in its
measurements, takes up half the space of its heavenly prototype. Langdon,
Oxford Editions of Cuneiform Inscriptions, p. 53, lines 13-14. This may well
be the oldest illustration of that impulse toward an increase in the ratio
between type and its antitype.

late Hellenistic poem *aitheros eikōn*.[3] This sort of mythological-speculative typology remained almost entirely foreign to ancient Israel. Only in the later writings of the Old Testament do certain reminiscences of such conceptions crop up. The clearest example is the *tabnit*, the model of the tabernacle that was shown by God to Moses on Sinai (Exod. 25:9, 40). One might also think of the scroll that was handed to Ezekiel (Ezek. 2:8 ff.); his message had thus a pre-existence with God as a heavenly book. But what we have here is scarcely more than a rudimentary relic of that all-embracing mythological conceptual world, with which Yahwistic faith plainly could establish no real relationship.

The Old Testament, on the contrary, is dominated by an essentially different form of typological thinking, namely, that of the eschatological correspondence between beginning and end (*Urzeit und Endzeit*). Isaiah and Amos speak of the eschatological return of paradise (Isa. 11:6-8; Amos 9:13), Amos of the return of the pristine David ("as in the days of old," Amos 9:11, R.S.V.), Hosea and Deutero-Isaiah of the return of the wilderness days (Hos. 2:16-20; Isa. 52:11 f.), and Isaiah of the return of the old Davidic Jerusalem (Isa. 1:21-26). But what is generally known need not be repeated here. To be sure, many distinctions in detail should be made in this connection. One should distinguish between the recapture of a primeval state, and the repetition of primeval events, whereby the *Urzeit* is at a stroke pushed into the beginning of Israel's *Heilsgeschichte* (Passover, wilderness period, David); and it should be asked whether, and for what reason, the second of these two ideas is the dominant one. And the relationship of the prophetic predictions to this form of typological thinking ought to be generally investigated. Is every Messianic prophecy a prophecy of the return of David, as it indeed seems to be in Isaiah 11:1, and certainly is in Jeremiah 30:9 and Ezekiel 34:23 f.? Where, and since when, was there the impulse to a heightening in the relationship between type and antitype (compare Isa. 52:12, "not in anxious haste," with Exod. 12:11)? The night visions of Zechariah (Zech. 1-6) exhibit a quite

---

3 O. Eissfeldt, *op. cit.*, pp. 109 ff.

unique mixing of mythical-speculative, and historical-eschato-
logical, typological thinking. Zechariah beheld in a single night,
compactly yet fully, the final events of *Heilsgeschichte,* and it
is thereby made clear that all eschatological benefits are already
pre-existently present in heaven, although on earth no sign
could yet be seen of God's zeal for the completion of his purpose
in history (Zech. 1:11).

Whether one must, with Bultmann, connect this sort of typological thinking first of all with the ancient Oriental theory of
world-periods is, however, very questionable.[4] Is the linear way
from type to antitype really to be designated as a cyclic occurrence? The components of every Old Testament witness, so
inalienably historical in character, do not at all permit a consistently developed notion of a repetition. Indeed, one must see
the basic ideas of typology less in the notion of "repetition" than
in that of "correspondence." In the one case, the earthly gains
its legitimatization through its correspondence with the heavenly;
in the other, the relationship of correspondence is a temporal
one: The primeval event is a type of the final event.

3. The new thing in the New Testament is the application
of this theological thought-form to a book, to the canon of the
Old Testament, although this theological-eschatological, analogical way of thinking itself is, as we have seen, prepared for in a
far-reaching way by the Old Testament's own self-understanding.
It is, in our opinion, the merit of Goppelt's book that it pointed
out the prevalence and the variety of this typological way of
thinking in the New Testament.[5] The New Testament narrators, often expressly, but often tacitly, parallel Old Testament
events, and they presuppose of the reader that he will know of
this (as said, often hidden) relationship of correspondence, and
will reflect upon it. This referring to the typical in the Old Testament goes far beyond the use of actual citations—just as one
often finds himself at the limit to which he may go with the
very notion of citations in this connection. (Is "And he gave

4 ThLZ (1950), p. 205.
5 L. Goppelt, *Typos (Die typologishe Deutung des Alten Testaments im
Neuen)* (1939) ; further, C. T. Fritsch in *Bibliotheca Sacra (A Theological
Quarterly)* (1947), pp. 87 ff.

him to his mother," Luke 7:15b, r.s.v., a citation from 1 Kings 17:23, or merely the place at which the narrator in his account moved especially close to the Old Testament model?) It is clear how this theological way of thinking accorded to the Old Testament prototype no less than the character of a source for the portrayal of the final consummating event. In the Passion narrative, as is well known, Psalm 22 is called upon, even to biographical details, as a source for the suffering of the eschatological Anointed One. On the other hand, the New Testament in manifold ways witnesses to the impulse toward a heightening between type and antitype. Everyone knows that in it no impossible attempt is made to set forth the gospel at any price in Old Testament dress. Neither Matthew nor Paul was hindered by the typological way of thinking from expressing what had come to pass with Christ that was different and new.

Allegory, on the other hand, falls strikingly into the background in the New Testament. Hermeneutically, a quite different evaluation is to be placed on allegory, for it is characterized by a much more rigid attachment to the text, indeed to the very letter of it, quite as much as it is by its unbridled freedom in matters of spiritual interpretation. Typology, on the contrary, shows itself to be astoundingly free of attachment to the word or the letter, yet bound to a much greater degree by the historical sense.[6] Indeed, with its much stronger attachment to history, it is concerned with tying onto facts, not with spiritual truths. Allegory is a much more rationalistic phenomenon.[7]

Having thus stressed the great importance of the New Testament's typological way of understanding things, the astounding fact must be pointed out on the other hand that the New Testament—as open as it was toward the Old—nevertheless fails al-

---

[6] Goppelt, *op. cit.,* p. 8 ; Cullmann, *Christ and Time,* pp. 131 ff.

[7] Joh. Gerhard gives the following definitions: *"Typus est, cum factum aliquod Vet. Test. ostenditur, praesignificasse seu adumbrasse aliquid gestum vel gerendum in Nov. Test. Allegoria est, cum aliquid ex Vet. vel Nov. Test. exponitur sensu novo atque accomodatur ad spiritualem doctrinam s. vitae institutionem. Typus consistit in factorum collatione. Allegoria occupatur non tam in factis, quam in ipsis concionibus, e quibus doctrinam utilem et reconditam depromit."* *Loci Theologici* (Cotta) Tom. I, p. 69, cited by A. T. Hartmann, *Die enge Verbindung des Alten Testaments mit dem Neuen* (1831), p. 632.

most entirely to provide any norm, any handy rule, for its interpretation. The New Testament thus stands as no milepost in the history of hermeneutics, unless it was that it saw in Christ the end of all methodical scribal learning. They who are "in Christ" have themselves already been drawn into this end-time, and they rely only on the Spirit of the Resurrected One, who interprets the Scripture for them with sovereign power.[8]

4. Our present-day theological point of view concerning the Old Testament still exhibits throughout the character imparted to it by the revolution brought about by rationalism. Luther, through his return to the literal sense, inaugurated for those who came after him a new epoch in the typological interpretation of the Old Testament; and Calvin, with his far more methodical exegesis, created a whole tradition of typological interpretation of the Old Testament which, as is well known, reached a particularly high point with Cocceius (1603-69).[9] But this typologizing, practiced on a broad basis by those of the Lutheran and Reformed traditions alike, came to a sudden end in rationalism, particularly through the work of Michaelis and Semler. From this point on, typology—with which, indeed, the church had even previously found itself no longer happy—was fully discredited. About 1755, to be sure, Michaelis wrote an *Entwurf der typischen Gottesgelahrtheit;* but this very book showed with special clarity the change that had come about, for, while Joh. Gerhard had linked typology with facts, Michaelis is concerned with "the religious truths" symbolically enshrined in the Old Testament.[10] Nothing is more characteristic of this degenerate sort of typology than the relinquishment of the attempt to relate the types to the New Testament (that is, their limitation to the Old), already observable in Michaelis. The spiritual truth contained in this Old Testament symbolism was,

[8] G. Ebeling, *Evangelische Evangelienauslegung,* pp. 101-110.
[9] On Luther, H. Bornkamm, *Luther und das Alte Testament,* pp. 74 ff. On Calvin, H. H. Wolf, *Die Einheit des Bundes (Das Verhältnis von A. und N. T. bei Calvin)* (1942). On Cocceius, G. Schrenk, *Gottesreich und Bund im älteren Protestantismus* (1923).
[10] J. D. Michaelis, *Entwurf der typischen Gottesgelahrtheit* (1763). At this time a clear distinction had ceased to be made between type, allegory, and symbol. Cf. C. T. Fritsch, *op. cit.,* pp. 216 ff.

without further ado, to be interpreted for itself. And Semler said of typology, "He who assumes no types . . . is deprived of nothing whatever; and even he who is most fond of typology cannot, for all that, place it among the fundamentals of Christianity."[11]

It was at this time that Old Testament interpretation lost all connection with the facts witnessed to in the New Testament, and this it has not won back until today. What was left was a connection with the teachings of the New Testament, with its religious ideas, with the "fundamentals of Christianity."[12] What now comes into play in the interpretation of the Old Testament is another form of analogical thinking: that of historical method. Troeltsch has expressed it with great clarity:

> Historical method, once . . . applied to biblical study, is a leaven that transforms everything, and finally shatters the whole framework of theological method as this has existed hitherto.
>
> Three essential points are in question here: habituation to historical criticism in principle, the significance of analogy, and the correlation that exists between all historical occurrences. . . . The means whereby criticism is possible at all is the employment of analogy. The analogy of what takes place before our eyes . . . is the key to criticism. Delusions . . . the formation of myths, fraud, factions, which we see before our eyes, are the means of recognizing similar things in the traditions. Agreement with normal, customary, or at least repeatedly attested ways of occurrence . . . as we know them, is the mark of likelihood for occurrences which criticism can acknowledge as actually having happened. Observation of analogies between similar occurrences of the past makes it possible to ascribe to them likelihood, and to explain what is unknown from what is not. This almightiness of analogy, however, in-

---

[11] A. H. Sykes, *Paraphrasis des Briefes an die Hebräer,* tr. by J. D. Semler (1779), p. 86, note 96.

[12] The great exception, the theology of J. Chr. Karl Hofmann—its closeness to the tasks set for us today and its distance from them—cannot be discussed here in such brief compass.

cludes in principle the similarity of all historical events, which is, to be sure, not likeness . . . but presupposes in each instance a kernel of common similarity by virtue of which even the differences can be sympathetically grasped.[13]

For our considerations, the statement about the significance and almighty power of analogy is important. It is superfluous to remark that it was through this method that the picture of Israel, its history and literature, which we consider historically adequate, was first developed. It is superfluous, therefore, to rush to the defense of this historical method. That this "almightiness of analogy" could not stop short of the investigation of inner and spiritual concepts, thus of Israel's religion, was only logical. There is, therefore, no cause for complaint that a more and more methodical science of comparative religion arose, for in this area, too, that new analogical way of thinking has bestowed upon us insights with which we would never be willing to part. The thing became insidious only where there lay at the bottom of this comparative procedure a hidden theological *pathos,* where Israel's religion was placed at "the peak of all ancient religions" and recognized as "the flower of all ancient religions" which "in the hand of the Master became the tool for shaping the absolute religion."[14] What is odd about such statements, and countless similar ones, is not the comparative method as such, which is everywhere employed; what is odd is rather the change in the object with which theology is now occupied. In order to give an account to Christendom of its belief with regard to the content and significance of the Old Testament, theology now points to Israel's religion. But that is right off to be accounted simply as a quite insidious reduction of the content of the Old Testament as it actually speaks to us. An entire dimension—the fullness of its witness to history—is excluded. Characteristic of this reduction is its seizing upon the spiritual, upon teachings, truths, conceptions of God, the world, man, sin, and the like. But it is nevertheless, as will be shown below, nothing more than a mere reduction.

---

[13] Ernst Troeltsch, *Über historische und dogmatische Methode* (1898); *Gesammelte Schriften,* II, pp. 729 ff.
[14] R. Kittel, ZAW (1921), pp. 96 ff.

Now it is our opinion that, in this regard, in spite of numerous changes in the posing of questions, as well as in the results achieved in the area of Old Testament theology, nothing fundamental has been altered even today. L. Köhler says in the first sentence of his *Theologie des Alten Testaments,* in his precise way, "One can call a book a theology of the Old Testament if it offers a compilation, justified by its contents and rightly organized, of those ideas, thoughts, and concepts of the Old Testament which are, or are capable of being, theologically important."[15] Procksch, to be sure, gives the "world of history" considerable space in his large work, but, aside from the fact that one can seriously question the theological relevance of the representation of history as Procksch gives it, he too devotes more space to his second part, which he entitles "The Thought World," than he does to this first part.[16] But, we would ask, is the object of a theology of the Old Testament correctly fixed if we see our task as that of stressing "thoughts, ideas, and concepts," or in describing a "thought world" of the Old Testament? We still stand here under the sway of that notion of religion which stems from rationalism, and which ought to be submitted to a much sharper criticism than it has been; and in such a reorientation the Old Testament is to the highest degree helpful to us.

5. The Old Testament is a history book. It portrays a history brought to pass by God's Word, from creation to the coming of the Son of Man. It may not be superfluous to remark that even the prophetic books are "history books," insofar as they do not seek to transmit teachings, truths, or the like, but rather to portray eschatological events in advance.

We see how the ancestors of Israel were called by the divine Word, and how in obedience to further divine words they wandered thither and yon; we see the promise of great posterity come to fulfillment, and Israel become a people. Then we see this people wandering at God's direction, and we see offices and institutions coming into being within it, founded by God's Word. In other words, we see this people continually driven, moved

---

15 L. Köhler, *Theologie des Alten Testaments,* p. v.
16 O. Procksch, *Theologie des Alten Testaments* (1950).

about, shaped, reshaped, destroyed, and resurrected through the
divine Word that ever and again came to it.[17]

This is one thing. The other is that we see prophets who in
ever more concentrated fashion predicted the consummation of
history; and these predictions, again, are concerned with this
same people of God, its institutions and offices, only now in the
last and final form in which God will establish them after apocalyptic judgment. This type of prophecy is for Christian theology
naturally the principal link between Old Testament and New,
since the witness of the New Testament itself designates Christ's
appearance in the flesh as the fulfillment of the prophetic predictions. But the question now has to do with the scope that we
may accord to the concept of prophecy. Certainly one must begin
with the prophetic predictions, that is, those prophetic utterances
that are directed toward the future. But Christian belief also
asks after the redemptive significance of the Old Testament's
witness to past history and present, that is, after the significance
of those passages that treat of the numerous facts of history already brought to pass by God's published Word. Indeed, it must
ask after these things, for prophetic prediction is related to these
witnesses to history in the most intimate way. Prophecy proceeds,
in fact, precisely from the creative Word of God, as the sole
power that can bring about judgment and redemption; for its
own part, it speaks ever and again of those very institutions and
offices which God had to begin with founded within the framework of Israel's history. It is therefore merely the connecting link
that binds together the witness to God, and to his judgment and
redemption (which, as said, had already broken into Israel's
history continually), and projects it into the eschatological, in
that—constantly basing itself upon what God had already accomplished—it speaks of God's final work with relation to Israel. But
since this is the case, can any fundamental theological distinction
be made between prophetic prediction on the one hand, and
witness to past history on the other? This article, however, aims

---

[17] We speak here only of the understanding of her history which Israel
herself set down as a witness.

primarily at posing the question of the redemptive significance of the Old Testament witness to past history and present.

6. We begin with a view of the matter which is certainly widely held today, and which Althaus, for instance, has formulated in a programmatic way: "The Old Testament has a pastoral significance for Christendom insofar as it is the deposit of a history of faith, under God's tutelage, which moves away from the bonds of nationalism and particularism, on toward the gospel."[18] Now that is certainly an aspect of the matter, the correctness of which is not to be contested. The Old Testament is indeed the picture book of a history of faith, and one of inexhaustible fullness. But if one asks what it finally and truly is, above all if one questions it regarding its own kerygmatic intention, the concept of a history of faith no longer suffices.

The Old Testament historical work whose theological tendency we can most easily grasp is the Deuteronomistic history. If we question it—especially the two books of Kings—as to its purpose, that is, as to what theological concern this exilic historical school had, the concept of a "history of faith" is at once excluded, while that of a cult—or temple—history is seen to be equally inappropriate. Rather, one sees that what is given here is a history of the creative Word of God, that is, a course of history is described which is determined by a whole pattern of mutually corresponding prophetic promises and divine fulfillments. What interests these historians is the precise functioning in history of the Word as proclaimed by the prophets. In a positively classical manner the concept of *Heilsgeschichte* is here sketched as a course of history which is kept in motion, and guided to its God-ordained goal, by the constantly intruding divine Word.[19] The older historico-theological delineations are to be distinguished from the Deuteronomic only in that the theological-programmatic element is lacking in them, or at least is not explicitly evident. The great history of the "Succession to the Throne of David" (2 Sam. 6—1 Kings 2) shows the first outworkings of

---

[18] P. Althaus, *Die christliche Wahrheit*, I, pp. 229, 240.
[19] In greater detail, von Rad, *Studies in Deuteronomy*, pp. 52 ff.

Nathan's prophecy (2 Sam. 7).[20] And it is well known how Yahwist and Elohist trace a history that is set in motion by the
promise to the patriarchs and guided on to the conquest of the
land. The word to Abraham in Genesis 12:3a ("I will bless those
who bless you, and him who curses you I will curse," R.S.V.) is of
great importance here, for it means to say: God's judgment and
redemption have now entered history; judgment and redemption
are determined by the attitude adopted toward the historical fact
of Israel. According to Deutero-Isaiah, too, the peoples confess,
"God is with you only, and there is no other" (Isa. 45:14, R.S.V.).
So Israel understood the course of her own history; she saw it not
as a history of faith, but rather she saw herself snatched up into a
divine history in which she was continually led by God's Word
from promise to fulfillment.

Before we continue this line of thought, a critical remark
must be made regarding the exegesis of historical texts of this
sort. The very return from an exegesis based on the history of
religions to a theological exegesis has led us in our day into a new
danger zone, for exegesis now feels itself under the necessity of
drawing from the narrative some "meaning," some "ideology," or
whatever you wish to call it, that can be entered on the credit
side of the ledger, theologically speaking. An excellent example
of this sort of thing is the interpretation of the Genesis narratives
by H. Frey (in many respects very useful). This is marked by a
very lively theological interpretation of each and every detail;
every single situation, every action or failure to act, every turning
this way or that, is—with the aid of penetrating interspersed comments based on the psychology of religion—brought into play
theologically. Yet, for all that, one has to ask whether the patriarchal narratives do not rather quickly set fixed limits to direct
theological interpretation, in that the narrator as a rule refuses
with a positively heroic firmness to give us any foothold for a
spiritual interpretation, but rather confines himself to portray-
ing the events in a dramatic way. The story of Hagar (Gen. 16),
or that of Abram's endangering the life of Sarai, ancestress of the

---

[20] L. Rost, *Die Überlieferung von der Thronnachfolge Davids*, pp. 82 ff.

people (Gen. 12:10-20), or that of Jacob's trickery (Gen. 27), and many others of the sort, seem like tightly closed mussels in their lack of any interpretation at all. To be sure, the entire Hexateuch, and especially the traditionary complex of the patriarchal narratives, is organized around quite definite theological themes; but these are anything but an adequate key for the interpretation of the intricate pattern of the stories and happenings in detail. They do suffice to let us see the event as a divine event, but they do not remotely suffice for an understanding of the "How" and the "Why." Did these narrators (with the exception of P) really mean to say anything essentially more than this: It happened then just so, for so Yahweh ordained it? That raises the question if we, with our hankering after interpretations that will establish some additional meaning, some truth over and above the facts given, do not overlook something quite essential, namely, the strongly cryptic character that these narratives to such a large degree have. What the Yahwist himself had in mind in these narratives is often impossible to determine. To what degree was he conscious, to what degree was Jacob conscious, of the significance of the events of Genesis 27? And what do we understand of the life of Isaac? We read only a few stories and then, later, the notice of his death—thus that he who had been laid by his father on God's altar carried the secret of his life with him to the grave. Where can any interpretation find firm footing here? The intelligible factor, the contribution of the narrator to interpretation, is for the most part minimal. In order to interpret such deeply cryptic happenings, must one not go much farther, rather than looking for an interpretation from the Yahwist himself? The fact that he has clothed the narratives in a dress seemingly so untheological represents, certainly, a far greater achievement than if he had charged them with the profoundest of reflections. And so we are threatened here with a new spiritualizing, not much better than that old "religious" spiritualizing which we think ourselves fortunate to have outgrown. Both of Israel's late theologies, the Priestly Document and the Chronicler's history, could teach us a lesson here: The way in which they tap about the rock-hard shell of the tradition might cause us to ponder, and give us a new impression of how profoundly hidden the divine meaning of this history is. One likes to talk of ancient Israel's encounter with God. But was the human partner in this encounter then really conscious of this and in control of it? Is the gripping narrative of the Yahwist, in spite of the long history of tradition that lay between him and the event, much more than a preliminary sketch of God's footprints in the early history of Israel? What did he know of the cultic theology of the Priestly Document, or of prophecy, or of the sufferings of Job? Who, then, in ancient Israel really encountered the God of Israel, the Father of Jesus Christ?

7. We return now to the words "only in you is God" and to our rejection of the concept "history of faith" [that is, as a description of the content of the Old Testament].* Just what does this *'ak bāk 'ēl wᵉēn ʿōd* (Isa. 45:14) embrace, in detail and in particular, if one would bring out its meaning? If one were to answer this question as many of our theologies would, one would say: What was peculiarly Israel's was its "idea of God," or a peculiar form of relationship with God ("God and man"), or a peculiar form of religious and moral sensibility, or the like. In other words, we have defined this indwelling of God in Israel almost exclusively in terms of the intellectual and spiritual. But, though such formulations are not without support in the Old Testament, they nevertheless require decided supplementation. If one frees himself from the associations of this spiritual conception of religion, one sees that the Old Testament depicts the peculiar thing vouchsafed by Yahweh to the people Israel in quite another way. It lies in the marvel of the real indwelling and gracious presence of God (Exod. 29:42 ff.; 1 Kings 8:12 f.); it lies in the revelation of his righteous will, in the *doxa* of his redemptive dealings in history, in the promise and constant provision of all sorts of redemptive benefits, etc. It is, in our opinion, precisely of these latter things that Old Testament theology ought to say a great deal more than it has. In the patriarchal narrative of the Yahwist it is the promise of great posterity and possession of

---

* Translator's addition.

the land that runs through the whole like a *cantus firmus* (the "I will be your God," Genesis 17:7, is introduced first in P). In Deuteronomy the gifts promised to Israel are the land, blessing, and rest from all enemies round about (Deut. 12:9; 25:19). Further to be mentioned are gifts conditioned by special historical situations, such as the manna in the wilderness, protection in holy war, and, finally, the eschatological prophecies:

> For behold, I create new heavens and a new earth; and the former things shall not be remembered or come into mind. But [they will] be glad and rejoice forever in that which I create; for behold, I create Jerusalem a rejoicing, and her people a joy. I will rejoice in Jerusalem, and be glad in my people; no more shall be heard in it the sound of weeping and the cry of distress. No more shall there be in it an infant that lives but a few days, or an old man who does not fill out his days, for the child shall die a hundred years old, and the sinner a hundred years old shall be accursed. They shall build houses and inhabit them; they shall plant vineyards and eat their fruit (Isa. 65:17-21, R.S.V.).

The same thing is true of the benefits which the individual expects from Yahweh: life (*ḥayyim*) and well-being (*shalom*). Nowhere do we encounter the material and this-worldly quality of the Old Testament redemptive benefits in so striking a way as in those accounts that concern the purchase of land.[21] Into the circumstantial realism of such transactions no pious syllable intrudes; and yet everything is supported by an emotion that is sacral through and through. Here are the stable givens, about which the thought and the theological reflection of the earliest as well as the latest periods revolve. In the Old Testament's view of the matter, it is for the sake of these things, that is, for their realization, that the *Heilsgeschichte* itself takes place. Naturally Israel had a religious "thought world" too, that is, a concern to comprehend these redemptive benefits, an effort to understand and appropriate them. And since succeeding generations posed

---

[21] Gen. 23 ; Jer. 32 :7 ff. ; Gen. 33 :18 f. ; 2 Sam. 24 :24 ; Ruth 4 :3 ff.

the problem of apprehension afresh, one cannot, for that reason, speak of that thought world as a static thing, but rather as something variable and changeable. Just how is it with all the various complexes of ideas relating to God, man, death, sin, and forgiveness? It cannot fail to strike one how much of this was given Israel only for a fixed term, only until it was once more shattered by perplexing upheavals from the depths. But that is only to say that this thought world was always something secondary as over against what happened to Israel along the way, and as over against the redemptive benefits held out before her. And to all of this there attaches the hermeneutical consideration that we can on the basis of the sources reconstruct a religion of Israel, and her world of piety, for the most part only indirectly, that is, by abstracting from the actual kerygmatic intention of the writings—which, as we have seen, are concerned with emphasizing the acts of God.

8. If one wishes to be fair to the theological thought world of Israel, one must mention its constant reference to the real redemptive benefits. Israel did not, indeed, rest content with a single fixed understanding of these historical gifts. Rather, a continual process of reworking is to be observed, one that was never finished but ever led to new interpretations. The gift of manna was understood in the older tradition as a miracle of physical feeding, and the occurrence has there the gravity of something once-for-all in redemptive history (Exod. 16:1-5, 13b-16a). The source P, on the contrary, sees in the transaction something typical, something that occurred ever and again as God's people received his gifts (that each got his share, that none had too much and none too little, that it could not be stored up, Exodus 16:6-13a, 16b-26). Again, Israel attached to the figure of Samuel almost every office that was in any way adaptable to him: that of seer, of judge, of prophet, and of Levite.[22] Again and yet again she felt impelled to explain this phenomenon within *Heilsgeschichte,* as if what took place in Israel in and through Samuel could be satisfactorily subsumed under none of the

---

[22] 1 Sam. 9:11 ff.; 7:15 f.; 3:20; 1 Chron. 6:18 ff.

offices that stood ready to hand. (Would not the Christian understand and approve of this searching and groping and pondering? But more of that later.)

There is yet another peculiarity having to do with the promised benefits themselves. It is not at all as if such promises only, so to speak, moved on before Israel, and remained till the end something to be hoped for. On the contrary, Israel told of manifold instances of divinely given fulfillment that had already been brought to pass in history. The most outstanding example of all is the fulfillment of the ancient promise of the land, concerning which the book of Joshua asserts in a positively pedantic fashion that everything promised had been fulfilled, and that nothing was lacking (Joshua 21:43 ff.; 23:14). Yet this historical fulfillment notably did not diminish the actuality of the promise that had once been given; it did not fall before the law of history. Rather, the promise of land, in spite of its initial fulfillment, remained in force for Israel. In Josiah's day, Israel is addressed by Deuteronomy as if she stood in every respect still prior to the fulfillment of the promise of land, as if "rest from all your enemies round about" (Deut. 12:9; 25:19, R.S.V.) had not yet been given. And Balaam depicts the blessings of Israel's well-watered and fertile land so exuberantly that one might suppose that he was not speaking of the niggardly Palestinian hill country at all, but positively of paradise:

How fair are your tents, O Jacob, your encampments, O Israel! Like valleys that stretch afar, like gardens beside a river, like "oaks" that the Lord has planted, like cedars beside the waters. Water flows from his buckets; his posterity has plentiful water (Num. 24:5-7).

It was through the prophets that a division of God's dealings with Israel into an initial and a final phase was then carried out. Thus Deutero-Isaiah prophesied of a second Exodus, which would take place to the accompaniment of yet more marvelous signs than did the first (Isa. 52:11 f.). Hosea, too, set the first wilderness sojourn over against a final one: Yahweh would again lead Israel into the wilderness, where his people, once more having been made entirely dependent upon him, would then accept the life-giving benefits from his hands, not from the gods of fertility (Hos. 2:16-20). From such passages as these, and many other similar ones, one sees that already within the Old Testament the dumb facts of history had become prophetic, and had come to be viewed as prototypes to which a new and more complete redemptive act of God would correspond. Thus all is in motion. Things are never used up, but their very fulfillment gives rise, all unexpected, to the promise of yet greater things (for example, so the monarchy founded by God gives rise to the promise of the final Anointed One). Here nothing carries its ultimate meaning in itself, but is ever the earnest of yet greater wonders.

In this connection still another characteristic peculiarity of the portrayal of God's dealings in history, and of the redemptive events, must be mentioned. The narrators are so captivated by the *doxa* of the event that once happened, they see and point out in the event the splendor of the divine gift in so exclusive a way, that they thereby manifestly misdraw the historical picture. There is, therefore, in the portrayal of the facts very frequently something that transcends what actually occurred. The narrator, or better—since it is something that for the most part took place on a far broader basis—the "tradition," is so zealous for God that the event is straightway broadened into the typical. It is precisely sober exegesis that must come across things of this sort and make the effort to understand what has taken place. In the book of Judges, the judges are portrayed as charismatic bearers of a theocratic office that embraced all of Israel—something that went far beyond their actual territorial sphere of influence. Yet the text itself lets it be seen quite clearly how much more limited, in time as well as space, their activity was. In the book of Joshua the entry into the Promised Land under Joshua is so described as if Israel entered Canaan *en bloc* under unified leadership. That contradicts the older portrayal, according to which the conquest was achieved through individual action on the part of separate groups (Judges 1:1 ff.). In such cases interpretation must concern itself, perhaps more than heretofore, with what is intended by that later portrayal. Clearly a *credendum* has here been projected into history. That is to say, the redemptive activity of God toward Israel has been portrayed as the unity that it was believed to be; a *doxa* is heaped on the event which reaches far beyond what actually occurred, for what is believed in is placed on view as something already effectuated in history. Conversely, the statements of the Psalms of lament far transcend any individual's personal experience, to the point of drawing a paradigmatic picture of the misery of being utterly forsaken by God. To be sure, an exceeding of the facts aimed at pointing up some glorious act of God that has been made manifest, occurs more frequently in the Old Testament. But, one way or the other, such statements tend markedly toward the radical. If one asks what human motives were involved, a certain exuberance, or that natural impulse to magnify or glorify historical events, may assuredly have played a part. But the exegete cannot pass over the fact that these statements are nevertheless now set forth with the claim to witness to a unique action of God in history. And for that reason one must, if one has taken careful cognizance of this entire phenomenon, speak quite precisely of an eschatological impulse in such portrayals, insofar as they introduce a definitive action of God as something already real in history.

9. At this point the question automatically imposes itself: What part have I in the Old Testament as a Christian believer, and what part has the church, if it cannot be that I identify myself, at least partly (it was never a question of more than that!), with the religion of ancient Israel? If I yield myself to the Old Testament's own kerygmatic intention, I must, as we have seen, ask what part I have in its witness to historical facts, and to the redemptive benefits promised to Israel. But I belong to none of the twelve tribes, I do not offer sacrifice in Jerusalem, nor do I hope in terms of Isaiah 2:1-4 for the glorification of the Temple mountain. I am not even a proselyte, and so able to appropriate for myself the greathearted consolation of Trito-Isaiah (Isa. 56:1-8). In other words, I have not "come to a mountain that can be touched" (Heb. 12:18). God's gracious provisions, so lavishly bestowed on Israel, seem to pass me by, because I do not belong to the historical people Israel; and the Old Testament maintains its connection with this historical Israel to its very last word. Is it

not possible that a great unease will once more make itself felt
in many of our congregations, instructed as they have been for so
long, an unease from which this inadequate teaching of the religion of Israel has up till now protected them?

The result of our reflections concerning the Old Testament's
various witnesses to past history and present (those that are
directly prophetic have concerned us only peripherally) can,
therefore, not be that we recognize in them a thought world that
is "very nearly that of the New Testament." Rather we see everywhere in this history brought to pass by God's Word, in acts of
judgment and acts of redemption alike, the prefiguration of the
Christ-event of the New Testament. That is the only analogy—
to return to the problem of analogy posed at the beginning—that
offers itself for a theological interpretation of these texts. This
renewed recognition of types in the Old Testament is no ped-
dling of secret lore, no digging up of miracles, but is simply
correspondent to the belief that the same God who revealed himself in Christ has also left his footprints in the history of the Old
Testament covenant people—that we have to do with *one* divine
discourse, here to the fathers through the prophets, there to us
through Christ (Heb. 1:1). We must now, in a few words, define
more precisely what this means:

(a) Typological interpretation will thus in a fundamental way
leave the historical self-understanding of the Old Testament texts
in question behind, and go beyond it. It sees in the Old Testament facts something in preparation, something sketching itself
out, of which the Old Testament witness is not itself aware, because it lies quite beyond its purview.

(b) Typological interpretation has to do with the entire Old
Testament; any restriction of it to a "high religion," or any
blocking out of the "priestly, cultic religion," is impossible.
Wherever one of God's dealings with his people, or with an individual, is witnessed to, the possibility exists of seeing in this a
shadow of the New Testament revelation of Christ. The number
of Old Testament types is unlimited.

(c) But typological interpretation has to do only with the
witness to the divine event, not with such correspondences in

historical, cultural, or archaeological details as the Old Testament and the New may have in common. It must hold itself to the kerygma that is intended, and not fix upon the narrative details with the aid of which the kerygma is set forth. It is precisely at this point that, as it is used in the church, it frequently runs wild and becomes an overly subtle exhibition of cleverness. Typological interpretation, both in Old Testament and in New, does not fix upon historical or biographical details, but confines itself to the *credenda*. Yet the reference of Old Testament statements to the New is not restricted to the person and life of Christ, but embraces the entire Christ-event as this is witnessed to in the New Testament, including its ecclesiological aspect.

(d) Typological interpretation is aware of the difference between the redemptive benefits of the Old Testament and those of the New; it is aware of the way in which limitations upon salvation are removed in the new covenant; above all, it is aware of the incompleteness of the old covenant, in which God had not yet implanted his precepts in the hearts and wills of men (Jer. 31:31 ff.); it is aware both of the lack of complete obedience and of the preponderance of the law in the Old Testament. But it sees in the time-conditioned benefits (land, rest, long life, and the like) foreshadowings of eternal salvation. It sees, too, in the manner in which God provides, in his mysterious leading, in the postponement of his gifts as well as in the marvel of his help, prefigurements of the grace and providence extended to those who are in Christ. Even in details, both the Christian community and individual Christians see in the temptations as well as in the consolations that came to the Old Testament people of God a prefigurement of their own existence in this world.

(e) But though typological interpretation transcends the self-understanding of the Old Testament text, it is not on that account to be divorced in any fundamental way from the process of exegesis. Naturally, it cannot serve as a heuristic principle for the elucidation of particular philological and historical problems. Yet an equally earnest warning must be issued against a sharp separation of typological interpretation from the historico-critical exegetical process, as if the one began only when the other had finished its work. As a matter of fact, both processes—that is, both of these seemingly mutually exclusive forms of analogical thinking—interlock. We face the undeniable fact that so very often even the best "historical" exegesis is achieved from a theological point of view—that is to say, in the final analysis, from the side of the Christian faith. At what other place would Old Testament exegesis reckon with Paul's word about the veil (2 Cor. 3:7 ff.)? At what point in its interpretive process does Christian interpretation think itself distinguishable from Jewish?

(f) Typological interpretation frees Old Testament exegesis from the compelling constraint always, in order to be theologically relevant, to bring into the discussion some meaning, some truth beyond that inherent in the event itself. But exegesis not infrequently has to do with texts that describe events but that give little or no interpretative comment. Exegesis must face up to this; and in the very fact that it makes it clear how this phenomenon—that the narrator has offered only a bare event—is to be understood, it shows itself theologically significant.

(g) Regarding the handling of this sort of typological interpretation in the case of individual texts, no pedagogical norm can or may be set up; it cannot be further regulated hermeneutically, but takes place in the freedom of the Holy Spirit.[23]

(h) Typological interpretation confronts today a much more complicated state of affairs, exegetically speaking, than formerly, and must for its part pass on to yet finer theological distinctions. Whether the term "typology" will be retained permanently for what has been outlined in this article, whether the very word is perhaps too heavily burdened with wrong connotations, or has here been so far broadened beyond its established usage as to complicate rather than to further the discussion, is an open question. It has been used here because it seemed the part of candor thus to establish a link with the old hermeneutical tradition, which ever and again shows itself to be more appropriate to the Old Testament witness than our theological spiritualizing. Should the term

---

[23] Concerning the only standard that Calvin names in this connection, the *communis lex Dei*, cf. H. H. Wolf, *Die Einheit des Bundes (Das Verhältnis von Altem und Neuem Testament bei Calvin)* (1942), pp. 123 f.

prove to be intolerable, it will then be equally incumbent on its opponents and on its friends to be prepared to give their precise reasons for this.

One must therefore—at last to use the controversial word—really speak of a witness of the Old Testament to Christ, for our knowledge of Christ is incomplete without the witness of the Old Testament. Christ is given to us only through the double witness of the choir of those who await and those who remember. There is an estimate of, and a verdict with regard to, the "truth contained in" the Old Testament that betrays from the outset a false understanding, for it proceeds from the assumption that Christ is given to us, and known by us, in the New Testament, and that one then needs only to define the worth of the Old Testament and its posture with regard to this Christ. But the Old Testament must first of all be heard in its witness to the creative Word of God in history; and in these dealings of God in history, in his acts of judgment as well as in his acts of redemption, we may everywhere discern what is already a Christ-event.

The beginning of the road that might lead us out of the confusion and the weakness of our understanding of the Old Testament would appear to look something like this.

2.

THE INTERPRETATION OF
THE OLD TESTAMENT
A Historical Introduction
by *Claus Westermann*

translated by Dietrich Ritschl

First, a general picture should be drawn of the background of the present discussion about the understanding of the Old Testament. The Christian faith as such does not demand the scientific investigation of the Old Testament. The church, before and after the Reformation, was able to live without the scientific discipline of Old Testament studies. Neither Luther nor the Roman Church of his day had a particular view of the Old Testament or a set of particular questions concerning it.[1] These only emerged when the church encountered the scientific study of history.

The Western world received through the Enlightenment the consciousness of historical periods and interrelations. This was comparable to the disclosure of a new dimension. For a church based on Scripture, this analysis of thought in terms of historical periods and correlations had to be important. The hearers of the Bible at the time of the Reformation were basically unaware of the interval between the Old and New Testaments; the obvious historical facts and the chronological sequences were of course seen by the Reformers and the orthodox theologians, but no theological importance was attached to them. When, however, all events of history came to be seen in historical perspective, the events reported in the Bible could no longer be ignored. The central events of the Bible are too closely connected with historical data to exclude them from the increasingly fluid picture of history and to continue to regard them as being on one

---

[1] *Vide* H. Bornkamm, *Luther und das Alte Testament* (1948).

plane, as was done before the disclosure of the new historical dimension.[2]

Two conclusions result from this fact. We cannot turn back from this disclosure of deep dimensions of history. We cannot turn back from the knowledge that the words and stories from Genesis to Malachi are not on a plane, as it were, but part of a path. We cannot turn back from the knowledge that much has been changed on this path—language, the forms of community, in a certain sense the thinking and the thought-forms, and the relation of Israel to the world around it. For instance, we can no longer disregard the fact that the prophet Amos lived in the eighth century and the prophet Haggai in the sixth: one before, the other after, the Exile. The historical environment of the prophecy of the former as well as the latter cannot be regarded as irrelevant for our understanding of the words of prophecy, and it can never become so again. We cannot bypass the fact that the forms of worship as depicted in the work of the Chronicler belong to a later period, that is to say, the sacrifice of Isaac would have been impossible at that time. The words of Ecclesiastes breathe so unmistakably the spirit of a later time that it is no longer possible for us to think of them as deriving from early Israel. This distinction of periods became something indispensable for us. It does not change the situation even when the setting of a text of the Bible is not certain for us.

On the other hand, however, we must not absolutize the historical point of view. It would be a distortion of the facts if we said that before the time of historical research the biblical stories were understood wrongly and after it they were understood correctly. One could speak so only in the enthusiasm of the

---

[2] The question about the relevance of historical periods for the study of the Bible was seen for the first time clearly and with all implications by Johann Philipp Gabler in his academic inaugural address at Altdorf in 1787: *"De justo discrimine theologiae biblicae et dogmaticae regendisque recte utriusque finibus."* He advocated there for the first time a complete separation between biblical theology and dogmatics; this implied that he demanded that biblical theology be understood as a historical science (p. 183): *Est theologia biblica e genere historico.* . . . All essential principles of such historical investigations are already present: distinction between authors, time periods, and even the historical description of concepts. Moreover, even form analysis is understood in principle, when Gabler demands that the *singula dicendi genera* be examined.

Enlightenment with which we should by now have become disenchanted. If one thing is clear, then, it is this: Our historical view is conditioned by our time and has its limitations in this fact. Listening to the Bible with historical judgment (i.e., critical listening) has become a necessity for us. But it would be wrong if we claimed to have found in this the only correct, absolute, and always valid method of biblical interpretation.

But the most significant change in the understanding of the Bible since the Reformation has not been the coming of historical criticism as such; rather it was the concept of history of religion which followed it. The Reformers were not in the least aware of the question which is posed to the Christian church by the existence of the many religions. It was not before the Enlightenment that the critical mind faced the existence of the religions. The concept and the practice of tolerance, which accepts as a fact variety of religions, is only thinkable in a time of enlightenment. And it was in fact at this time that the modern concept of "religion" was molded: religion as a concrete fact, and this always in a plural form, as, by analogy, the phenomena of different languages. These religions were seen as a part of history in this newly discovered sense. They had come into being and had passed away, and in their coming and going one could observe laws which correspond to the laws of historical growth and decline. The religions in their manifold appearances and historical dynamics were the content of what is called "history of religions." This was a discovery which the Christian church could not disregard. The plurality as well as the historical movements of the religions could not be denied. This new understanding of the history of religions soon began to gain the upper hand even deep within theology. It became manifest, for example, in Old Testament studies, when the so-called theology of the Old Testament changed over into the history of religion of the Old Testament, and later to the religion of Israel. This implied that the Old Testament was but the historical source of one of the many religions, and that the religion of Israel became but a sector of the general history of religions. One deliberately neglected the fact that this book was still for the major part of mankind an authentic authority, namely, part of their Bible. The "history of religions" school considered this fact as unimportant for the understanding of the Bible, many times even an obstacle.

With all this it should not be said that the "religio-historical school" has not brought to light and made understandable much in the Old Testament which was hidden before and which will have to be maintained as an essential achievement not to be surrendered. But for the whole understanding of the Old Testament this school's limitation was in its all-determining concept of "religion."

Now something very strange happened: The very foundation upon which the concept of history of religions had developed and which had been the basis of the theological work of the teachers and scholars of this school began to be shaken. The basic presupposition was challenged and threatened in such a way that it could no longer be maintained that the foundations of our own faith could be leveled and relativized as merely one religion among many others. Powerful forces emerged which insistently raised the question: Are we historians of religion actually dealing with something that gives us life and is worth dying for? "How is our own God, that is, our own faith, related to this history of religions?" This question emerged quite unexpectedly from a new direction. The historians of religion were forced from the outside, as it were, to face the question of whether the God of their section of history of religion was really that God who could today give shelter and consolation to the distressed. At this turning point it is primarily the appeal of Rudolf Kittel that deserves to be mentioned. Soon after the First World War he confronted the scholars in the field of Old Testament with this basic question.[3] Now, a regressive trend occurred: Old Testament theology began to move back into the center and it was generally felt that an "Old Testament history of religion" would not suffice. But a real clarification was not reached by this new turn. There came a long period of transition during which no basic

---

[3] R. Kittel, "Die Zukunft der alttestamentlichen Wissenschaft," ZAW, 39 (1921), pp. 84 ff., and F. Baumgärtel, *Verheissung. Zur Frage des evangelischen Verständnisses des Alten Testaments* (1952), p. 135.

solutions were produced. This is well exemplified by the fact that the "history of religion" school was the last one in Germany to produce great commentaries, and that only in our day, after thirty years, preparations for new commentaries are being made. This period of transition is characterized by an unsolved and unclear parallel position of history of religion and theology.

It is against this background that one must understand the present situation that seems to be just the beginning of the search for the understanding of the Old Testament. Our situation is determined on the one hand by the discovery of the historical perspective which also includes so-called religion, and on the other hand by the realization that we must inevitably speak of the Old Testament theologically, answering the question of whether and in what way the God of which and for which the Old Testament speaks is the same God on whom Jesus calls in the New Testament and the God of the creed of the Christian church.

If we ask what all these new approaches have in common, we are literally pushed to the answer that basic to all approaches is the insight that the Old Testament reports history or a story or events that happened.[4]

Noth: ". . . the biblical witness according to which God reveals himself in historical events, and not in ageless myths or in a system of propositions. It ignores the fact that the Old Testament, to a surprisingly large extent, consists of historical narratives . . ." (p. 78).

Von Rad: "The Old Testament is a history book. It portrays a history brought to pass by God's Word, from creation to the coming of the Son of Man . . . even the prophetical books are 'history books' . . ." (p. 25).

Zimmerli: "When we survey the entire Old Testament, we find ourselves involved in a great history of movement from promise toward fulfillment" (pp. 111-112).

". . . the hidden knowledge of being underway from promise toward fulfillment in the framework of the history of Yahweh with his people . . ." (p. 109).

---

4 This, it seems to me, is also the presupposition of Bultmann's work.

Two more scholars should be mentioned to show that the same basic thesis has also moved into the foreground in other camps.

The first one is Martin Buber: "What is preserved for us here is to be regarded not as the 'historization' of a myth or of a cult drama, nor is it to be explained as the transposition of something originally beyond time into historical time: a great history-faith does not come into the world through interpretation of the extra-historical as historical, but by receiving an occurrence experienced as a 'wonder,' that is as an event which cannot be grasped except as an act of God. . . . Something happened to us . . . we can only believe it" [*The Prophetic Faith*, Harper Torchbooks, p. 46].

Or a comment on the Temple sermon of Jeremiah (Jer. 7): "His words here simply mean this, that God does not attach decisive importance to 'religion'! . . . He desires no religion, He desires a human people" [p. 172].

"YHWH is a God living in history. He does not fix history from the sphere on the yonder side and strange to it. He does not allow history to be unrolled as a scroll, but He Himself enters into it, and conquers it" [p. 211].

It is obvious that M. Buber is also concerned with God's history with his people in the Old Testament. However, there must be a reservation: It sometimes seems as if this very simple fact, the acting of God in history, were pushed into the background in favor of the human side in terms of "history of faith." He says in the introduction: "The history of Israel's faith is narrated . . . in the Bible." This shift of the accent to the human side of history is elsewhere even more strongly expressed; cf. especially H. J. Kraus, *Evangelische Theologie*, 12 (1952/53), pp. 59 ff.: "*Gespräch mit Martin Buber.*" Nevertheless, it can be said generally that Buber sees in the Old Testament the record of a history, of the history of God with his people.

From a totally different direction comes the work of G. Ernest Wright, *God Who Acts* (London, 1952), in which the Old Testament is still in a stronger and more embracing way conceived of as a record of the history of God with his people. He says in his introduction: ". . . Biblical theology, while it is not propositional and systematic dogmatics, is nevertheless a defensible entity of its own kind. . . . It is a theology of recital or proclamation of the acts of God . . ." (p. 11); or: "Hence it is here maintained that Biblical theology is *the confessional recital of the redemptive acts of God* in a particular history . . ." (p. 13).

"The realism of the Bible consists in its close attention to the facts of history and of tradition because these facts are the facts of God" (p. 38).

The author is primarily concerned with demonstrating the significance of this view of the Old Testament to theology and the church in general. In the wholeness of the acting of God he sees the essential relation between the two Testaments. ". . . one of the most important tasks of the Church today is to lay hold upon a Biblically centered theology . . . in which both Testaments are held together in an organic manner" (pp. 29-30). Such a biblical theology, in his opinion, can no longer be a system of thoughts, but a theology of recital, in which determinating events in one's own history are recited as the saving act of God in his history with his people.

In the light of the fact that all these new approaches are more or less opposed to the mere historico-religious view of the Old Testament, it is at first sight really surprising that the concept of history plays such an important role in all the quotations mentioned above! This is only understandable if—consciously or unconsciously—the significance of the notion of history has been changed. When von Rad says: "The Old Testament is a history book" (p. 25), he makes it clear in the next sentence that he uses a concept of history different from that of the historian of the 19th century. "It portrays a history brought to pass by God's Word, from creation to the coming of the Son of Man." The same absolute connection between history and the Word of God is stressed by Zimmerli: Christ is the final fulfillment insofar as in him "the Word of God . . . has become wholly event, and the event that is the Word of God, wholly and completely" (p. 113). Noth, too, says (pp. 87 ff.): ". . . to which saving acts belong also the promising and the demanding Word of God . . ." (though the connection between Word of God and history of God is not so stressed here).

Here is the decisive point. We ask: What is "a history caused by the Word of God"? What is history if it is understood as the movement between promise and fulfillment, i.e., between the Word that comes from God and the fact that is caused by God? One must be aware that this definition and concept of history denies the 19th-century concept of history.

It may become clear at this point that we are actually concerned with a new beginning. On the one hand, the science of Old Testament studies has acknowledged without reservation the movement toward historical thinking. It is accepted as a fact that the Old Testament can never again be interpreted without reference to the historical interrelations as did the fathers of the Reformation and the period of Orthodoxy. On the other hand, however, Old Testament scholarship has liberated itself (or is in the process of doing so) from embracing a concept of history which believes it can exclude the question about the working of God while examining and describing the history of mankind. Therefore it can no longer be admitted that the history reported in the Old Testament is "history of religion" or "history of salvation" in the sense of a sector of history. On the contrary, it is a part of history, a part of world history, within which no single factor proves objectively that in it God works in a unique way— least of all the Word of God as a controllable and available entity!

This is to say that neither the religion of Israel nor its piety, nor the thoughts about God contained in the Old Testament; neither the sum of all statements about God, cast into a kind of system, nor an all-determining theological principle, makes this book the witness of the history of God with his people, but only —daring and risky as it may sound—the acting of God which cannot be grasped in any of these categories. His acting can only be witnessed and confessed and can only be passed on in witness and confession!

But one can only speak meaningfully about this intervention of God in history if it is connected with the Word. Those who experienced the deliverance at the Red Sea, and later generations, could *not* confess, praise, and pass on this event as an act of God, solely because they *believed* God had acted, or because they had a conviction or a feeling. They could do this only for the *sole* reason that this salvation had word-character, i.e., because this deliverance was promised them in the hour of distress, and they could therefore experience it as fulfillment of the promise, or as the happening of the predicted. This connection is of decisive importance for the understanding of the Old Testament. The fact that a historical event is witnessed to be an act of God can in the Old Testament never—at least never exclusively—be proved because the people who were involved had certain thoughts, experiences, or beliefs. This is not a sufficient foundation to carry a creed! Rather the only basis for a creed is this: that a *factum* is recognized as a *dictum*. The saving act at the Red Sea *began* with this—that a Word came to a man (Exod. 3:7 f.): "I have *seen* the affliction of my people who are in Egypt, and have *heard* their cry because of their taskmasters; I know their sufferings, *and I have come down to deliver them out of the hand of the Egyptians . . .*"

Only through the relation with the promising Word and solely through the relation with it does the historical fact become God's acting; it is only in this way that a "history of God with his people" comes into being. The continuity of this history lies in nothing else than in the overarching connection which binds the promise to the happening of the promised. This is why in the present discussion about the interpretation of the Old Testament the double concept of promise and fulfillment stands in the foreground.

The first one of these concepts indicates a speaking, the second one a happening (or an acting). And here is the basic problem in the present search for understanding the Old Testament: How is the Word of God, addressed to man, related to the (historical) event? How are God's Word and history related? The period of Orthodoxy thought the Word of God in the Old Testament was available without any concern for history. Without any hesitation words were taken out of their context and served as proof texts for statements in dogmatics. The exact opposite happened in the period of theological work which began with the Enlightenment. What was actually and essentially valid was no longer the Word of God, but history. "God's Word" became dependent upon historical thinking. If it contradicted the historical event or development which had been proved as true, it could not have been correct. Both periods did not really listen to the Old Testament, because both claimed to know about it in advance. One time it was on the basis of a timeless and valid dogmatics, the other time it was because of a dogmatical concept of history which assumed that the human spirit could grasp and master history by way of thinking. The time of these two extremes is over, and now begins the laborious task of asking step by step what actually the Old Testament itself is saying in its texts about the relation between the Word of God and history.

3.

PROPHECY AND FULFILLMENT*
by Rudolf Bultmann

translated by James C. G. Greig

I

The primitive Christian community lived in the conviction that the prophecies of the Old Testament had been fulfilled in its time, that is, the appearance of Jesus Christ, in his death and Resurrection, and in the same way in its own existence and destinies; or, insofar as the fulfillment still remains outstanding, that they will shortly be fulfilled in the *parousia* of Christ.

According to the conception which prevails in the New Testament and in the tradition of the church, prophecy is understood to be the forecasting of a future happening, and fulfillment is the occurrence of what has been forecast. And if the prophecy is authorized by God, it is to a certain extent a promise of God's, which finds its fulfillment in what happens later.

For the New Testament a double truth is self-evident in this: (1) The future with which the Old Testament prophecies are concerned is the *eschaton*, the Messianic age, and this has *become the present* for the Christian community, the *ekklēsia* of God. (See 1 Cor. 10:11.) The prophecies of the Old Testament are, therefore, in this sense all Messianic prophecies.

(2) The Old Testament does not contain prophecy only in those passages which are prophecies in the proper sense of the word, that is, in the threats and promises of the prophets; rather is it a *book of prophecy as a whole*, the utterances of which, whether they are reports or complaints or whatever they may be, become recognizable as prophecies. In this sense Paul says: "For whatever was written in former days was written for our in-

---
* *Studia Theologica*, II (1949), pp. 21-44, and again, *Zeitschrift für Theologie und Kirche* (1950), pp. 360-383.

struction . . ." (Rom. 15:4, R.S.V.), that is (following vs. 3), because we can learn from it that what happened in Christ corresponds to prophecy.

If the New Testament in the first instance, i.e., in the understanding of the prophecies of the prophets as referring to the
eschatological age of salvation, follows *the Jewish tradition of
the Old Testament,* in the second instance it follows the Stoic
tradition of Hellenistic culture. This *last* developed the tradition
of *investigating* old texts vested with authoritative value for
truths, which were far from the minds of the authors of these
texts themselves and were actually not contained in the texts at
all, but must be read out of them—or, better, read into them!—by
more or less artificial or forced interpretation, by *allegorizing.*
This method was taken over by Hellenistic Jewry and applied to
the Old Testament. Where Philo uses the method of allegorizing
to derive from their reading of the Old Testament timeless
truths of theology, cosmology, anthropology, and ethics, the New
Testament uses it to find Messianic prophecies. In every case it is
clear that what is already known is derived from reading of the
texts. But people want to find it in the old texts so that it can
count as authoritative truth. The difference between the New
Testament and Philo is simply that, throughout, for the former
it is not a question of giving validity to general truths, but of
demonstrating that the events of the present are based—and so
predetermined—on God's plan of salvation, thus taking from
these events any offensiveness that might be theirs, and indeed
turning the offense into its opposite, into a confirmation of the
certainty of salvation. But the method is the same.

Some examples may illustrate what has been said.

The first form—seeing the fulfillment of *prophecies of the
prophets* as having come to pass in the story of Jesus—is the one
which is typical for Matthew, as it is expressed in the often repeated and varied formula "All this took place to fulfil what the
Lord had spoken by the prophet . . ." (1:22, R.S.V.), a formula,
of course, which he also applies when he interprets a text from
the Psalms as prophecy (13:35).

He finds the prophecy of the Virgin Birth (1:23) in Isaiah
7:14; and that of the Massacre of the Innocents (2:17 f.) in

Jeremiah 31:15; and according to 8:17, Jesus' healing miracles are foretold in Isaiah 53:4; while his speaking in parables is foretold according to 13:35 in Psalm 78:2; as a prophecy for the entry into Jerusalem (21:5), Zechariah 9:9 has to serve; Judas' betrayal for thirty pieces of silver (27:9 f.) is foretold in Zechariah 11:12 f.

The following examples show how random passages of the Old Testament are understood as prophecies:

(a) From the Psalms (besides the passage already quoted in Matt. 13:35): According to Romans 10:18, the mission to the Gentiles is foretold in Psalm 19:5. And Paul (in 1 Cor. 15:27) finds a prophecy of the consummation of Christ's eschatological Lordship in Psalm 8:7.

(b) From the law: In Romans 10:6-8 Paul interprets Deuteronomy 30:11-14 as a prophecy of justification by faith. In 1 Corinthians 9:9, Deuteronomy 25:4 as a prophecy has to serve as the prescription that the preacher of the gospel can claim the right of being received by the congregations.

(c) In 1 Corinthians 10:1-4 the prophecy about the Christian sacraments is taken from the *history of Israel*: The crossing through the Red Sea and the march under the cloud are prototypes of baptism, and the manna and the miraculous drink from the rock are prototypes of the Lord's Supper. So far then, as in vss. 5-7, Israel's fate in the desert has to serve as a warning; Israel's situation in its wanderings is a prototype of the situation of the Christian community.

To talk of this kind of prophecy and fulfillment has become impossible in an age in which the Old Testament is conceived of as a historical document and interpreted according to the method of historical science. The New Testament understanding of it may well be right in those cases where it conceives of the eschatological promises of the Old Testament as prophecies of the "age of salvation." It is, however, also clear in these cases that the prophet did not think of these events in which the New Testament finds the fulfillment—e.g., the fulfillment of Zechariah 9:9 in Matthew 21:5, or of Isaiah 59:20 f. in Romans 11:26 f., or of Jeremiah 31:31-34 in Hebrews 8:8-11.

The impossibility of the New Testament and the traditional understanding is, however, clear in the numerous instances where the Old Testament text only becomes of use when it is understood in a sense contrary to its original meaning, and above all when it is quoted quite contrary to the original wording, according to the LXX text, in instances where the Hebrew wording would not be appropriate.

Isaiah 7:14 (Matt. 1:23, *supra*) can only be used in the LXX text as a prophecy of the Virgin Birth, because in it the Hebrew *'almāh* (young woman) is translated as *parthenos*.

From Jeremiah 31:15 comes Rachel's lamentation (Matt. 2:17 f., *supra*) on the Jews led into captivity, to whom return was moreover promised.

The servant of God of Isaiah 53:4 is laden with plagues and does not take them away as does Jesus, who heals (Matt. 8:17, *supra*).

Psalm 78, from which is proved in Matthew 13:35 (*supra*) that Jesus' speaking in parables is in fulfillment of prophecy, is not a prophecy at all! The Psalmist wishes to proclaim wisdom, that is to say, God's wonderful deeds in the past of the people. The teaching on wisdom is designated *māšāl* and *ḥîdāh*, and because *parabolē* in the LXX serves as the translation of *māšāl*, the explanation with regard to speaking in parables is possible.

Nor is the passage from the prophet Zechariah (11:12 f.) a prophecy, in the way it has to serve in Matthew 27:9 f. It is an allegorical description of conditions among the people. When he breaks his covenant with the owners of the flocks, the prophet, playing the role of shepherd, throws the miserable wages of thirty pieces of silver into the Temple treasury—*'el hā' ôdṣār* as we have to read with the Syriac in the Targum, while the M.T. offers us *'el hayyôṣēr*—"to the potter." The explanation in Matthew presupposes both variants—Judas brings the money into the Temple, and for it the priests buy the potter's field.

The words from the Psalm quoted in Romans 10:18 (*supra*) are not a prophecy of the mission to the Gentiles, but say that heaven and earth praise God's glory night and day.

And Psalm 8 is not speaking of Christ's eschatological Lordship (1 Cor. 15:27, *supra*), but of man's high estate, which is God's gift to him.

In Romans 10:6-8 (*supra*) Paul relates what in Deuteronomy 30:11-14 is said of the law to the preaching of justification by faith.

Deuteronomy 25:4 (in 1 Cor. 9:9, *supra*) prescribes suitable treatment of the ox treading the corn, and can only be related to the preachers of the gospel by allegory.

When Paul in 1 Corinthians 14:21 interprets the prophecy of Isaiah 28:11 f., he is perverting its meaning rather to its opposite, as the original meaning is that God will abandon the people of Israel to peoples who speak in foreign tongues.

Hebrews 2:6-8 brings in Psalm 8:5-7 as a prophecy of the temporary humiliation of the pre-existent Christ. In the original text these words describe the dignity of man.

Psalm 40:6-9, which is understood as a prophecy of Christ's self-surrender as a sacrifice in Hebrews 10:5-7, can be used to this end only in the LXX text. In its original intention the Psalm speaks of God's demanding no animal and food sacrifices, but obedience, and in this sense it means "Mine ears hast thou opened." But instead of *'oznayim kārîtā lî* the LXX reads *sōma dè katērtisō moi*.

Again, Hebrews 12:26 quotes Haggai 2:6 as a prophecy of the eschatological catastrophe. In the original text it is meant figuratively, that peoples are to be set in motion and bring their treasures to Jerusalem. It is capable of use only in the LXX wording, to which the *eti hapax* goes back.

It is clear that in all these cases the writers in the New Testament do not gain new knowledge from the Old Testament texts, but read from or into them what they already know. If one follows their intention one is obliged to say that the Old Testament becomes clear as prophecy as a result of fulfillment. And so prophecy is recognized as such in fulfillment! But what would be the point of such a proceeding on the part of God? The purposes of the primitive Christian community would, of course, be served by it, for both in its anti-Jewish polemics and in its mission to the Gentiles it was able to overcome stumbling-blocks, to answer questions, to adduce proofs, having the ability to represent objectionable or astonishing facts as predestined and prophesied.

But is that theologically tenable? Can the offense of the cross of Jesus be overcome by recognizing it as long-prophesied and decided upon by God—or only by grasping its meaning and significance?

Furthermore, what then is the criterion by means of which it becomes possible to find prophecies in the Old Testament? What safeguard is there that the sense one wishes to find is not being arbitrarily imported? In reality this method of finding prophecy —whether with or without allegorizing—abandons the text of the Old Testament to the mercy of arbitrary choice, and the grotesque examples in the apostolic fathers are simply the consequence of the method of the New Testament authors. Thus it is when in 1 Clement 17:7 the scarlet cord which Rahab the harlot hung out of the house is explained as a prophecy of redemption through the blood of Christ or when Barnabus 9:8 finds in the three hundred and eighteen servants of Abraham a prophecy of the cross of Christ. Even if the arbitrary nature of the interpretation is limited by the fact that the exegete cannot derive from what he reads in the text anything he likes, but may only take from it truths of Christian kerygma and dogma, that is not only a completely superfluous effort—as these truths are already known as it is—but it also conceals the real stumbling-block which belief has to overcome, and so the right way to overcome it.

II

In the years 1841-44 there appeared the two volumes of the work *Weissagung und Erfüllung (Prophecy and Fulfillment)* by Joh. Chr. Konr. Hofmann. His thesis is that it is not the *words* of the Old Testament that are really prophecy, but the *history* of Israel, to which the Old Testament testifies. This history is *prophetic history* which is fulfilled in the story of Christ and his community. Prophecy, then, is not the prediction of coming events for the realization of which we have to wait. Prophecy is rather history itself, insofar as this is a movement leading to a goal, and constantly bears within itself this goal as prophecy or promise. In fulfillment, history is understood as prophecy, in the significance of its movement becoming clear. That is naturally something quite different from when, in accordance with the traditional view, prophecy becomes understandable from fulfillment, in the sudden coming to light of a secret meaning of words which in their context had originally meant something quite different. On the contrary, every word—like every event—of which the Old Testament has something to say, has in its historical position its unambiguous sense, and only takes on the character of prophecy by the fact that the course of the history to which it belongs is prophecy when taken as a whole. Since for Hofmann, Christ is the goal of history, history is prophecy of Christ,[1] and fundamentally is not just the history of Israel, but that of the world in general. "If it is true that all things, great and small, serve to bring about the unification of the world under its head, Christ, then there is absolutely nothing in the history of the world in which something divine does not dwell, and so nothing which must necessarily remain foreign to prophecy" (*Weissagung und Erfüllung,* I, p. 7).

Hofmann gives an example: "Something which is to take place in the future may well be delineated in an earlier event and be represented in anticipation. Every triumphal procession which went through the streets of Rome was a prophecy of Caesar Augustus: For what Augustus constantly represented, the triumphant general did on his day of honor—the god in man—Jupiter in the citizen of Rome. In Rome's according to her victors this particular honor, her future revealed itself as one in which she would master the world through her Emperor, revered as a god. After the Apostle John has told of how it came about that on the cross Jesus' legs were not broken, he adds, 'so that

---

[1] H. Schlier takes up the view in his article "Weissagung und Erfüllung," *Die Religion in Geschichte und Gegenwart,* V, pp. 1813 f., when he says that only when in Christ the end of the ages had come—when Old Testament history was completed—did that which previously took place become manifest as something referring to Christ and fulfilled in this.

the prophecy might be fulfilled "not a bone of the Passover lamb is to be broken." ' Thus he sees a prototype of Jesus in the paschal lamb, and in what happens to Jesus there is fulfilled in his case a prophecy or intimation of what is to come—given in the Passover meal. The meaning of triumph is not fulfilled in the many recurrent triumphal processions, nor of the Passover in the Passover meals taking place every year, but the real content of one and the other, in which the truth of each consists, is not to appear till a future time, and so only then to confirm for itself the prophecy contained in it" (*Weissagung und Erfüllung,* I, pp. 15 f.).

Moreover, Hofmann also finds within the Old Testament, and so within the history of Israel itself, prophecy and fulfillment. When we find in Genesis 15:6 "Abraham believed God, and it was counted unto him for righteousness," that is a prophecy which found its fulfillment in the occurrence reported in Genesis 22, namely, in Abraham's being ready obediently to sacrifice his son. Faith is obedience; but Abraham's faith is not perceptible as such in Genesis 15, but becomes so only in Genesis 22.

Hofmann's way of speaking about prophecy and fulfillment is manifestly a *philosophy of history* which is influenced by Hegel, and gains its Christian character only because for him *Christ is the goal of history.* And in other ways, too, the outlook which is determined purely by considerations of the philosophy of history is subject to certain limitations. An example of this is the interpretation of Adam's exclamation about Eve in Genesis 2:23: "This *is* now bone of my bones, and flesh of my flesh: she shall be called Woman, because she was taken out of Man" (k.j.v.). According to Hofmann, this is the first prophecy. For since the relationship of man and woman expressed in this exclamation did not as a consequence of the fall (which actually does not come into Hofmann's conception of things) remain undisturbed, it required to be restored in higher perfection. "What man was to woman but has not continued to be, Christ is eternally to the human race. He is the head of the community, as the man is the head of the woman. In fellowship with him she

knows and so also controls everything" (*Weissagung und Erfüllung*, I, p. 71). Here again Hofmann's basic view is maintained
insofar as the intention of the beginning of history, according to
his interpretation, is realized in its end. The prophecy here, too,
consists in the fact that in Adam's exclamation the intention of
history which points to its *telos* becomes perceptible from the
telos.

As against Hofmann's view, however, we have to ask ourselves *what its theological relevance is*. It naturally cannot provide a proof of the validity of Christ, as Christ must first of all be
recognized as the goal of history before the interpretation of
Israel's history as *sub specie Christi* can become possible. But if
we sought to say that a confirmation of Christ is actually made by
the fact that such an interpretation becomes possible, then that
simply means we are confirming Christ by a consideration in the
realm of the philosophy of history. Now, does faith demand such
considerations—has it any need of them? Is Hofmann's view,
interesting as it is, not a concern with the history of Israel which
is theologically irrelevant? But may something which is right
not perhaps lurk in the question he puts—first of all, that is, in
his desire to understand as prophecy not the individual words of
the Old Testament, but the history of which it tells us; and so
in his desire to interpret this history on the basis of Christ, its
"end," as prophecy? Does his error not lie in his effort to reach
this understanding with the aid of the philosophical idea of
history as a process of development, in which tendencies originally active in whatever takes place attain their realization in the
natural course of events? According to the New Testament,
Christ is the end of salvation history (*Heilsgeschichte*) not in the
sense that he signifies the goal of historical development, but
because he is its eschatological end. Can Old Testament history
perhaps be legitimately understood as prophecy on this basis?
The attempt to answer this question is to be undertaken in such
a way that three concepts are examined, in which the New Testament picks up decisively important concepts of the Old Testament and yet interprets them in a new sense—that is, eschatologically.

III

1. The Covenant Concept

The covenant concept is a primary Old Testament concept, designating the relation between God and the people: And in speaking of God's covenant with the people, something real is meant, in contradistinction, let us say, to the concept of marriage, which describes this relationship figuratively. Naturally God and the people are not equal partners in the covenant; yet their relationship is a covenant, which rests on mutual loyalty and which makes such loyalty binding; God demands the loyalty of the people, and the people can rely on the loyalty of God, which has chosen this empirical and historical people. The covenant originally gained its validity through sacrifice, and is constantly maintained and so renewed by the right sacrificial worship.[2] And if in the popular mind it is therefore reckoned to be unshakable provided the people will only offer to its God the worship demanded of it, the preaching of the prophets protests against this. First of all it protests against the tying down of God to the land in which the people have found a home and with which they become more and more one. In the same way it protests against seeing God's link with the people as an irrevocable one, and says that the validity of the covenant depends on the obedience of the people, seeing this obedience, however, not (or not only) as the faithful cultic worship of God, but as obedience to his moral requirements, which demand justice and righteousness. If he wishes, God can reject the people he has chosen. Israel has no claim to preference over other peoples:

"Are ye not as children of the Ethiopians unto me,
O children of Israel? Saith the Lord.
Have not I brought up Israel out of the land of Egypt?
And the Philistines from Caphtor, and the Syrians from
    Kir?" (Amos 9:7, K.J.V.)

Naturally that is not a protest against the idea of election as such. It is retained when we read:

---

[2] Cf. Nils A. Dahl, *Das Volk Gottes* (1941), p. 9.

"You only have I known of all the families of the earth:
Therefore I will punish you for all your iniquities."
(Amos 3:2, K.J.V.)

The protest is only directed against Israel's regarding her
position of privilege over other peoples as an assured possession,
and not reckoning with the possibility of its revocation. The
covenant is broken if one of the partners does not fulfill his
covenant duties.

If, then, it is a question of God's covenant with a people
as a real, empirical, and historical entity, the validity of the
covenant can be made to rest only on conditions which can be
fulfilled by such a people, as a people; that is, on the celebration
of the official *cultus,* and, in later Judaism, on the maintenance
of a particular order of life. A covenant with a people made to
rest on the fulfillment of moral requirements as a condition of
the covenant is an impossibility in the reality of the historical
situation. As it is, there is a contradiction in terms in speaking
of a covenant which distinguishes an empirical and historical
people and assures it of God's help, if the validity of the covenant
is bound up not with the existence of the empirical and historical
people as a people at all, but with the moral attitude of the individual in the people. What then is the basis of the security of
that individual? Is it in the fact that he belongs to the "chosen
people"? This is, of course, the naïve and natural idea that comes
from the idea of election—that the people is chosen as a whole,
by God, and that the individual gains his security from his membership in the covenant people. Such was the naïve consciousness
of Israel, against which the prophets' protest is raised, and against
which John the Baptist later protests:

"And think not to say within yourselves, We have Abraham to *our* father: for I say unto you, that God is able of
these stones to raise up children unto Abraham." (Matt.
3:9, K.J.V.)

But if that is the case, and the validity of the covenant depends
on the moral attitude of the individual, then the idea of God's
covenant with the people is done away with. That and nothing
else is, in fact, what Jesus says in the saying:

"And I say unto you, That many shall come, from the east

and west, and shall sit down with Abraham, and Isaac, and Jacob, in the kingdom of heaven. But the children of the kingdom shall be cast out into outer darkness." (Matt. 8:11 f., K.J.V.)

God's covenant with a people whose individuals suffice for the moral demands of God as members of the people is an eschatological concept, because such a people' is not a real empirical and historical, but an eschatological, dimension.

In this way, then, the concept of the covenant in prophecy becomes an *eschatological concept*. Since the old covenant has been shattered by the guilt of the people, God will conclude a new one in the coming age of salvation. But this covenant, like the age of salvation in any event, has a wonderful character:

"Behold, the days come, saith the LORD, that I will make a new covenant with the house of Israel, and with the house of Judah: not according to the covenant I made with their fathers in the day *that* I took them by the hand to bring them out of the land of Egypt; which my covenant they brake, although I was an husband to them, saith the LORD: but this *shall be* the covenant that I will make with the house of Israel; After those days, saith the LORD, I will put my law in their inward parts, and write it in their hearts; and will be their God, and they shall be my people. And they shall teach no more every man his neighbour, and every man his brother, saying, Know the LORD: for they shall all know me, from the least of them unto the greatest of them, saith the LORD: for I will forgive their iniquity, and I will remember their sin no more" (Jer. 31:31-34, K.J.V.).

"Moreover I will make a covenant of peace with them; it shall be an everlasting covenant with them: and I will place them, and multiply them, and will set my sanctuary in the midst of them for evermore. My tabernacle also shall be with them: yea, I will be their God, and they shall be my people. And the heathen shall know that I the LORD do sanctify Israel, when my sanctuary shall be in the midst of them for evermore" (Ezek. 37:26-28, K.J.V.).

Is such a covenant still a real historical possibility? Is the idea of an eschatological covenant not a sign that God's covenant is in its essence an eschatological dimension which is not to be realized within the world? Are Ezekiel and Jeremiah not being inconsistent when still they conceive of this eschatological covenant as one with a future empirical people of Israel?

In any case the New Testament draws the conclusion from the idea of the eschatological covenant, in its belief that the promise of Jeremiah has now been fulfilled for the Christian community (Heb. 8:8-12; 10:16 f.). But this community is not a people as a historical entity within the world. And so, too, the foundation of the new covenant is not any more an event in the history of the people than the old one is. It is founded in the death of Christ, and the individual is received into it by baptism and participation in the Lord's Supper, in which the body and blood of Christ are consecrated in bread and wine. The death of Christ as an *inaugurating event* does not come into the history of the people like the Sinai event; it is at the most an episode in that history. Rather does it call man out of the community of the people and found a society, which is not bound to the world. "Wherefore Jesus also, that he might sanctify the people with his own blood, suffered without the gate. Let us go forth therefore unto him without the camp, bearing his reproach" (Heb. 13:12 f., K.J.V.). In coming together for the Lord's Supper, this community is a community of worship. But the worship no longer has to do with a people, like the festival of the Passover lamb. The Passover lamb had been replaced by Christ, who has been slain "as our Passover" (1 Cor. 5:7). The synoptic tradition expresses this by placing Jesus' last meal, in which it sees the institution of the Lord's Supper, on the eve of the feast of the Passover, while John, in order to express the same idea, places the Crucifixion at this time.

According to Paul, the contrast between the old and the new covenant is that of the "letter" and the "spirit" (2 Cor. 3:6-18). The new covenant as the "lasting" one, that of the "spirit" (*pneuma*) and of "righteousness" (*dikaiosunē*), outshines the old in "glory" (*doxa*). But this glory is not visible in the world like the old and does not become the lot of a people as such, as is the case, say, in Deutero-Isaiah (e.g., 60:19 f.), but only of such as turn to the Lord. And these are changed "from glory unto glory," in receiving knowledge of his glory from the preaching of the gospel. But they only have "this treasure" in "earthen vessels" (2 Cor. 4:7 ff.), i.e., only want and death are to be seen in them, and in this world the "life of Jesus" is only shown forth in *them.* So it is clear that the new covenant is a radically eschatological dimension, that is, a dimension outside the world, and to belong to it takes its members out of the world.

The worship and ritual of the old covenant have their counterparts in the new. Already we have seen in reference to the feast of the Passover the idea that Christ has been slain as the Passover lamb of the new covenant: "Therefore let us keep the feast, not with old leaven, neither with the leaven of malice and wickedness; but with the unleavened *bread* of sincerity and truth" (1 Cor. 5:8, k.j.v.). The Epistle to the Hebrews develops the theory that the Jewish cult is a type of the Christian institution of salvation which has been abrogated from now on— a "shadow of good things to come" (Heb. 10:1, k.j.v.; cf. 8:5).

The covenant sign of the old covenant, circumcision, is abrogated: "For he is not a Jew, which is one outwardly; neither *is that* circumcision, which is outward in the flesh: but he *is* a Jew, which is one inwardly; and circumcision *is that* of the heart, in the spirit, *and* not in the letter; whose praise *is* not of men, but of God" (Rom. 2:28 f., k.j.v.; cf. 1 Cor. 7:19; Gal. 5:6; 6:15). Christians are circumcised not with a circumcision made by hand (Col. 2:11). What it amounts to is this: "For we are the circumcision, which worship God in the spirit, and rejoice in Christ Jesus, and have no confidence in the flesh" (Phil. 3:3, k.j.v.).

In this way the contrast of the covenant people to other peoples has lapsed, "For there is no difference between the Jew and the Greek: for the same Lord over all is rich unto all that call upon him" (Rom. 10:12, k.j.v.). "For as many of you as have been baptized into Christ have put on Christ. There is neither Jew nor Greek, there is neither bond nor free, there is neither male nor female: for ye are all one in Christ Jesus" (Gal. 3:27 f., k.j.v.; cf. 1 Cor. 12:12; Col. 3:11).

2. The Concept of the Kingdom of God

As in other Semitic people, God is represented in Israel as
a king: Since when, is debatable; there are indisputable signs of
it in Isaiah 6:5, yet we can with great assurance infer its existence
at an earlier time. The significance of the Kingdom of Yahweh
is that he is the Lord of the people, who imposes his will on the
people by his statutes and commandments (*miṣwōth*). As judge
(*šōphēṭ*) he settles disputes by his pronouncement, and so he is
the preserver of law within the people, as he is without it, in
directing Israel's war and showing himself generally to be its
protector and helper. The realistic representation of the Kingdom of God is shown by the competition with the worldly kingdom, which we shortly have to discuss in more precise terms.

There seems to have been in Israel a festival of Yahweh's
enthronement as a New Year's festival. "Yahweh has become
King" is the cry of the festival (Pss. 47, 93, 96, 97, 99). He is
praised as supreme over all other gods and as Lord of the world.
In the cultic festival, the pious congregation experiences his
kingship. But just as the Royal Psalms became eschatological
Psalms, so, too, the concept of the Kingdom of God becomes an
eschatological concept. In the time of the Exile when God
abandoned his people, the establishment of his Kingdom of the
future, which will bring salvation, is expected. In this way
Deutero-Isaiah regards the liberation of Israel from exile as the
dawn of the age of salvation. The messenger of joy, whom the
prophet sees in the spirit, announces: "How beautiful upon
the mountains are the feet of him that bringeth good tidings, that
publisheth peace; that bringeth good tidings of good, that publisheth salvation; that saith unto Zion, Thy God reigneth!" (Isa.
52:7, K.J.V.)

In the period after the Exile the pronouncements about God's
present and future kingship continue on parallel courses, and in
its further development it is not regarded as exclusively in the
future. In a certain sense it is always present, a faith finding expression in prayers, and also lying behind the rabbinic formula
"to take the yoke of the kingdom upon oneself"; for that means

taking the law upon oneself—reciting the Shema.[3] But the conviction is prevalent notwithstanding, that God's kingship in the world has not been established now. The hopes of Deutero-Isaiah and the postexilic prophets had been deceptive. There is still nothing to be seen in the glory of the era of salvation. Foreign peoples hold sway in the world and are even the masters of God's people. And particularly when the representation of Satan as ruler of the world penetrates Judaism, a renewed yearning and hope for the future realization of the Kingdom of God comes into being. The apocalyptic writer dreams of that age:

"Then God's rule over all his creation will appear, and then the devil will come to his end." (Assumption of Moses 10:1)

The prayer goes up:

"Let thy glory be revealed
And the splendour of thy greatness be known!
Let thy glory be revealed, yea, now,
And do not delay thy promise!" (Syriac Apocalypse of Baruch 21:23, 25)

"And may God establish his Kingdom
In your life and your days,
In the life of all the house of Israel
Right speedily and soon!" (Qaddish)

The dawn of God's Kingdom, with which the dominion of Satan comes to an end, is at the same time the beginning of the new *aeon*.[4] The future age of salvation, awaited by the prophets as a new historical epoch, although one introduced and shaped by wonders, and as a definitive age of salvation, now becomes simply a supernatural era of salvation. The judgment of the world precedes it, a judgment which no longer takes place as it

---

[3] Cf. Strack-Billerbeck, *Kommentar zum Neuen Testament aus Talmud und Midrasch*, I (1922), p. 608.
[4] Here, where it is simply a question of the basic idea, I can leave out discussion of the varying elaborations of the eschatological hope and especially of the distinction of the Messianic age (as a prelude) and the new *aeon*, which is frequently met with.

did in the expectation of the prophets, within the history of the nations, but one which is a forensic act of justice, at which the whole world has to answer for itself in the presence of the judge. At this act, the resurrection of the dead follows the "woes of the Messiah," preceded by the consummation of the old *aeon,* as all diabolical wickedness and all distress reach their climax.

In Jesus' preaching, too, the Kingdom of God is no longer understood in the sense of Old Testament theocracy, as the dominion of the divine king in the liberated land, over the people of Israel, now elevated to power and prosperity, but as the wonder of a new era for the world breaking in from heaven. This no longer appears as the ideal picture of the life of a people which, with Jerusalem in its midst, dwells peaceably in its fields under its fig trees and its vines. Nor does some idealized picture depict the glamour and the delights of the coming *aeon,* as in the case of the apocalyptic wonders. There only remains the phrase "the dominion of God" and the idea of a community in which God's name is hallowed and his will is operative. That this community is no longer tied down to the boundaries of the people can be seen in the comment already quoted of the many who will come from east and west (Matt. 8:11 f.); and in the same way it can be seen in the story of the Good Samaritan (Luke 10:30-37). The demands of the Sermon on the Mount, the command to love, do not reveal any sort of interest in people and the organization of the people; the law is overruled by love, and the judge will ask some day in the tribunal only about what "you have done unto one of the least of my brethren" (Matt. 25:31-46).

But is such a rule of God realizable within this world? Is it not by its very nature simply eschatological, so that we cannot expect it to be realized in any temporal future period?

The New Testament has made the idea of the eschatological rule of God its own in such a way that it sees in the existence of the community the realization of the rule of God, the coming into force of the new *aeon,* seeing in the community a dimension which is at one and the same time within and beyond the world. In this the rule of God is, naturally, not conceived of as an idea which becomes realized progressively and more closely in the course of history; it takes place as God's act in history; it is what is present. Yet it is so not in the old sense—not within the history of the people and in the forms of the national community—but beyond it. It is realized by Jesus' having been made King through his Resurrection, and it is a reality where he is recognized as King. If, as is probably the case, the title *kurios* comes from Hellenistic worship, it is nevertheless clear in Paul that devotion to worship took on an eschatological significance, and that the *kurios* is an eschatological Lord. He is already ruling now and will rule till the *parousia,* at which he will give up his dominion to God, so that God will then be all in all (1 Cor. 15: 23-28), when death is annihilated at the resurrection of the dead. Till then Christ, as it were, represents God, exercising dominion in the meantime in his stead.

The era of salvation is the present for Paul, as the age of Christ's royal dominion (cf. 2 Cor. 6:2). His glory is already effective in those who believe and are justified. Paul is led through the world by God "in Christ," so that he may everywhere spread the "savor of his knowledge," and so death and life (2 Cor. 2:14-16). Righteousness and life need not be expected only of the judge's pronouncement in the coming judgment of the world, but already become the lot of those who acknowledge Christ as their Lord.

The rule of God and so of Christ is therefore something completely different from what Old Testament prophecy had expected. It is eschatological and supramundane in its entirety; and the man who has a part in it is, as it were, already taken out of the world, so that he lives no longer "according to the flesh," however much he still lives "in the flesh" (2 Cor. 10:3). And if with Paul the eschatological event remains inconsistently apportioned between present and future, in the case of John it is thoroughly brought home to us. Here we have the basic formulation when the Jesus of the Johannine writings speaks: "My kingdom is not of this world" (John 18:36). The judgment of the world is not to be expected as a future one; it comes to pass in Jesus' having come into the world as the "light," and in the fact that this coming of his means decision about death and life for everyone. Those who believe in him will not be judged, and those who do not are judged already. Those who believe in him are already risen and have crossed over from death into life (3:16-19; 5:24 f.; 8:51; 11:25 f.; 12:31; 14:6).

The world is convicted of sin, the Messiah is the "just one," that is, the victor, the "prince of this world" is judged (16:8-11). The fact that Jesus has overcome the world (16:33) is not obvious from within the world, but is shown in the very fact that the world is still given over to itself. But Jesus' victory is continued in the triumph of faith over the world (1 John 5:4).

3. The Concept of the People of God

The kingdom of this world is in a peculiar rivalry with the Kingdom of God.[5] A people whose King is God cannot actually tolerate any earthly king, as is clearly expressed in what Gideon, according to Judges 8:23, says to the Israelites: "I will not rule over you, neither shall my son rule over you: the LORD shall rule over you" (K.J.V.). Only against opposition was the secular kingdom introduced into Israel, and in the judgment of the prophet, Israel's guilt originated in Gilgal, where Saul (according to 1 Sam. 11:14 f.) was anointed king (Hos. 9:15). Even if the secular kingdom were not as such further opposed by prophecy, after it had become popular through David, yet the inner contradiction between the idea of the people of God and the secular kingdom soon comes to light.[6] The secular kingdom is a form of state organization. There are certain necessities which go along with it, as 1 Samuel 8:10 ff. reminds us: a civil service and an army, financial resources and therefore taxation. External politics demand in certain circumstances leagues with Gentile states—all of which are things having nothing to do with the idea of a people of God: They may represent nothing more than the means of organizing a secular people. The interests and forces placed in them can only distract from the investigation of what God's will is, and the consciousness of power which arises

---

[5] Cf. Joh. Hempel, *Das Ethos des Alten Testaments* (1938), pp. 175 ff.
[6] Cf. Walther Eichrodt, *Die Theologie des Alten Testaments*, I (1950), p. 237.

with the consciousness of the state leads to the forgetting of the limitation of man and people by the power of God. Added to this are the moral consequences which arise on account of the transformation of the old patriarchal, tribal organization; uncertainty in regard to the law, class conflict, and the unleashing of ambition and egoism.

The prophetic reaction is directed against the forms and consequences of the new state organizations.[7] But it is clear that the kings, if ever they are willing to bear the responsibility for the state, do not have the possibility of carrying on their rule in the cause of the prophetic idea. They have to see to armament and to the fortification of towns; they have to concern themselves with alliances, and so on. By contrast, the prophets cannot be representatives of the idea of the "people of God" in a form such as would allow it to be implemented in the secular kingdom. They demand the execution of law and justice, but link this demand to the idea of patriarchal, tribal organization which prevailed before the days of the state, and so what they demand inevitably miscarries. Where their ideals lead to some legislation or other, this outlines the picture of a utopia—for the constitution outlined in Deuteronomy, like that of the Priestly Code, is utopian; that is, they fail to recognize the real necessities of the organization of the state and are only capable of implementation at the price of the people constituted in accordance with these ideals not leading any independent existence *as a state*.

After the Exile, then, the ideal of theocracy was also implemented, but Israel, the people of God, is no longer a state. It lives subject to foreign dominion and can indeed only so live if it wishes to be the people of God as an empirical people. This is again clearly demonstrated in the turning away of the pious from the Hasmonean Dynasty, as soon as that dynasty, after liberating the land from Syrian domination, grasps the necessity of acting as a state. In the same way it is demonstrated by the voluntary submission of the pious to Roman dominion, when Pompey enters Jerusalem. That is to say, the people of God has acknowledged that it can no longer exist as a state, if it wishes

---

[7] Cf. Hempel, *op. cit.*, pp. 88 f., 121, 179 ff.

to realize itself in that capacity, but only as a religious community, as a kind of church.

Can we, however, seriously designate the Jewish "church" of the Persian and Roman era as the realization of the people of God? On the one hand, it is a community which is held together and molded not by the forces and forms of a natural life, but by the laws of a theoretically conceived *cultus* and ritual, which more and more loses its significance for real life. On the other hand, it is linked to the empirical Jewish people and shuts itself off to other peoples, actually with the help of that ritual. It is only now that circumcision and the Sabbath take on that historical significance. And so Judaism, which desires to be the people of God and the national community at one and the same time, is a self-contradictory phenomenon.

The contradiction in the hope expressed is symptomatic of this. They pray:

"Blow the great trumpet for our liberation,
And raise the banner for the assembly of our exiles.
Bring back our judges as at the first
And our counsellors as in the beginning,
Have mercy, Yahweh, our God, on Jerusalem, Thy city,
And on Zion, the dwelling-place of Thine Honour,
And on the Kingdom of the House of David,
The Messiah of Thy righteousness."

(Eighteen Blessings)

Thus they expect the restoration of the independence of the people as a state and curse the Roman overlordship, which was, nevertheless, still needed. But they are far from wishing to bring about the restoration by political and warlike activity, expecting it, on the contrary, through God's miraculous intervention, and expecting an independent Jewish world empire without it existing actually in the form of a state. Insofar as the representation of the national ideals which this hope gave rise to generally loses its color and is suppressed by the hope of the new *aeon,* in which the forms of existence as a state have generally lost their meaning, it is characteristic that contradictory representation of a "hope" is alive in Judaism.

Another symptom is the inconsistent idea of the Messianic hope in the narrower sense of the term. If there are prophecies of a coming Messiah, a king of the era of salvation, of the seed of David, also in the pre-exilic period, yet the actual development of this Messianic hope falls within the postexilic period; and corresponding to this is the notion (which is in itself impossible) of a Davidic king of the era of salvation, who is not to be thought of as an actual ruler, but must remain a shadowy figure, a symbol. This figure must fundamentally compete with the idea of God's kingship and, practically speaking, with the rule of the priests, as what is in practice the only possible form of theocracy. Actually the figure of the Messiah is often not to be found in the pictures of the future and has basically lost its significance. And so the Messianic representative of the Davidic line is suppressed by the mythical figure of the "Son of Man" and the Messianic era is lowered to the status of a prologue to the real salvation era.

The development we have just sketched shows the contradiction between the idea of a people of God and a people constituted as a state; it illustrates the illusion of making an identification of the people of God with an empirical and historical people. The idea of a people of God corresponding to the royal dominion of God cannot be reconciled with that of a people as a nation, constituted as a state, but explodes it. It is the peculiar paradox of Judaism that it makes the attempt to reconcile the two. It had to give the empirical people on the one hand the form of a theocracy, and on the other hand to make the people of God an eschatological concept; it has to expect both from the Messianic era—and so from the new *aeon*.

In the New Testament everything has been brought into a new light by the assertion that the new *aeon* has dawned in the Christ-event. Just as the eschatological Kingdom is present in the Lordship of Christ, so the people of God, the true Israel, is present in the Christian community. And so the people of God is no longer an empirical historical entity—it does not exist as a people requiring institutional ordinance for its organization. Hence the state, too, insofar as it is really a state, that is, a legal ordinance, is made irrelevant (Rom. 13); it is, so to speak, released from the sphere of interest of the people of God (cf. 1 Cor. 6:1 ff.). From this there then naturally arises the peculiar dual existence of the Christian in church and state with its problems, which however have not become a subject for reflection as yet in the New Testament.

The real people of God is the *ecclesia*, which is an eschatological unit, and in that capacity is manifested both in the individual local community and in the totality of communities. There is access to it not by birth or because one belongs to a people, but through the impact of the gospel's call, and as a result of being called out of the world and sanctified by baptism, which incorporates the person baptized into Christ as the "body" of the *ekklēsia*. Thus the members of the people of God are the "called" (*klētoi*), the "elect" (*elketoi*), the "saints" (*hagioi*); they belong to Christ (*einai Christō*) and they are in Christ (*en Christō*). As the people of God, the *ekklēsia* is the "Israel of God" (Gal. 6:15; cf. Phil. 3:3; Rom. 9:6-8; James 1:1) in contrast to the Israel "after the flesh" (1 Cor. 10:18). The "fathers" and the promises belong to it, and the Jews can even be reproved as the "synagogue of Satan" (*sunagōgē tou Satana*).

IV

How far, then, does Old Testament Jewish history represent prophecy fulfilled in the history of the New Testament community? It is fulfilled in its inner contradiction, its miscarriage.[8] An inner contradiction pervades the self-consciousness and the hope of Israel and its prophets. Israel is concerned with being regarded not simply as an empirical dimension within the world, but as the people of God; it claims to see God's activity and guidance in its history, and not simply the product of human planning, arbitrary human choice, and blind necessity. The

---

[8] From the essay by L. Goppelt, "Typos" (1939), p. 14, on the work of Patrick Fairbairn, *The Typology of Scripture*, Vol. 2 (Edinburgh, 1857), which, Bultmann says in the German edition, was not accessible to him—he thinks he can deduce that Fairbairn's view is moving in the right direction [Trs.].

drift of this is, therefore, toward a transcendent God and his activity. But we find the contradiction in the fact that God and the activity are not conceived of in the radically transcendent and eschatological sense, but are brought into line with the empirical history of the people. There is a miscarriage of history in this contradiction. The idea of a covenant of God with a people shows itself to be an impossible development within history and becomes an eschatological idea. The idea of the rule of God is shown to be unrealizable within the world, and the attempt to realize it is reduced to absurdity by the grotesque form of a priestly and legalistic theocracy. The idea of the people of God shows itself to be unrealizable in an empirical national community, as this requires for its historical existence forms of state organization, law, and authority. It must therefore constantly run counter to the idea of a people of God, if the people of God is to be considered as identical with this empirical people.

In its very demonstration of this impossibility, the miscarriage of history actually amounts to a promise. There is nothing which can count as a promise to man other than the miscarriage of *his* way, and the recognition that it is impossible to gain direct access to God in his history within the world, and directly to identify his history within the world with God's activity.

This miscarriage is, of course, to be understood as a promise only on the basis of its fulfillment, that is, on the basis of the encounter with God's grace, which makes itself available to those who understand their situation as one of impossibility. Fulfillment can, therefore, not be regarded as the consequence of historical development, for that is actually nothing else than this miscarriage. And that would be the end of it, if God had not made a new beginning in Christ, who, we have to admit, does not inaugurate a new historical development but is a "new creation" in the eschatological sense—a beginning which from now on is available for every age to those who become aware of the fact that their way was leading to miscarriage—their way, in which they desired to realize within the world the eternal significance of their life. The encounter with the grace of God teaches man to conceive of God's activity as eschatological in the true sense, that is, as an activity withdrawing him from the world; and it endows him with the possibility of faith as that of eschatological existence in the world and in time.

In the light of this we get the right to conceive of this Old Testament history of miscarriage as a promise, that is, the way in which God has led the people of the Old Testament; and we get the right to interpret that conflict not as that of two human ideas, but as one which belongs to human existence as such—the conflict of being created for God and called to God, and yet of being imprisoned in secular history.

If we interpret Old Testament history in this sense we are following Paul's interpretation of the law. The law is the "tutor unto Christ" (Gal. 3:24) because it led man into this miscarriage of his endeavors. "The scripture hath concluded all under sin, that the promise by faith of Jesus Christ might be given to them that believe. But before faith came, we were kept under the law, shut up unto the faith which should afterwards be revealed" (Gal. 3:22 f., K.J.V.). "For God hath concluded them all in unbelief, that he might have mercy upon all" (Rom. 11:32, K.J.V.).

The law as it confronts man in the form of the law of Moses is the way in which man comes to grief in sin: Christ is the end of the law (Rom. 10:4). Yet the law is God's holy and good will (Rom. 7:12). Then the idea of a people of God in a covenant with God as its King and the hopes which go along with this are such as to seduce man into an identification of God's eschatological activity with what happens in secular history, or of the people of God with an empirical people, and so it is the way to the miscarriage of the human situation.

In this way we get an answer to the question of what *theological relevance* there is in the whole of what we have been considering: why we give up the naïve, traditional meaning of prophecy and fulfillment, and go on indeed to ask if we may legitimately speak of prophecy and fulfillment at all. What is the purpose of speaking of it? Is it not a superfluous speculation —a religious philosophy of history?

It is, just as much or as little as what Paul says of the law; what faith means as the way of salvation is wholly understood only by those who know the false way of salvation which we find in the law. Paul's doctrine of the law is not a piece of apologetics wrung from him by the necessity of his situation, bespeaking his anxiety to balance against each other the pronouncements that the law does not justify and yet that it is given by God. Rather does faith, to be sure of itself, require us to know about the significance of the law—otherwise it would constantly be subject to temptation through the law—in any form whatever. In the same way faith requires the backward glance into Old Testament history as a history of failure, and so of promise, in order to know that the situation of the justified man arises only on the basis of this miscarriage. Thus faith, to be a really justifying faith, must constantly contain within itself the way of the law as something which has been overcome; it must also, in order to be an eschatological attitude, constantly contain within itself the attempt to identify what happens in the secular sphere with what happens eschatologically, as something which has been overcome.

4.

THE "RE-PRESENTATION" OF THE OLD TESTAMENT IN PROCLAMATION
by Martin Noth*

translated by James Luther Mays

It is not difficult to demonstrate that the Old Testament is wholly and in every respect a product of history. This is true even of the Old Testament "canon," for it exists in a variety of historically conditioned forms. Therein lies a problem, particularly for the Reformed church who read the Old Testament in the translation of Luther. For Luther's Bible did not follow in its selection of "canonical" writings the ancient and medieval and current ecclesiastical tradition which adopted the Old Testament "canon" used in the Hellenistic synagogue and passed on in the Latin translation. Luther, rather, with regard to the compass of the Old Testament, reverted to the "canon" of the Hebrew synagogue, which until then did not have the church's legitimation. This historicity characterizes the entire text of the Old Testament which demonstrably and evidently has been affected by the passage of time, just like any other work of literature handed down to us as manuscripts from ancient times. It is true of the individual books of the Old Testament, all of which clearly raise the question about the historical situation in which they emerged. In fact, it is true of every single word in the Old Testament, formulated as it is in a language which had its own time and history and which, therefore, is not fully intelligible unless its time and history are known. The recognition of these facts does not depend on some one particular approach to the

---

* This article appeared originally in *Evangelische Theologie* (Jahrgang 12, 1952, Juli/August), Heft 1/2, pp. 6 ff.

Old Testament, selected out of several which are possible; these facts simply are given with the Old Testament and cannot be disregarded as a matter of preference.

Above all, and here is the real center of the matter in question, the entire content of the Old Testament is inseparably bound to an age in history which has now passed, which had its own ideas and views of life. Yet, on the other hand, the Old Testament is one part of the Christian Bible, the basis for Christian proclamation to the present; therefore, it must have a direct contemporary relevance. And here that fatal chasm yawns between a "historico-critical" exegesis which feels obligated to fix its eye rigidly on the given facts and a concern for relevance which approaches the matter from the standpoint of the requirements set by contemporary proclamation, because it believes it must. This chasm divides theological science precariously. Systematic theology is able only in exceptional cases to participate in the presuppositions and methods of scientific exegesis, while pastoral theology in the large disregards the fundamentals of exegetical studies altogether. The chasm divides theological education, for in systematic and pastoral seminars the student often thinks he had better forget what he may perchance have learned in exegetical seminars. The chasm separates an essential part of the endeavors in scientific theology from the work in the pastorate.

Here something is obviously wrong. It would be idle to ask who is to blame for it. The difficulty lies in the matter itself, and thus it is certainly more appropriate to inquire into the way the matter itself puts the problem. This problem is bound up with the fact that in the biblical witness we deal with a revelation of God which has occurred within history, while, after all, God cannot be limited to history and time. From the perspective of this insight one must consider the various questions that are raised with regard to the situation in theology which has been described.

First of all, there is the question whether in exegesis the historical method was not an erroneous procedure from the start, since it begins with the principle that no fundamental distinction should be made between the biblical witness and other literary traditions. In fact, the opinion is widely prevalent that practical interpretation cannot begin with historical exegesis, because it merely ascertains "accidental truths of history" but nothing binding or valid. This opinion, however, disregards the biblical witness according to which God reveals himself in historical events, and not in ageless myths or in a system of propositions. It ignores the fact that the Old Testament, to a surprisingly large extent, consists of historical narratives which for their part originated in the course of exactly the same history they narrate. Because of these facts, *historical* exegesis is positively indispensable. To dismiss them would mean that the biblical revelation must be different from what it is. *Historical* exegesis, however, necessarily means historico-critical exegesis, for the problem of what really happened in history cannot be settled except by "discriminating" and "testing." The Christians in Berea are commended for their *anakrinein tas graphas* (Acts 17:11), and this remains an essential task. Paul's request to "sensible men," *krinate humeis ho phēmi* (1 Cor. 10:15), is applicable not only to his own sayings but as well to all biblical witnesses. It is certainly to be conceded that historico-critical studies often have been pursued with a presumptiveness inappropriate to the subject. Nor have their results always been described in a way which makes it easy for the non-exegete to understand their basic presuppositions or to put a significance on its conclusions which they indeed deserve. It is urgently to be desired that historico-critical exegetes present their studies in such a way as to make apparent their necessity and appropriateness and, therewith, their theological relevance and productiveness. But the shortcomings of historico-critical exegesis are in no case an argument against its fundamental justification.

So the question remains: Is there a legitimate path leading from this *historico-critical* exegesis to a genuine proclamation in the present day and for the present day? Can that chasm really be bridged? After all, the real historical involvement of the entire Old Testament is not just a garment to be taken off in order to unveil a hidden, timeless "content" of relevance; this involvement is rather part of the entire form of the Old Testament. The procedure of eliminating the "sub-Christian" and "pre-Christian" elements of the Old Testament which belong to the history of re igion, in order to retain as the essential "core" the pallid and uncompelling phenomenon of an "ethical monotheism," a "moral religion," is hardly worth discussing today. This procedure simply misses the concrete content of the Old Testament, which is concerned with events in history.

But if the historical character of the Old Testament cannot be set aside in exegesis at any point, what is to be done? Since the Old Testament by tradition is part of the Christian Bible, is there anything left but to jump across that chasm into some kind of "practical exegesis" which simply disregards the necessity of historico-critical exegesis and in the end learns to live with a somewhat guilty or, at least, a weak scientific conscience by repeated practice at the *sacrificum intellectus*? It is no exaggeration to say that this sort of "practical exegesis" is widely in vogue. Then, what is the point of adhering stubbornly to the validity of the Old Testament in Christian preaching in opposition to the period when the Old Testament was despised and condemned for political reasons? Is the Old Testament really valid as it is, and as it was read by Jesus Christ as a witness to himself, and as such handed down to his followers? Would it not be more honorable to accept the hardly obsolete thesis of Adolph von Harnack's?[1] He called it a great misfortune that "the Reformation was unable to avoid the fate of retaining the Old Testament in the sixteenth century." He thought it "the consequence of religious and ecclesiastical paralysis" that "since the nineteenth century the Old Testament is still conserved as a canonical document of Protestantism," for in the nineteenth century *Religionsgeschichte* showed how the Old Testament was conditioned by historical and religious development.[2] If we reject this thesis of Adolph von Harnack's—and most would agree in doing so today—and consequently "continue to use" the Old Testament, our decision will be valid and based on fact only if

---

[1] *Marcion,* 2nd ed. (1924), p. 217.
[2] *Op. cit.,* p. 221.

we are determined to read the Old Testament in the form in which it is given. It is the conviction that the Old Testament cannot be read just in the form in which it has been handed down to us, which gives rise to the demands for a specially qualified *ad hoc* method of exegesis. It is interesting that such demands for a special method of exegesis are not raised to the same extent with regard to the New Testament. In reality there can be only one method of exegesis—an exegesis whose work is defined by its subject. Such exegesis may be more or less perfect—and as the work of human beings it will always be imperfect—but there is no choice between different kinds of "exegesis."

All these reflections force this question upon us: Is there a "re-presentation"[3] of the Old Testament which is exegetically legitimate, one not "made up" for some purpose, but founded on the very subject itself? For an answer, we have to turn to the Old Testament. In fact, the Old Testament itself knows of the process of a "re-presentation" of historical events. We shall focus our attention on the two questions, what is "re-presented," and in what way it is "re-presented."

In ancient Israel there were three great annual festivals of pilgrimage, during which all men were to appear at the sanctuaries of the country. Two of these festivals which were taken over from the cultic tradition of the country were given a partly new interpretation in Israel—they were "historized"; that is, related to certain events of history. The festival of Passover-Unleavened Bread originally was a combination of an apotropaic sacrificial rite (probably a custom of nomadic herdsmen performed when they set out for their summer pastures) with an agricultural festival celebrated in order to dedicate the grain at the beginning of its harvest. But in Israel it came to be celebrated, year by year, in that month in which Yahweh had delivered Israel from Egypt (Deut. 16:1). It now was celebrated "in remembrance of

---

[3] To avoid the constant use of German terms, "re-presentation" and "re-present" are used by the translator to translate the words *Vergegenwärtigung* and *Vergegenwärtigen*. As used in this article, these words are technical terms which mean "to actualize in the present." Both the notion of "contemporizing" and of "making relevant" are involved. Any English word is admittedly inadequate.

the Exodus from Egypt" (Deut. 16:3), and unleavened bread was eaten to re-create the original situation of anxious haste. So annually Israel re-created the situation of being prepared for the setting-out which, according to Exodus 12:11, was part of the Passover directly before the Exodus. The entire Passover-instruction of Exodus 12:1-20 undoubtedly was designed for a Passover to be celebrated every year (cf. Exod. 12:24, 25).

A somewhat similar development occurred in the case of the Feast of Tabernacles. It originated in the people's custom of living in "booths" for the purpose of harvesting fruit from the orchards. But in Israel the living in "booths" was re-enacted "that your generations may know that I made the children of Israel to dwell in booths, when I brought them out of the land of Egypt" (Lev. 23:43, K.J.V.). Thus, in both these festivals the situation of the Exodus from Egypt was again and again contemporized in certain details. Because these festivals originally were connected with the agricultural year, they were repeated annually; their being "historicized" led to an annual "re-presentation" of certain elements of past historic events.

Because of the relations between "myth and ritual" and "cult and drama" set forth in *Religionsgeschichte,* there is nowadays a tendency to assume a distinct "dramatic" element in the Israelitic cult, albeit in this case it is a matter of "dramatized history" rather than of "dramatized myth." Supposedly, at the Festival of the Passover-Unleavened Bread and at the Festival of Tabernacles the "Exodus from Egypt" was "performed" in the cult, in a "sacral drama," the details of which have not come down to us. In such a way these respective events are said to have been "re-presented." I hesitate to attribute to this supposition a value which is given it by many today. But certain features of "re-presenting by performing" are surely present in the Israelite cult in the Old Testament in view of what has been said so far. But there is something else to be said on this matter which is of its essence in the Old Testament. In the instructions given for the celebration of Passover, already mentioned above (Exod. 12:24 ff.), it is commanded that the act of worship should be interpreted by simply retelling the story of the Exodus from Egypt, in order

that its tidings might be passed on from generation to generation (vss. 26, 27a). Thus, the narration of the event of God's
wonderful act is a necessary part of the "re-presentation."

"Re-presentation" by the spoken word occurs also in connection with the proclamation of the law which, according to
Deuteronomy 31:10-13, was to be repeated at the Feast of Tabernacles every seventh year. Can we posit a "Feast of the Covenant," at whose recurring celebrations the events of Mount
Sinai were performed and, together with it, the law proclaimed?[4]
The historical value of assuming such a regular "dramatization"
of the events of Mount Sinai in the cult is debatable. Yet one
can see, particularly from the Deuteronomic law, that the repeated proclamations of the law, which indeed took place, were
always formulated in such a way as to make Israel hear the law
as if it were for the very first time. Indeed, the Deuteronomic
law is formulated as Moses' speech addressed to the Israel of his
time, and originally to Israel standing at Mount Horeb. This
could be done because later Israel was identified with the Israel
of the wilderness, and the Deuteronomic law could receive the
form of the address of Moses even when it arose in a post-
Mosaic time. Particularly illuminating in this matter is the
formulation of Deuteronomy 5:3, which appears in a secondary
introduction-piece to the Deuteronomic law: "Yahweh made
not this covenant with our fathers, but with us, even us, who
are all here alive today." There is no reason for supposing that
this statement, formulated as the speech of Moses, is meant to
be an argument against the idea of another covenant which preceded the one made between Yahweh and Israel at Mount Horeb.
The author simply "forgets his part" and for a moment drops
the projection of the Deuteronomic law back into Moses' time
to think of the later generations of Israel who, when the law
was proclaimed, were expected to listen to the law just as if they
themselves—and not their ancestors—were standing at Mount
Horeb to receive the demands of their God. The frequently occurring expression, "today," in Deuteronomy is to be understood

---

4 Cf. especially S. Mowinckel, *Le decalogue* (1927) ; also G. von Rad, *Das
Formgeschichtliche Problem des Hexateuchs* (1938), pp. 13 ff.

in the same sense.[5] It is not meant to shift the historical environment of Deuteronomy, but rather to furnish the situation for the repeated proclamation of the law. This is especially true of the solemn paragraph Deuteronomy 26:16-19: *"To-day* Yahweh thy God commandeth thee. . . . Thou hast declared Yahweh *to-day* to be thy God. . . . Yahweh hath declared thee *to-day* to be a people of his own possession . . ."

In fact, we may include as texts of this kind those passages primarily liturgical in character, in which, by using "we" or "ye," Israel is addressed as if it were in the situation of ancient Israel although it is, in fact, the later generations that are in the mind of the writer. When the children ask what is the meaning of the ordinances, they shall be answered: "We were Pharaoh's slaves in Egypt; and Yahweh brought us out of Egypt with a strong hand . . ." (Deut. 6:20 ff.). The formula of confession in Deuteronomy 26:5 ff. is in the same vein: "The Egyptians dealt ill with us . . . and Yahweh heard our voice . . ." Again and again this word is spoken: "To-day if ye will hear his voice, harden not your heart, as at Meribah, as in the day of Massah in the wilderness . . ." (Ps. 95:7 f.), as if those who are addressed here had been present at Meribah and Massah.[6] These statements are hardly to be explained merely by reference to the idea of the solidarity of the whole people throughout all the periods of their historical existence.[7] Particularly, the emphatic "to-day" of Deuteronomy is not explicable in terms of so general an idea. It is, rather, a matter of a continuing "re-presentation" of past events.

Such "re-presentation" in the Old Testament can also refer to events of the future, and not only to those of the past as has been the case in the examples adduced so far. We leave out of account the special case of the prophetic oracle, in which the prophet speaks of events to come, which he in vision and audi-

---

[5] Rightly pointed out by von Rad, *op. cit.,* pp. 25 ff.

[6] Of course, the following verse speaks of "your fathers"; but the very abruptness of the transition shows that those addressed were put in the situation of their ancestors.

[7] This idea in the particular sense of a solidarity in guilt may be present in those prayers of confession in which, by using "we," those who pray confess the guilt of the past as their own (Neh. 9:33; Dan. 9:5 ff.).

tion already had experienced as being present; the prophetic experience is a subject in its own right. However, in the sphere of the cult, future events were spoken of as if they had already occurred. The Psalms of the "enthronement of Yahweh" are a case in point.[8] Their characteristic formula of enthronement, "Yahweh has become King,"[9] is pronounced as though the enthronement of Yahweh happened at that very moment. Of course what is meant by the enthronement of Yahweh in these Psalms is an open question. Probably these Psalms are developed from the idea that God became King in the primeval past, an event cultically "re-presented" in them (for example, Ps. 93). But there is scarcely any doubt that thought about the past (*Urzeit*) was related to the idea of the final time (*Endzeit*); in some of the enthronement Psalms—I think in particular of Psalm 47—the center of interest is the eschatological reign of God.[10] Like other Psalms, the eschatologically interpreted enthronement Psalms were meant to be sung in the cult; and thus in the cult the primeval and eschatological accession of God to rule could be announced as if it were a present event.

This theme of cultic "re-presentation" in the Old Testament (which appears to have consisted primarily of interpretative narration and also of the constantly repeated Word of God as his demand on Israel, accompanied by certain elements of dramatic action) can and must be developed further. This may suffice, though, for raising the question about the basis of such a "re-presentation." The realm in which the "re-presentation" took place was the cult. Since the Israelite cult in many respects depended on traditions of Canaanite agriculture, and thus on the cult of the ancient Orient as a whole, it may well be asked whether it is related to the "thinking in cycles" prevalent in the ancient Orient, according to which every event repeats itself periodically, in the course of a year or any other space of time, and is thus, again and again, "re-presented." As a matter of fact, in Babylon, at the great Feast of the New Year, year by year the

---

[8] We can be certain that these hymns were used in the cult without settling the intricate problems involved in their date and interpretation.

[9] Cf. H.-J. Kraus, *Die Königherrschaft Gottes in Alten Testament* (1951), pp. 2 ff.

[10] Cf. also Kraus, *op. cit.*, pp. 99 ff.

great enthronement cry, "Marduk has become king," resounded, and the epic of creation was solemnly recited in order to "re-present" the great act of creation. It would be a denial of evident facts to reject any connection between the matters in the Old Testament here in question and ancient Oriental cultic practice and its widespread notion of continuous repetition of events.

But on the other hand—and here is a most essential distinction—the "re-presentation" at the periodical feasts of ancient Israel does not involve some timeless myth, but something which by nature is a unique historical event. It is primarily, as has been demonstrated, the Exodus from Egypt. Here is something peculiar to the Old Testament, due to its general orientation to history rather than myth. How was "re-presentation" possible in the Old Testament on this particular basis? Will it be necessary to think in terms of a special "concept of time" for the Old Testament, or perhaps for the Bible as a whole? It would be a profitable task to investigate in exhaustive fashion the concept of "time" in the Old Testament, as well as in the New; however, it seems to me quite doubtful whether our problem would be clarified by detecting a special "concept of time" in either of the Testaments, especially since conceptual thinking is quite alien to the Old Testament. In any case, the particular manifestation of "re-presentation" in the Old Testament is inseparably linked with the subject of this "re-presentation"—God acting, and, indeed, God acting in history.

As in all history, so *this* history is especially involved in the tension between the course of time and the presence of God which is not bound to time, between the "mediateness" (*Mittelbarkeit*) and the "immediateness" (*Unmittelbarkeit*) of all history to God, of which K. Barth speaks in discussing God's unending creation.[11] "Re-presentation" is founded on this— that God and his action are always present, while man in his inevitable temporality cannot grasp this present-ness except by "re-presenting" the action of God over and over again in his worship.

Herewith the question posed above is answered positively. In

---

11 *Die Kirchliche Dogmatik*, Vol. III, Part 1 (1945), p. 83.

the Old Testament—and the same could be proved for the New Testament—there is the legitimate appearance of a "re-presentation" of past events, namely, in the realm of the cult and worship. This is exegetically demonstrable; what remains is to develop the consequences of this exegetical finding. If Christian proclamation means to take its biblical basis seriously, it will have to follow the biblical witness also in the question of the "re-presentation."

"Re-presentation" in the Old Testament deals with the acts of God in history, his saving acts, and his demands. This is an important conclusion also for practical purposes. At the Passover, it shall be told that Yahweh "forbearingly passed over the houses of the Israelites in Egypt" (Exod. 12:27); the Passover shall be celebrated in the month in which "thy God brought thee out of Egypt by night" (Deut. 16:1); the living in booths at the Feast of Tabernacles is intended to be a reminder that "I made the Israelites live in booths, when I brought them out of the land of Egypt" (Lev. 23:43). All this implies certain negative, but distinct, conclusions.

A legitimate "re-presentation" cannot use the individual human figures of biblical history as its subjects, either as ethical "models," which they in fact never are,[12] or as exemplary "heroes of faith" since in the biblical narratives they are never so presented,[13] or as representatives of true humanity whose experiences, psychologically or phenomenologically or sentimentally, are to be imitated and depicted in terms of contemporary man. All these figures are individuals of times now past, whose human lives and ways we know but little, and it cannot be the task of genuine proclamation to fill out their picture.[14] Perhaps there is no need to be emphatic about what has just been said as there will be general, though not complete, agreement about it. Emphasis on the next negation is more crucial.

---

[12] The one exception is the reference to the "long-suffering of the prophets" and the "patience of Job" in James 5:10 f.

[13] In Romans 4:1 ff. the faith of Abraham is discussed, not to hold up Abraham as an ideal, but to answer the question concerning what God reckons as righteousness. Even in Hebrews 11, the emphasis is placed on what faith is able to do, rather than on the list of men as models.

[14] Of course, a poet can undertake this task, for instance, Thomas Mann in his novel about Joseph and his brothers.

A legitimate "re-presentation" cannot use specific historical situations which emerge in the Old Testament as its subject. For historical events happen but once. Though this proposition is naturally not formulated just so in the Old Testament, the historical narratives of the Old Testament in their entirety presuppose its validity.[15] It is certainly not biblical to think in terms of the movement of oscillations or cycles which bring about the periodical return of all things. As in individual human life, so every event in history is a unique and irrevocable occasion.[16] An illustration will clarify the point. According to Isaiah, chapter 7, in the years 733 B.C. King Ahaz was offered that famous word, "If ye will not believe, surely ye shall not be established," together with that famous "sign," to support his faith. This historical situation never happened again in Israel's history and will never happen again in any history. In those days a decision was reached once and for all. It is a frivolous question to ask what might have happened if Ahaz had had "faith," and what the course of history—in this case, the saving history of God—would have been. The Word of God, delivered then as message by the Prophet, stands as valid Word; but the historical situation in which it was proclaimed cannot be identified with any other situation in history. The same "opportunity" never returns. The history of Israel is not repeated in the histories of other nations, nor in the history of the universe. Principles of a *"Weltpolitik Gottes"* cannot be derived from God's dealing with the people of Israel.

According to the Old Testament, the subject of a legitimate "re-presentation" can be only the saving acts of God himself, to which saving acts belong also the promising and the demanding Word of God, and the punitive judgments of God. These saving acts, though they have entered into the "mediateness" of history and are perceptible to us only in this "mediateness," yet are always present as the "immediate" acts of God. And we, as men caught in the time-process, can do nothing but "re-present"

---

[15] Only in the eschaton, at the edge of history, does the historical deed of God repeat itself in a different way and on another plane. Cf. the role which the miracle of the Exodus plays in the eschatological proclamation of Deutero-Isaiah.

[16] Cf. K. Barth, *Die Kirchliche Dogmatik,* Vol. III, Part 4 (1951), pp. 652 ff.

again and again. And in what way do we "re-present?" By proclaiming the saving acts of God, by "telling" them. The elements of dramatic action which are found in the "re-presentations" of the Old Testament gave rise to the question "Why?" (according to Exod. 12:24-27a), and thus occasioned the proclamation of the saving acts of God. That which is to be proclaimed is given in a "tradition." It is helpful to put the matter as simply as Karl Barth once did:[17] "In revelation we deal with a 'news report,' or better said, with a 'sheaf of news reports,' and these 'news reports written in words' appear in a 'book, the book of the Old and the New Testaments'; and we have to ask what these 'news reports' say, and we have to pass them on just as they are."

But how can we read these "news reports" which have been handed down from ages past, fixed in a language belonging to history? The answer to this question is exegesis, historical exegesis appropriate to the matter, yes, even "historico-critical" exegesis, that is, exegesis which knows how to test and to "discriminate." It is the task of such exegesis to prevent these "news reports" from being conveniently compressed into a short "resumé" that is monotonously repeated again and again, and to make plain the variety of voices with their manifold nuances which speak in these "news reports." Human voices can tell the saving acts of God only "by divers portions and in divers manners" (Heb. 1:1); we would be impoverished if this manifoldness were not continuously probed.

---

[17] "Das christliche Verständnis der Offenbarung" in *Theologische Existenz heute*, N. F., 12 (1948), pp. 9, 13 f.

5.

PROMISE AND FULFILLMENT*
by Walther Zimmerli

translated by James Wharton

The question concerning the connection between the Old and New Testaments has been opened for our generation in a new way since critical study in both Testaments has disclosed new perspectives. A particularly striking way in which the New Testament conceives of the relationship of both Testaments is the language of promise and fulfillment.

It would be a sharp criticism of the New Testament language of promise and fulfillment from the very outset if we were forced to conclude that it had been pressed upon the Old Testament as something foreign, something not current in the Old Testament itself. Thus the first task must be to determine, through an investigation within the Old Testament, to what extent this New Testament language corresponds to authentic Old Testament forms, and to what extent it may be considered legitimate interpretation of these forms in its appropriation of them.

I

It is methodologically in order to begin with that which formed the core of Israel's confession—the Pentateuchal traditions. In 1928 Galling[1] called attention to the fact that a peculiar twofold aspect of the statements about the election of Israel may be discerned in the Old Testament. Alongside the talk of Israel's election in the event of the deliverance from

---

* This article appeared originally in *Evangelische Theologie* (Jahrgang 12, 1952, Juli/August), Heft 1/2, pp. 6 ff.
[1] K. Galling, "Die Erwählungstraditionen Israels," BZAW, 48 (1928).

Egypt, which may be found evenly distributed throughout all the different parts of the Old Testament, there stands the insistence (attested on a much narrower basis) that the election of Israel is grounded in the election of its patriarchs Abraham, Isaac, and Jacob. Galling[2] interpreted the proclamation about the patriarchs as a secondary structure, deliberately created in the early period of the monarchy and derived from a "greater Israel" ideology. As early as 1929 Alt[3] had shown that the word about the "God of the fathers" (more specifically the God of Abraham, the God of Isaac, the God of Jacob) may have retained original elements of tradition from the preconquest period of the tribes. In them lie catalyzed the recollections of encounters between the individual patriarchal figures and God, recollections which were formerly at home among different tribal groups and independent from each other. Considering the sociological type of these groups (to be identified as semi-nomads, alternately seeking pasturage in desert and arable land), the supposition lies near at hand that the promise of possession of their own land played a role in the earliest form of this body of tradition.

In the course of time this complex of patriarchal tradition underwent in many respects a process of shaping and concentration, not to mention the heavy addition of material that bears the marks of the postconquest period.[4] Through combination with the word about the deliverance of Israel from Egypt and the conquest of the land (which unquestionably stands at the center of the Israelite credo[5]) the patriarchal tradition was pressed into a unified succession of historical events. Abraham, Isaac, and Jacob no longer stand parallel to each other as separate figures proper to different tribal groups (which was probably the case at one time). They are condensed into a genealogical order, each patriarch embodying all Israel, the son carrying on the divine Word of promise given to the father.

---

2 *Ibid.*, pp. 64 f., 74 ff.
3 A. Alt, "Der Gott der Väter," BWANT, 3, Folge, Heft, 12 (1929).
4 Here belong, above all, the cult legends which are connected with the patriarchal figures and point to holy places within the arable land.
5 On this idea, see G. von Rad, *Das formgeschichtliche Problem des Hexateuch*, BWANT, 4, Folge, Heft, 26 (1938), *Ges. Studien z. AT* (1958).

There is only one history of Yahweh with his people Israel,[6] rather than many diverse histories. Structural accommodation to the Exodus story (itself already having been amplified by the account of a covenant ratification on the mountain of God) may be seen further in that now a covenant-ratification scene, accompanied by phenomena of fire and smoke,[7] intrudes into the patriarchal narratives with the first member Abraham, hinting at the hidden norm of the Sinai-event. Moreover, the strong stylization of the introductory portion of the Abraham story[8] (apparently composed *de novo* by the Yahwist) under the Exodus motif may be understood from this standpoint. In Genesis 15:7 one can hear the echo of the formula of Yahweh's self-disclosure known from the introductory sentence of the Decalogue, "I am Yahweh, who led you out of Ur of the Chaldeans."

In the passages just cited, there is an unmistakable intention to make the patriarchal narratives parallel the Exodus tradition. In the light of this, it is all the more remarkable, on the other hand, to see at another point the increasing emergence of a basic element of the patriarchal stories which was originally quite independent of the Exodus tradition—the element of promise. This element of older tradition proved able not only to establish and maintain itself, but also to become dominant in the entire breadth of the patriarchal narratives, pervading normatively even those areas in which the traditional material itself was of a quite different sort. As early as the time of the Yahwist, the entire patriarchal history appears under the sign of promise.

In this connection it must be made clear that this talk of promise is nothing rigid or crystallized. Even though it is precisely in these important passages that the ceremonious formula of promise appears, nevertheless the formula does not remain fixed, but evinces a turbulent history of extension and reinterpretation on a deeper level.

The original content of the promise to the fathers may have

---

[6] Cf. the basic analyses of M. Noth, *Überlieferungsgeschichte des Pentateuch* (1948).

[7] Gen. 15:7-12, 17-18 (J).

[8] Gen. 12:1 ff.

consisted in the pledge of the land. In Deuteronomy the promise
in this form may still be discerned clearly in later times.[9] Very
early, however, the pledge of a great posterity was ranked alongside it. The extensive elaboration of this element, so powerfully
emphasized through the use of the suspense-building motif of
the childless wife in all three patriarchal stories,[10] was probably
due to the combination of patriarchal history with the Exodus
tradition. There is a sharp contrast between the fathers, on the
one hand, singled out and separated from their clans, and, on
the other hand, the existence of Israel in its fullness as a whole
people.[11] In humble, astonished confession, the biblical writers
express this in the symbolic figures of the stars of the heavens,
the sand of the sea, and the dust of the earth.[12]

The vitality of the conception of promise may be seen in
another way in the introductory passage of the Abraham story
formed by the Yahwist. The word of Yahweh to Abraham which
introduces the Abraham story[13] indeed sounds the note of land
and posterity as elements of promise, but it clearly places them
in the shadow of the pledge of a blessing (unmistakable in the
fivefold use of the root *brk*). "Blessing" here means more than a
mere numerical increase. This theme of the patriarchal history,
newly composed by the Yahwist, can only be understood against
the background of the theme of the "curse" stories in Genesis
3-11, which have been placed before it. The recognition of a
specific intent in the composition of the Yahwist does not remove, even in this passage, the pertinent question, "What, from
the point of view of content, is expressed through this transcending of the promises of land and posterity which are concretely unfolded in later chapters?" It can hardly be denied that
we encounter here an expression of a deepening interpretation

---

[9] G. von Rad, "Verheissenes Land und Jahwes Land," ZDPV, 66 (1943),
pp. 191 ff. (On p. 192 von Rad has placed together all the promise passages
and their various contents.)
[10] Abraham-Sarah, Gen. 11:30; 15:2 ff.; 17:17; 18:11 f.; Isaac-Rebeccah,
Gen. 25:21; Jacob-Rachel, Gen. 29:31; 30:1 f.
[11] This contrast-motif is used in a different way in the arrogant speech of
those who remain in the land (Ezek. 33:24).
[12] Stars, Gen. 15:5; 22:17; Exod. 32:13; cf. further Deut. 1:10; 10:22;
28:62; Neh. 9:23; sand on the shore, Gen. 22:17; 32:13; cf. also Isa. 10:22;
48:19; dust of the earth, Gen. 13:16; 28:14.
[13] Gen. 12:1-3.

of the simple land and posterity promises. Here it is said: Beyond the promise of land and increasing posterity, there is promised, in the coming history of Israel, a fullness of blessing thoroughly capable of constituting a universal counter-history to the world-wide history of curse related in Genesis 3:11 (J). The old patriarchal history, which looked forward to fulfillment in the Conquest, is thereby placed in the tension of a much farther-looking expectation of fulfillment. For Abraham's posterity finally to become a people and to possess the land of Canaan—this alone would not mean the full realization of the promise. The program of the Yahwist is here greater than the fulfillment about which he himself will later tell. Beyond his account of fulfillment, promise yet unredeemed will remain open.

In another way, the Priestly document deepens the content of promise indicated above. Yahweh's revelatory address to Abraham also mentions the promise of increase and land (Gen. 17: 6-8), but adds to it a third aspect—the promise that God wills to be the God of Abraham and his posterity. In this address the first half of the covenant formula is cited, "I will be your God and you shall be my people."[14] The gift of the land and of increase (so the P document wants to say) are only the earnests of a greater promise—Yahweh wills the achievement of the reality of God's own people, and he wills to be God who is near to his people. To sketch the mounting realization of this goal is the theme of the total narrative of the P document. This narrative shows, then, that the Priestly author achieves the combination of the patriarchal narratives with the Exodus story under the arch of tension of promise/fulfillment on a much narrower basis than did the Yahwist. Whereas the Yahwist (intent on a parallel elaboration of the patriarchal and Exodus stories) did not hesitate to speak of a covenant of Yahweh with Abraham and a second covenant with the Israel of Moses' time, the P document, on the other hand, senses in this twofold form of the word about the covenant a language that is not fully appropriate to the word of promise and fulfillment. Consequently the P author

---

[14] G. von Rad, "Verheissenes Land und Jahwes Land," ZDPV, 66 (1943), p. 196. *Ges. Studien z. AT* (1958).

speaks not a word about a covenant in the time of Moses.[15] The desire to present the element promise/fulfillment in a pure form has asserted itself here over the tendency to stylize the patriarchal and Exodus stories in parallel to each other. Thus the strange phenomenon can be observed that the word about covenant, which was probably originally anchored in the account of the Sinai events, first intruded (through the Yahwist) into the Abraham story; afterwards, however (in the P document), it was suppressed in the very place where it originally inhered.

After this glance at the turbulent elaboration of the promise to the patriarchs, perhaps now it is possible to give a more specific answer than has previously been given to a quite basic question: "Why were the patriarchal narratives, so understood, included in the complex of stories in which Israel related its primeval history as a folk?" In accord with the investigations of Alt concerning the "God of the fathers" one may answer first of all, simply: "Here certain ancient and authentic traditions have persisted." This answer is important, but it is probably not sufficient. One can perceive clearly enough in other passages how various groups within Israel were able to forget old memories without a backward glance, eliminating them from the tradition when they did not fit the great context of the Yahweh history in which Israel believed.[16] Alt has shown further that the way in which the gods of the fathers were connected to specific human groups (families, clans, tribes), and their movement toward social and historical functions, must have been favorable to the combination of the patriarchal traditions with the Yahweh faith.[17] From another standpoint Noth has established the fact that the common way in which the patriarchal history and the conquest tradition point to possession of arable land must have brought both complexes of tradition close together.[18] Beyond all of these historical and traditio-historical considerations, how-

---

[15] Von Rad has pointed to this fact emphatically (*Die Priesterschrift im Hexateuch*, BWANT, 4, Folge, Heft, 13, 1934, 176 f.).

[16] How completely, for example, have the immigration traditions of the Galilean tribes disappeared!

[17] *Op. cit.*, p. 66.

[18] *Op. cit.*, p. 59.

ever, the theological statement must be essayed: In the language about promise, which in the patriarchal era already precedes the election of the historical Israel, the Israelite faith apparently recognized a fully authentic, indeed necessary (from the standpoint of content) exegesis of that which is properly intended in the Exodus credo. The word about the promise to the fathers is understood by the faith of Israel (which in the first line pointed toward Yahweh, the God who had led them out of Egypt), not as a competing or endangering element, but as an unfolding development pertinent to the genuine meaning of the Exodus confession, and indeed securing it. Only in this way can one understand that the word about the promise of Yahweh to the fathers seeps into almost all the patriarchal narratives like a liquid dye, giving them the quite specific coloration which distinguishes them even in a superficial reading.

With this consideration, however, the question concerning the theological meaning of the category promise/fulfillment comes insistently to the fore. What is it that gives this language such indispensable significance in the innermost circle of the Old Testament credo?

A first consideration is easily recognized: The category promise/fulfillment serves to secure the irrevocable validity of the gift bestowed by God. Behind the gracious favor of Yahweh, which Israel had experienced in the deliverance from Egypt, in the covenant ratification on the mountain of God, and in the leading into the land, there stands not merely a momentary impulse of Yahweh, which can be reversed capriciously tomorrow, on a new impulse; what happens to Israel is that which Yahweh has promised of old in his word. The fulfillment of such promises proclaims the faithfulness of Yahweh which remains steadfast throughout all time.

In order to judge adequately the uniqueness and the importance of this word, we would do well to ask how peoples surrounding Israel described the validity of a fundamental religious givenness in similar relationships. Why is Babylon the holy city? It is because, at the time after the battle in which Marduk conquered the chaos-dragon and built heaven and

earth, the Annunaki in gratitude built the temple Esagila and
the temple tower as a dwelling for Marduk, and so brought
Babylon into being.[19] In the Assyrian period, in the city of
Asshur, the same narrative was taken over as the basis for the
holiness of the city and its temple Esharra.[20] Why is Thebes, the
city of Amon, the holy center of Egypt? It is because it is
the "honorable hill of the Primeval beginning, the beneficent
eye of the Lord of all, his beloved place, which bears his beauty
and surrounds his entourage."[21] Hermopolis and other Egyptian
cities made similar claims.[22]

Israel answers the question as to the validity of the honor of
its own land thus: It is the "sworn" land, that is, the land
pledged to Israel through the promise. In Israel the category
promise/fulfillment takes the place of the mythical orientation
which prevailed in its environment. Faith in the gracious favor
of God toward Israel made visible in the gift is not substantiated
by tracing the human in an unbroken line back to the divine,
erasing the limits of space and time. Rather this substantiation
is found in the reference to the word of promise which precedes
in history the event of realization. Yahweh substantiates his act
through his word, and alongside this there is no impersonal
obligation of Yahweh, grounded in mythical relationships, which
could help toward substantiation.

If we attempt now to define the category promise/fulfillment
more deeply in terms of its content, a primary point to establish
is this: Promise and fulfillment encompass in every case a
specific historical space. They are bound inseparably to history;
not merely to a "historicity" conceived as having no extension
in either direction, but a history which is extended in time. Without such a history, promise/fulfillment is inconceivable. This
category is an unlimited safeguard against every attempt at self-
redemption from this temporally extending course of history,
subject as it is to the lowliness of ever-recurring accidental and

19 *Enuma elish*, VI, 34 ff. (Gressmann, AOT², pp. 122 f.; Pritchard,
Ancient Near Eastern Texts, pp. 68 f.).
20 AOT², p. 132.
21 H. Kees, "Ägypten. Religionsgeschichtliches Lesebuch²," 10 (1928), p. 3.
22 *Op. cit.*, pp. 3 f.

unfathomable events. Anyone who knows of promise and fulfillment is responsible to a yesterday about which he has heard something, and he walks toward a tomorrow. This category guards against every flight into a timeless, mystical understanding of God's nearness, as well as against an understanding of encounter with God reduced to a single existentialistic point without historical relatedness. Israel has been given the land and has been called to its proper being through a word of promise; when Israel speaks of fulfilled promise, it knows about its historical origins in the patriarchal period.

A second point is implicit in this: the recognition that this historical path stands under a definite tension. Anyone who speaks of promise and fulfillment knows of veiled purposes and distressed waiting; he knows of walking, and not only of standing still; he knows of a summoning, and not only of a looking on. History receives a declivity toward that which is yet to come. But this is not merely a declivity determined by empty motivating powers, but one which stands illuminated by clear words.

All of these moments emerge clearly in the language about promise and fulfillment. Through the appropriation of the patriarchal tradition and in the placing of it before the Exodus tradition, the credo of Exodus and conquest undergoes not only an enrichment but a substantiating explication. It is obviously then understood only when it is heard in this aspect of motion and authentic historicity.

II

Until now we have followed the language of promise and fulfillment in the innermost circle of the Old Testament credo. It would be remarkable if it did not appear also as a structural line in the other Old Testament statements.

In his *Studies in Deuteronomy*, von Rad has also thrown light on the theology of history in the books of Kings.[23] He has shown

---

[23] G. von Rad, *Deuteronomiumstudien B: Die deuteronomistische Geschichtstheologie in den Königsbuchern* (1947), *Ges. Studien z. AT* (1958). Translated by D. Stalker in *Studies in Biblical Theology*, No. 9 (SCM Press and Alec R. Allenson, 1953).

how the entire history of the monarchical period is shaped, according to the Deuteronomistic understanding, in terms of the fulfillment of a prophetic word which always recurs anew. The prophet has an unmistakably functional significance in this historical work. The promise of Nathan to David runs through the entire royal history of Judah. The threat of Ahijah of Shiloh and the promise to Jeroboam foreshadow the coming event of the division of the monarchy and of the independent Northern Kingdom; the word of the unknown man of God from Judah foretells the pious King Josiah from afar; and so it continues throughout all the named and unnamed prophets until the end of the kingdom of Judah.

When we compare this group of statements with the promise to the fathers, we see on the one hand that the language of promise and fulfillment here no longer attaches only to the great basic affirmation of the bestowal upon Israel of its existence as a people and the bestowal of the possession of land; but this language has dared to move out into the separate branches of the history of Israel. Alongside the great pervading promise to David, which existed from the time of 2 Samuel 7, maintaining its force in the entire subsequent history, there appear also the small episodic events of dynastic changes in Israel,[24] the rebuilding of Jericho,[25] the Josianic reform,[26] and Josiah's death,[27] all clarified by prophetic words which precede them. In a certain sense this represents an exemplification, worked out in individual cases, of the fact that the total history of God's people, also in many separate decisions, is stretched in an arc of tension from promise to fulfillment.

On the other hand, it is also plain here how much the knowledge of promise and fulfillment entails a journey, a "being on the way." The Deuteronomic history may well have been written during the Exile, at the time of the collapse of Israel's history. It is clear that its author understands this event not merely as a catastrophe which has stripped history of its meaning,

---

[24] 1 Kings 14:6 ff./15:29; 16:1 ff./12:21, 23/2 Kings 9:36.
[25] Joshua 6:26/1 Kings 16:34.
[26] Does 1 Kings 13:2 envision 2 Kings 23:30?
[27] 2 Kings 22:15 ff./23:30.

a catastrophe which now hangs timelessly over him; he has a Yesterday. The collapse which lies behind him is the judgment of Yahweh, which, in its character of fulfilled prophecy, is more than an anonymous fate. But he also stands before Tomorrow—even if this tomorrow is characterized only by the despairing question as to whether the promise to David has lapsed completely.

The comparison with the promise to the fathers also touches on another aspect. A new content emerges in the promise. In the statements of promise in the books of Kings the note of judgment and doom is sounded. The question as to how this new content of promise is to be evaluated must be our concern in later connections.

Finally, this point ought to be made: In the patriarchal stories the Word of promise was spoken personally by God to the one receiving it; here the Word is bound, for the most part, to a specific group of men who can be described in terms of an office. The prophet has become the bearer of the office of mediating the promise.

This is the place to pause and allow room for a parenthetical consideration. Until now, promise/fulfillment has been described as a category peculiar to the Old Testament. But does not this category indeed extend into the area of a much broader relationship in the history of religion? Individuals who bring divine oracles interpreting the future are found not only in Israel. Mesopotamia knows a very elaborate soothsaying tradition, over which Shamash rules as lord of the oracle and master of divination.[28] In the form of the auditory oracle or the dream, Assarhaddon and Ashurbanipal receive definite advice in specific historical situations.[29] There are texts from Egypt which tell of the choosing of a young king to become monarch in a way reminiscent of elements in the books of Kings.[30] We have texts from Egypt and Mesopotamia which foretell times of doom or prosperity coming upon the entire land.[31] It is clear from the

---

[28] B. Meissner, *Babylonien und Assyrien,* II (1925), pp. 242 ff.
[29] H. Gressmann, AOT², pp. 281-283 ; J. B. Pritchard, ANET, pp. 449-451.
[30] J. B. Pritchard, ANET, pp. 447-449.
[31] AOT², pp. 46-55 ; Pritchard, ANET, pp. 441-446.

polemic introduction of the Deuteronomic law governing prophecy[32] that there was no lack of such persons having to do with prophecy also in Israel's more immediate environment.

In view of all this information, the first thing to establish is that, phenomenologically, these figures have some things in common. We see how near one can come to the other in such incidents as the coming of the seer Balaam from a foreign land, fulfilling the function of a man of God at an important juncture, throwing light upon the coming history of Israel in his prophecy;[33] or the witch of Endor taking over the function of a prophet of doom against Saul (although this function is interrupted by the figure of Samuel whom she has conjured).[34] Unmistakably, the phenomenon of a word-bearer who interprets the future—acknowledged as a phenomenon widespread in the history of religions (van der Leeuw talks here of a "speaker"[35]) —has become in Israel an office which has to do especially with prophecy.

But one must add immediately that, in spite of all phenomenological similarities, the root of the matter in the Old Testament is something different when prophecy is heard. The sort of prophecy that one encounters in Israel's environment always gives the impression of isolated assertions. They do not combine to form a total history overarching the generations and determined by a unified will. It is rather a question of prosperity for the individual king, Ashurbanipal, or the proclamation of a time of distress, rescue from which will be achieved by a single saviour-king; at the court of this king, the formulation of prophecy was probably composed *post eventum* for his glory.[36] One can discern elements of this kind also in Old Testament prophetic words, but all of these words are sustained in a quite different manner by a knowledge of a great history which includes every individual dynasty, in which Yahweh's will for

---

[32] Deut. 18:10 f.
[33] Num. 22-24.
[34] 1 Sam. 28:3 ff.
[35] G. van der Leeuw, *Phänomenologie der Religion* (1939), pp. 204 ff.
[36] The text found in AOT[2], pp. 283 f., and Pritchard, ANET, pp. 451 f., for example, speaks about the alternation of periods of blessing and of doom without any deeper motivation.

justice is being worked out in a manner far transcending the figure of the specific king in question. Blessing or rejection occur not in the free capriciousness of history, but each king stands always in a recognizable relationship to this all-encompassing will of God for his people which is oriented in terms of a definite divine justice. The word of Balaam and even the act of the witch of Endor (without her conscious intent) must accede to this orientation, just as in the patriarchal narrative the blessing of Isaac, in its content of promise, had to submit to the will of Yahweh against the subjective will of Isaac.[37]

But we cannot speak of such matters only with reference to the narrative books. We can no longer pass by the figures in whom promise in the Old Testament is most openly expressed— the written prophets. They must now be dealt with quite fully in their own terms.

The specific form in which the prophetic word appears is the messenger's address.[38] The prophet understands himself above all as a messenger. He must bring news of that which is to come. Everything else he may have to say, whether diatribe, cries of woe, admonition, or exhortation to conversion, is secondary to that principal function, no matter how valid it may be in its own content. It belongs to the essence of the messenger that he is the forerunner of the thing which he announces. The messenger is superfluous when the coming event instantaneously announces its own arrival. Thus the messenger's word always sets up a tension-laden interval between the message and the occurrence of that which is announced. This time interval which is granted in the sending of the messenger is then properly understood by the listener when he understands it as a time in which it will be possible for him to bend himself to the will of the one who sends the message. This can be recognized particularly well in the prophetic paradigm-story of Jonah, for example, where the precise duration of the time interval is stated: "Yet forty days and Nineveh will be destroyed!"[39] Therefore the promise here, as

[37] Gen. 27.
[38] For its form, cf. L. Koehler, "Deuterojesaja," BZAW, 37 (1923), pp. 102 ff., and also his *Kleine Lichter* (1945), pp. 11-17.
[39] Jonah 3:4.

always, sets up a unique interval for freedom. This is true even
of the preaching of Isaiah "lest they see with their eyes and hear
with their ears . . ." No matter how much it was rejected by the
masses, this preaching was able to assemble a circle of disciples
about Isaiah, disciples who may have been the ones intended in
the preaching about the Remnant. The confrontation of Isaiah
with Ahaz also makes this time interval visible. Even for the
proclamation of Ezekiel to the "stiff-necked house that will not
hear,"[40] what we have said holds true. The very fact that this
prophet understands his office as the office of the watchman who,
in view of the coming judgment, must warn the godless individual at the cost of his own life,[41] shows that he also knows
about the interval which is held open.

The preaching of the prophets which precedes the coming
event, then, takes away from it the anonymity of a meaningless
stroke of fate. That which is to come will be a word-become-
history. This must be amplified immediately by a further distinction in order to be fully accurate. There is also a form of
prophecy which cannot be freed from fatalism. The prophecy of
Cassandra in Aeschylus' *Agamemnon* points to an impersonally
happening event in which an old curse is inexorably fulfilled.[42]
The prophetic message, by contrast, alludes again and again to
an event which is personally brought to pass by God, and therefore an event which is supremely personal in its intention.[43] Thus
the soothsaying elements in the prophetic proclamation—that is,
the elements which point to the events in history which are yet
to come—can often fall strangely into the background, and can
be retained with an almost lukewarm indefiniteness. Anyone
who tries to discover from the words of Amos a fortune-teller's
unambiguous picture of that which is to come will find himself
in difficulty. Does Amos foresee earthquake or plague or crop-
failure or military distress or extermination of the people or
exile? The proclamation of Amos becomes completely unam-

[40] Ezek. 3 :7.
[41] Ezek. 3 :16 ff. ; 33 :1 ff.
[42] *Agamemnon*, 1072 ff.
[43] W. Zimmerli, *Gericht und Heil im alttestamentlichen Prophetenwort* (Der
Anfang, Zehlendorfer Vorträge, 1949), pp. 21-46.

biguous, however, when he proclaims in that which is to come, the *one* who is personally coming. "Prepare to meet your God, O Israel!"[44] With irritating carelessness Hosea can place the threat of being carried away into Egypt right alongside talk of being carried away into Assyria.[45] But when he talks about the *one* who comes in history, whether Assyria or Egypt be given the upper hand, all ambiguities cease. "I am like a moth to Ephraim and like dry rot to the house of Judah . . . I will be like a lion to Ephraim and like a young lion to the house of Judah. I, even I, will rend and go away, I will carry off, and none shall rescue."[46] "I, even I . . ."—this is the unambiguous center of all coming events. In the talk about the coming Day of Yahweh, which the prophets appropriate from the popular expectation and fill with new content, this personal center of the coming event becomes most transparent, from the terminological point of view. Yahweh himself is the future about which they speak.

How is this Yahweh-event to be described, then, in terms of content? It is a bit off course to speak here of "the prophets" in a comprehensive way, since very strong differences can be perceived in the structuring of the message at given points; moreover, there are differences between the preaching in the Northern Kingdom and in Judah which must not be overlooked. First of all it is plain that the coming Yahweh-event heralded by the prophets is decisively directed toward Israel as the people properly addressed by it, the people to whom its primary vengeance is turned. It is an event in which the God of Israel from Egypt,[47] the Holy One of Israel,[48] confronts his people.

In this event the terrifying work of the Holy One of Israel, whose wrath burns in judgment upon his people, stands unmistakably in the foreground in the public preaching of the earlier prophecy. Because the work that Yahweh announces in his promise is nothing less than the work in which Yahweh, the Holy One of Israel, is himself fully involved and in which he purposes

44 Amos 4 :12, R.S.V.
45 Hos. 9 :3, 6.
46 Hos. 5 :12, 14, R.S.V.
47 Amos 3 :1 f. ; Hos. 12 :10.
48 Isa. 5 :19 ; 43 :3.

to be glorified, therefore it becomes ever plainer in the prophetic promise that Israel will not be able to survive in this event. The reality of the people of God can actually survive only in their death before the Holy One who has drawn near, in which everything given to them in the strength of the old promise—land, posterity, monarchy, and Temple—are swallowed up together in judgment, and the covenant of Yahweh with Israel comes to an end. In Ezekiel, who carries Hosea and Jeremiah's historical-theological points of departure through to their ultimate and most bitter consequences, this hopelessly-trapped existence of the people of God becomes visible in the sharpest form.[49] In the Exile it breaks in upon Yahweh's people in the historical event visible throughout the world.

But alongside this dark language of promise there runs a different-sounding word, at times only quite softly audible, then breaking out fully, but never totally silent. Because Yahweh himself is there in the event announced by the messengers, it will never carry within it only the condemning fire of his holiness, but also his holy, primeval loving-kindness[50] and his jealous will to complete what he has begun. Thus the well-known elements of promise appear again at this point. The recollection of the promise to David determines Amos 9:11 f., and the talk of the saviour-king is normative for Isaiah 9. The word about the shoot from the severed stump of Jesse[51] attempts to make visible how judgment and salvation stand alongside each other in fulfillment. The new interpretation of the "steadfast, sure love for David" of Isaiah 55:3 recalls in its freedom of expression the deepening interpretation of the promise to the fathers which we characterized earlier. The knowledge of the election of Zion[52] (perhaps connected with the election of David) determines the Zion affirmations of Isaiah, which hint at fulfillment rather than describe it. This knowledge also stands behind the image of eschatological realization in Ezekiel 40 ff., in which the old promise of the land

---

[49] W. Zimmerli, "Das Gotteswort des Ezechiel," ZThK, 48 (1951), pp. 249-262.
[50] Hos. 11:8 f.
[51] Isa. 11:1 ff.
[52] H. J. Kraus, *Die Königsherrschaft Gottes im Alten Testament* (1951), pp. 50 ff.

is impressively connected with the thought that all salvation and healing in the land comes from the place where Yahweh has newly bestowed his presence.[53] In Deutero-Isaiah the old elements of the gift of the land, the increase of the people (contemporarily interpreted as the ingathering of the diaspora to Zion), and the "steadfast, sure love for David" are actualized anew. All this is also related here to a central point—the presence and the glorification of Yahweh. Again there stands alongside this promise the event of historical fulfillment—the miracle of the resurrection of the people who were dead in the Exile[54]—in the return and rebuilding of the Temple in Jerusalem. Is this the fulfillment of the prophetic promise?

We must answer, "No." Rather it ought to be made clear that there is no such thing as *the* prophetic promise which can be compressed into a unified formula. The prophetic word promises death and it promises life. Neither will it do to reduce the two opposing assertions to a single line through a historical construction by proposing the formula: The Old Testament prophetic promise develops from prophecy of doom to prophecy of salvation. We see in the postexilic prophecy not only how expectation of full salvation is maintained (Haggai, Zechariah), but also how the message of judgment begins to recur (Malachi). Prophecy ends in a disquieting dissonance. *The* Yahweh-event, which would unite the elements of death and life proclaimed by the prophets in a conclusive fulfillment, has not yet come to pass.

The prophetic promise proclaims at its deepest level not a coming *something,* after the manner of the fortune-teller, but *he* who comes, as he kills, as he calls to life. The remarkable freedom in the fulfillment of the prophetic word, as over against any predetermination of the coming event according to the calendar, can be understood only from this central point of view;[55] only from this central point can one understand the often striking change of the historical content of the message. Isaiah's language can move from the hard assurance of total desolation of the

---

[53] Ezek. 43:1 ff.
[54] Ezek. 37:1 ff.
[55] Apocalyptic (Daniel) no longer shows the same freedom.

land[56] and the destroying day of Yahweh, to the comforting,
". . . do not fear . . . it shall not stand, and it shall not come to
pass."[57] Deutero-Isaiah's message apparently changed from the
announcement of the eschatological coming of Yahweh, who
miraculously leads his people back through the desert, to the
concrete historical assertion of the liberation through Cyrus.[58]
This raises the purely psychological question: How is the un-
shaken certainty of the prophet to be explained, in spite of a
changing message? An "experience of disillusionment" exists only
in certain literary studies in the prophets,[59] not at all in the
prophetic word itself. The single exception is that of the man
who is characterized in the prophetic canon precisely as the
typical example of the recalcitrant prophet in a didactic story:
Jonah. Here the prophet (who would have enjoyed being proved
correct in the word which he proclaimed, a word in fact understood as the fortune-teller's sort of prediction of coming historical
events) turns scoldingly against Yahweh because the ensuing
Yahweh-event moved in a quite different direction as judged from
outward appearances. The genuine prophet of the Old Testament
knows, on the other hand, that in the last analysis he is no soothsayer (even though the actual words of his promise always refer
to a definite history), because he proclaims the coming work of
the one who remains Lord over the way in which his will is to be
realized. His wisdom remains the supreme wisdom, even in
instances where the individual announcements with which he

---

[56] Isa. 6 :11 f.

[57] Isa. 7 :4, 7.

[58] J. Begrich, "Studien zu Deuterojesaja," BWANT, 4, Folge, Heft, 25
(1938).

[59] The hypothesis of an experience of disillusionment based on the narrow
ground of Isa. 51:9-16 (probably not quite accurately interpreted) constitutes the weakest point in the otherwise so distinguished and challenging
study of Begrich on Deutero-Isaiah. There is a phenomenon of doubt-ridden
temptation (*Anfechtung*) which emerges from the freedom of Yahweh over
against his history and which is interpreted by the people again and again
as the inability of Yahweh and of the prophetic word (Isa. 5:18 f.; Jer.
17:15; Ezek. 12:22). This should not be confused with an experience of disillusionment. Doubt-ridden temptation and disillusionment are two different
things. The one who is tempted by doubts stands in the tension of a life
which gives God the glory and concedes that he is in the right even where
human understanding is unable to see clearly (Jer. 12:1). Doubt-ridden
temptation endures this tension. Disillusionment, on the other hand, has
given up faith in the truth of God in his original Word, even though it may
be able to find it again on a different level.

sends the messenger are full of contradiction. Isaiah sought to clarify the deed of Yahweh figuratively in the parable of the farmer who does different things at different times, and yet whose total activity is the expression of a profound wisdom.[60] Yahweh remains in the right even when the messenger does not understand the secret relatedness of the individual messages. Jeremiah's remarkable waiting and restraint in his proclamation is also to be understood from this standpoint.[61] The prophet is never in control of Yahweh's word; Yahweh remains free. The prophet can only await each new receiving of the message. When this has happened, then, of course, the message must be delivered with all certainty.[62] The prophetic message is never fixed, as it must be for the soothsayer; it can never be authenticated merely in terms of its material correspondence to a predicted set of facts; rather it is always the proclamation of the personal work of Yahweh. This is indicated precisely in the extraordinary certainty of the prophet. Only Yahweh himself can legitimately interpret his promise through his fulfillment, and the interpretation can be full of surprises even for the prophet himself. For the prophet, the certainty of his message does not lie in the objective authentication of its "soothsaying" content, which could be measured against a neutral norm;[63] but this certainty rests alone in the event of the renewed personal address of Yahweh, the event of the word.[64]

For the prophet, this does not mean that the promise was called in question. Rather, all Old Testament prophecy lives from the certainty that the Yahweh-history, however opaque it

---

[60] Isa. 28 :23 ff.

[61] Jer. 28 :11b.

[62] Jer. 28 :12 ff.; cf. also 42 :1 ff.

[63] Cf., for example, the word of Jeremiah to Hananiah (Jer. 28 :7-9), which is by no means imperative, but simply challenges him to a consideration.

[64] The tangential criterion of genuine prophecy found in Jer. 28 :9 (occurring again in Deut. 18 :21 f.), pointing to an objectively observable coming to pass of the prophetic word, must not be allowed to confuse the issue. In Deuteronomy, it is already plainly relativized in 13 :1. We never encounter the use of this criterion in Jeremiah ; in fact it is a criterion which can never be used *in actu*, because of its very nature. Its point can never be a matter of subjecting Yahweh in his word to an objective test-case. Much rather, the prophet probably intends, also here, that Yahweh, the Lord of history himself, will publicly demonstrate the truth of his word of promise only through its fulfillment in the coming event.

may be, nevertheless takes place under the informing word of
Yahweh; for this very reason the Yahweh-history is properly understood only as the residuum of his all-powerful word. "Surely
the Lord God does nothing, without revealing his secret to his
servants the prophets."[65] This certainty is most triumphantly expressed in Deutero-Isaiah, the prophet who confronted the gods
of the world powers in the time of Israel's utter humiliation.
Yahweh speaks: "I am the first, and I am the last; besides me
there is no god. Who has announced from of old the things to
come [conjectured text]: Let them tell us [conjectured text] what
is yet to be. Fear not, nor be afraid; have I not told you from of
old and declared it? And you are my witnesses! Is there a God
besides me? There is no Rock; I know not any."[66] If one relates
these words only to the predictive content of Deutero-Isaiah and
the earlier prophets, he must conclude that this passage speaks in
an incorrect and exaggerated way. Also in this case the true
pathos and the massive assurance are anchored basically in the
unshakable certainty of the power of Yahweh's promise; this is
a certainty which cannot be attacked by pointing to individual
"mistaken prophecies," and yet a certainty which nonetheless is
grounded completely upon Yahweh's deed and word in history.
His word, which announces history, also forms and shapes his
history. "I, I am the Lord, and beside me there is no saviour. I
declared and saved and proclaimed; no stranger was among you;
and you are my witnesses, says the Lord, and I am God."[67]

III

Let us take a summary glance at the Pentateuch and the prophets.
The Pentateuch is the charter of Israel, giving information about
the origin and the ordering of this people. Some prophetic dia-
tribes indicate how this people, knowing itself as the people of
God under the rubrics—election of the fathers, covenant, and
law—runs the risk of thinking of itself as an entity which is

---

[65] Amos 3:7, R.S.V.
[66] Isa. 44:6-8; cf. further, 41:22-24, 26; 43:9.
[67] Isa. 43:11 f. [Translator's note: Zimmerli interprets the Hebrew of one
phrase quite differently from the Revised Standard Version.]

accomplished and realized. Prophecy is aware that it is commissioned to oppose this kind of thinking. It knows of an imminent new Yahweh-event. It calls the people anew into the movement of a history which presses from promise toward fulfillment. The element of promise/fulfillment became for the great prophets the major theme, unveiled in a new way. This is not to say that this theme had not been normative as early as the patriarchal narratives, but when the later Israel looked upon it merely historically as an inherited "possession" it stood in danger of being historically buried.

Is this prophetic alarm legitimate from the point of view of the Old Testament? Or must it be characterized as only a fanatic marginal note? A closer look shows that the hidden knowledge of being underway from promise toward fulfillment in the framework of the history of Yahweh with his people occurs more often than might appear at first glance. It lies dormant also in texts which at first seem to speak simply about present affairs or even events already past. Some of the phenomena which have been described as "utopian" (thereby putting the question as to their actual meaning perhaps a bit prematurely) may go back to this basic structure of Old Testament language.

At this point we must take a second look at the Pentateuch. Why is the entire Deuteronomistic account of the giving of the law (in contrast to the Book of the Covenant, which actually deals with the same matters in part) cloaked with an air of expectant waiting, and why do the benefits of the blessing, of life, and of rest appear as great promises in the parenesis? Is there not an overtone here of a hope which is yet unrealized, even for the times of the Deuteronomist?[68] This sort of thing reposes in an even more hidden way in the historical scheme of the Priestly document.[69] But when the erection of the tent sanctuary by Moses is described as the goal of the Priestly history; when, in remarkable anticipation of history, certain elements of the Jerusalem Temple are placed in the tent sanctuary; and when, further, the

---

[68] Cf. the guarded statements which point in the same direction in von Rad, *Deuteronomiumstudien,* pp. 50 f.

[69] Indications to this effect may be found in Noth, *Überlieferungsgeschichte des Pentateuch,* pp. 263, 267.

presence of Yahweh in the midst of his people is described as the supreme fulfillment—is all of this only a historiography which romantically transfigures its subject, a portrayal of the "good old days"? In this connection it is certainly not without significance that all of these holy ordinances (including the measurements of the Temple presented in eschatological and not in contemporary historical form) are taken up in the book of Ezekiel. Here they are a part of the expected event in which Yahweh will be present in his Temple; and from the standpoint of this presence, the entire land (including that geographical puzzle of Palestine, the Dead Sea) will be made whole. The P document can hardly be interpreted rightly without reference to Ezekiel 40-48. What appears to be historical possession in P is in reality also hope. The Chronicler's work must also be mentioned in this connection.[70] The extravagant description of the empire of David and Solomon (who, according to 1 Chronicles 28:5, shall "sit upon the throne of the kingdom of the LORD over Israel," K.J.V.) can be properly understood only when one sees here also the expression of hopeful expectation of that which is yet to come, breaking through the contemporaneous historical presentation. One has only to place Herodotus alongside this history-writing in order to recognize the unique character of the Old Testament historiography, which is committed to faith in God's promise (something which probably deserves to be investigated again on a broader basis).

A brief observation concerning the Psalms is in order at this point. The discussion as to whether eschatological elements are not present above all in the Psalms, which sing the praises of Yahweh, has been under way for a considerable length of time. Gunkel brought these elements together and discussed them under the title "The Prophetic Aspect in the Psalms" ("Das Prophetische in den Psalmen").[71] This designation is accurate to the extent that the prophets are decisively responsible for the recognition that the center of everything that is promised is the

70 Cf. in this regard, G. von Rad, *Das Geschichtsbild des chronistischen Werkes*, BWANT, 4, Folge, Heft, 3 (1930), esp. pp. 119-132.
71 H. Gunkel and J. Begrich, *Einleitung in die Psalmen* (1933), pp. 329 ff.

coming Lord himself. It is too narrow, however, in that the so-called eschatological Psalms are by no means to be understood as the further development of the proclamation of the written prophets. In these Psalms the faith of the Old Testament people of God unfolds on a much broader basis, appealing also to the declarations of the very salvation theology which was attacked by the prophets. It becomes clear that, alongside all of the elements of retrospection into the creation and Israel's *Heilsgeschichte* with Yahweh, the talk of Yahweh's kingship, for example, is a language full of promise. A comparison with the Babylonian psalms, which are in other respects so closely related, may serve to clarify certain points. An analogous observation can be made in the Royal Psalms. Over the king in Jerusalem stands the old promise to David. Accordingly, at a time when the Davidic monarchy has disappeared, one can hear the passionate questioning of Yahweh about the fulfillment of the promise which still tarries.[72] But also in those instances where the contemporary king is spoken of, it is repeatedly noticeable how the language transcends contemporary description in the direction of a superlative which is by no means completely realized. This is not to be dismissed by ascribing it to the exaggerations of court style. Rather, because the anointed one has a significance in the historical purpose of Yahweh on the basis of the word concerning David, a superlative word about the king's righteousness and power and responsible relationship to God enters into the language about the contemporary king; and this is a language which arouses the expectation of a greater one who is yet to come.[73] The same phenomenon can be perceived in Deutero-Isaiah's words about the servant of Yahweh, in which he seeks to sketch the existence and office of the prophet in their ultimate meaning.[74]

When we survey the entire Old Testament, we find ourselves involved in a great history of movement from promise toward

[72] Ps. 89.
[73] G. von Rad, "Erwägungen zu den Königspsalmen," ZAW, 58 (1940/41), pp. 216 ff.
[74] H. W. Wolff, *Jesaja 53 im Urchristentum* (2. Aufl., 1950) ; W. Zimmerli's article on *pais theou* in ThW (1952).

fulfillment. It flows like a large brook—here rushing swiftly, there apparently coming to rest in a quiet backwater, and yet moving forward as a whole toward a distant goal which lies beyond itself. At the same time the Old Testament refers again and again to historical realizations which have happened and are happening. This probably appears most fully in Joshua 21:45, where it is said with reference to the fulfillment of the promise of the land: "Not one of all the good promises which the Lord had made to the house of Israel had failed; all came to pass." Here the brook appears to have come to a standstill. But in fact this is only apparent; in what follows the book of Judges will make clear the aspect of watching and waiting for the "helper" who will make room and give Israel rest. Farther along, the story of Saul's anointing by Samuel will name the one who will bring rescue to the beleaguered folk;[75] but how history is to be set in motion by the anticipation of the obedient fulfillment of the role of the anointed, over and beyond the promise to David!

It would not do to construct a fixed systematic of fulfillment. The following observations can be made, however, concerning the fulfillments of which the Old Testament speaks. These fulfillments never lead out of the historical realm into an ahistorical world. They are fulfillments for and in the midst of the historical Israel or the peoples which have to do with Israel. These fulfillments are always the will of God which has become event. Thus the question concerning further fulfillment always involves the more pressing question of the still further, the ultimate will of Yahweh. But because this is so, every Old Testament event receives increasingly the character of a fulfillment which in turn presses the question of deeper fulfillment. All Old Testament history, insofar as it is history guided and given by Yahweh's word, receives the character of fulfillment; but in the fulfillment it receives a new character as promise. At the same time the promise knows that it must allow itself to be corrected through the freedom of the divine fulfillment, because Yahweh himself is the center of all promise. No summons which would call this

---

[75] 1 Sam. 9:16.

history to its conclusion can be heard in the Old Testament. On the contrary, we can observe that some prophecy remains inert, and that some prophetic utterances are mutually contradictory in terms of their immediate contents. At one point the fulfillment of the role of the earthly messiah is expected; at another, the perfection of the kingship of Yahweh is spoken of without mention of any earthly king. Here the radical extinction of Zion is hinted;[76] there its ultimate glorification at the end of the age is expected.[77] One cannot calculate from the Old Testament a smoothly developing summation of all promises.

IV

The New Testament message of fulfillment thus stands over against this situation in the Old. In Jesus Christ the Apostles attest the Word of God which has become wholly event, and the event that is the Word of God, wholly and completely. In him (as Paul formulates it) all promises are yea and amen.[78] In his cross, the impossibility (which the prophets had proclaimed) of a righteousness of Israel's own, and the end of the covenant conceived in the law emerges radically. The judgment against sin, promised by the prophets, falls here in such a way that neither Jew nor Greek can avoid it. In the Resurrection of Christ, however, the remnant-event of Israel occurs. From the standpoint of the Resurrection the remnant-event is made visible as resurrection from the dead[79] and new creation[80] in a radicalness only rarely conceived by the prophets. Here Israel undergoes its deepest humiliation and at the same time the deepest confirmation of its election, in the one rejected by the masses of the historical Israel. Here the old covenant is finished in that the new covenant is established in the midst of Israel in the sacrifice and Resurrection of Christ; now, however, the covenant is established in a freedom which involves the extending of an invitation to

---

[76] Mic. 3:12.
[77] Isa. 2:1 ff.; Mic. 4:1 ff.
[78] 2 Cor. 1:20.
[79] Ezek. 37:1 ff.
[80] Isa. 43:18 f.

those who stand without. Here every prerogative of Israel according to the flesh is ended, in order that the Israel of God[81] may
take shape in the body of the Resurrected One.

What is the situation with regard to the question of promise
and fulfillment? First of all it is quite clear that the core of the
New Testament good news is the preaching of the Today of
fulfillment. The king's shout is here sounded, in view of the
present reality. This affirmation can be heard most radically in
the Johannine writings. In Christ, life, resurrection, and salvation are present in history. Along with this, however, it remains
clear that the Christ-event into which the believer is ingrafted
through faith stands against a world of death and sin from which
the believer is not removed.[82] Faith is nevertheless the organ of
contact with and growth into the new. Paul develops this in the
formulation, "For we walk by faith and not by sight."[83] Unmistakably, then, the existence of the believer in Christ comes
to stand in a new way under an arc of tension between promise
and fulfillment,[84] precisely through this fulfillment which the
entire New Testament proclaims as a "once for all,"[85] an unrepeatable and also unsurpassable fulfillment. In a new and much
more serious manner there begins a running toward the goal
which lies ahead.[86] In its prayer the congregation is commanded
to beseech in a new way, "Thy kingdom come. . . . Deliver us
from evil." With all of its knowledge of fulfillment, it never
occurred to those of the Christian faith to alter this supplication
into an affirmation in the perfect tense, and to dispense with the
prayer. But the new aspect of awaiting fulfillment is that fulfillment can bring nothing more than the open unveiling of that
which is already fulfilled. All supplication for fulfillment in the
congregation of the new covenant merges in the single plea,
"Come, Lord Jesus!"[87] Every effort to run toward the goal and to

---

[81] Gal. 6:16. G. Schrenk (*Judaica*, 5, 1949, pp. 81 ff.) would like to relate
the passage only to the Jews who believe in Christ, however.
[82] John 17:15.
[83] 2 Cor. 5:7.
[84] For the proclamation of Jesus, cf. W. G. Kümmel, *Verheissung und
Erfüllung* (1945).
[85] Rom. 6:10; Heb. 7:27; 9:12; 10:10.
[86] Phil. 3:12 f.
[87] Rev. 22:20; 1 Cor. 16:22.

lay hold of it becomes a running toward him who has already laid hold of the believer, before all of his running.[88] Every cry for redemption is a cry from the mouth of one who knows that he is redeemed. So the history after the event of fulfillment in Christ (sealed on Good Friday and Easter), anticipating fulfillment in none other than just this Christ who will come again, becomes a history of a special sort. Its end, toward which the promise presses, can be nothing other than its beginning in Jesus Christ.

Looking back at the Old Testament from this point, it is clear first of all that in Christ the Old Testament is at an end. The Old Testament history does not simply extend into the New Testament history in an unbroken line. Christ is the end of the old covenant and its promise. But this is not so in such a way that he has denied the Old Testament, thrusting it aside as an alien book and abrogating the form of its historicity as a false one.[89] Christ is at the same time the fulfillment of the Old Testament, in which it comes to its ultimate honor. The Old Testament does not sink into something nonessential in Christ, even though it is at an end in terms of its own word. Christ in his kingship is not fully understood except as one relates the Old Testament proclamation of promise to him, even though now he alone can be the legitimate interpreter of the Old Testament language of promise.

Here again we find repeated in a remarkable way the procedure which was the starting point for our discussion of the Old Testament. Just as Israel, which knows Yahweh as its God who delivered it from Egypt, found the legitimate explication of its confession of faith in the incorporation of the promise to the fathers into its credo, so the primitive Christian faith, born of confrontation with the living Christ, found the legitimate explication of the Christ-event upon which it depends by incorporating the Old Testament promise. By the appropriation of the category promise/fulfillment, any mythical orientation of the election and covenant events was done away with, and all of the mythical vocabulary and conceptuality which came in subsequently at this

---

[88] Phil. 3 :12.
[89] Cf. W. Kamlah, *Christentum und Geschichtlichkeit* (2. Aufl., 1951), ch. 1, "Die Überwindung der israelitisch-jüdischen Geschichtlichkeit."

or that point[90] was subordinated to authentic historical interpretation, and demythologized. In a similar way, because of the Christ-event, there is achieved the same defense against direct mythical understanding and the same quality of interpretation from the standpoint of historical promise. Everything which happens afterward in the dispute with the Hellenistic and Gnostic environment is carried on under the presupposition of this genuine historical interpretation. Lord, Son of God, Word-become-flesh—this is he who now first and foremost is called the "anointed," the Christ, also in the Greek-speaking world. This name points to one who fulfills all Old Testament promise. When the church then held fast to the Old Testament alongside the New in its canon, it was not merely obeying the law of historical inertia. When the church today holds fast to the Old Testament as a part of the canon, this is not merely the "result of a religious and ecclesiastical paralysis."[91] Rather, she confesses thereby her obedience toward the grace of Christ bestowed in genuine history, in opposition to all philosophical and mythological immediacy in the understanding of the Christ-event.

V

In his essay "Prophecy and Fulfillment"[92] Bultmann posed the question as to how far the category prophecy/fulfillment is still usable in theology, in view of present-day knowledge of the New and Old Testaments. His conclusion is that the Old Testament/Jewish history can only be called prophecy in its inner contradiction, in its failure (p. 72). In its fulfillment-citations the New Testament reads the Old Testament word partly in the Old Testament/Jewish tradition as allusion to the fulfilling eschaton,

---

[90] For example, the designation of Jerusalem as the Mountain of God in the north (Ps. 48:3), as the navel of the world (Ezek. 33:12); the designation of the king as God (Ps. 45:7) or as the son of God (Ps. 2:7). Cf. also the talk about creation as a battle with a dragon (Isa. 51:9 f., and elsewhere).

[91] A. von Harnack, *Das Evangelium vom fremden Gott* (2. Aufl., 1924), p. 217.

[92] Cf. Bultmann's article in this book. Since Bultmann speaks (under the heading of "prophecy") about most of the matters with which we have dealt under the somewhat broader term "promise," a criticism of Bultmann's theses in the present connection is not beside the point.

and partly as allegorically disguised allusion to events of the
Christ-history, in accord with Hellenistic/Stoic conceptions.
Neither of these alternatives, according to Bultmann, can be
maintained any longer, in view of the present-day level of historical knowledge. In this judgment Bultmann measures the Old
Testament words from the perspective of the soothsaying word,
and establishes thereby how they fall short of the fulfillment in
Christ. One can see in Old Testament prophecy (and not only
there) how the soothsaying element is plainly relativized in favor
of the promise of the personal Lord who is drawing near. Anyone who sees this must conclude that Bultmann has not done
justice to the Old Testament's own understanding of the word of
promise at this point.

Bultmann further attempts to demonstrate from the Old
Testament ideas of the covenant, the royal lordship of Yahweh,
and the people of God, how these three central spheres of proclamation tend to become questionable in their relationship to
Israel, the people of God, even in the Old Testament proclamation itself. Actually, they can only be realized eschatologically.
But even the eschatological formulations of the prophets do not
surrender their relatedness to the historical Israel. Thus the New
Testament proclamation begins here with the radical eschatolo-
gizing which dissolves every connection with the ethnic entity Israel, and proclaims covenant, royal Lordship of God, and people
of God as present in Christ and his congregation, in eschatological contemporaneity (and thus "de-secularized"). In this way, Old
Testament history can only become promise in the sense that it
is a history of failure. Bultmann believes that he is simply following the Pauline interpretation of the law with this conception:
"Rather does faith, to be sure of itself, require us to know about
the significance of the law—otherwise it would constantly be
subject to temptation through the law—in any form whatever.
In the same way faith requires the backward glance into Old
Testament history as a history of failure, and so of promise, in
order to know that the situation of the justified man arises only
on the basis of this miscarriage. Thus faith, to be a really justifying faith, must constantly contain within itself the way of the

law as something which has been overcome . . . in order to be an
eschatological attitude" (p. 75).

It is strange how Bultmann, whose presentation of the three
spheres of conceptuality one must accept gratefully as a masterly
summation of Old Testament materials, obscures some most important matters at a decisive point in his reading from the New
Testament standpoint, and is simply not able to see them. Certainly the New Testament speaks of the failure of all legalistic
attempts to come to God, and thus also of the collapse of ethnic
prerogatives of Israel based upon the law. But does it not say in
the same breath that Jesus Christ, who was born of the people
Israel according to the promises, is the center of the eschatological
congregation? Can this King be understood at all apart from his
people, the "lost sheep of the house of Israel," to whom he sends
his twelve[93] (however true it may be that he then calls his Israel
and also the Gentiles)? The King who was born in Israel according to the promises includes his people with himself, even though
they be disobedient to his call which invites them into a Kingdom
which is not of this world. He does not deny his people, even on
the cross which is erected in Jerusalem. The church has always
forgotten this to its hurt in its dealings with the synagogue. Certainly the New Testament speaks of the failure of the covenant
grounded upon the law alone, but precisely in so doing does it not
establish decisive elements of Jeremiah 31, in the sovereign freedom with which a king "fulfills" the herald's decree? It fulfills and
does not only shatter. Is that which the Old Testament says about
the faith of Abraham really only destroyed (remembering that
according to Paul this does not belong to the time characterized
by the subsequent giving of the law, but stands in the sphere of
evangelical promise)? The Old Testament speaks about the grace
of the forgiveness of sins;[94] about the raising from the dead of
the people which had become as dry bones in its death, because
of its guilt;[95] and about the gift of a new heart and a new spirit.[96]
Is all of this really only shattered in the New Testament, in such

---

[93] Matt. 10:6.
[94] Ps. 103:8 ff.
[95] Ezek. 37:1 ff.
[96] Ezek. 11:19; 36:26.

a way that this formula (failure as fulfillment) really covers everything that can be said about the New Testament fulfillment? Is there not fulfillment here, even in the midst of the shattering?[97]

Bultmann points above all to the idea that all of the declarations in the Old Testament are still bound to the earthly people Israel or its fathers. The actual "shattering" which takes place through the New Testament proclamation is said to happen in the matter of "de-secularization" *(Entweltlichung)*, the stripping away of that which pertains to the world. If we are thinking and speaking of the term "world" here only in the framework of the Johannine language about the *kosmos,* in the sense that the Christian is delivered from being at the disposal of the powers of this world, there can be no objection against this. But if we should also intend that the Christian is delivered from history, which continues to stand under the tension of promise and fulfillment (now, of course, the tension between the Resurrection and the coming of Christ)—history subject to the total humiliation of today, tomorrow, the day after tomorrow—then one cannot suppress his misgivings against this description of the New Testament proclamation. This language could only be appropriate if one placed alongside the insistence upon "de-secularization" the further insistence upon a radical "secularization" of the congregation of Christ.

Does there not lurk in Bultmann, however hidden it may be behind every intent to cling to the New Testament message in its historicity, the desire to strip *history* away from the Christ-event-history, with its opaque and accidental events, which nevertheless in the Old Testament are illuminated again and again through the accompanying word and so are transformed into promise? Does Bultmann not do this in order to elevate the Christ-message purely out of history in existential interpretation, placing it over

---

[97] In order to avoid any misunderstanding, let it be made clear that this cannot be a matter of a simple appropriation of the New Testament statements about fulfillment. It is our task to comprehend the concept of fulfillment in a new way, on the basis of the present-day view of the Testaments. But the content of the biblical statements of fulfillment is not fully understood in the unilinear talk about "shattering," as the texts themselves indicate also from more recent viewpoints.

against the Old Testament in the same remoteness as the Greek tradition? Must this way not end with a new Christ-myth?

The Old Testament, about which the New Testament insists that it is not only shattered, but also fulfilled, is the unconditioned assurance of the real historicity of Christ. It guards against every Christ-myth. As long as the gospel is bound up together with the Old Testament, it will never permit itself to be singled out as a timeless element of proclamation.

VI

Two considerations may serve to conclude the entire discussion. One has to do with the question posed for systematic theology: whether it must not incorporate the Old Testament promise into its Christological considerations in a stronger measure. This is not intended in the sense that one ought to make the Old Testament statements contemporaneous with the Christ-message by means of allegory, which would destroy real historicity. Nor is it intended in the sense that one ought to seek an apologetic proof of Christ out of the Old Testament;[98] nor yet in the sense that one ought to make a forced construction based upon the scheme of *Heilsgeschichte*. Rather it is intended in the sense that one must make a legitimate interpretation of the mighty event of faithfulness which has taken place in Jesus Christ on God's initiative. Christ is the eschatological event of the faithfulness of God, because the promise which, "In many and various ways God spoke of old to our fathers by the prophets" (Heb. 1:1, r.s.v.), is fulfilled. It is not fulfilled in the literal sense of the coming to pass of a prediction that can be documented in individ-

---

[98] What Bultmann has said about the impossibility of a strict proof from prophecy in his essay "Die Bedeutung des Alten Testaments für den christlichen Glauben" (*Glauben und Verstehen*, 1933, p. 335) may be fully underscored. Precisely when the sovereign freedom of the divine fulfillment, of which even the prophets were aware, is recognized in the Christ-event, it will become clear that Christ will never permit himself to be "deduced" from the Old Testament promise-material, which is of such diverse expression. It is the genuine problem of the one whom Matt. 11:9 calls "more than a prophet." This does not exclude the fact that faith in Christ afterwards recognizes in the Old Testament a book full of genuine allusions to Jesus Christ. One ought to inquire in this connection whether the New Testament "proof from Scripture" (as over against Bultmann) is not to be understood in this direction, in terms of its ultimate purpose.

ual occurrences after the manner of the fortune-teller; but it is indeed fulfilled in the promise of the divine person, about which all Old Testament promise revolves, including the material promises such as the promised land, posterity and life, the holy place, kingship, and righteousness. ·Here is fulfilled the name magnified by God, the blessing upon the nations (Yahwist), the God-with-us ("I will be your God," Priestly document), the servant of God who suffers for the many. Here is fulfilled the condemnation to death and the salvation unto life, in which the "I, I" of God can be heard.[99] All of this is fulfilled as an event of faithfulness, as the promise which has come to expression in history. Therewith also is truly fulfilled the proclamation of the Lordship of God in the midst of history and the triumph over the idols, which are not able to illuminate history through their word (not to speak of being able to create history by it).[100] As the Christ of Israel, and only as such, is he the Son of God, Word become flesh, the firstborn of all creation. Must not systematic theology think through this material in a much more fundamental way?

With this we come to the second consideration. If Christ is to be understood in the way which we have indicated, in his proper nature as the fulfillment of the promise to Israel, then a certain conversation is unavoidable: the conversation with the historical Israel. Today this Israel has come to life anew in a way undreamed of, also upon the political scene of our day. It speaks today incomparably more audibly than did the synagogue which was overpowered politically by the Christian church and accordingly ignored from the theological point of view. As yet the Christian church has taken astonishingly little notice of this, on the whole. In present Israel the Old Testament is claimed as the book of this people. The fact that this takes place mostly in quite secular forms does not alter the basic claim.[101] Less and less will

---

99 Hos. 5 :14/Isa. 43 :25.
100 Isa. 44 :6-8.
101 It may well become a matter of far-reaching consequences for the spiritual situation of Judaism, however, that the prophetic word, which has been virtually suppressed by synagogal orthodoxy, unmistakably receives more weight in the new Israel.

the church be able to avoid the question as to what is involved in this claim to be Israel, the question as to where its right, its limits, its temptations lie. The church will have to express itself more clearly than it has until now about whether it wants to abide by the answer of Harnack, or whether it wants to risk anew the full New Testament answer. The latter answer, to be sure, will also bind it together with the synagogue in a quite new, inseparable relationship in its witness, its service of love, and its entire hope.[102] It seems to me, moreover, that Bultmann does not offer the equipment adequate for this conversation, which can no longer be postponed for any length of time.

---

[102] Rom. 11.

6.

REMARKS ON THE THESES OF BULTMANN AND BAUMGÄRTEL
by Claus Westermann

translated by Dietrich Ritschl

The Introduction by D. C. Simpson to the collection *The Psalmists* (London, 1926) provides a typical example of the attempt to read into the Old Testament a preconceived notion of history which has been lifted from an alien context. The significant passage is this:

> The Higher Criticism, once feared as the enemy of Revelation, has long since proved itself the ally alike of faith and of reason. It has led Old Testament theologians to formulate a theory of the gradual growth of the Hebrew Religion from lowly origins at Sinai into the strong and vigorous system of the post-exilic Judaism which forms the background of the Christian Gospels. This theory is now generally accepted in its broad outlines, however much individual scholars may differ in regard to details. So far from leading to a denial of the truth of the Divine self-revelation vouchsafed to the Hebrew people in preparation for the Incarnation, it provides a reasonable conception of the Hebrews' slowly increasing consciousness of that preparatory revelation. It shows conclusively that to Moses there was apparent at the most only a faint glimmer of the light of God's self-revelation, a light which shone more clearly for the eighth century prophets, was reflected in the Deuteronomic Law Book of Josiah's reign, and illuminated with even more intense splendour the thought of the exilic prophets, throwing into bold relief the lights and shadows of Jewish life, and revealing the ever-

increasing consciousness of the barrier of sin and also
the ramifications of Jewish legalism as the result of its
attempts to thrust this barrier aside. Still later some Jewish seekers after a fuller revelation of God found help in
what they called 'Wisdom' as the medium between God
and man, while others, the Apocalyptists, endeavoured to
pierce the veil and visualize a more or less spiritual Kingdom. The end of such a process of development, and the
climax of the whole, was the advent of the Perfect Mediator and his establishment of the Christian Church
(pp. vi f.).

This all too smooth line of a steady development of the
Israelite religion from primitive beginnings under Moses to a
climax in the origin of Christianity, which was thought to be
generally accepted (rightly so?) by Old Testament scholars in
1926, is hardly acknowledged by a single scholar in the field
of Old Testament today. It is significant that this approach was
related to a certain method, namely, "the higher criticism,"
or the historical-critical method. But obviously a seemingly critical approach is here tied so intimately to a specific dogma of
historical development that everything is actually determined by
this dogma; the arrangement and also the evaluation of events
are absolutely fixed.

Rudolf Bultmann

It is illuminating and instructive to compare this sketch with
the contribution made by Bultmann in the present volume.
Bultmann begins with the historical-critical method (so he says
himself, p. 52). But he reaches the opposite conclusion. The line
of a definite upward development in the first approach corresponds here to an equally definite downward development: The
history of the Old Testament is a history of foundering and failure. As such, it is also a history of promise, but this can be seen
only from the New Testament point of view.

First of all, I would like to draw attention to two points in
Bultmann's work which seem to me important for further discussion:

1. The way in which the New Testament interprets single verses in the Old Testament as "predictions" can no longer serve as the general guide to our understanding of the Old Testament.[1] One may modify this first thesis of Bultmann, or one may limit it. But in general it cannot be denied unless the entire Old Testament scholarship from the conservative to the critical camp is disclaimed at the same time.

2. If we can no longer find the decisive relation between the Old and New Testaments in the Old Testament quotations as such, then we must search for the way in which the important and overarching concepts of the Old have moved into the New Testament. This is the method of a New Testament scholar, Bultmann, while an Old Testament scholar, Baumgärtel, starting with the same presupposition, goes the opposite way; he wants to determine and define what is essential and relevant to us in the Old Testament by using a New Testament concept (*epaggelia*). Here one must agree with Bultmann that the exegesis of the Old Testament must begin with the Old Testament concepts even when one is concerned with the question of its relation to the New Testament. It seems to me that Bultmann points in a direction which from now on must acquire essential importance in theological work: *exegesis of concepts which embrace both the Old and New Testaments.* There are already available quite a number of detailed studies which follow a single concept through the whole Bible. We still lack, however, a survey of the basic concepts in the Old and New Testaments which, looking at them in *terms of their history,* sees them in unity and totality, and inquires about the manner in which they describe the acting of God as a whole.[2] In this survey the relation of these concepts to one another will be of crucial importance. Which central concepts of the Old Testament are lacking in the New or standing at the periphery, and *vice versa?* Where does a new concept emerge, and where does an important concept change or

---

[1] Bultmann and Baumgärtel agree in this point; cf. pp. 41 ff.; similarly also Zimmerli and others.

[2] Cf. Wright, who has the same concern on this point (pp. 45 f. of this book). It may be necessary to point out in this connection that the *Theologische Wörterbuch zum Neuen Testament* has laid a necessary and excellent foundation, but has not made superfluous what is demanded here.

lose its meaning or disappear totally? A close connection between the history of concepts and form-analysis would then become necessary. This kind of approach would actually make it apparent that we are serious in our listening to the Bible as a whole. This all-embracing view, it seems to me, is present in Bultmann's approach, and one can only hope that this line will be pursued further in New as well as Old Testament studies.

3. I cannot accept, however, the conclusion which Bultmann reaches in his exegesis of the three concepts of Covenant, Kingship of God, and People of God. Nevertheless, it seems to me that his conclusions come much closer to the texts of the Old Testament than the opposite results by Simpson, who believes he can construct a linear upward movement. But a comparison of the two approaches suggests at once the question of whether the Old Testament is pressed into too linear a line of development in both cases—with Simpson upward, with Bultmann downward. These attempts do not do justice to the facts.

One can, of course, say that the covenant of God with his people is broken, that the kingship of God is denied by his people, that the people of God founder as God's people. But Bultmann, in his conclusions, turns these facts, which are indeed the result of the history of God with his people, into an inherent principle of history which determines the whole history: "An inner contradiction pervades the self-consciousness and the hope of Israel and its prophets" (p. 72). This is a generalization which obscures important facts. The end result is superimposed upon the whole, when Bultmann says: "But we find the contradiction in the fact that God and the activity are not conceived of in the radically transcendent and eschatological sense. . . . There is a miscarriage of history in this contradiction." It is hardly by accident that Bultmann finally summarizes the history of *concepts* thus: "The idea of a covenant . . . the idea of the rule of God . . . the idea of the people of God shows itself to be unrealizable. . . ." According to this, the contradiction would be one between an idea and its realization, but this involves a departure from the initial basic understanding that the Old Testament records deal with God's acting with his people. This is no longer history, but an abstraction from history.

Bultmann's concluding generalization, that especially in its failure the Old Testament as a whole receives the character of promise, also leads to the dangerous denial of its character of the report concerning a way—a way leading from promise to fulfillment in which neither moment can be balanced against the other, a way which cannot be summarized in a formula (Zimmerli) as a tangible result. Just as one cannot say that the Old Testament in general is a history of failure, neither can it be said that in general it is a history of promise. Both would be abstractions from the factual reports; both would be crystallizations of an idea. Bultmann is consistent in concluding his presentation of the inner contradiction in the history of the people of God with the admission that this is the "conflict . . . which belongs to human existence as such." At this point it becomes still more obvious that the history of God's people, recorded in the Old Testament, is to Bultmann ultimately only an illustration, an *exemplum* of human existence; the events which are recorded do not have the character of uniqueness. The "theological relevance" does not lie in the happening as such, but rather in this: that here an example of the failure of the history of salvation meets the believer just as the false way of salvation is shown to him by the law, so that he does not fall victim to this temptation. By placing the speaking of promise and fulfillment in parallel with Paul's speaking of the law, the data of the promise and the facts of the fulfillment are deprived of their simple historicity. The course of events within which God has truly given promise and fulfillment is replaced by the two realms of a false and a true way to salvation.

It should be stressed again that this criticism applies only to the conclusion of Bultmann's work. Having denied the applicability of the New Testament usage of promise passages, Bultmann concludes—by investigating three Old Testament concepts —that there nevertheless exists a relationship of promise and fulfillment between the Old and New Testaments. This essential result of Bultmann's work is not dependent upon the thesis which he produces at the conclusion. If one cannot accept his thesis that the history of the Old Testament is in general a history of foundering and, as such, a history of promise, one can substitute for it a much simpler one: Second Corinthians 1:20 says, "For as many promises of God [there are], in him [they are] the Yes." The context makes it clear that "promise" is here simply to be understood in the sense of promising something (as Bultmann says at the very beginning of his essay). One cannot draw from this the conclusion that words actually given Israel were later redeemed by acts and events. This, of course, does not refer to what the New Testament formulates *in retrospect* as promise and fulfillment, but rather to the whole history of the announcements which were addressed to Israel. The fact that Jesus of Nazareth is the fulfillment of this history of promises in the Old Testament can in no way be proved, not even— here one must agree with Bultmann—by a proof through prediction passages. This is precisely the point where only the believer—Bultmann has also stressed this—can confess: "Thou art . . ." But when someone says so either today somewhere in our world or at that time by the Sea of Galilee, he accepts with this confession of Christ *necessarily* God's history with his people whose fulfillment God has given to them in Christ. "Here Israel experiences her radical coming to naught and at the same time the strongest confirmation of her election in the One who was rejected by the people of the historical Israel" (Zimmerli).

Friedrich Baumgärtel

In his book *Verheissung*[3] Baumgärtel poses the question of how the Old Testament should be understood as a whole. Baumgärtel's question is focused upon one point: He sees the fundamental error of the new approaches of the last decades in the lack of a distinction between prediction and promise. His own exegetical work in the Old Testament has led him to make a radical distinction between these two concepts. Promise has God as its subject; prediction has man as its subject.

Prediction unfolds knowledge. It is a word of man; therefore, it is relative; its fulfillment must still be experienced. It is an announcement of a coming event.

---

[3] Baumgärtel, *Verheissung* (1952), pp. 28 ff.

Promise is a present benefit of salvation; it is the reality of the life in fellowship with God. It can only be received by faith through grace. Promise is an address from God, but it is also the benefit of salvation (pp. 7 ff.). The Old Testament contains a basic promise which embraces all possible promises: "I am the Lord, your God." But this pregnant concept of promise is taken from the New Testament. It has no counterpart in the Old Testament and cannot have. It is the concept of *epaggelia* which occurs only in the New Testament. Baumgärtel finds the clearest definition of this concept in Ephesians 3:6, the "promise in Christ," i.e., the promise which has become reality in Christ.

This juxtaposition leads to the decisive conclusion that *only* the promise in the Old Testament is relevant to our faith, but not the prediction. That which is relevant to our faith in the Old Testament can only be defined in a term taken from the New Testament. With this the traditional understanding of the Old Testament in terms of the scheme of promise-fulfillment is left behind. It has lost its meaning for us and should disappear completely. Concerning this thesis I would venture the following:

1. The question of decisive importance is whether one can strip the Old Testament predictions or promises of their reaching toward the future without changing substantially their meaning. Most exegetes agree that this is impossible. To clarify the present discussion, one would do well to distinguish the two propositions which are contained in Baumgärtel's thesis:

(a) It is not the predictions but the promises of the Old Testament which are relevant to our faith.

(b) The prediction requires the fulfillment for its confirmation; the promise itself, however, carries the fulfillment. When God says, "I am the Lord, your God," then what is promised in this sentence is already present for those who accept it by faith through grace.

Consequently, in the case of a promise the reaching into the future dimension is dropped. But this means that the message of the Old Testament is no longer the report of a history; or at least this history is no longer relevant to us.

2. Promise (*epaggelia, Verheissung*) in German as in Greek

can have quite different meanings depending on where one puts the emphasis: (a) on the event of promising, or (b) on the content of the promise. Undoubtedly, Baumgärtel places all the emphasis upon (b). Promise is to him primarily the content of the promise. This corresponds certainly to Ephesians 3:6, but does it represent the facts in the Old Testament? One cannot deny that in the Old Testament the happening of the promise —or let us now say announcement—belongs necessarily to the content and that without the happening of the promise all which is announced cannot be understood. If, for example, in the case of the prophets one would envisage only that which is announced, one would receive a totally insufficient and even false picture of the prophets.

3. According to Baumgärtel the promise is a pledge, and this is absolute and never conditional. It can only be a pledge of salvation (examples, pp. 7 ff.), in contrast to the prediction which can prophesy salvation or doom. In *epaggelia* the concern is only for salvation. At this point Baumgärtel gets into difficulties, for his point does not hold good even for the "basic promise" of the Old Testament—the sentence "I am the Lord, your God." This sentence has rather, as Baumgärtel himself points out, an aspect of grace and of wrath. It can be a pledge toward salvation, but it can also be the opposite: the threat of God's wrath (this cannot possibly be denied with regard to the main passage, Exod. 30:2-3). Hence, it is precisely the basic promise of the Old Testament which does not correspond to the definition of the concept of *epaggelia*.

What Is Promise?

Baumgärtel's work has, nevertheless, in my opinion, a special significance in the present discussion about the understanding of the Old Testament. The importance lies in the fact that he has radically posed the question: What is promise? In his opinion there are two basically different events; one, the *epaggelia* (promise), is relevant to us, while the other, *propheteuein* (the prophesying) is not. The main reason is that one is

Word of God; the other, word of man: "God does not prophesy" (p. 33). "God promises, but man does not" (p. 33). The basic distinction, according to Baumgärtel, that God *alone* is the subject of *epaggelia* and never of *prophēteuein,* is unquestionably proved by the texts and is of essential importance. But *only* for the New Testament! This is so because not only is the basic concept *epaggelia* taken from the New Testament, as Baumgärtel himself stresses, but also its counterpart, *prediction = prophēteia.*

What Baumgärtel says on pp. 28 ff. and 71 ff. about the limited or even annulled significance of the "prophetic proof text" in the New Testament (in the historical books as well as the epistles) can be gainsaid only in small part. These "prophetic proof texts," generally speaking, do not have for us the convincing power which they had for the people of the New Testament (so also Bultmann, cf. pp. 51 ff.). One might agree, perhaps with some reservations, with Baumgärtel's radical conclusion: "For us today this method is impossible, because we know that the Old Testament words did not mean this. References like this are not relevant to our faith" (p. 84). This statement, however, is concerned with the understanding of the prophetic proof within the New Testament. But this understanding of prediction as a proof does not exist in the Old Testament, or at best it is at the periphery. There is no *epaggelia* in the sense of the New Testament usage of the word, as Baumgärtel says himself ("*epaggelia* has no roots in the Old Testament").

One must also stress, with the same emphasis, that there is no *prophēteia* in the Old Testament (or only at the periphery) in the New Testament sense of the word (contrary to the statement of Baumgärtel on page 28: "With regard to the concept 'prophecy' there is no difference between the Old and New Testaments"). The main criterion for the distinction is not applicable in the Old Testament. "Prophecy" is certainly not word of man, but word of a messenger who speaks with the claim to utter the words of God (*kōh 'āmar YHWH*). Surely, it is the word of Yahweh in the mouth of men, but this is also the case with the "basic promise," the announcement of salvation! The prophecy of the Old Testament is not prediction of a future happening. This has been worked out beautifully and clearly by M. Buber in his work *Der Glaube der Propheten* [*The Prophetic Faith*]. The following quotations can only sketch the connections:

"But the connection of the *nabi* with the future is not that of one who predicts" (p. 2, Harper Torchbooks, 1960).

"He announces a latent fate, which is based upon the alternative dynamics of the present hour and at the same time is directed toward it" (p. 9).

"The Israelite prophet utters his words, directing them into an actual and definite situation. Hardly ever does he foretell a plainly certain future" (p. 103).

Zimmerli means the same when he says: "The prophetic promise proclaims at its deepest level not a coming *something* after the manner of the fortune-teller, but *he* who comes"— Yahweh.

"The genuine prophet of the Old Testament knows . . . that in the last analysis he is no soothsayer . . . because he proclaims the coming work of the one who remains Lord over the way in which his will is to be realized."

Here it is emphatically stressed, and in my opinion absolutely rightly so, that the concept of "prediction" which Baumgärtel elaborated in contradistinction to "promise" is missing the point of the prophecy.

Baumgärtel must be asked the question: Can one so easily separate the promise to the people of Israel from the happenings of the promise? Can one abstractly crystallize the *promissum* out of the *promissiones*? Precisely this is what Baumgärtel deliberately does as he insists all through his second chapter: What is relevant is only that which was promised to the people of Israel, i.e., the fellowship with God. Irrelevant to us is all that was unfolded out of this "basic promise" by way of single "time-bound" predictions (but he can also say: in time-bound promises; e.g., p. 19: "Since these Old Testament promises concern us and appeal to us not in the least, they really have no relevance for us . . .").

With this it is stated quite clearly that the history here reported has no significance for us. What is actually important for us is that which is distilled from history, that which undergirds the concrete, historical prophecies which unfold it, but does not depend upon the concrete prophecies and can be separated from them; it is the *timeless* basic promise "I am the Lord, your God." This is an abstraction from the concrete historicity of the Old Testament. The idea that we are permitted to do this must be rejected on the basis of the Old Testament as it has come down to us. If someone ventures to interpret the Old Testament from the prospective gained in Christ, then he only accepts the creed of the church of Christ; he accepts the place wherein he hears the Old Testament. If someone ventures to interpret the Old Testament on the basis of New Testament *concepts,* then he shows that he already knows from the New Testament everything that the Old Testament had to say to the church. Thus he actually denies the significance of the way in which God has led his people from the calling of Abraham through Deutero-Isaiah up to the hour "when the time was fulfilled." Ultimately he admits, then, that the church could also live without the Old Testament. But this is only the simple consequence of the fact that for Baumgärtel the overarching tension between promise and fulfillment, the existence of which cannot very well be denied through the whole Bible, is focused into the one single point: "promise." That which God in Christ has given to men, to the world, is, according to Baumgärtel, essentially not fulfillment (this concept is almost entirely absent in his whole work) but promise (*epaggelia* in the sense of that which is promised). But if one takes away from this overarching tension (cf. Zimmerli!) the undergirding importance for the whole Bible, and if one thinks that this tension can be reduced to a single point, then one deprives both the Old *and* New Testaments of their historical character. That which is promised in the Bible is not essentially and not primarily the content of the promise, but it is event. The promise is event, and the fulfillment is event. All attempts to distill from these events a nebulous positive and objective "essence" do not make the Bible what it is—a book of stories, the report of an event.

7.

THE HERMENEUTICAL PROBLEM OF THE OLD TESTAMENT*

by Friedrich Baumgärtel

translated by Murray Newman

These four theses will be developed in the following discussion:

1. The simple Christian understanding of the Old Testament is based on a prior understanding. Because he has been grasped by the gospel of Jesus Christ, the Christian understands the Old Testament as witness of Jesus Christ. For the evangelical faith only with and in this prior understanding is there an affinity to the Old Testament witness as a word working effectively in the contemporary situation. Without the introduction of this evangelical prior understanding the Christian remains merely a spectator of the active power which the Old Testament Word indeed has for the Old Testament man who "understands," i.e., for whom the Old Testament Word once was indeed powerful. His understanding, however, was an *Old* Testament understanding, outside the gospel, and therefore not our understanding, i.e., our being grasped through the Old Testament witness.

2. Basically theological understanding can only be the Christian understanding just characterized; it happens out of this prior understanding. It is theological insofar as it guarantees the validity of understanding by a methodical and systematic use of understanding. Theology is obliged to develop a method, therefore a hermeneutical principle, which will lead the simple understanding of the Christian out of personal individualism, with all its possibilities of error and subjectivism, into a com-

* This lecture, which was given April 1, 1954, on "Theologians' Day" in Berlin, is presented here in a shortened and greatly modified form.

mon, valid understanding, and one which will also prevent sectarian caprice. For working out the hermeneutical method the general principles of scientific understanding are authoritative.

3. For this understanding we cannot eliminate the fact, derived from study of the history of religion, that the Old Testament is a witness out of a non-Christian religion; its self-understanding is not identical with the evangelical prior understanding (although the affinity is experienced under such a prior understanding). It is just that which gives the Old Testament its character of *Old* Testament; its witness does not come out of the gospel. It is just that which brings about the necessity and the task of the hermeneutical question today: To what extent does the evangelical faith hear the Word of God through the Old Testament witness by experiencing this difference and affinity?

4. The Old Testament Word is the active Word of God, the power of God to the Old Testament and New Testament man alike. However, it can have power for the evangelical man as Old Testament Word only as a witness which is conditioned by historical and religious development and which moves outside the gospel in its self-understanding. It cannot have power for the evangelical man as evangelical Word, because it is not evangelical Word. And it is Old Testament Word in its character of being conditioned by historical and religious development and in its power for the Old Testament man in his self-understanding. Only as Old Testament Word in this sense, only as the witness outside the gospel, can it be a witness of the gospel for us. By the initial establishment of the method of understanding it must be made clear that the Old Testament witness, the witness from outside the gospel in its self-understanding, has power for the Old Testament and evangelical man alike.

Concerning Thesis 1

The Christian whose heart is devoutly open in faith to the Word of Holy Scripture, upon hearing Isaiah 6, will reverently bow down under the worshipful antiphon "Holy, holy, holy is

the LORD of hosts"; he will fold his hands, and in his heart he
will worship, too. God is present. And as he perceives the presence of the holy God it can easily happen that he sinks to his
knees with the prophet: "Woe is me! For I am lost." And out of
such a sense of being lost in the presence of the majesty of God
the words of the Psalmist press upon our own lips: "Create in
me, O God, a clean heart and give me a new and steadfast spirit,
cast me not away from thy presence" (Ps. 51).

What has just been described is no phantasy, nor is it a
theologoumenon; we all know that such does happen. The sim-
plest Christian can testify to it. But *what* happens here? Something takes place for the man who listens with the participation
of his whole being. The Word of Scripture has power for him.
But this power takes place only for the *believing* man, i.e., for
the one who knows himself to be in a trusting encounter with
him in whom he believes as the Holy One. Thus in and from
faith the Word of Scripture is experienced as active, as sanctifying, as the "Word of God." Completely in the sense of Romans
1:16: The gospel is a power of God which brings salvation to
everyone who believes. Under the Word of the Old Testament
the believing hearer comes into a sphere of power and strength.

One cannot object that this is not a convincing argument because a poem or musical work on occasion can create just such
a spell.[1] Not everyone who hears a poem "enjoys" it. There are
prosaic people who regard aesthetic sensitivity as childish senti-
mentality. And an unmusical man never comes under the spell
of a musical composition. He indeed hears, but he does not
understand, i.e., he is not encountered. For "understanding" a
certain sensitivity (*sensorium*) is necessary which comes out of
the inner participation in the meaning of that which is being
understood. In order to understand the Word of Scripture, participation in the meaning of the Word of Scripture is necessary;
faith is necessary. Congeniality, in the sense of affinity, is necessary in order to understand; and "understanding" means to be

---

[1] Such an objection by H. W. Hertzberg, "Ist Exegese theologisch möglich?",
Für Arbeit und Besinnung (Flensburg-Kiel, 5. Jahrg., 1952), No. 11.

drawn into the Word's sphere of power. Dilthey once asserted[2] that intuitive perception (*das Divinatorische*) in exposition rests in such a determination (*Bestimmtheit*) of the understanding.

Once more the question: *What* happens here? The answer: It is "understood"—not in the sense of a theological interpretation, but in the sense of being immediately drawn in under a power which faith knows as *the* Reality. For this Reality the simple Christian yearns, albeit in fear and trembling, as for the total support of his life. This trusting affinity to the Old Testament Word lives continuously out of a committed and committing intercourse with the *whole* Bible; it is a matter of the "practice" of faith in this sense.

Let us note here in a preliminary way that the hermeneutical circle, of which Schleiermacher and Dilthey[3] speak, emerges at this point. For, beside Romans 1:16 the word in Romans 10:17 also stands just as firmly: "Faith comes from *akoē; akoē*, however, through the word of Christ." How else could faith come! But the prior apprehension (*Vorfindlichkeit*), namely, believing knowledge of that reality which opens hearts to *akoē*, cannot be denied either.

Under the Word of the Old Testament, however, it also happens in quite a different way. According to 2 Kings 9, at the command of God (vs. 6) the prophet Elisha has the field captain Jehu anointed king. And then this soldier leaves a deep blood-filled trail on his way to the throne to which God has appointed him. When all this dreadful business is completed, God's approval is announced to Jehu because he has acted so zealously in accordance with the divine purpose. The simple Christian? He does *not* understand. He understands the logical relation of the words to one another, but he does not understand what is meant. He has no sense of an inner relationship to this event which was willed and confirmed by God. He has no affinity to it. When he hears, he becomes distant from that which is to be understood, and distance is a barrier to understanding.

---

2 Wilh. Dilthey, "Die Entstehung der Hermeneutik," *Ges. Schriften*, V (1924), p. 332.
3 Cf. Wilh. Dilthey, *op. cit.*, p. 330.

An example from the Psalms: "Vindicate me, Lord, for I walk in purity, I wash my hands in innocence" (Ps. 26). I am willing to accept as correct the position of von Rad in the Bertholet Festschrift (1950)[4]: Such expressions portray types; the prototype of the ṣaddîq is depicted in them. Human possibilities of fulfillment are far transcended, and in a cultic act a man represents himself as the exemplary ṣaddîq. Even if the simple pious man could grasp that, there is no affinity here to Christian faith, only strangeness. If in the evangelical faith we represent ourselves before God, then it can only be in the way that the Lord has taught us. Thus are we to pray: "And forgive us our debts." So on hearing Psalm 26 the simple Christian will confess: I do not *understand;* this Psalm has no power for me. Woe is me if it had power for me.

It should be clear at this point that only with the prior understanding of the evangelical faith, only because he has been grasped by Christ, does the simple Christian receive the Old Testament Word with understanding, i.e., it becomes actively present for him.

On the other hand, this must now be said: The Old Testament has its power, first of all, in another religion.[5] There it was understood, for affinity was there. That understanding did not come from the gospel, but in the context of the Old Testament self-understanding. The bloody triumph of Jehu was the triumph of God himself, and the Israelite hearer of this story was drawn mightily under its spell. And the yearning desire of the pious

---

[4] G. von Rad, *"Gerechtigkeit" und "Leben" in der Kultsprache der Psalmen* (Festschrift Bertholet, 1950, pp. 418 ff.) ; Ges. Studien z. AT (1958), p. 225.

[5] This characterization "another religion" made a somewhat unfavorable impression on the hearers when originally used in lecture form. Nevertheless, this designation from *Religionsgeschichte* must be maintained. There are many books concerning the "History of the Israelite Religion." Do not these books with their attempt to depict the course of a religion, which is nevertheless not the Christian religion, continue with perhaps some reason? No one resists such effort. The religious historian can indeed proceed in no other way. That the Israelite religion has genetical and substantive connections to the Christian religion is certainly as little to be questioned as the fact of such connections between the Islamic religion, on the one side, and the Christian and Israelite religion on the other. However, this fact makes it all the more necessary, first of all, to grasp the three religions in their uniqueness as phenomena in the general history of religion. The hermeneutical question today demands this necessary task first of all. Cf. further "Concerning Thesis 3."

man of the Old Testament was as fully and completely open to the prototype of the *ṣaddîq* in Psalm 26 as this transcendent prototype is completely strange to the Christian faith. What in the Old Testament self-understanding was in no way a surpassing self-righteousness—there it was the reaching out of the self for the highest good, for the grace of God in the Old Testament sense—to the simple Christian, who knows his Sermon on the Mount, must seem plain blasphemy; he withdraws with no understanding of it at all. He views this Old Testament event simply "without understanding," i.e., it has no active power for him.

Concerning Thesis 2

The observations to this point have been derived from a consideration of the simple understanding of the simple Christian who prayerfully reads his Bible. With these observations, however, we have not yet advanced to the *theological* question. In the discussion above "understanding" was dealt with simply as a general phenomenon, and at least this much was shown: In all understanding a prior understanding is included; in all understanding there is a prior apprehension (*Vorfindlichkeit*). Before I seek to understand a work of literature or a work of art, before I seek to interpret it in an intelligent way, I already like it. It is the same thing with two people who love each other without really considering why it is so. Prior apprehension is precisely the liking, perceiving as good, respecting, and appropriating in advance what is to be understood. In glancing at our simple Christian: He loves from faith. However, faith is not without him who is believed. And he who is believed is he who reveals himself to us through his Word, i.e., he who has already grasped us through his Word. The Christian seeks to understand the Old Testament because he already loves it as the witness of the Word of God (the hermeneutical circle).

Simple understanding in every area is personal and subjective. It is the attempt of all science to lead the simple understanding out of such personal individualism and such eclectic acceptance (our simple Christian accepts Isa. 6 and Ps. 51, but moves away from the Jehu story and Ps. 26) over into an understanding based on principles. Thus science seeks to ensure the *validity of understanding* (our simple Christian must understand every word of the Old Testament as presently effective for him!). Where there is no principle and, therefore, no orderly system, there is chaos.[6] The science which, although recognizing completely the relativity of human cognition, intends to speak validly (and must do so if it is to have any meaning at all), is orderly and systematic. Validity of understanding occurs only where the individual case, having been ordered in a logical and systematic arrangement, is understood in terms of the whole. Logical and systematic understanding, based on principles, is methodological understanding, which alone ensures the validity of understanding. Not all simple understanding of the Old Testament is valid. A person may have a direct understanding of a biblical passage which has great power for him, and he may personally experience a real affinity with the particular Word. But it can still be very questionable whether his personal understanding can be regarded as generally valid. In the use of understanding displayed by sectarians—which is very important for them—innumerable examples of the lack of validity are quite evident.

Theology is science. In order to establish the validity of its statements, it is therefore necessary to develop a methodology of understanding, a theory of exegesis (hermeneutics). Only in this way can it lead the personal individualism of understanding the biblical Word into a common, valid understanding, into a community (*gemeindliche*) understanding. This, therefore, differentiates theological understanding from the simple understanding previously developed, that it is methodological, i.e., logical and systematic, understanding. In such understanding (and this is what constitutes its scientific character), the general laws of human thought, cognition, and understanding are involved; it is the task of philosophy to investigate these laws. If theology is science—no matter in what sense—it will authenticate its character by being logical, methodical, and systematic in its understanding and will reject any attempt which would permit unme-

---

[6] Concerning the necessity of methodological principle, cf. my article "Ohne Schlüssel vor der Tür des Wortes Gottes?", EvTh, 13 (1953), pp. 413 ff.

thodical procedures in the process of understanding, because this would call its innate character into question. In view of certain deviating efforts,[7] this must be said with great emphasis for the sake of the purity of theological thought.

The theological method is developed under that prior understanding which was understood from observing the simple Christian understanding. This prior understanding, which is not justified by the Old Testament itself, constitutes the uniqueness of the theological understanding of the Old Testament; it is parallel to all scientific understanding, which (in accordance with the peculiarity of whatever is being understood) is always methodological understanding developed with a prior understanding. In order that the method should not undermine the freedom of understanding as a prior decision, it is essential that it (again parallel to all scientific understanding) be worked out in the *process of understanding* by means of critical, i.e., discriminating and evaluating, reflection on the material that is to be understood.[8] That hermeneutics has been called the teaching of an art is connected with the intuitive perception which in the process of understanding is included with a sense of being drawn into a sphere of power and strength, and with an awareness of affinity. The subjectivity of every method of understanding, therefore also of the theological, is grounded in this intuitive impulse.

That the point just developed is not aimed at a dogmatic understanding of the Old Testament witness indeed requires no particular mention. However, mention of something else in this connection cannot be avoided. Without candor on this point, we cannot proceed. Within theology the fundamental prior understanding may differ. It is not important here to develop this matter in relation to Catholic interest in that which is being understood. But the division of confessional groups within evangelical theology quite clearly has a very important effect on hermeneutics. Lutheran exegesis has a different understanding from Reformed, and that makes dialogue difficult. It is not at all my

---

[7] Most recently by G. von Rad and H. W. Wolff; cf. on this point my article mentioned in footnote 6.

[8] Cf. my article mentioned in footnote 6, pp. 418 ff.

desire to open up a breach here. Our concern is the truth of the matter. The understanding of Scripture is different on both sides, and this has its effect on the manner of understanding and on the development of the method of understanding. To me it does not seem fortuitous that typological interpretation is principally at home on the Reformed side. However, I should not venture into an area where we Old Testament scholars are in urgent need of help from systematic and historical theologians. I do not regard the difference as unfortunate, but as natural, since I am fully convinced of the actuality and necessity of that prior understanding. Yet it must be clearly seen that today the confessional difference is included in the hermeneutical problem of the Old Testament.

Since, in addition to prior understanding, the general scientific principles of understanding are constitutive for the theological *methods* of understanding, these principles are formed from contemporary thinking. There is a counter proposal which often enough is raised: The New Testament has already understood the Old out of that prior understanding; therefore, the manner of understanding developed from the New Testament could and indeed should be the plumbline for the theological understanding of the Old Testament. Here the answer would be as follows. That prior understanding is certainly to be taken from the New Testament witness: the "Word of God," i.e., Christ as grasping us in faith. The New Testament's method of understanding, however, can no longer obtain for us today. The intention of the New Testament method of understanding remains inviolable; it corresponds to that prior understanding. But the methodological principle of understanding which the New Testament offers is no longer acceptable today. The New Testament's principle of understanding can be characterized in two directions. Here I will content myself with a few comments, since recently in another place I expressed myself on this complex question in detail.[9]

[9] In my book *Verheissung. Zur Frage des evangelischen Verständnisses des Alten Testaments* (1952), which generally might be consulted for further explication of the theme treated in the present essay.

First of all, the proof by prophecy in the New Testament represents no methodological help for us today. Contrary to the popular view, proof by prophecy has a very limited function and is not at all a general principle of understanding in the New Testament. The New Testament uses it merely in an effort to present proof that Jesus of Nazareth—contrary to outward appearances—actually is the Messiah. For that matter, it serves precisely the same purpose for the opponents of Jesus who desire to prevent the acknowledgment of his Messiahship with such proof. And quite apart from the very limited use of this principle of understanding (if one can use this expression in this respect at all!), the presentation of a proof by prophecy has no active power for us today—power, in the sense explained above, which becomes real in "understanding" (i.e., in being encountered). Where the reason *(ratio)* comes into play, intelligent knowledge by encounter *(das verstehende Beteiligtsein)* ceases.

The other principle of understanding in the New Testament is *typological re-presentation* of the Old Testament witness. Re-presentation in this sense means that the type has happened *for us* and is written *for us*. The *parakalein* is included in the type: written for us, warning for us, comfort for us.[10] This New Testament manner of realization of the Old Testament Word is therefore no longer possible for us today, because our contemporary historical thinking demands of us—for the sake of truth as it confronts the historical thinker—that the literal meaning of the Old Testament witness be "understood." It must, therefore, be *the literal meaning* which has power for us today and not a meaning interpolated into the witness. This is quite apart from the fact that the proof of a typological parallel addresses itself to the reason and, therefore, can never draw us who are in the Christian faith into its spell. The Christian can certainly never

---

[10] The newer typologists must be made aware of this. It is not a matter of the unlimited establishing of typological parallels. In any case, that is not in accordance with the New Testament outlook. The New Testament continually has a kerygmatic intention in establishing a typological parallel: realization of the wrath and grace of God. The typology of the New Testament throughout is within these limits. From the standpoint of the New Testament, the introduction of a typological parallel of itself accomplishes nothing at all. It must be demonstrated to what extent the *parakalein* dwells within the typological parallel.

enter into a sphere of power by considering a typological parallel
—actually, he can only consider it. The simple Christian will
never find a typological parallel by himself. If it is shown to him,
he can blandly disregard it without the slightest effect upon his
faith. For us today the type lacks the power to achieve a re-
presentation. The New Testament was able to achieve such a
re-presentation in its recital of the type, for it did not see the
Old Testament as a historically conditioned witness (today we
cannot at all see it otherwise!) but as the inspired Word of God
in a formal sense (which it can no longer be for us today).

Because they are conditioned historically, the New Testament's methods of understanding cannot be accepted by contemporary theological thinkers. Having accepted the intention of
the New Testament's methods of understanding (prior understanding), theology works out the principle of understanding by
the intelligent penetration of the Old Testament witness by
means of the general scientific principles of understanding which
obtain today.

Concerning Thesis 3

Our thinking today is historical thinking. When I say that, I
am expressing a thesis which is not uncontested.[11] I well understand that one can see limits and dangers here. But I still do not
see that we can extricate ourselves from this fateful imprisonment
with a good conscience; above all, I do not see *how* we can extricate ourselves. In any event, it must be conceded even by those
who are able to view the matter more optimistically that we still
are not able to manage without historical thinking. As long as
kerygma is just not conceivable without historical report, just
so long will historical thinking be of considerable importance. In
any event, it must be conceded that the very long period of
historical thinking cannot be eliminated; rather, it will remain
influential, even if it should sometime be completely superseded.

---

[11] Cf. most recently the discussion Gogarten-Kinder, ELKZ, 7 (1953), pp.
318 ff.

Historical thinking separates us today from the methodology of the New Testament, as well as from the Reformers' understanding of the Old Testament. From the perspective of our contemporary thinking about the hermeneutical question the fact cannot be eliminated that the Old Testament is a witness from a religion outside the gospel and therefore from a religion strange to us. Viewed historically, it has another place than the Christian religion. This is therefore a statement of quite extraordinary importance, because it means that the *self-understanding* of the Old Testament (which is the document concerning the other place) must be taken into the evangelical understanding. Consequently the experience under the gospel must occur at the same time as the experience outside the gospel. Only that which in his time actively took place for the Old Testament man in his "understanding" can actively take place in the evangelical "understanding" of the Old Testament Word for the Christian faith. Because of our historical thinking, no other re-presentation of the Old Testament witness is any longer possible for us today. The *parakalein* for us today must be present in the *parakalein* which confronted the pious man of the Old Testament (cf. concerning Thesis 4).

The simple understanding described above does not understand thus unquestioningly. Indeed, often it does not even understand at all, i.e., many an Old Testament Word does not draw the simple Christian into its spell, even when under the same Word the pious man of the Old Testament felt himself in its sphere of power. Often enough the simple Christian simply has no access to the understanding of the pious man of the Old Testament. He is not able to accept for himself the *parakalein,* which is present in the Old Testament event for the Old Testament man. This simply means that in many passages of the Old Testament he is not able to perceive the Word of God, and often enough he is cut off from the "understanding" of the pious man of the Old Testament. He necessarily proceeds eclectically, subjectively, and therefore not validly. The simple understanding does not reckon with the character of the Old Testament witness mentioned above as conditioned by historical and religious de-

velopment, which for theological understanding cannot be re-
linquished. Theological hermeneutics should lead to valid understanding, for it must seek to understand the *whole* Old Testament
as the Word of God in a methodical way, avoiding any eclecticism
and also any harmonizing. Basically, one should be able to proclaim the gospel from any Old Testament witness (even if it
were not practical to do so!).

After all this has been said, the way which hermeneutical
procedure should take seems to me to be clear. First, the "understanding" of the pious man of the Old Testament must be made
transparent (understanding in the sense of his being grasped—
the sphere of power). Only when the Old Testament self-understanding (in which the Word of God becomes actively powerful
for the Old Testament man) is made clear, can the question be
asked: To what extent can the Old Testament Word in its self-
understanding be actively powerful for us in faith? The Old
Testament man *did* understand. He lived under the "Word of
God" (which is event) in a relationship to God; he experienced
himself as in the sphere of power. That his understanding was
different from the New Testament understanding and from our
contemporary understanding, that he stood in a living fellowship
with God in another way than the New Testament man or we
today, that he was in another situation in the history of piety—
this all has its basis in the historically conditioned character of
the Israelite religion, which is just not the Christian religion.
It is the task of hermeneutics, first, to bring about a clarification
concerning this *situation in the history of piety,* i.e., concerning
the inner structure of the relationship of the pious man of the
Old Testament to God.

The "understanding" of the Old Testament man occurs
under conditions which the Christian understanding does not
know:

1. In the relationship to God in the Old Testament it is a
matter of a God-people relationship. The Old Testament religion is a cult-religion. The "community" (*Gemeinde*) is the
political and cultic group (*Gemeinschaft*) in one. The view that
an individual relationship to God gradually developed in

Israel is false. In every period of Israelite religion the individual basically has access to God only as a member of people and cult. This is true however many individual notes are sounded. In this connection, the circle seems to become ever smaller when one considers the extension of the research of Gunkel and Mowinckel being penetratingly carried on by von Rad, Weiser, and others, which has revealed that the Psalms are to be separated from the individual and are to be understood as cultic in character.

2. The Israelite religion knows no living fellowship with God after death. The relationship to God is limited to the earthly life. At death in the Christian faith the door to eternal and living fellowship with God is opened, but in the Israelite faith God excludes the pious man from living fellowship with him for all eternity.

Therefore, the Old Testament is the witness of faith from a strange religion. Viewed from this perspective, "understanding" the Old Testament Word is necessarily impossible for our faith. And that is true—this must be seen—fundamentally and continuously. *Nothing* in the Old Testament is excepted, not even Isaiah 6 and Psalm 51, to remain with the illustrations already used.

In view of this situation, the recently imparted advice[12] becomes very questionable: We must knock unwearyingly on the door of the Old Testament Word until we hear something. The simple understanding does that easily; it proceeds without discrimination. But to knock theologically? We are knocking there not on a door slightly ajar, but on a thick concrete wall. Patient knocking does not help at all there. The "hermeneutical crowbars" must certainly be brought in (which Wolff rejects with such horror), i.e.; there an attempt must be made to develop a hermeneutical method which will take into our "understanding" as a constitutive element the hard fact that Old Testament "thinking" comes from a completely different situation in the history of piety. (This is in contrast to typological exegesis, which

---

12 Cf. H. W. Wolff, "Der grosse Jesreeltag," EvTh, 12 (1952), pp. 78 ff.

avoids the whole difficulty by simply ignoring the character of the Old Testament witness as conditioned by historical and religious development.) Consequently, the way of progress toward achieving theological statements concerning the Old Testament certainly becomes long, time-consuming, and difficult (again in contrast to the typological procedure). It provides occasion for complaint today on the part of the impatient. However, determining the *validity* of theological statements takes precedence over any impatient haste.

The means to the clarification here desired is research in the history of piety. By "piety" I mean the inner attitude in the presence of the living God. Research in the history of piety is research in the history of religion. It produces no theological statements, but one has need of it in order to arrive at theological statements. Von Rad[13] is fearful that investigation in the history of piety will be carried on in order to examine the Old Testament testimonies in regard to their "religious" content and their "ideas," and then to present as cogently as possible that which comes closest to the Christian position in this respect, and thereby to demonstrate adequately the theological significance of the Old Testament. History of piety is not history of ideas, but something quite different. It is the illumination of the inner structure of the pious existence of the Israelites in order to penetrate their understanding, which is not our understanding. Thereby it seeks to aid in exploring the distance of our understanding and, on the other hand, the contemporaneity of our understanding. Research in the history of piety is a historical and scientific aid which is indispensable for the hermeneutical process. That it has already been completed, unfortunately cannot be maintained. The new science of the phenomenology of religion must definitely be used here in addition to comparative history of religion.

The whole problem of the history of piety cannot be broached here. It may suffice to return to the illustrations mentioned at the beginning (Thesis 1) and to explain briefly

---

[13] G. von Rad, *Genesis* (1961), pp. 41 f.; see also G. von Rad, "Typological Interpretation of the Old Testament," pp. 17 ff.

what is involved. The pious man of the Old Testament "understood" the Jehu story. It must be made clear from the perspective of the history of piety what this narrative (which, of course, does not intend to narrate merely history) means within its boundaries in the history of piety, and to what extent the pious man of the Old Testament "understood" what was meant, i.e., to what extent it was actively sanctifying him. The *movens* and *agens* in the attitude of the pious man, which stems from the limitations resulting from its place in the history of religion, must be shown so that the statement can be made that God reveals himself as the living and holy God in the sinister and murderous deeds of Jehu. Moreover, it must be shown how, in hearing this story, the Old Testament man with the full involvement of his being experiences God as the holy God. Concerning Psalm 26 *mutatis mutandis* the same: It must be made clear to what extent the Psalmist can (and must) say before God, "I wash my hands in innocence," and to what extent the pious man of the Old Testament who hears this Psalm read, folds his "hands" and joins in saying as his prayer the words of the Psalm, which are filled, but not overflowing, with self-righteousness (words which certainly are not at all the representation of himself in self-righteousness, but a seeking of the living God). In the vindictive Psalms, to some extent under the limitations mentioned above, are attitudes formed from sheer necessity in which the most fearful thoughts of vengeance and a sense of not being forsaken by the living God lie organically together as one—such a completely "strange" Word of God! It is self-evident that the passages to which affinity can immediately be found (cf. above concerning Isa. 6 and Ps. 51) are to be examined in the same way in regard to the motivation and necessity of their statements.

Only when the whole problem of the history of piety is recognized does one understand the difficulty of attaining the hermeneutical way in which the Word of the Old Testament can be understood theologically, i.e., evangelically ("understanding" in the sense of being grasped through the Old Testament witness). Our contemporary insight into the character of the Old Testament statements, being conditioned by historical and religious development, inexorably compels us to this research in the history of piety. For our contemporary theological knowledge this constitutes precisely the character of the Old Testament as *Old* Testament: Its witness does not come out of the gospel, but out of a religion which lived under different historical and religious conditions. With this recognition, the typological and Christological methods of interpretation fall; they had their place in times of spiritual history which did not know historical thinking. Simply to eliminate a fact which for us today cannot at all be denied, as do these two methods, is certainly very tempting, for this way spares one the difficult burdens involved in the obligation of thinking things through theologically. But for the sake of scientific veracity, typological and Christological interpretation today is an anachronism which cannot be permitted.

Concerning Thesis 4

Research in the history of piety reveals within the Old Testament witness a unique movement of experience (*Erfahrens-Ablauf*) which is different from that under the gospel. It is conditioned by certain limitations in the realization of the relation to God on the part of the pious man of the Old Testament. The evangelical faith concludes that under those boundaries already mentioned there is a limitation. The affinity which the evangelical understanding nevertheless feels to the Old Testament Word is real, and it must be connected with the fact that there is fundamental accord in the basic tendency of experience. Because of this basic tendency a development frequently occurs in the Old Testament experience into which evangelical faith feels itself immediately drawn (our examples: Isa. 6; Ps. 51). At the same time, however, there are movements of experience in Old Testament piety in which the boundaries have such a serious effect that they cause the simple, evangelical understanding to withdraw in alienation (the Jehu story; Ps. 26).

What then does the Christian actually and *fundamentally* experience in his faith in Jesus Christ when he knows himself confronted and grasped by the reality of God? The following experience of the Christian cannot be separated from his appropriation of the grace of God and receiving it in faith:

1. The experience of the existence of God, his transcendence and power, together with the experience 'of his own situation within the world, his own weakness and brokenness.

2. The experience that the revelation of God obtains for me and is directed to me as an unconditional demand; also the experience that I seek to extricate myself from such a demand.

3. The experience that with this manifestation of God the divine judgment comes to me over the opposition of my will and brings me into a situation with no exit; and that the self-disclosure of God in his judgment then opens the way for me into a living fellowship with him.

This fundamental evangelical experience can be summed up and expressed in this way: God the Lord, the Lord my God. Such an experience is foundation and promise in one. And the fundamental experience of the Old Testament? There can be no doubt that it is the same. "I am the *Lord* thy God, I am the Lord *thy* God"—on that rests the old covenant, and that is the promise which comes with the old covenant. In this same fundamental experience, and in the evangelical knowledge through faith that the fundamental promise of the old covenant has been realized in Jesus Christ, is anchored the affinity of the Christian faith to the Old Testament Word. This is true even if the experience of the pious man of the Old Testament under the boundaries already mentioned develops in a way which must appear impeded and frequently in error from the evangelical point of view.

Here, in my opinion, one must begin if one asks questions concerning the Old Testament in accordance with the hermeneutical principle, and therefore in accordance with methodological exegesis.[14] Considering everything, it would be

---

14 I have developed this thesis in detail in my book mentioned in footnote 9.

hermeneutical to proceed in such a way that at least the following points of view may be maintained in the evangelical understanding of the Old Testament witness:

1. The Old Testament witness must be understood from the standpoint of the gospel. Only as he who is grasped by Christ does the theologian "understand" the Old Testament Word as the Word of God (the prior understanding!). Understood from itself, in its self-understanding, the Old Testament Word is indeed "understandable" in terms of the history of religion, or the history of piety, but not theologically; it remains a strange word from a strange religion, without power, which can only be objectively considered, but it does not meet us.

2. The Old Testament Word is to be taken into the evangelical understanding as the *Old* Testament Word, i.e., as witness with a meaning from the time and for the time which obtained then; therefore it is the Word outside the gospel, the Word which in its character as conditioned by historical and religious development has power for the Old Testament man, by which the Old Testament man was encountered. In evangelical understanding the Old Testament must remain the *Old* Testament. Typological and Christological understanding is excluded because it does not take the Old Testament Word into the evangelical understanding with its self-understanding, but with a meaning not justified by this self-understanding.

3. The Old Testament Word is to be understood as gospel, i.e., it must be made clear that, as conditioned Word outside the gospel, it is powerful for us, the active power of God for us; it is a witness which encounters and meets us in our existence together and as one with the evangelical witness. When a hermeneutical methodology is introduced, it must be shown to what extent the Old Testament witness (in its conditioned situation in the history of piety as characterized above) has active power for the Old Testament and the New Testament man at the same time. If this process of clarification is achieved methodologically, then the Old Testament is "understood" theologically, i.e., from the gospel.

4. The fundamental promise "I am the Lord thy God" must

be recognized as a valid foundation for comprehending the "to-gether and as one." In this promise the Old Testament and the New Testament witness have the common root of their life, the Old Testament by faith expecting its realization, the New Testament knowing by faith that in Jesus Christ it has been realized.

Theologically this "together" must be understood in two ways:

1. The testimonies of the Old Testament which are "strange" to our evangelical faith with its more developed religious under-standing—are they really so strange to us? Do not we ourselves again and again step into the conditioned situation of the Old Testament, forgetting that the realization of the fundamental promise in Jesus Christ has long since released us from these Old Testament boundaries? Are not we ourselves Jehu, who was a fighter for his church? In any event, the history of Christianity is full of triumphs over the "enemies of God." Throughout the history of the Christian church this bloody trail has been traveled in the name of the living God and for his glory. These are gross matters. There is a more refined "trail of blood," and we our-selves travel along it daily. Do we not really "understand"? And Psalm 26: "Vindicate me, O God!" And the self-representation of the *ṣaddîq*—does that really happen only in the piety of Israel? And the vindictive Psalms—do we not say *"Raca"* to-gether with the pious of the Old Testament? And our evangeli-cal certainty, not that we *must* die (together with the pious of the Old Testament), but that we *are permitted* to die? Is the Old Testament hopelessness in the face of bitter death really so utterly strange to us at all times? And God and Germany? Do we really have no "Old Testament" temptations *(Anfechtungen)*?

We understand very well what the Old Testament Word in all that means *for us*. We see ourselves as in a mirror. Thus we are "Old Testament" men in the fore-court of the gospel, and so completely released from the evangelical prior understanding. Here we experience the Old Testament witness as present mightily for us; it becomes judgment for us. Really no affinity? Really no "together" with the Old Testament Word? However, at the point where the pious man of the Old Testament knows himself to be completely in God's vise, it is terrifyingly clear to us who experience this "together" that we are in flight before the holy God who desires to grasp us in Jesus Christ. That is difficult for the evangelical Christian. But in any event, such a witness of the Old Testament is powerful and humbling for him; in withdrawing from the gospel's sphere of power he is brought over into his "affinity" with the Old Testament.

But in experiencing the judging power of the Old Testament witness we also experience at the same time and under the same Old Testament Word the gracious and comforting knowledge that these are words *outside* the gospel, words from limited and restricted circumstances, and Christ has long since released us from them. And if our temptation ever is to fall back into them, nevertheless, when we experience these testimonies as actively bringing judgment upon us, in the same experience we come again into the gospel's sphere of power. Thus we come to understand what the abolition of the Old Testament testimonies means. We no longer need to cry for our vindication, as the Old Testament petitioner *must* do (Ps. 26), for God has long since given us our "vindication" in Jesus Christ. No longer do we need to be so zealous with the imprecatory Psalms of the Old Testament for the triumph of God over the enemy; God's triumph over all that opposes him has long since been revealed in the cross and Resurrection. Thus the Old Testament Word becomes a joyous message to us; it brings us to our broken situation before God and at the same time assures us that in the midst of the "Old Testament" testing of our faith we may have confidence that God has already freed us from this situation. Thus ever again we can find ourselves in the sphere of power under the evangelical Word, and that is the comfort which is given to us when Old Testament Word, which is abolished Word, judges and humbles us.

Thus the Old Testament witness together with the gospel is powerful for us. That was made clear in the Old Testament testimonies from which the simple understanding immediately draws back. On the other hand, that the simple understanding can say, "I understand completely" (Isa. 6; Ps. 51), rests on the fact that at such points the common fundamental experience "I am the Lord thy God" is fully present in its pure and original form. There the Old Testament Word has power to humble and establish and is present for the Old Testament man and Christian man in one unbroken unity (at least fundamentally). Between that "I do not understand" and the "I understand completely" lie the immeasurably abundant gradations which result from the effects—sometimes stronger, sometimes weaker— of the limited and conditioned character of the Old Testament piety. They range from complete strangeness and antithesis to the gospel, to testimonies in which, viewed from the history of piety, the antithesis is dissolved into a striking nearness to the New Testament witness (as Pss. 51, 73).

2. The other line which is to be drawn in order to make the "together" clear is the *Heilsgeschichte* one. Here it can only be touched upon, not because it is less decisive than that treated under the first section, but because I have recently expressed myself in detail on this point in another place.[15] I would like to be permitted to refer to that for supplementation and clarification of the statements which follow.

Understood from the standpoint of the gospel, *Heilsgeschichte* is this: "The Word became flesh." He who is grasped by Christ "understands" this *Heilsgeschichte*. This means that the history (*Historie*) of Jesus is experienced by us (together with the early community) in faith as God's judgment and salvation being actualized for us by God and as the realization of living fellowship with him. The Old Testament event belongs in this "the Word became flesh." It must be comprehended from the event of Christ. It can be "understood" as *Heilsgeschichte* event, therefore, only from the standpoint of the gospel and never from the standpoint of the *Heilsgeschichte* self-understanding of the Old Testament. The Old Testament event can be conceived of as *Heilsgeschichte* event only insofar as it calls us into question in

---

[15] Cf. my article "Das alttestamentliche Geschehen als heilsgeschichtliches Geschehen" in *Geschichte und Altes Testament*, Festschrift für Albr. Alt (1953), pp. 13 ff.

our existence before God and establishes us in our existence. Moreover, with the Old Testament event it is not just a matter of the outward event; rather, an inner event takes place in the outward movement. It is thus exactly the same as with the New Testament event. This inner event and the attitude of the pious man of the Old Testament are likewise to be illuminated through research in the history of piety. Such research must make clear to what extent and how the outward event is reflected in the believing testimony of those for whom it occurs as an active event, as an event which encounters the inner existence, which humbles and establishes (the Old Testament self-understanding). Only when this happens can one comprehend to what extent this encounter of Old Testament man affects our own existence before God, and to what extent this encounter is our own encounter (together with Israel) under the gospel (the evangelical understanding). Only when this is the case is the Old Testament event *Heilsgeschichte* event. Only then is it included in this: The Word became flesh.

The whole gravity of the contemporary problem concerning the Old Testament comes from the fact that the historical-critical research implicit in our contemporary historical thinking has sharply recognized the Old Testament as the witness of a religion outside the gospel. It almost seems as if many have not even comprehended that today we must first just lose the Old Testament completely, i.e., comprehend it in its self-understanding as completely separate from the New Testament and in no way "justified" through the gospel!—in order to win it back again at all. The problem concerning this winning it back again is the hermeneutical problem today. This "losing" inexorably involves the loss of "contents" of the Old Testament which the New Testament and the Reformation accepted from the Old Testament as completely self-evident. This is a very serious situation, above all because the widespread traditional-ecclesiastical view holds that these contents must unconditionally be preserved in the sense of the New Testament and the Reformation. This view takes a stance which rejects the history of religion and phenomenology of religion, fully failing to recognize what extraordinary help modern critical research means for proclamation. To desire to build theological bridges here by renewing typological and Christological ways of understanding, which stem from times when the Old Testament (far removed from any penetration by means of history of religion or any historical thinking at all) was understood in the sense of verbal inspiration,[16] means basically to exclude modern historical-critical thinking from the process of understanding. One should consider that in doing this he fully precludes access to an understanding of the Old Testament for the modern man (understanding in the sense of encounter). Therefore he paralyzes proclamation. This is quite apart from the fact that the failure to incorporate the relativity of the Old Testament resulting from its historical and religious development affects scientific veracity.

I am quite conscious that in my discussion I have wandered along some precipices. For fundamental questions of theology in general are involved here: theology as science, historical thinking, the relation of biblical science and systematic theology, matters in the history of theology, faith—revelation—Word of God, understanding of Scripture, confessional limitations of the theologian—I could easily continue. That the systematic theologians especially will be painfully aware of the omissions and limitations in this discussion is only proof of how very much biblical science urgently needs help from the side of systematic theology. From the side of Old Testament science we must eagerly ask that such help come. For the sake of the truth of the whole matter, I should certainly be permitted to add: If such help should prove fruitful, then the systematic theologians will have to take notice of what happens in Old Testament science in a completely different way than previously. The painful feeling that my colleagues from the field of systematics will have in the face of my discussion takes hold of the Old Testament scholar when he seeks to fathom how modern knowledge in the

---

16 With good reason Wehrung characterizes such attempts as "expression of a prejudiced book-faith." Cf. Georg Wehrung, "Theologie, Kirche, Kirchen-leitung, von der kirchlichen Aufgabe der Theologie," ZSTh, 22 (1953), p. 165.

history of religion works out, let us say, in the field of systematics. One reads again in Karl Barth how he deals with the Virgin Birth. The main point from the standpoint of the history of religion, which weighs so heavily upon us Old Testament scholars here (Isa. 7:14), he simply dismisses with a few sentences in this way: There is no need to deal with the *hieros gamos* here —from the standpoint of comparative history of religion it is not a question of the *hieros gamos* complex, but the two other themes of virgin—mother—child and redeemer—king. In just such a way two disciplines live apart from one another, although they are very closely dependent upon one another. This is a point which is compellingly worked out in Ebeling's valuable article on the historical-critical method.[17] An autarchy of exegesis is the consequence. The consequence of this is that one accomplishes a theological short circuit from exegesis to proclamation or forgoes a serious exegetical substructure in proclamation.

In another respect also I have come to a narrow ridge in my discussion: biblical science and church. The tension which I have already alluded to previously is—I am carrying coals to Newcastle—notorious. Old Testament science is certainly not without guilt in this regard. But the church must be entreated to leave its attitude of mistrust and defense and enter into the theological enterprise from the standpoint of its present state and necessities. This would be commensurate with the church's own and correct thesis, which is often heard, that theology is a matter not only for the theological faculties but for the whole realm of the church. The church must comprehend that some risk is involved in theology, as faith itself is a risk. And it must concede that risk involves the possibility of errors and mistakes; that there is temptation also in science; and that, in spite of everything, all research is concerned with the truth in the evangelical sense. There is certainly erring faith and temptation also in the church. Nevertheless, for the church the main concern is the truth in proclamation. The church must be helped decisively to the insight that in the face of the demand for

---

[17] G. Ebeling, "Die Bedeutung der historisch-kritischen Methode für die prot. Theologie und Kirche," ZThK, 47 (1950), pp. 1 ff.

theological statements which will disturb no one the effort must continue for assured and valid theological statements. This is necessary even if the way may be long and not without the painful awareness that it will lead us out of the children's land of reverent and submissive silence before the Holy One into a critical and disturbing obligation to speak. Of course, it must be recognized in the beginning that such speech will be only a broken stammering before the Object with which it deals with its weak human powers.[18]

---

[18] For the question concerning biblical science—church, special reference should be made to the articles by Ebeling and Wehrung mentioned in notes 16 and 17.

8.

THE HERMENEUTICS OF
THE OLD TESTAMENT*

by Hans Walter Wolff

translated by Keith Crim

The Problem of Methodology

Anyone who attempts to discern the basic rules for understanding the Old Testament will do well first of all to make clear the boundaries of this task in order to be able to establish the rules in a useful way within these boundaries. We are confronted with a double question: In what sense is hermeneutic methodology to be rejected? and, in what sense is it to be promoted?[1]

1. *Every method of exposition, which by some principle would make itself master of the text and its context instead of entering into the service of the text, is to be rejected.*

(a) The multiplicity of the Old Testament texts resists any principle of exposition which seeks to determine the contents of the texts according to a predetermined schema. The turning away from the fourfold sense of Scripture and the turning to the literal meaning which took place at the Reformation[2] is to be

---

* This article appeared originally in *Evangelische Theologie* (Jahrgang 12, 1952, Juli/August, Heft 1/2), pp. 6 ff.

[1] Fr. Baumgärtel, "Ohne Schlüssel vor der Tür des Wortes Gottes?" EvTh, 13 (1953), pp. 413-421, calls for a clarification of the question. It should be noted that this article which sings the praises of methodology proceeds in the following manner: From "methodological considerations for the exposition of an Old Testament pericope" (EvTh, 12, 1952/53, pp. 78-104) he deals with the introductory and concluding principles which should indicate the boundaries of all methodology in order to arrive thereby at the "consciously practiced unmethodologicalness" of the author (p. 415). The real methodological discussions remain unnoticed for all practical purposes, above all on pages 97 ff., precisely where he sought to protect the attempt at typological exposition against arbitrariness. Nevertheless, this author, as well as the whole circle of workers on the *Biblischer Kommentar,* is grateful to Fr. Baumgärtel

carried out afresh in the face of every hermeneutic principle that denies to the manifold texts their own proper message.[2a] The historical research on the Old Testament and recently, above all, the analysis of the texts according to form criticism and history of transmission, have shown us ever more clearly that the individual types of text are to be interpreted differently according to their different *Sitz-im-Leben*. The great works of history are to be read differently from the cycles of stories that celebrate the Credo of Israel; the hymns and laments, which are there to be repeated, differently from the prophetic oracles which arouse Israel's attention; the law books, which serve the community of life of the people, differently from the proverbs, which bring in the harvest of everyday experience. It no longer occurs to any of us to force from each of these texts in the same manner in addition to the literal, historical meaning, a moral, an ecclesiological, and even an eschatological meaning. It must be determined on the basis of the meaning of the words whether the text raises its voice for the path of the individual or for the life of the people of God, whether it calls to praise of God's deeds or to obedience, whether it awakens penitence, love, or hope. Any other hermeneutic principle has just as little right to regulate the declarations of the Old Testament according to thematic points of view as has the teaching of the fourfold meaning of Scripture. There is always the inherent danger of doing violence to the texts if the wide variety of Old Testament texts is shoved into the press of some unified question that is

---

for the stimulus to rethink the foundation, methodology, and limits of methodology of typological exposition. In recent years he has concerned himself with the problems of Old Testament hermeneutics as no other has. In addition to his book *Verheissung* (1952) and the above mentioned article see also "Das alttestamentliche Geschehen als 'heilsgeschichtliches' Geschehen" in *Geschichte und Altes Testament*, Festschrift for A. Alt (1953) ; "Das hermeneutische Problem des Alten Testaments," ThLZ, 79 (1954), pp. 199-212 ; "Der Dissensus im Verständnis des Alten Testaments," EvTh, 14 (1954), pp. 298-313.

2 Cf. H. Bornkamm, *Luther und das Alte Testament* (1949), pp. 69 ff. ; H. H. Wolf, *Die Einheit des Bundes* (Das Verhältnis von Altem und Neuem Testament bei Calvin, 1942), pp. 101 ff. ; G. Ebeling, "Die Anfänge von Luthers Hermeneutik," ZThK, 48 (1951), pp. 175 ff.

2a The hermeneutic principles current today (see below notes 3-5 and 101a) proceed of course altogether from the literal meaning but are fond of determining the relevance of the text for us from outside the text.

foreign to the text, whether it be, What does the text say of the office of Christ?[3] or, To what extent does it, as a part of the law, clarify the contrast to the gospel?[4] or, Does it offer "promise in Christ"?[5] Every such hermeneutical principle allows at best only a fraction of the texts to speak. It evaluates, and mostly devaluates.[6] It declares one text relevant and many others beside it irrelevant.[7] So through methodological regulation the Old Testament becomes an invariable unit that has little in common with the real unity of the thoroughly manifold texts. For the most part, the texts themselves with their historical word quickly bring hermeneutic principles to ruin by shaking off the muzzle that has been placed on them.[8]

(b) The real unity of the Old Testament texts is simply given in the fact that they are all documents of the history of Israel before Christ, and that the uniqueness of this history is determined by Yahweh's speaking and dealing as Israel's God. In reference to the nearness of these documents to Yahweh's speaking and dealing in Israel's history, appreciable differences can be seen. It is no slight difference whether the Song of Deborah or the Song of Miriam sings Yahweh's deeds of salvation permeated with the hot breath of the events themselves, or if the Deuteronomic theologian, who collects the historical traditions, teaches that Israel's path is to be understood as God's Word become history. It is a different matter whether prophetic words announce as the word of Yahweh God's deeds, or whether prayers of lamentation full of despair await Yahweh's word and deeds. What a contrast it is when on the one hand the Yahwist testifies

---

[3] W. Vischer, *Das Christuszeugnis des Alten Testaments* (1934), pp. 7 ff.

[4] E. Hirsch, *Das Alte Testament und die Predigt des Evangeliums* (1936), pp. 11 and 78 ff. "Thus exactly because the Old Testament is the powerful historical antithesis of the New, it fits so well as the first part of the Christian Bible," p. 83.

[5] Fr. Baumgärtel, *Verheissung*, pp. 143 ff.

[6] G. von Rad, "Verheissung," EvTh, 13 (1953), pp. 410 ff.

[7] Baumgärtel, *op. cit.*, pp. 36 ff., 91 ff., 115 ff.

[8] All hermeneutics can always be improved only by better detailed exegesis, just as exegesis can always be improved only from the text. Cf. G. Eichholz, "Der Ansatz Karl Barths in der Hermeneutik," in *Antwort*, Festschrift Barth (1956), p. 54. "Exegesis can, like all theological work, only serve the text. Because it is so, the text continually overtakes the exegesis . . . rounds out the theological knowledge of yesterday, gives it new insights, forces it to new vocabulary with which to express them."

to God's being in daily conversation with men, and on the other hand Israel's proverbial wisdom in the secular life of every day mentions only as an exception its presuppositions of belief in Yahweh! These appreciable differences, however, in the character of the documents as witnesses, do not change at all the common presupposition that the history of Israel can be understood only as the history of the people of Yahweh. These documents then are all—more or less fragmentary, from near or far —reflexes of Yahweh's speaking and dealing in Israel. They would not exist as texts if they did not witness to Yahweh as Lord. Yes, they all stand directly or indirectly in the service of the Word of God and the deeds of God for Israel. Scarcely a piece of the Old Testament has become literature in any other manner; no single piece has been transmitted to us literarily in any other manner.

Here the other limit of every hermeneutic method becomes visible. If the texts stand, by origin or by adoption, in the service of witnesses to the God of Israel, and if no other than the God of Israel is God today, no hermeneutic principle can force the text to testify to God today. But it is just for this reason that for proper understanding it must be said, no method can replace the Spirit of the living God as the proper expositor of the texts.[8a] Here passionate protest now flames up, as if we were speaking of a "pneumatic method" and thus in principle of "unmethodicalness"![9] Therefore we are concerned with clarification of the question which must be asked of every careful methodology, namely, what can be done by methodical hermeneutics and what cannot. It is not my intention to propagate a "pneumatic method" of understanding.[10] For it, as a human method, could as little as any other replace the free action of the Spirit of God, who makes the historical words speak as the Word of God today. But the interpreter of any text, which as a historical text stands today in the service of the living God, should be conscious of the

[8a] Cf. O. Weber, *Grundlagen der Dogmatik*, I (1955), pp. 341, 347 f., and also his article "Hermeneutik" in EKL, II.
[9] Baumgärtel, EvTh, 13 (1953), pp. 417 f.
[10] Cf. also Chr. Maurer's article, "Exegese," 114b, EKL, I, p. 1229.

limit of every methodology.[11] Therefore Luther says, *"Omnis scriptura infinitae intelligentiae."*[12] No text which serves as a witness can, from the point of view of method, be done with once for all, however surely preliminary questions of understanding can be solved more or less conclusively. The witnessing word waits on its encounter with each new hearer. Therefore the texts are ever to be preached anew. The multiplicity of preaching is less a practical necessity than it is an objective demand, for the real understanding of the text remains a charismatic event. Where in the service of Israel's God the historical word becomes the voice of God today, charisma takes place.

He who is afraid here of the breaking in of sectarian caprice has turned the matter exactly upside down. For where charisma is active it is not that the interpreter has done violence to the text, but that the text has overpowered its interpreter.[12a]

This result, which cannot be forced methodically, in which the door of the text opens from within, is something that each hermeneutic can learn to await in as far as it remains conscious of its own proper task. If it takes into account that the text is in the service of Israel's God as the living God, then methodology is given the clear task of subordinating the hearer to the given text. Here is the wide field of scientific labor that is ready for service.

2. *Therefore a method of exposition is to be sought for, that seeks with all available means to understand the text in its*

---

[11] Baumgärtel, *op. cit.*, p. 414, astonishes one through the unqualified comparison, "methodological and theological are the same." Even when he finally thinks of the "relativity of all scientific methods" (p. 421), the problem of the limits of each method in the face of the peculiar and illusive objects of theology does not seem to move him. I am glad to be taught by Baumgärtel that our only possibility is methodical hearing and that therefore methodology must be considered and practiced as carefully as possible. But insofar as the biblical text bears witness to the God who is God for us today, insofar, therefore, as the historical text stands in the witnessing service of the present God, before him I can only declare myself, together with all methodology, an unprofitable servant. Our methodology is to listen; to speak remains his free activity. Our methodology remains knocking from outside; but the door is opened from inside, if there is to be real understanding.

[12] WA, IV, pp. 318 f.

[12a] Fr. Baumgärtel in EvTh, 13 (1953), pp. 413 ff., misunderstood my marginal comment in EvTh, 12 (1952/53), pp. 78 f., in this sense, as if (prayed for) charisma endangered methodical work. Charisma, as the free gift of God, however, does not exclude methodical work on the part of the

historical context, and is concerned to eliminate arbitrary inter-
pretations.

(a) It must first of all see to it that the expositor gives himself
to the peculiar character of the Old Testament text. It is not his
task to bring the text over to the position of the expositor, but
to betake himself to the place of the text. In this he will, in as far
as he is able, avail himself of the possibilities of philological,
historical, and literary interpretative technique. He will en-
deavor to discover the place in Israel's history where the text is
at home. He will seek to learn the occasion and intention which
caused the author of the text to speak. He will be concerned to
establish exactly the proper message of the text in the light of
the individual words, and the individual words in the light of
its proper message. In short, he will honestly work historically
and critically,[13] and certainly all the more carefully, the more
earnestly he reckons with the fact that the history of Israel, from
which his text comes, is the stage of the witnesses of Yahweh,
the God of Israel. In general there is no quarrel among us over
the necessity of this historical work of interpretation in reference
to the individual texts. But it is, however, most vigorously disputed among us in what total context the Old Testament texts
are to be seen. At this point, methodological considerations must
be pushed forward resolutely, however difficult the task is.

(b) For it belongs to the incontrovertible basic rules of
hermeneutics that a section of text can be understood aright
only in its *context*. This rule has not been adequately observed
if only the immediate literary connections have been investigated.
We cannot avoid the question of the total meaning of the Old
Testament.[14] It immediately brings with it the other question,

expositor, but includes it. It does not supplement a human method with
human caprice, as Baumgärtel fears, not without some justification, but
gives a foundation to relevant human research, and gives the fruit of understanding that results from the presence of the Spirit. The expositor can no
more produce this fruit by himself than he can the text, through which the
fruit is given to him. Cf. 1 Cor. 2:11 ff., and note 93 below.

13 In this connection compare the details in EvTh, 12 (1952/53), pp. 79 ff.

14 Thus Hirsch, *op. cit.*, p. 72, with good cause. His complaint about his
teachers, that they "dealt with the Old Testament as a complete compendium
of strange as well as ordinary, great as well as small, historical, literary,
and religious curiosities" (p. 3), hits upon a continuing danger and embar-
rassment of Old Testament science.

which is in the last resort decisive: In what context does the
Old Testament as a whole belong? In what historical connections
does it belong? Where are the analogies that illuminate what it
says of itself? There are three conflicting points of view. The
first affirms that the Old Testament can be understood only as a
document of a folk religion in analogy to the neighboring cul-
tures of the ancient Orient;[15] the second, its peculiar character is
grasped only in its historical connection with late Judaism and
the synagogue, where it is also conceived of as canonical;[16] the
third, the New Testament is the obvious context where the total
meaning of the Old Testament is first discovered. So general history of religion, synagogue, and church strive with one another
for the Old Testament.

Where else should the quarrel be decided but in the Old
Testament itself?[17] To find for whom and against whom it raises
its voice, to determine in which context it can express itself
truly and fully, that is the final and decisive task of all scientific
concern with the Old Testament. That this necessity is widely
evaded in the midst of many specialized studies constitutes the
serious dilemma of Old Testament science. We can give here
only some indication of what nevertheless is beginning to be
established as the result of research, but which must be subjected to still further investigation.

---

[15] Thus the opinion that for decades has come to be regarded as self-
evident, and which remains unattacked by Baumgärtel. "The Old Testament
is the witness of a strange religion," a "cult religion," in which "the concern
is for the relation of God and people." ThLZ (1954), p. 206. Cf. EvTh (1954),
pp. 311 ff.

[16] So, interestingly enough, E. Hirsch, in complete agreement with the
synagogue. Op. cit., p. 72. See below.

[17] That corresponds to the New Testament view. "Nothing were falser than
the thought that the early Christian exegesis was less literal than that of
the Rabbinical exegetes. It can be seen that the New Testament exegesis
itself can be particularly literal. It is therefore our task in conversation with
Judaism, to affirm the authority of the Old Testament, yes, even to restore
and re-establish it, but not to limit it or twist it. Jesus fell in battle for the
law as rightly understood, not as a rebel in battle against the law, Matt.
23:23." O. Michel, "Das Alte Testament im Neuen Testament," in Bahnauer
Hefte, 5, p. 45. Cf. also W. Vischer, op. cit., p. 33; "In case Jesus is truly
the hidden meaning of the Old Testament writings, then an honorable philological exegesis must in some way deal with that fact." In view of the
vigorous and fashionably pursued attacks on Vischer's work, which were
essentially caused by the detailed carrying out of his exegesis, thanks for
the basically relevant stimulus of this book should never cease to be given.
Anyone who rereads its basic deliberations will be surprised how many of our
present problems are dealt with there. Cf. especially op. cit., pp. 32 f.

The Special Starting Point of Old Testament Hermeneutics

1. The more distinctly the old Oriental religions are reconstructed before our eyes, the more clearly we see that the Old Testament actively resists the attempt to understand it in analogy to the cults of its environment. This is all the more surprising since the connection of Israel with its environment in matters of a general world view, of profane and sacral usage, of cultic institutions, yes, even of prophetic phenomena, is constantly becoming clearer.[18] But even though it is a child of the ancient Orient, in its essentials it can still not be understood in terms of its environment[19] as shown in the following: The basic strata of Old Testament literature in the Pentateuch, in the historical books, and in the prophets bear witness to an acting and speaking of Israel's God, which is throughout directed to Israel in the midst of the nations of the world. This thoroughgoing nature of the witness of faith which is strictly related to history finds, quite apart from all parallels in detail, no explanation in terms of the literary types of the surrounding world, for which the mixture of god-myths and cultic legends on the one hand, and royal annals and similar historical documents on the other, is characteristic. Of course, in individual cases even Shalmaneser III can ascribe the victory of Karkar to his gods Ashhur and Nergal;[20] or the prophet-priest of the god Dagon can command the king of Mari to build a city gate or to make preparations

---

[18] Herein lies the relative correctness of Baumgärtel's view, see above, note 15. See also M. Noth, *Geschichte Israels*, 2nd ed. (1954), p. 10.

[19] Cf. Noth, *op. cit.*, p. 11: "And still just in the light of these connections and possibilities of comparison (i.e., with the environment of Israel) Israel appears as a stranger in this its world. To be sure, Israel wore its garb and behaved in the way that was customary in it, but yet was different from it in essence; and that not only as every historical entity has its individual character, but rather that in the center of Israel's history phenomena appear for which there are no longer any possibilities of comparison. This is certainly not because materials for comparison have long since disappeared, but because after all that we know, such things are not at all encountered in the rest of history. Making this clear must be one of the tasks of a presentation of the history of 'Israel.'" G. von Rad now asks, "Whether the book has attained this goal set for it." *Verkündigung und Forschung 1953/55* (1956), pp. 133 f. It remains the great problem confronting our generation, and can be dealt with only in the community of work of historians and theologians.

[20] TGI, 46; AOT, 341.

for war.[21] But for the writing of history[22] to be entirely removed from courtly glorification of the king and made into a
unified testimony to faith in Yahweh, the God of Israel, and by
the same measure for the witness of faith to be removed from
mythology, and even the cult pressed into service as a witness to
Yahweh's actions in history—for this no analogy can be found in
Israel's environment. Ethnology cannot explain this peculiarity
in the face of the demonstrable kinship of Israel with its environment.

First, following the signposts of the Old Testament itself, we
must seek to understand it on the basis of the peculiar nature
of Yahweh, the God of Israel. In his essence, Yahweh is not a
figure of mythology in the sense that one could speak of him in
the manner of the myths of the neighboring lands, which chat-
ter so much of the "private life" of their gods and of their life
together in the pantheon.[23] Yahweh is the one beside whom no
other is God, and before whom all the others are shown to be
no gods. And of him as the One, there is really nothing else to
say but that he has approached men, and in particular that he
acts in history for his people Israel.[24] It is because he has revealed
himself as God in Israel in this way that the witness of faith in
Israel has such a decided connection with history. Here the writing of history exists only as praise of Yahweh or as confession of
guilt before him;[25] even the mythical narrative forms must
underscore that Yahweh is not God among gods or God for himself, but that he comes into the daily life of real men.[26]

So then Yahweh does not live by the Israelite cult, any more
than he dies when it is extinguished, but Israel lives from the

[21] Cf. W. von Soden, *Welt des Orients* (1950), pp. 396-403, and also EvTh,
15 (1955), pp. 448 ff.

[22] Cf. R. Rendtorff's article, "Geschichtsschreibung," EKL, I.

[23] Tablet XI of the Gilgamesh Epic remains exemplary. In it the gods in a
thoughtless mood play at having a flood, only later to flee into heaven from
their own undertaking, and to "cower down like dogs." After the waters have
abated they are seen greedily "gathering like flies over Utnapishtim's sacrifice." Cf. for the text, A. Parrot, *Bibel und Archäologie*, I (*Sintflut und
Arche Noahs*, 1955), pp. 17 ff.

[24] It is here that the differences from the "monotheistic tendencies in the
Egyptian religion" are to be sought; cf E. Otto in *Welt des Orients* (1955),
pp. 99-110.

[25] G. von Rad, *op. cit.*, p. 133.

[26] Cf. for instance the Yahwistic narratives, Gen. 2 f., 11, 18, etc.

deeds and from the words of its God. In this connection two phenomena are illustrative, which show Israel to be a stranger in its environment. First, Israel is not so much determined through a special cult with the functions of priests and the service of sacrifice, as it is rather through the fact that it lives from the beginning under a *divine law,* which is continually proclaimed anew.[27] It has the function of keeping Israel near to the God who freed it and gave it gifts, and at the same time, by the rejection of unrighteousness, it has the function of ordering the whole life of the people as a community of mutual help. In this way, the God who saved Israel from its foes and gave it the land assures also the free life of the Israelites among one another. Second, prophecy occurs in Israel.[28] In this also Yahweh shows himself as the God who alone makes history (Isa. 43:8-13). In incomparable manner the prophets proclaim that even the great powers must serve only the activity of God concerning Israel, in judgment and salvation. They proclaim anew that Israel does not live by its own accomplishments and independent undertakings, but by Yahweh's intervening for his people and by his instruction.[29] Finally, this is also indicated by the strange political structure of Israel in the course of its history, in which the *kingship* appears remarkably late and as unprecedentedly secular,[30] and very quickly comes to an end without its own beginning and end being identical with the beginning and end of the Israelite state. Before and behind, it is unified through the name, the deeds, and the word of Yahweh; throughout its course it is accompanied by the singular opposition of Yahweh's word through the prophets, and so at every point distinguished from its environment.

In so saying, we have mentioned only a few of the phenomena

---

27 Cf. M. Noth, *op. cit.,* pp. 97 ff.
28 *Ibid.,* p. 232.
29 Cf. W. Zimmerli, "Das AT als Anrede," BEvTh, 24 (1956), p. 54. "In the smoking ruins of Jerusalem, according to the testimony of Ezekiel, the justice of God in relation to his people becomes evident. In its special history it was the people of mankind, and now for the sake of its covenant with the Holy One, it can make the justice of the covenant Lord visible only through its death."
30 Cf. N. Noth, *op. cit.,* pp. 152 f., and "Gott, König, Volk im Alten Testament," ZThK, 47 (1950), pp. 157-191. This important article is circumvented

that make it impossible to understand the history of ancient Israel
and the Old Testament literature in its essential characteristics
in terms of its environment. Careful investigation shows it is a
stranger. The historian of the ancient Orient can only recognize
it as such. But where are the relatives with the same features?

2. The synagogue calls: Here, only here! We are the sons. In
us you can recognize the fathers again. Who could mistake the
historical continuity? Indeed, the synagogue with its Bible must
be a witness that God has spoken to Israel as to no other people in
history. But has the Old Testament truly come to its goal in the
synagogue? Is its "total meaning" only to be grasped "from the
standpoint of the community which has gathered, selected, and
edited it from among the written traditions of its people"?[30a] Is
it therefore correct to say that the "Old Testament-Jewish religion (including the figure of Abraham, the prophets, and the
Psalms) has in the *Law* its center which determines all else"?[30b]

What does the Old Testament itself say about that? In as far
as the exegetical labor of the last decades has worked out with
even approximate correctness the leading themes and main
strands of the Old Testament tradition, we can say today unequivocally that it stands in opposition to this reduction of its
total meaning as a completely erroneous viewpoint.[31] The ab-
solutizing of the law in the synagogue tears it out of the context
in the Pentateuch in which it is firmly surrounded by God's
saving deeds for Israel and his covenant with Israel, and is given
as God's help for life.[32] How differently from the rabbinical
casuistry do the great historical works and the prophetic proclamation measure Israel's life![33] The prophetic word shows that

---

in an astounding manner by Geo Widengren, *Sakrales Königtum im Alten
Testament und im Judentum* (1955). The theses presented by Widengren
had been previously shown by Noth to be very questionable.

[30a] Hirsch, *op. cit.*, p. 72.

[30b] *Ibid.*, p. 76.

[31] Cf. above all, M. Noth, *Überlieferungsgeschichte des Pentateuch* (1948),
and G. von Rad, *Das formgeschichtliche Problem des Hexateuch* (1938).

[32] Cf. above all, M. Noth, *Die Gesetze im Pentateuch, ihre Voraussetzungen
und ihr Sinn* (1940), for the whole group of problems. Cf. also G. von Rad,
"Literarkritische und überlieferungsgeschichtliche Forschung im AT," *Verkündigung und Forschung* (1947/48), pp. 172-194, and H. J. Kraus, *Freude
an Gottes Gesetz*, EvTh, 10 (1951/52), pp. 337-351.

[33] The casuistic exegesis of the law as condition for life misses first of all

there is no salvation for Israel outside of the thankful and obedient life with Yahweh in the covenant. It recognizes that Israel makes a failure of its life by its total and incorrigible disobedience. But it testifies above all that Yahweh's word and deeds continue to work in Israel, for he cannot forsake them. Where they refuse to obey him and show this disobedience as incorrigible, there God announces that through judgment and forgiveness he is preparing a new covenant for Israel.[34] So God's work with Israel goes forward. That he himself comes to Israel— that remains the message.[35]

Judaism itself, if it read further in the Bible, had to regard it as a fatal distortion of the biblical message to consider the individual's being brought on the way to exact fulfillment of the law as the essential point. So in addition to this there appeared the philosophical interpretation which regarded the Torah as the source of all wisdom; *kolla' bah,* "Everything is in it."[36] Now both important and unimportant things become universally valid. In the sum of the words one finds all the truths of the world expressed. This strange honor completely silences the Old Testament. How unhistorical this singular book of history has now become! Where can we still hear that Israel is confronted by the deeds of salvation of its God; that he himself seeks Israel and works with it through his Word? Has a mystic, Chassidic Judaism understood it better? Martin Buber sees the "eternal

---

the old meaning of Torah as instruction in life out of the previously proclaimed free choice and gracious act of God (cf. G. von Rad, EvTh, 1953, p. 409), and in addition avoids completely the prophetic event which breaks into the old covenant, and which sees Israel therefore as judged by the radically proclaimed divine law, because Israel has rejected its only helper. Characteristic for this is the construction of the great Israel Oracle, Amos 2:6-8, 9-10, 13-16; 3:1-12. Compare also W. Zimmerli, *op. cit.,* pp. 46, 80: "The reduction of the Old Testament word to the concept of law is simply exegetically false and may not be taken over from the synagogue."

[34] It is significant that M. Buber cannot really accept the total announcement of judgment of the prophets, but must reinterpret it as the call to repentance (*Glaube der Propheten,* 1950). To be sure, he overcomes the casuistry, but his concept of dialogue distorts the prophetic relationship of deity and mankind. Cf. H. J. Kraus, EvTh, 12 (1952/53), pp. 72 ff., and H. W. Wolff, "Das Thema Umkehr in der alttestamentlichen Prophetie," ZThK, 48 (1951), pp. 129-148.

[35] Cf. W. Zimmerli, "Promise and Fulfillment," p. 105, "The prophetic promise proclaims at its deepest level not a coming *something,* after the manner of the fortune-teller, but *he* who comes, as he kills, as he calls to life."

[36] Cf. F. Maass, "Von den Ursprüngen der rabbinischen Schriftauslegung," ZThK, 52 (1955), p. 137.

reality" in the mystery of the proclaiming letter.[37] Where then
is Yahweh, who is proclaimed as so invariably personal, as the
One who acts, who speaks, who is coming? And if he means that
the meaning of the biblical history is fulfilled in its total reality,[38]
where then is the secret of the choice of Israel, where is the guilt
of those who have fallen away from the covenant, where is the
hope for renewal of the covenant as an act of God?

3. We are not able to recognize in these Jewish sons the witness
of their fathers in its full meaning. So there remains then only
the question about the other sons, whom Paul addresses as the
Israel of God.[39] Is the church really comparable to the old
Israel? Does the New Testament witness correspond to that of
the Old?

(a) Is not the old covenant valid for Israel alone, but the new
essentially valid for the Gentiles? As an antithesis this question
is not to be answered affirmatively on the basis of either the Old
or the New Testament. It is the great testimony of the Yahwist
in his composition of primeval history and patriarchal history
that with the calling of Israel Yahweh wants to prepare the
blessing of a new life for the world of the nations, which is
fragmented and subject to death.[40] Prophecy awaits the eschatological pilgrimage of the peoples to the salvation which God
has prepared on Zion.[41] So Israel also knew how to sing in its

---

[37] In this connection, H. J. Kraus, "Gespräch mit Martin Buber," EvTh, 12
(1952/53), p. 62.
[38] Cf. M. Buber, *Königtum Gottes* (3rd ed., 1956), pp. lxiii f., and W.
Vischer, *op. cit.*, p. 39. Highly instructive for the position of the present state
of Israel toward the Bible is Schalom ben Chorin in the article, "Judentum
II," EKL, II, which speaks of a return to the Bible. In this the Bible is the
"Book of the history of the nation, source of its language, guide to its land,
key to its national self-understanding." But where does one hear what the
Old Testament itself has to say of God's dealing and speaking? S. ben Chorin
certainly expects a Jewish reformation from the return to the Bible. He sees
that at present "the religious side of the Bible is often neglected," but believes it could be "reactivated." "The Jewish people will have to show themselves creative again in their own field." Does that mean, listen to the Old
Testament? Where is one waiting for the eschatological acts of God, which
the Old Testament tells us to wait for? Where are they recognized?
[39] Gal. 6:16.
[40] Gen. 12:3b.
[41] Isa. 2:2-4.

hymns that the foreign nations would become witnesses to the salvation of Israel not only as spectators and helpers, but would even be drawn into the benevolent, helpful lordship of Yahweh and so become the saved of Yahweh also.[42] Naturally this does not at all change the fact that in the whole of the Old Testament Israel is the real partner of Yahweh, but the Old Testament gives prominent expression to the thought that God's special dealings with Israel in history have their goal in the Gentile world, yes, that they have the whole world in mind from the first.

And what does the New Testament say? Are not the call and the acts of Jesus Christ directed quite definitely and at first exclusively to the lost sheep of the house of Israel?[43] And is it not that the congregation from among the Gentiles is grafted among the branches of the old, noble olive tree Israel, only as the new Israel?[44] Indeed, is not the whole congregation from among the nations, from the calling of the Twelve in the Synoptic Gospels to the Apocalypse of John, constituted consciously as the new people of the twelve tribes?[45]

There is no question but that all along the line in the New Testament Israel, as Yahweh's covenant people, is, as a whole and in detail, a type of the *ekklēsia* of Jesus Christ. As a community from among the Jews and the Gentiles, the church is a stranger among the peoples just as the old Israel was in its environment, and only as the stranger who is called does it become a blessing to the world.

While the synagogue seeks, but mostly in vain, to make proselytes at the time that it is dispersed among the nations, and seeks to assert itself among the nations, or more recently, alongside the nations of this world, the New Testament shows the true correspondence to the Old Testament witness. Most certainly the New Testament people of God is not identical with the Old. True progress can be seen, for, just as the New Testament testifies, in Jesus Christ God's dealings and speaking have

---

42 Pss. 96, 98.
43 Matt. 10 :6.
44 Rom. 11 :17 ff.
45 Mark 3 :14 ; James 1 :1 ; Rev. 7 :4 ff. ; 21 :12-14.

come to their goal. This progress contains also antitheses in some details.[46] But the main thing is to observe the remarkable analogy: The church of Jesus Christ can understand itself aright only as the eschatological Israel of God.

(b) Yet we must now ask further: Can the way of salvation and the foundation of salvation in the Old and New Testaments be understood only antithetically? Is it not that the Old Testament Israel comes to ruin on the imperative of the covenant law, while the New lives out of the indicative of the act of Christ? In the Old, therefore, Israel itself is brought to judgment, and in the New, Christ for Israel. As an antithesis this proposition also is substantiated by neither the Old nor the New Testament. To begin with, the Old Testament people of God, too, is constituted by God's fight for Israel, by his love. The imperative of God's law is surrounded by the indicative of God's action.[47] To be sure, Israel breaks away from the covenant and must experience ruin as a result of this guilt. It is then confronted in manifold ways by the God of Israel. Not only is it confronted by the call to turn again, but, since that remains futile, by God's own turning from wrath again in compassion; the rejected love flames forth and heals the rebellious ones through judgment and compassion.[48] Even the ceremonial of sacrifice, into which too little research has even yet been done, must be largely understood in Israel as the offer of the God of Israel to declare anew righteousness to the unrighteous.[49] And finally, beside the path of erring Israel stand many and various figures that cannot be ignored: Moses, who intervened, suffered, and interceded for his people, who renews the broken covenant; or quite differently, King

[46] Among the greatest of these is that for the present, Israel as a whole does not belong to the new people of God, that the "not my people," the object of grace, by whom Hosea means the old Israel (2:1-3) is applied in the New Testament to the Gentiles (1 Peter 2:10; Rom. 9:25).

[47] See notes 32 and 33 above, as well as W. Zimmerli, *Das Alte Testament als Anrede*, pp. 22 f. The relationship of God's covenant and God's law in the Old Testament corresponds largely to the relationship of gospel and *paraklesis* in the New Testament. Cf. in this connection, E. Schlink, "Gesetz und Paraklese," in *Antwort* (Festschrift Barth, 1956), pp. 323-335.

[48] Hos. 3; 11:8 f.

[49] Cf. G. von Rad, "Gerechtigkeit und Leben in der Kultsprache der Psalmen" (*Festschrift Bertholet*, 1950), pp. 418 ff. "In old Israel, the predicate *ṣaddik* was scarcely bestowed any other way than through the cult" (p. 423). "Again and again the ones praying describe themselves as living com-

Josiah with his renewal of the covenant on the basis of the newly discovered Word of God in Deuteronomy; and once again, entirely differently, the Servant of God, who bears the sins of the many and heals Israel by his death.[50] Of course, this does not at all change the fact that faithless Israel must pass through the darkest judgment and at the end of the Old Testament seem to be almost overcome by heathendom. But the Old Testament gives expression in the most manifold ways to the fact that the God who has called his people in love and given them gifts, cannot let his people go even amid faithlessness and judgment, indeed, that his final action for Israel still remains to be taken.

This final action is proclaimed by the New Testament. Jesus Christ is the last Paschal Lamb that is offered for Israel.[51] He is the last King, who through his free act of love in his death renews with finality the broken covenant.[52] He is the last Priest of Israel, who through his own sacrifice takes away the sin of the people.[53] Now he is here in body, he whose shadow so often fell upon the old Israel.

But is he not at the same time the new Moses, who announces with final authority the law of the Kingdom of God, in that he proclaims it anew as the law of the covenant?[54] Can even an Apostle announce the gospel of the new covenant without setting up in his exhortation the imperative of the "law of Christ"?[55] Yes, cannot it be said of the new covenant as of the old, he who fails to keep it will be judged? "He who has not the Son has not life."[56] And again it holds for the whole, as Yahweh's people proved to be a type of the *ekklēsia,* so the old founding and renewing of the covenant in Yahweh's deeds and word corresponds

---

pletely with God, as having placed all their confidence in him, and having been completely obedient. That is not an inconceivably hardened self-righteousness, but the cult has shown them it is in this way they should lay hold on God's good pleasure offered to Israel" (p. 424). Cf. also, G. von Rad, "Die Anrechnung des Glaubens zur Gerechtigkeit," ThLZ, 76 (1951), 129 ff.

50 Deut. 9 :8 f. ; 2 Kings 23 :2 f. ; Isa. 53.

51 1 Cor. 5 :7 ; John 19 :14, 36 ; and also R. Bultmann, *Das Ev. d. Joh.* (1952), p. 525.

52 John 19 :19.

53 Heb. 7 :23 ff.

54 Matt. 5. See J. Schniewind, *Matthäus* (NTD), p. 37.

55 Gal. 6 :2.

56 1 John 5 :12.

to the founding of the new covenant in the saving act of God in Jesus Christ.[57] The people of the new covenant can, like that of the old, enter history only by virtue of the liberating action of its God; the new covenant has its permanence, as Jeremiah promised in the old, only through the forgiveness of sins. It could not be God's covenant any more than the old could if God's kingship were not proclaimed over all its members as pointing the way of life.

While the synagogue forsakes God's path of life, which he began in the old covenant, while it separates God's covenant law from his covenant acts and seeks in vain to fulfill it in legal casuistry, the New Testament points out the true correspondence to the Old Testament kerygma. The final great act of God in the New Testament is most certainly not to be equated with his manifold and various acts of old. Moreover, it must be said here that God's previous action and speaking have reached a new stage of their history—they have attained their goal. This very progress, however, involves antitheses in some details.[58] The main point to be seen, however, is the decisive analogy: The church of Jesus Christ is constituted, brought safely through perils, and renewed by God's saving act, just as Israel was. And Jesus Christ restores the connection—broken by the Rabbinate—of the law of God with the covenant of God as a guide for the life of the covenant people.[59]

(c) But are not these analogies which have been brought forward merely formal? Do they not conceal the decisive antithesis which still remains, namely, that God's covenant gifts in the Old Testament are entirely different from God's gifts in Jesus Christ? Israel's Credo acknowledges as gifts of the covenant none other than deliverance from enemy powers, good farm land, fruitful vineyards, numerous posterity. And did the prophets have basically any other blessings to announce than victory over foes,

---

[57] Mark 14:24; 1 Cor. 11:25.

[58] The most valid of these is that Jesus Christ goes to death for his people; no priest or king of the Old Testament does that, nor does any prophetic Messianic figure.

[59] Cf. H. Diem, "Jesus, der Christus des AT," EvTh, 14 (1954), p. 444.

dwelling in peace under vine and fig tree, and social righteousness? On the other hand, Jesus Christ is the first to provide spiritual gifts, forgiveness of sins, righteousness before God, and fellowship with himself. He conquers death and calls us to eternal life, and of this the Old Testament has almost nothing to say. But even this antithesis—here material, national, and temporal gifts, and there spiritual, individual, and eternal gifts—cannot be maintained on the basis of either the Old or the New Testament.[59a]

The old Israelite Credo praises Yahweh for the deliverance from Egypt and the gift of the Promised Land for the very reason that Yahweh by so doing has revealed himself as the covenant God of Israel. If Israel receives the gift aright, it then prays to Yahweh as its own God.[60] The Priestly document stresses that the historical act of deliverance from Egypt is understood only when Israel comprehends in it Yahweh's covenant will to be the God of Israel and for Israel to be his people.[61] In the cult also Israel must hear the warning that the gift of peace in the land will be taken away if, as the people of Yahweh's pasture, it does not heed Yahweh's voice.[62] From Amos and Hosea on, the prophets proclaimed judgment because Israel took the gifts as booty and rejected the giver. It is for this reason that Yahweh coaxes his faithless wife into the desert to woo her anew as a fiancée and to win her to full companionship, to an eternal

---

[59a] Cf. Fr. Baumgärtel, *Verheissung*, pp. 20 f. "The promises which God has placed in the law according to the Old Testament understanding" (life, possession of the land, richness of crops, general welfare, victory over foes), "are in direct opposition to the promise in Christ . . . for they are bound to the Israelite *nomos*, and this does not concern us." L. Koehler has already commented on these remarks relevantly in "Christus im Alten und Neuen Testament," ThZ (1953), p. 250, "Here it seems to me, the Achilles' heel in Baumgärtel's presentation becomes visible for the first time. He understands the Old Testament from the point of view of his understanding of the New Testament and does it violence or even reduces its value because it does not fit into his will for seeing things." It is highly desirable that Baumgärtel's approach to the New Testament be scrutinized. With this should be compared also C. Westermann, "Zur Auslegung des Alten Testaments," in *Vergegenwärtigung* (1955), pp. 108 f.

[60] Deut. 26:1-11.

[61] Exod. 6:7; 40. The real goal of his deeds and gifts is, for the Priestly document, the "preservation of his very personal presence." Cf. K. Elliger, "Sinn und Ursprung der priesterlichen Geschichtserzählung," ZThK, 49 (1952), p. 127.

[62] Ps. 95.

betrothal, which is based on his mercy and his gift of righteousness as engagement presents, and which will be maintained through his constancy.[63] The thoroughly personal character of the prophetic message is determined by the pressure of Yahweh's "I" on Israel in judgment and salvation. This tendency of all the concrete threats and promises must be seen: "I come, and I will live with thee." "Prepare to meet thy God, O Israel!"[64] Out of the certainty that life is specially and totally bound together with Yahweh there even grew up, though only in a narrow segment of the Old Testament, the certainty that the one to whom Yahweh himself grants life for his own possession can never fall victim to death.[65] Naturally that does not at all change the fact that in the whole of the Old Testament material, collective and temporal blessings stand in the foreground. But the Old Testament from beginning to end is not silent about the fact that everything depends on one's being bound to God, and for this reason the individual is addressed by God more and more in the Old Testament. Indeed, in this lies the germ of the certainty of victory over death.

And what does the New Testament say? Without question it regards Jesus Christ as the gift of all gifts (2 Cor. 9:12; Rom. 8:32). But does it know a Jesus who passed material needs by? Do not the healings of the sick take up a surprisingly large amount of space in the whole New Testament? And how important the poor are in his sight! For Paul it is correspondingly important that the community in Christ send financial help to the poor in Jerusalem.

Do the Beatitudes not specifically renew the promise of land for the poor?[66] Jesus did not call any disciple into his fellowship without providing for him on "this side," yes, even with great promises of houses, children, brothers and sisters, and fields for the present time.[67] Yet these details are merely indications that

---

[63] Amos 2:6 ff.; Hos. 2:16 f., 21 f.

[64] Zech. 2:9, 14; Amos 4:12.

[65] Pss. 16, 73. In this connection see G. von Rad, "Gerechtigkeit und Leben in der Kultsprache der Psalmen," *op. cit.*, pp. 432 ff.

[66] Matt. 5:5. Cf. also H. Wildberger, pp. 419 ff.

[67] Mark 10:29 f.; Luke 22:35. Cf. also H. Bardtke in the article, "Glück und Schicksal," EKL, I; D. Bonhoeffer, *Widerstand und Ergebung*, p. 254:

the God of the New Testament is not less concerned with the "this side" of human history than is the God of the Old Testament. And is the New Testament basically more, or perhaps even exclusively, concerned with the individual? Does Jesus not constitute the new people of God even by his calling the Twelve? Are not all who are called to him through the gospel called into his community, addressed as members of his body?[68] This community has also its new social life.[69] It is under way as the wandering people of God, even as the old was.[70]

We must see that the unspeakable gift in Christ is all too quickly misunderstood as spiritual, individualistic, and transcendental if we do not hold before our eyes its original in the covenant Yahweh granted to Israel. He who gives himself to his community through forgiveness of sins in his death and in his Resurrection, so that he is forever Lord and Shepherd, is also concerned with giving gifts for and directing its temporal life in this world.

At the same time in that the synagogue does not recognize that it was God who afflicted Jesus Christ—and therefore Judaism grasps at the earthly gifts culminating in the new possession of the land in Palestine while rejecting the Giver—or on the other hand transposes the Old Testament Word into the mystic or ethical, the New Testament demonstrates the true correspondence to the Old Testament kerygma. To be sure, the gift of salvation in Christ is not identical with that in the Old Testament. A new deed of God has truly taken place, even as the New Testament also proclaims the gift of Christ as the final fulfillment of the Old Testament promises, which as such conserves the old blessings in itself.[71] But the conclusive analogy remains dominant: The new covenant in Christ corresponds to the covenant

---

"In this respect the difference between the Old and New Testaments lies only in this, that in the Old Testament the blessing also includes the cross, and in the New Testament the cross also includes the blessing."

68 Acts 2:41 ff.; 1 Cor. 12:12 ff.
69 1 Cor. 6:2; 2 Cor. 8 f.; 1 Peter 4:8 ff.
70 Heb. 4.
71 Circumcision, the old calendar of festivals, and the pronouncing righteous in the sacrificial cult are abolished (Gal. 2; Col. 2:16 ff.; Heb. 12:18 ff.).

will of Yahweh as its fulfillment in the same way that marriage
corresponds to engagement.

So we are confronted by the conclusion that the old Oriental
environment and the Jewish successors of the Old Testament Israel, while presenting us with numerous aids to understanding
details, still do not provide anything comparable to the essential
total meaning of the Old Testament.[72] *Only the New Testament
offers the analogy of a witness of faith to the covenant will of God
—a witness founded on historical facts—who chooses out of the
world a people for himself and calls it to freedom under his Lordship.* I stress, an analogy. This is not identity, for while covenant
is covenant, old is not new. In the old covenant Israel is the partner, in the new the congregation from among Israel and the
nations. In the old, witness is born to God through many and
various servants, institutions, and events; in the new through the
Son. In the old God deals provisionally, in examples, in passing;
in the new finally, comprehensively, inalterably. In this way the
historical distinction is seen by the analogy.[72a] But even so we
are not dealing with analogies in separate areas, for Yahweh is
the Father of Jesus Christ.

Thus the analogy of the Old and New Testaments is supported by the historical relationship. The old covenant moves
forward toward the new; Israel is called for the sake of the
Gentiles. The new covenant comes from the old; Jesus Christ is
the Son of David and the Paschal Lamb. It is the analogy of way
and goal, of shadow and body, of picture and object, of promise
and fulfillment, of engagement and marriage.[73] This analogy in

---

[72] The "material of history of religion" must as a matter of basic principle
not be utilized "in eclectic fashion" as Baumgärtel fears (EvTh, 1954, p. 311,
note 11). But his principle that "all Old Testament statements are conditioned by history of religion" can hardly do justice to the fact of Israel's
being a stranger in its environment; the nature of that stranger can be
understood only in the light of the New Testament.

[72a] Otto Schmits, "Das Alte Testament im Neuen Testament" (*Festschrift
Heim*, 1934), speaks of a "remarkable dual relationship of history-of-salvation dialectic," "which is determined in a unified manner . . . through the
present salvation situation. The old covenant is shown by the new to be
inadequate, but as old *covenant* even in its inadequacy it points beyond
itself. And this in such a manner that the newness of the new covenant as
well as the inadequacy of the old, and also the fact that the old points beyond itself to the new, are derived from the new creation and the newness
of life and spirit which has taken place in Christ."

[73] Rom. 10:4; Col. 2:17; Heb. 10:1; Heb. 9:24; 1 Cor. 10:6, 11; 1 Peter

a historically unique relation, which is not without a decisive moment of intensification toward the *eschaton,* we call typology.[74]

When the relationship of the Testaments is thus determined the special approach of Old Testament hermeneutics is given. In the New Testament is found the context of the Old, which, as its historical goal, reveals the total meaning of the Old Testament; also the correspondence in the details helps one to understand the witnessing intent of the Old Testament contexts.[75] If it is shown to be true that no other historical document is comparable to the Old Testament in the way the New is, and that there also exists between the two Testaments a singular mutual relationship, then the typological approach is indispensable for an exegetical methodology that seeks to understand the historical context of the Old Testament texts and is concerned to eliminate arbitrary interpretations.

But how is it to be effective in the explanation of individual texts of the Old Testament?

The Carrying Out of Typological Interpretation

1. What does typology mean for the exposition of the Old Testament?

On the basis of tradition it is feared that typology would lead

---

3:21; 2 Cor. 1:20; Hos. 2:21 f.; Eph. 5:23. In this connection, W. Zimmerli, *op. cit.,* p. 81, "Jesus Christ comes as the one who fulfills the Old Testament proclamations. Not in the way that one would fulfill a responsibility of monetary debt—whereby one is thereafter free from his responsibility, but· in the way that the promises of an engagement are 'fulfilled' in marriage, so that in the fulfillment all that was meant before, the promise, is made full."

74 I have considered whether hermeneutic discussion would not be freed from a burden if the concept "typology," which has been overburdened and unjustifiably misunderstood in the sense of allegory, were allowed to disappear. But I see no other concept which, in spite of everything, is similarly adapted to designate so well the special relationship of analogy between the two Testaments. It is the question of the relevant context of the Old Testament which in the end forces me to introduce this concept which I have held back as long as possible. Cf. L. Goppelt, "Typos," *Die typologische Deutung des Alten Testaments im Neuen* (1939), p. 244: "Each typology is constituted through correspondence and intensification. . . . The establishment of individual typological relationships must be held to the following principles: Figures, events, institutions, may be interpreted in as far as they are expressions of a relationship with God, and therefore not just any worldly immanent, external individual features of Old Testament events or accounts." Such typology is not subject to a scheme of continuity like the linear style of history-of-salvation thought. E. Fuchs, *Hermeneutik* (1954),

to arbitrary importations, which would introduce a hidden meaning in which the historical meaning would not really be taken
seriously.[76] In opposition to this it must first of all be established
that the comparative consideration of the eschatological analogy
of the New Testament is intended neither to replace nor to supplement the historical meaning of the text; rather it should
serve above all in inquiring into the historical meaning. Typology is intended not to suspend historical-critical work, but to
support it in a relevant manner. The question of exposition remains firmly directed toward the meaning of the text that the
authors had in mind in their time. The concern is that just this
meaning may be missed through neglect of the New Testament
context.

I see at least three aids that will accrue to Old Testament
exegesis through typology.

(a) Consideration of the New Testament correspondences
has a heuristic function. Albrecht Alt used the assistance of
analogy in a masterful manner to determine historic facts when
he showed how to understand the patriarchal belief in God
through the aid of Nabatean records from Roman times.[77] How
much more it must be possible to draw on the New Testament

---

pp. 198 f.: "The new meaning of the past is given only in examples" (p.
200). If I speak in the following pages of "typological interpretation" it is
not because I regard a "specially qualified method" of Old Testament exegesis as necessary. C. Westermann, *op. cit.*, pp. 109 ff., justly opposes that.
The term "typological" will rather first of all only underscore the fact that
the Old Testament is to be understood in the relation to the New Testament
that is proper to it; it therefore above all reminds the exegete of the Old
Testament that he must pay attention to its relevant context. That means
no more and no less than that New Testament exegesis, in order to be
relevant, must also listen to the context of the Old. At the same time the
term "typology" is intended to bring to mind the task of proper understanding. It confronts the exegete with the question of what the Old Testament
text in its historical meaning means for the present-day reader after the
New Testament kerygma stands beside it. Because the Old Testament sciences need this reminder today we regard the term "typological" as helpful.
G. von Rad, "Typological Interpretation of the Old Testament," pp. 17 ff., has
shown anew on the basis of both Old and New Testament facts that it is
relevant. It is not intended to propagate a qualified special method of Old
Testament exegesis, but to present the given facts, which relevant exegesis
should not overlook.

[75] 2 Cor. 3:12 ff. shows itself anew as true in the present-day exegesis
of the Old Testament.

[76] Cf. J. Fichtner's article, "Exegese I," 2 f. EKL, I, p. 1224.

[77] For the methodology of the work of Albrecht Alt compare W. Zimmerli
in *Göttingische Gelehrte Anzeigen*, 209 (1955), pp. 88 ff.

documents to explain the Old Testament than to draw on any other area.[77a] The theological setting of the law in the Sinai tradition, Exodus 19-24, and in Deuteronomy has only recently been rightly determined again with the help of form history studies, which show it as the covenant gift of Yahweh, who had previously chosen Israel through his historical acts of salvation to be his people.[78] How could there have been for so long those stiff-necked misinterpretations in the exposition of the laws in the Pentateuch if the analogy of the Pauline exhortations or of the Sermon on the Mount had been used as heuristic aids in discovering the state of affairs in the Old Testament? In our days it is time to stress that because of the similarity of the matter, more essential help can accrue to Old Testament science from the New Testament than from the ancient Orient.[79] The numerous aids to understanding which Oriental studies continually offer us in details threaten to obscure our view of the heuristic aids which can accrue to us from the decisive "parallels" when we consider them more carefully. That is the intention of typology. It sees in vigorous contact with New Testament science genuine aid to research.

(b) Consideration of the eschatological analogy of the New Testament promotes the investigation of *intention* in the explanation of a text. Interpreting the texts only backwards and sidewards must be recognized as an obviously erroneous method

---

[77a] The establishment of this point should not at all mean that the analogies from history of religion are underestimated as aids to understanding. They are basically of a different type than those of the New Testament. We may not demand from the environment of the Old Testament that which only the New Testament is able to provide; and we must just as little seek to wrest from the New that which only the religious-historical environment of the Old has to offer.

[78] See above, notes 31 and 32.

[79] Cf. for example, the approach of W. Zimmerli in his study, "Ezekiel ein Zeuge der Gerechtigkeit Gottes" in *Das Alte Testament als Anrede*, pp. 38 and 60, where he compares the Lucan and Johannine concept of witness with Ezekiel. Cf. also O. Michel, *op. cit.*, p. 45: "The eschatological factor has truly become critically decisive also in reference to the Old Testament. . . . The authority of the Old Testament is not set aside by Jesus, but rather defined anew and thus in the eschatological sense 'fulfilled' (Matt. 5:17-20). Now major and minor commandments can be distinguished (Matt. 23:23; Mark 12:28), as can human ordinances and the basic will of God (Mark 10:1 ff.)." Paul recognized the proper order of rank of promise and law (Gal. 3). Compare Rom. 10:4 ff., "Righteousness by law has been displaced by righteousness by faith."

in Old Testament research.[80] In explaining such old Oriental building stones as religious-historical motifs and literary forms, institutions, or customs in terms of their origin and their parallels, something necessary was certainly done, but this was only preparation for the real exposition of the text. This is carried to completion only when it is made clear for what building the stones have been gathered together here, what functions the forms and institutions take on, what declarations the author intended to make with his material.[81] In the history of science it is probably not accidental that attentiveness to the transformation of the traditional materials and to the kerygma, which is to be heard with the *traditum* in the present context of the text, occurs at the same time as a new consideration of typology.[82] In the final analysis, the Pentateuch sources are voiceless if we do not hear how they lead Israel through the witness to God's deeds and gifts which laid the ground for the future, doing this in one way in the early period of the monarchy (J) and differently in the Exile (P). The great works of history remain voiceless if we do not hear how in the midst of judgment they lead Israel to repentance (Deut.) and so to a truly new beginning (Chron.). The words of the prophets would not have been transmitted if they had not been designed to lead to constant repentance and to the sure expectation of the new deeds of God.[82a] The constant consideration of the New Testament *eschaton* helps the expositor to interpret the Old Testament texts in a way that is true to the material, in a forward direction, in the direction of the actual witnessing intent of the texts in their contexts.[83]

---

[80] Model examples of this are Gunkel's Genesis commentary and the more recent Scandinavian research—for example, the book of G. Widengren referred to above in note 30.

[81] Cf. H. J. Kraus, "Zur Geschichte des Überlieferungsbegriffes in der alttestamentlichen Wissenschaft, Teil VI," EvTh, 16 (1956), pp. 379 ff. In particular the relationship of Albert Eichhorn to H. Gunkel should be observed.

[82] Cf. especially the work of G. von Rad, and now, W. Zimmerli, "Einzelerzählung und Gesamtgeschichte im Alten Testament," *op. cit.*, pp. 9-36.

[82a] Jer. 36:5 ff.; Isa. 8:16 f.; 30:8.

[83] That the Old Testament witness has essentially a forward drive finds a significant expression in the singular will to transmission, which has succeeded in maintaining an unbroken, living transmission and which is unknown in the texts of the surrounding nations, which have been rediscovered by archaeology. Cf. EvTh (1935), p. 450.

(c) Typology as a working hypothesis helps produce theological solidarity *vis-à-vis* the witnessing intent of the Old Testament, and warns the expositor against finding too quickly in the Old Testament texts testimony to a God who is foreign to the Father of Jesus Christ. The God of the prophets who judges his people is not foreign to the One who finally gives his own Son up to judgment, particularly since the one who does not believe the Son is judged already. Not even the bloodiest stories of the judges can be found *only* strange and gruesomely offensive. The story of Ehud who murdered the Moabite king Eglon is related with obvious pride in the ability and cunning of Ehud and does not shrink from the most gruesome details. But we would certainly not be letting the text speak in its present context if we were shocked morally and cultural-historically by these events and accounts that are truly foreign to us (as if our modern civilization does not know even much worse horrors!).[84] The whole story stands under the statement "Yahweh raised up a savior for Israel!" (Judg. 3:15). In the inclusion of the story in this context, is not—in all the details—the joy over the fact that God can free his people in the strangest ways from the mightiest tyrants still vivid? A moralistic consideration bars access to the proper self-assertion of the text; typology, which bears in mind what morally questionable figures carry on the affairs of the new covenant, is free to recognize even in Judges 3 the God who saves his people throughout the course of history.

This is some indication of how consideration of the New Testament analogies can serve the historical understanding of the Old Testament. It should be clear that typology is of help in approaching and carrying out historical understanding, and should not merely serve for concluding considerations of a meditative nature. The service of the typological method as thus understood will probably be accepted by many who otherwise dispute resolutely the immediate relevance of the Old Testament texts for the proclamation of the church. Many among us grant them validity in as far as they correspond to the "basic

---

84 Cf. Fr. Baumgärtel, *Verheissung*, pp. 94 f.

promise" of the gospel in the sense of the justification of the individual sinner. For the most part, they should serve as a mirror in which we find ourselves as standing in opposition to the gospel.[85] Whoever makes the attempt to weigh the Old Testament texts on the scales of theological formulae and dogmatic *loci*—even though he finds them so central that they become for him a hermeneutic principle—he experiences only that the scales cannot even hold the mass of the texts, but that they spill over to left and right. He experiences, above all, that his scales are smashed finally by the Old Testament if they have not already been smashed by the New.

If the essential presupposition of typology is correct, that the Old Testament does not bear witness to a strange god, but to the Father of Jesus, then it must be allowed to speak completely with the kerygma that is its own. But then typology does not lead only to historical understanding, but also at the same time to an exposition of the Old Testament that is *proclamation,* in as far as the God of Israel is the God of the church, is God today, in as far, therefore, as the character of the Old Testament as address is also relevant to us.[86] And with that we come to our final problem.

2. What does the Old Testament mean for the church's proclamation?

Once again we begin with a simple hermeneutical reflection. The final sentence of a text is to be understood in its proper content only in the light of what precedes. The 73rd Psalm closes with the words:

> But it is good for me to draw near unto God:
> I have made the Lord Jehovah my refuge,
> That I may tell of all thy works. (A.S.V.)

---

[85] Baumgärtel, *op. cit.,* pp. 84, 119, 143 f.; EvTh (1954), pp. 299 f.; E. Hirsch, *op. cit.*

[86] Cf. W. Zimmerli, *op. cit.,* pp. 65 ff. For the "irresistible inclination" of exegesis to proclamation that is to be understood anew today, cf. also G. Eichholz, *op. cit.,* p. 65. In the above line of thought and with all that follows, Baumgärtel's concern that typological exposition will pursue "an intellectualistic establishing of analogies," which have no value for proclamation, becomes irrelevant. (*Festschrift Alt,* pp. 18 ff.; *Verheissung,* pp. 83 f.). Cf. H. W. Wolff, *Alttestamentliche Predigten mit hermeneutischen Erwägungen* (1956).

This saying is rounded out so completely that it could be transmitted independently. But the movement that surges in it, its fullness and its intention, can be recognized only if we come to it from the whole Psalm with its frightening assaults and its reassuring discoveries. The following reminder leads even further. Just as surely as the Gospels would not have been written without the Easter-event and therefore, with their testimony of the road Jesus took, are not to be understood without their conclusion, so it is certain that the Easter accounts are understandable only in the light of the previously recounted words, deeds, and sufferings of Jesus. The Easter-event can be properly understood only as the Resurrection of the Jesus to whom witness is previously borne. The One who brings in the new era with word and deed has entered into his Lordship, but because of his Resurrection all the preceding chapters gain permanent significance. His call, his invitation, his forgiveness of sins, are words of final validity. The stories about Jesus and the words of Jesus which have been transmitted become types of his eschatological divine Lordship. It is as such that they are worth transmitting.

But this corresponds exactly to the permanent meaning of the Old Testament in relation to the Christ-event as a whole. As certainly as the history of Israel remains incomprehensible without its proper conclusion, so certainly is this conclusion, Jesus Christ in his unique movement, fullness, and intention, to be understood only in the light of the preceding history of Israel. As certainly as the historically related witness of faith of the Old Testament cannot be understood without its eschatological analogy, so certainly does the understanding of the great concluding chapter, the New Testament, stand in need of constant attentiveness to the preceding Old Testament context. It is all too easy to formulate falsely the scope of a text if the details of the entire text do not receive proper attention.

The proposition that the Old Testament can be properly understood only in the light of the New,[87] in order therefore to remain true, stands in need of its converse: The New Testament

---

[87] Fr. Baumgärtel, *Festschrift Alt,* p. 18 ; EvTh (1954), p. 299.

Christ-event can be fully understood only in the light of the Old Testament.[88] That is the permanent fundamental meaning of the Old Testament for the proclamation of the church, but for a long time we have been about to miss it.

We need to be reminded that no New Testament writer felt he was in a position to witness to Jesus Christ without constantly opening and quoting the Old Testament. Both the proclamation of Jesus and the preaching of the early Christians are unthinkable without the Old Testament.[89] Herein the application of contemporary methods of interpretation fluctuates. Typology prevails as a method of interpretation prepared in the Old Testament itself.[90] It leaves to the old testimony its historical position, but brings it into connection with the present and so recognizes its function as proclamation. Beside this stands allegory as practiced in the Hellenistic manner,[90a] which boldly attributes a new meaning to the old text. Furthermore, there is the "proof of prophecy" as practiced according to Jewish tradition, which not only relates the true prophecies of the prophets to the *eschaton* of the time of Christ, but also reinterprets quite ordinary words into prophecies.[91] These various means of interpretation are united by the certainty that now, in Jesus Christ, the Old Testament Word is recovered in its whole breadth, that now it will make itself heard anew if we will completely understand the history of Jesus of Nazareth as God's eschatological work, and will live in it.

This certainly has commended itself to us as true to the facts. This does not mean that we would have to take over the methods of interpretation of New Testament times, unavoidable though they were for the New Testament witnesses, but it does mean that we will not be able fully to understand and to live

---

[88] Cf. EvTh, 12 (1952/53), pp. 33, 54, 102.

[89] Cf. M. Dibelius, *Die Formgeschichte des Evangeliums*, 2nd ed. (1933); e.g., pp. 15 ff., p. 187; and also C. H. Dodd, "Die Grundlagen der christlichen Theologie," EvTh (1952/53), pp. 433 ff. "The earliest undertaking of Christian thinkers was the searching of the Old Testament in order to discover which passages had particular connection with the New Testament events, and what interpretation of the events they suggested."

[90] L. Goppelt, *Typos* (1939); cf. von Rad, EvTh, 12 (1952/53), p. 19.

[90a] E.g., Gal. 4:24 f.

[91] Cf. R. Bultmann, "Prophecy and Fulfillment."

with the history of Jesus of Nazareth without the Old Testament. This depends on the Old Testament itself, not on a proposed interpretation. Whether the Old Testament continues to speak among us depends on the Old Testament itself, as we can and must understand it with the aids to study that are available today.[92]

Accordingly, we are to listen to an Old Testament text in no other way than in accord with the meaning proper to it in its Old Testament context. We have seen that in this New Testament analogies are helpful in our approach. But in going on to attain proper understanding it becomes fundamentally indispensable to take the New Testament context into consideration. That does not mean superimposing on the historical meaning of the Old Testament text a second meaning, an allegorical one, or one that thinks entirely in terms of prophecy.[93] That would ruin everything. Rather we are to listen to how the historical meaning of the text continues to speak in the New Testament situation. Just as decisively as we must leave allegorical interpretation and interpretation in the sense of prophecy proofs behind, so decisively must we renew typological interpretation. If allegory counts on the identity of the Testaments, and prophecy proof counts on a continuity that can be shown within history, so typology sees before it the analogy of the revelation of God and of human existence. If allegory thinks punctiliarly in terms of eschatology, and proof from prophecy linearly in terms of history of salvation, typology thinks in examples in terms of history of salvation.

If Yahweh is the Father of Jesus, then the proper witness of the Old Testament has typological significance for the recognition of the New Testament facts. The Old Testament text has

---

[92] Many things we probably understand less well than the early Christians did, some things perhaps better, e.g., the law, which we can understand in part differently (as covenant law) from Paul (Gal. 3) in his dependence on Rabbinic interpretation of Scripture.

[93] But typological interpretation in this sense dare not "leave the historical self-understanding of the Old Testament text," as von Rad, *op. cit.*, p. 31, formulates in a manner easily misunderstood. I also have expressed myself in a manner open to misunderstanding and thereby called forth Baumgärtel's protest (EvTh, 13, 1953, pp. 413 ff.), which led me to this present attempt at a more far-reaching consideration of method.

been expounded in its context only when the typological contribution it, as a section of text, makes to the total message of
the Bible can be heard.[93a]

We are now able to formulate the central question of typological exposition as follows: To what extent is the New Testament kerygma illuminated by the history that precedes it (or,
apprehended only when the previous history is listened to along
with it)? Or, in reference to detailed exegesis, *What does the Old
Testament text in its historical meaning say to mankind living
in the eschaton of Jesus Christ?*

When asked this question, the Old Testament can truly give
expression to the fullness of its witness. But then its significance
for the proclamation of the church can hardly be comprehended
in formulas such as "Witness to Christ," or "Law," or "Promise,"
or "Theocracy,"[93b] which yield only a partial return. Instead
of this, we shall now, by way of example, bring together several
possible answers to this central question, each in accordance
with the different content of the texts.

(a) A great number of Old Testament texts are intended to
bear testimony to the will, the purpose, and the intention of
Israel's God. The Yahwistic version of the primeval history is
obviously governed by this. God, who in Genesis 2 establishes
and cares for the life of man by his personal labors, must already
in Genesis 3 put into effect the death penalty on the basis of his
command in 2:17. Yet only the serpent, and not man himself, is
cursed; the death sentence is suspended, and man is sent into
the fields for life-long hard labor, but not before God himself
has provided him with leather garments. Death enters not
through God's decree, but rather through man's hatred for his
brother. Yahweh lets even the murderer live on, an uneasy
fugitive, to be sure, but with the protecting sign on his forehead.

[93a] K. Barth (KD, IV, 2, pp. 21-25) has described typological interpretation as "Listening in on what is said indirectly, what is implicit in the
statement." If this is not heard, something important has been missed. It is
beyond question that in Old Testament science at the present the danger
of over-interpreting is not as great as that of under-interpreting, in which
the entire biblical context of an Old Testament text does not receive sufficient attention.
[93b] See below, note 101a.

Then after man's *hybris* has become unbearable in a new act of transgressing his bounds, the total death sentence seems to become unavoidable. Yet again Yahweh's strange purpose, the occasion of which is to be found only in himself and not in mankind, breaks through and lets Noah find grace in the sight of Yahweh. Obviously God cannot let his work go. Hope for a new humanity becomes apparent, a "comforter" in the midst of the accursed field (5:29). So he begins after the judgment and "plants a vineyard" (9:20), first pledge of peace, joy, and well-being. Yet even the new mankind comes under judgment for lust after fame and might; only dispersion and confusion of language can keep them from putting themselves in God's place. In this moment when the fate of mankind seems again to hang fully in the balance, the witness to the calling of the patriarchs begins with the key word "blessing" already repeated four times in Genesis 12:2 f. This blessing which Yahweh will establish with Abraham's posterity is intended to be shared by mankind, which is fragmented and subject to death.

If we let this characteristic witness of the Yahwist speak further in the total biblical context, it brings us above all to the insight that it is *God* who is at work in Jesus Christ, Yahweh the God of Israel and so the Lord of mankind. He labors and toils with these human beings, shows patience, and delays judgment, and even in the midst of necessary judgment shows mercy, and in the end gives blessing instead of the deserved curse. This Old Testament witness elucidates for us the Johannine witness that *God* had so loved the world that he gave his only Son so that each one who believes in him might have eternal life (3:16). The Old Testament stresses that *God* is acting in Jesus Christ. It shows that the Johannine witness is not a notion of his age, but that it corresponds to the purpose of Yahweh's will. To him testimony has long since been borne in Israel, and since the beginning, despite all man's guilt, he is working for a life of blessing for man. *This is the way in which the Old Testament text must continue to speak* with its characteristic witness, just in order *to show the Christ-event as an eschatological act of God, and to guard against false isolation and historization.*

Other texts do the same thing in a similar manner. On the great day of atonement, according to Leviticus 16:20 ff., in the cultic act all Israel's guilt is transferred by the priest to the scapegoat, who is then driven out into the wilderness to Azazel. In this way the otherwise inescapable connection between guilt and fate is broken by a ritual act. Israel is released from the obligation of a synthetic view of life, the obligation to bear the fate that it has brought about by its own guilt. The text is concerned to show that Yahweh the covenant God has established this possibility, and that Israel is bound to fulfill exactly this ordinance which was established for its salvation. Such a text out of the history preceding the New Testament is able to bear witness with its historical meaning to the sort of divine will that lives behind the Christ-event, to break the curse-laden connection of guilt and fate. At the same time such Old Testament rituals show us a twofold meaning: first, the new which appeared in Christ for Israel and the Gentiles and abrogated the old ordinances, yet in such a way that God's will which had been exemplified and witnessed to in them came to its proper goal; second, that salvation, here as there, is beyond the power of man but is bound rather to the established divine ordinance: "He who believes in Christ is righteous."

Again it is in a different way that the Priestly account of the Tabernacle witnesses in remarkably solemn formality to Yahweh's will to come together with Israel in the holy tent, to dwell in the midst of the Israelites and be their God, who sanctifies them (Exod. 29:42 ff.). In a very different manner Hosea says that God's mercy is in conflict with his wrath. "My heart is turned within me, my compassions are kindled together" (11:8). So the Old Testament with its preparatory historical witness to Yahweh the God of Israel helps in manifold ways to grasp and proclaim the Christ-event as the eschatological divine event.[94] The multitudinous Old Testament types bear witness in

---

[94] To this extent, typology takes up the valid meaning of the old prophetic proofs. Cf. W. Zimmerli, "Promise and Fulfillment," p. 95, "The category promise/fulfillment serves to secure the irrevocable validity of the gift bestowed by God." *Das Alte Testament als Anrede*, p. 84, "Listening to the Old Testament insures the true historicity of Jesus Christ, in that it makes visible not only the *kairos* of a 'today' but also a yesterday, and with it a tomorrow as well. Christ is 'the one who is to come.' "

the most lively fashion who the God is with whom the congregation of Jesus in dealing in the *eschaton.*

(b) At the same time they make clear the uniqueness and meaning of the sending of Jesus. We have hinted at this already in connection with the Yahwistic primeval history, the ritual of the great Day of Atonement, and the priestly account of the Tabernacle. We shall add here only a few examples of a different type. What do the prophetic threats of judgment in their historical meaning signify for the total scope of the Bible? "You only have I known of all the families of the earth; therefore I will visit upon you all your iniquities" (Amos 3:2). The prophet testifies that when God's covenant people reviles the Lord of the covenant, only judgment is left. How does this thought continue to speak in the New Testament community? If the proper content of the prophetic word is really to continue to sound forth we must not turn aside too soon to an antithetical interpretation that says: The judgment which Israel bore in the old covenant, Jesus Christ bears in the new for Israel. In the analogy to the decisive event of the New Testament the proper content of the prophetic words of judgment continues to speak in an entirely different manner. In the new covenant also judgment begins with the house of God (1 Peter 4:17), those who crucify the Son of God afresh are given over to disgrace (Heb. 6:6). Christ is to some the fragrance of death unto death, and to others the fragrance of life unto life (2 Cor. 2:16). So naturally those who reduce the New Testament to the formula of justification of the sinner, which they understand on all too small a scale and probably not in a New Testament manner, cannot any longer hear what the Old Testament has to say. The Old Testament helps us to see a full view of the mission of Jesus in opposition to any abbreviation of the New Testament.

The formulas of lament in the Psalter do this service in a very different manner when they help bring before God those typical troubles of the Israelite, or, by heaping up troubles, make sure that each one who prays in Israel can be included. In Israel the opportunity of coming before Yahweh with troubles and guilt is ever present. It can no doubt be said with

certainty of the 22nd Psalm that in Israel this formula awaited
the one who would bring before God in prayer in an exemplary
way the fullness of the troubles of the one forsaken by God as
expressed in this Psalm. Therefore in the meaning of its words
it illuminates as a document of the cultic history of Israel the
service of suffering of Jesus in Israel's *eschaton*. But even so,
it continues to offer itself anew to the members of the congregation. The offer to Israel is the offer to all men in spite of everything to present before God with confidence all their concrete
troubles in the community of the sufferings of Jesus. So these
hymns of lament and thanksgiving in the Psalter help us to grasp
the meaning of the mission of Jesus in the midst of life,[95] to experience the history of salvation as "the history in which all
other history is included" (K. Barth, KD, III, 1, p. 64). *The
Old Testament prevents the witness to Christ from being cor-
rupted into philosophy about Christ.*

(c) In numerous Old Testament texts, not beginning with
the Wisdom Literature but already in the great historical works
and the old law codes, it is not God but Israel who is the subject
of the declarations. Just as the Old Testament provisionally and
through examples discloses the purpose of God that is at work
for us in Jesus Christ, so it places before us again and again the
model case of God's covenant people, in whom, provisionally
and through examples, the nature and task of the eschatological
people of God is to be recognized. As the God of Israel cannot
be seen without his people, so the Old Testament prevents us
from seeing the New Testament Christ-event without the called
community, the head without the body.

If we listen to all that the story of the crossing of the sea
in Exodus 14 with its many strata has to say, it bears witness
that Israel was constituted as a free people of God exclusively
through the wonderful saving deeds of Yahweh. Israel's contribution was doubt, fear, and contradiction to God who spoke.

---

[95] The Old Testament Sabbath texts as analogies bear witness anew to
the meaning of the eschatological Christ-event. Cf. in this connection, E.
Jenni, "Die theologische Begründung des Sabbathgebotes im Alten Testament," *Theologische Studien*, 46 (1956), pp. 35 ff.

Faith resulted only from God's carrying them across, an event which took place despite the people's disbelief. It is in an entirely different manner that Ezekiel (ch. 37) in his vision of the field of dry bones depicts the model of God's people, which dies because of its sins, abandoned there by its God, but which through the Spirit of God, who awakens the dead to life, becomes a new reality. Again it is said differently by Deutero-Isaiah (43:8 ff.) concerning the exiled people which in spite of its own blindness is to be God's witness among the Gentiles, because to them alone has been entrusted the Word of him who makes all history.

Is it not inevitable that the eschatological people of God of the new covenant will misunderstand itself if it does not see presented before it these Old Testament examples in their historical meaning? Will it remain with the real Christ if the Old Testament witnesses only to "Christ and nothing else"?[96] What consequences it has can be clearly seen in the unfortunate dispute over the exposition of the 1st Psalm between Fr. Baumgärtel[97] and G. von Rad.[98] For Baumgärtel the "deep majesty" of the Psalm "from the point of view of the gospel" consists in our seeing ourselves in it as in a mirror, namely, as Pharisees, who with their piety seek to assert themselves as righteous before God. Here it is seen how a hermeneutical principle completely silences the proper witness of an Old Testament text, namely, the joy in coming under Yahweh's leading to a fruitful and protected life which is righteous only because of the word of Yahweh offered as a gift. Baumgärtel can grant no "theological relevance" to von Rad's exegetical discovery that the Psalm is based on an ordinance of grace[99] because he is governed by the premise that the Old Testament is the witness of "a *non-Christian religion*," which "in its self-understanding has *nothing* at all *to do with the gospel.*"[100] When Baumgärtel despairingly asks

---

[96] Fr. Baumgärtel, *Verheissung*, p. 127.
[97] *Ibid.*, p. 66 ; EvTh, 14 (1954), pp. 300 f.
[98] EvTh (1953), pp. 408 f.
[99] *Op. cit.*, p. 408.
[100] EvTh, 14 (1954), p. 312 (italics are Baumgärtel's!) ; cf. ThLZ (1954), pp. 205 f. ; *Verheissung*, p. 119.

von Rad how the Old Testament kerygma can then be theologically relevant to us, then the answer can only be because
Yahweh is God, the Father of Jesus. Even under this presupposition the Psalm that glows with wished-for good fortune must
not be twisted around into the dismal picture of a Pharisee, but
rather out of its own proper witness there appears the original
portrait of that righteous man whose meat it is to do the will
of God (John 4:34), and at the same time the original portrait
of a disciple band that is pure for the sake of the word of Christ
that is spoken to it, and which brings forth much fruit in unity
with him (John 15:1 ff.).[101] Because Psalm 1 portrays a typical
model of membership in the people of God even in the concrete traits of its provisional character it helps orient properly
the members of the Body of Christ. *The Old Testament guards
the Christian message from false individualizing.*

(d) There is still more to be said about the ecclesiological
meaning of the Old Testament.[101a] The great majority of Old
Testament texts offer not typical model cases of God's people, but
a colorful variety of ways, deeds, decisions, and sufferings of
God's people, nothing but individual situations of Israel and
of men. Fr. Baumgärtel fears that "typology would kill the interest in the relation of the Old Testament to history, in the
stirring historical reality."[102] That may be relevant to a certain
form of allegory which would like to read into the Old Testament text its New Testament knowledge of Jesus Christ. Ty-

---

[101] Cf. in detail H. W. Wolff, "Psalm 1," EvTh, 9 (1949/50), pp. 385-394.
[101a] To be sure, not in the direction of the theocratic interpretation of
A. A. van Ruler, "Die christliche Kirche und das Alte Testament," *Beitr. z.*
EvTh, 23, 1955. Van Ruler sees clearly how much depends on the proper
understanding of the Old Testament for the life of the Christian, the church,
and the world. "The common things of the world are—spiritually speaking
—the most important" (p. 32). But he paints a false opposition of the Testaments when he sees theocracy in the Old and "only" soteriology in the New
(esp. pp. 65, 82 ff.). The Old is primarily concerned with the *covenant* of
God with Israel and not with God's Lordship over the earth in itself;
the New with reconciliation in Christ for the establishment of God's Lordship on earth. Here also the point of view of typology can be seen: Because
God sets up his eschatological Lordship in Christ, correct "theocratic" proclamation is not to be separated from the proclamation of his saving will,
on the basis of either the Old or the New Testament. Cf. van Ruler in
reference to the discussion of his book by J. J. Stamm, pp. 200 ff., and Th. C.
Vriezen, pp. 211 ff.
[102] *Verheissung*, p. 142.

pology, however, which has brought the knowledge of the correlative analogy of the Testaments to a theologically relevant listening to the proper witness of the Old Testament, is most vitally interested in just these concrete historical facts, and in the testimonies of the Old Testament that are conditioned by their situation. It recognizes the concrete details of the Old Testament established by historical exegesis as aids for the eschatological community of Jesus Christ in finding the way to concrete obedience in history.

So it reads then with new eagerness the patriarchal stories and notes how there is a movement in them from promise to fulfillment through manifold errors and temptations. Here it finds exemplified the community that is born by the word of Christ, as in the real world it becomes God's people through disbelief and belief. Thus it reads the stories of the journey through the wilderness with its incessant temptations between the well-known fleshpots of Egypt and the unknown Promised Land, set on the march only by the word of a dubious messenger of God and some signs of God's presence. In the proper witness of these pericopes, which are always to be gone over in detail, the community which is led by the word of the Apostles and strengthened by certain signs of the presence of Christ finds typological guideposts for its own road. It reads the old covenant law of Israel and notes its passionate interest for the poor, the slaves, and strangers; it sees that the prophets stress in unmistakable manner that the God of Israel watches particularly over the rights of those who have no property. And so it sees itself on its road through history warned against a sentimental and merely private interpretation of Jesus' commandment of love, and with the help of the Old Testament recognizes anew that Jesus Christ has established again the *rights* of the poor.[102a]

[102a] Here also *antitheses* should not be overlooked. We can think of the contrast of Luke 9:54 f. and 2 Kings 1 and of the imprecatory Psalms. Jesus Christ drives out the spirit of revenge, but at the same time fulfills the boasting of divine election and promise and the waiting for his aid that are proper to the imprecatory Psalms as hymns of lament. Typology places the new by the side of the old, but it does not do this as if the old said the same as the new. It recognizes how the old furthers the full hearing of the new, and in this does not hide analogies. Therefore it is perhaps better to speak of *antitypes* rather than antitheses in relationship of the Testa-

One gains a new desire to go through the whole Old Testament in order to trace out[102b] how the Old Testament Word
continues to speak in the community of Jesus, even including
the good wishes for many children in Psalm 127, which teach
us to see the right relation of God's deed and man's work in the
midst of everyday life, even to the collections of proverbs which
offer a thousand practical aids to proper human relations, to
self-training, and above all to proper speaking and proper
silence, and which the eschatological community rejects only
when it does not find its joy in true and total life with Jesus
Christ in the fear of Yahweh. *The Old Testament keeps the
Christian message from transcendentalism.*

The final service of the Old Testament, however, which can
be exemplified by Job as well as by Daniel, is that it helps the
church to deal in a practical manner with "the problem of the
temporal nature of eschatological existence,"[103] where it is
theoretically so sorely needed, and intellectually can be explained only by vigorous inclusion of the Old Testament.

The Old Testament is an aid to eschatological existence in
the history of this world.[104] One of Dietrich Bonhoeffer's last
concerns was that we may prematurely abrogate the things of
this world because "we read the New Testament all too little

---

ments to each other, even in reference to texts such as 2 Kings 1 or imprecatory Psalms. These are to be heard not only in contrast to isolated
New Testament statements such as Luke 9:55, but in their own context,
whereby we can see the seriousness of judgment of actions opposed to God
still only in the light of New Testament correspondences.

[102b] In such "tracing out" the searching of the whole Old Testament as
done by the early church (cf. note 89 on C. H. Dodd) must be practiced
anew by us. Constant living in the Scriptures, plowing through all their various parts, leads to discoveries that drive us to proclamation. In the full and
ever-new meeting with the fullness of the texts the charismatic discovery
of the texts takes place. That the types in the old texts begin to speak cannot
be regulated hermeneutically (cf. von Rad, EvTh, 12, 1952/53, p. 33) in as
far as the texts begin here to regulate the community of the new covenant.
That does not restrict but rather challenges us to listen "methodically" and
scientifically.

[103] R. Bultmann, "Heilsgeschichte und Geschichte," ThLZ, 73 (1948), p.
666. On this question, see also H. J. Kraus, "Das Problem der Heilsgeschichte
in der 'Kirchlichen Dogmatik'" in *Antwort* (Festschrift Barth, 1956), pp.
69-83.

[104] To this belongs also the new waiting for the coming Lord, in whom
the church is included together with God's waiting people of the old covenant
in the time of fulfillment. As the old Israel was the shadow of the future,
so is also the present church *umbra futurae ecclesiae* (Luther, WA, 3, p.
306; cf. EvTh, 12, 1952/53, p. 103). In a similar manner Calvin sees "that

from the point of view of the Old."[105] "We live in the next-to-last things and believe the last things."[106] Therefore while we are under way in the *eschaton* of Jesus Christ we cannot do without the great number of manifold witnesses to the way, which are typical for the way of God's people in the world. Bonhoeffer was able to write down the sharp sentence, "He who too quickly and too directly would be and feel in accordance with the New Testament is, in my opinion, no Christian."[107]

The concern of typological interpretation of the Old Testament is to keep us from just that. It knows it can deal properly with the Old Testament only by practicing exposition which is historical, which compares the Old Testament with the New, and which is thus proclamation.

---

for the one who lives after the coming of Christ, the Word of God is binding also in the area of the *pueritia ecclesiae*" (H. H. Wolf, *op. cit.*, p. 133). Cf. also W. Zimmerli, *op. cit.*, p. 87. Further, E. Fuchs, *Hermeneutik* (1954), who, on p. 22 calls "the Pauline typology" a first "attempt at the interpretation of history out of association with time itself," an attempt "which hoped to meet the danger of the historicizing of the Christian hope." On p. 201, "Those who believe are not alone, even humanly speaking, in the historical attacks on their stand of faith. It is spiritualism to expect help under attack out of an isolated walk with Christ. Christ shows his might in the witnessing power of the fathers." O. Weber says cogently (*Grundlagen der Dogmatik*, I, 1955, p. 323): "Wherever in Christendom the Old Testament with its message was separated from the New, and no longer seen in its own message, there of necessity Christendom became only a band of esoterics, for whom the world was strange, foreign. Thus it was with Marcion. So it is in the last analysis also with those contemporary theologians who regard the New Testament and its message essentially from the point of view of the 'development' of the relationship with God."

[105] D. Bonhoeffer, *Widerstand und Ergebung*, 6th ed. (1955), pp. 227 and 182.

[106] *Ibid.*, p. 113.

[107] *Ibid.*

9.

JESUS CHRIST AND
THE OLD TESTAMENT*

A Review of A. A. van Ruler's book:
Die christliche Kirche und das Alte Testament
(*The Christian Church and the Old Testament*).

by *Johann Jakob Stamm*

translated by Ludwig R. Dewitz

The following article is divided into two parts: In the first, there is a repetition of my discussion of van Ruler's article from "Kirchenblatt für die reformierte Schweiz," 112 (1956), pp. 27 ff.; in the second, some new observations are added.

I

The author of the writing to be discussed occupies the chair of "Ecclesiastical Professor" at the University of Utrecht, and in this capacity he lectures on Dutch Church History, Liturgy, and Dogmatics.[1] A width of vision developed in a broad range of subjects is manifest in the book in its knowledge of the Old Testament field and the literature of many other disciplines. Along with various Dutch authors, Calvin, Kohlbrügge, and Brunner are repeatedly quoted, while, strangely enough, only occasional reference is made to the *Church Dogmatics* of Karl Barth. The work is divided as follows: Introduction, pp. 7-12; Chapter 1: The Old Testament and Its Exegesis, pp. 13-33; Chap-

* Arnold A. van Ruler has taken part in the discussion which was caused by the first publications of the contributors to "Biblischer Kommentar" (EvTh, 12, 1952/53, pp. 1-104) when he wrote his "Die christliche Kirche und das Alte Testament" (BEvTh, 23, 1955); his point of view differs from that of Fr. Baumgärtel. The contributions here given were presented at the spring meeting of contributors to "Biblischer Kommentar" from March 26 to 28, 1956.

[1] I am indebted to Professor H. van Oyen in Basel for this information.

ter 2: Does the Old Testament Behold the Christ?, pp. 34-68; Chapter 3: The Necessity for the Old Testament in the Christian Church, pp. 69-92.

In the introduction the difficulty and, at the same time, the importance of the clarification of the hermeneutic problem in the Old Testament are shown. The perspective in which the author addresses himself to the problem is stated in the following sentence (p. 9): "Our whole understanding of the Kingdom of God and with it of the catholicity of the Christian faith, the church, and Christianity is determined by what we think of the Old Testament and the way we deal with it." The difficulty of the matter is expounded by a list of not less than ten "solutions," by which the Christian church of the past and the present believed it possible to do justice to the Old Testament.

In the first chapter, four questions are discussed: whether both Testaments are concerned with the same God; granted that the Old Testament is revelation, what possibility and method are available for its scholarly apprehension; what is the purpose of God's presence in Israel; and what is the mutual relationship between our exegetical and homiletic studies in the Old Testament?

It would require too much space to review completely the richness and power of the ideas which van Ruler develops. Only a few matters can be selected.

In regard to the second question, recognition is given to the possibility of regarding the Old Testament as revelation on the basis of the fact that inspiration is not exhausted in the inspiration of the authors of the Bible, but that it is "at the same time inspiration of Scripture" (p. 19). The author bases his statement on a passage from Bengel's *Gnomon;* he could also have made reference to *Church Dogmatics,* I/2, pp. 514 ff. Old Testament revelation itself, viewed in that perspective, he sees (p. 22) in the "self-communication or the presence of God in the midst of his people in a sequence of actions . . ." In this connection it is stressed that "more is involved than the Word, involved is the communion of the Holy God with his elect people"; hence it is not possible to retreat simply to the piety or theology of the Old Testament (pp. 23 f.).

In considering the fourth question, which deals with the relationship of exegesis and homiletics, van Ruler comes to the conclusion (pp. 31 f.) that in preaching from the Old Testament "there takes place in the Pneuma an actual repetition of Israel. . . . We are made to become Israel, with Christ as the center, through the Spirit." From this perspective of contemporaneity with Israel the sermon must be an eschatological-theocratic one, proclamation of the Kingdom and not of Christ. "The sermon then deals with the same concrete earthly things with which the Old Testament is concerned" (p. 32).

The second chapter, dealing with the question of whether the Old Testament beheld the Christ, is essentially critical in nature; in it prominence is given to that which apparently separates or distinguishes the Testaments. Here the author stresses, among others, the following points:

1. The Old Testament, as a document whose history is driven toward the future through promises, contains a number of such promises, which may even contradict each other. Hence, Christ cannot be the one and only fulfillment of them all (p. 42), for he is only *one* act of God alongside the others in the people of Israel (p. 37). Correspondingly, there exists in the New Testament *one* way of reconciliation, in the Old Testament, on the other hand, many (p. 48).

2. In the Old Testament the Messiah is a man, in the New, God himself; hence the deity of Jesus cannot be derived from the former (pp. 46 f.).

3. The New Testament kind of missionary work through sending out messengers is not anticipated in the Old Testament, nor is the rejection of the Messiah by Israel foreseen (pp. 49 f.).

The path of such criticism, on which a detailed comment must for the present be held in abeyance, leads van Ruler to the position of denying not only the use of allegory as a hermeneutical principle, but also of typology, which is especially represented today by von Rad (*supra*, pp. 17 ff.), and which he regards as a threat in its appearance in Noth's Biblical Commentary. Typology is rejected because, as is apparent already from the statements of the first chapter, a Christ-centered ideology is denied to the Old Testament as a whole. The relevant passages which can be regarded as the heart of the whole book

are the following (p. 65): "Jesus Christ is an emergency measure
which God has delayed as long as possible. Therefore, one must
not do violence to the Old Testament to find him, not even
when one as a Christian theologian inquires after God in the
Old Testament." Just before this passage the question is put
(p. 64): "Is God really concerned in creation with grace, covenant, salvation, or is he not rather concerned in salvation only
with the created reality—that it might continue to stand before him?"

In the third chapter van Ruler endeavors to prove from his
presuppositions the necessity of the Old Testament for the
Christian church, by using the following concepts: legitimation,
foundation, interpretation, illustration, historization, and eschatology. It will suffice to show how the author interprets the first
and last of these words: To legitimatize Jesus, the Old Testament is necessary, because his claim to be the Messiah can only
be decided by answering the question whether Jesus really does
the works of God. "But what the works of God are can only be
established by means of the Old Testament" (p. 70). In regard to
eschatology it must be kept in mind first of all that van Ruler
understands the expression "eschatological" as pointing to the
fact "that originally and ultimately and therefore in all times the
concern is with God himself, and the world in the naked existence
of things" (p. 82). According to him this "flickers through once or
twice" in the New Testament. In the Old Testament, however,
this original and final factor—this faithfulness toward earth and
time—is shown much more clearly. In this respect we should
stress with great emphasis the more abundant value of the Old
Testament as over against the New. There we have a much more
positive concern with creation and the Kingdom, with sanctification and humanity, with culture, state, and society. For this
reason the Old Testament ought to be expounded not Christologically, but eschatologically or theocratically. "In it abides a
deep confidence in the goodness of the world, in the usefulness of
man, and in the possibility of sanctifying the earth" (p. 83).

Anyone who reviews the content of the book, feeling himself
secure in the possession of Vischer's *Witness to Christ* and Barth's
Church Dogmatics, may be inclined to indulge rashly in sharp

criticism. It is doubtful whether in this he would find the approval of Vischer and Barth. However that may be, I think it is right and proper to reserve critical judgment in order to ponder deeply van Ruler's intention. This intention must be seen in connection with the present state of scholarly research. Here Baumgärtel takes up a definite position with his publication *Promise. A Contribution Toward the Evangelical Understanding of the Old Testament* (1952). Only in contrast to Baumgärtel does van Ruler's study appear in its proper light. For the former, not much remains of the Old Testament with his overemphasis on spirituality and inwardness since he must break through the numerous barriers thrown up by its realism which present to the Christian an embarrassing liability. In the latter, we have a full and joyous affirmation of this realism, the down-to-earth concern with this world, and that to such an extent that the Old Testament surpasses the New Testament in its value for preaching.

Is it not fresh mountain air which blows here, and does one not gratefully appreciate the wide and free vision which opens far beyond spiritualizing anxieties? Does one not sense the profound and good understanding for the political responsibility of the church which guides van Ruler's attempt? Finally, might we not feel a little proud that on the basis of Reformed tradition such statements can be made concerning the Old Testament?

To be sure, when all of this has been said, critical questions remain. As has already been pointed out these will be concerned with details which are mentioned in the second chapter dealing with the difference between the Testaments, and especially with the problem of the so-called Christological exposition of the Old Testament. Is it really true that it can be pushed aside because of the Old Testament hope of the Kingdom which is regarded as more far-reaching and greater than Jesus' work of reconciliation —an emergency measure? Can it be doubted that in creation God is really concerned with grace, covenant, and salvation? Obviously, van Ruler has clearly seen the goal which is pointed out in the proclamation of the Bible, and he has stressed this impressively; but for long stretches he loses sight of the way which leads to it. Does not the whole Bible stand against him when he tries to reach the goal, certainly with Christ, but not entirely and completely through him alone?—the Old Testament in Yahwist and Priestly writing, with its knowledge of the covenant as the goal of creation, the covenant which is represented by the people, the remnant, the individual, and the New Testament with its message of the appearing of this One who has come to save Israel and the world?

What is at stake in this hermeneutical question we learn from van Ruler himself. At the end (p. 91) he raises the question of whether in God's plan for the world the people of Israel had still a role to play. This, he thinks, must be answered with a *non liquet*. This may be understandable from his presuppositions, but it shows, at the same time, where it leads when one gets away from the biblical line with its "through Christ alone." Van Ruler does this because he is afraid of curtailing the hope of the theocratic Kingdom. With him we agree that this hope should come to an increasingly full and rich fruition among us. We are gladly reminded by him of the service which the Old Testament here renders; but against him we have confidence that this actually happens when the Old Testament is properly expounded in a Christological manner according to its historical place in the history of salvation as preparation and foreshadowing of that which is to come, as a document pointing to the future, the promises of which are realized in Jesus and his church but are not yet finally consummated. For this reason the Old Testament is not only a witness of past history, but it also keeps alive and nourishes with its gifts the hope of the end.

How important the latter is, van Ruler has set before us afresh, and it is only right that our final word to him should be one of thanks.

II

I should like to add to what has been said by referring back to the content of the second chapter. As already mentioned, it is entitled "Does the Old Testament Behold the Christ?" Van

Ruler arrives here at a negative, critical conclusion by emphasizing that which in his opinion separates the Testaments. His
thoughts in this connection have been condensed in the three
points mentioned above (p. 202). I would like to refer to them
once more so as to comment on them in order:

1. The Old Testament, as a document whose history is
driven toward the future through promises, contains a number of
such promises which may even contradict each other. Hence,
Christ cannot be the one and only fulfillment of them all (p.
42), for he is only *one* act of God alongside the others in the
people of Israel (p. 37). Correspondingly, there exists in the New
Testament *one* way of reconciliation, in the Old Testament, on
the other hand, many (p. 48). Only in the New Testament—it is
also declared here—does the idea of substitution have its final
breakthrough.

2. In the Old Testament the Messiah is a man, in the New,
God himself; hence the deity of Jesus cannot be derived from
the former (pp. 46 f.).

3. The New Testament kind of missionary work through
sending out messengers is not anticipated in the Old Testament,
nor is the rejection of the Messiah by Israel foreseen (pp. 49 f.).

In the first point van Ruler will be supported by our normal
way of thinking when he draws attention to the contradictory
promises in the Old Testament. He perceives these contradictions
quickly and easily, and I must confess that he reminded me—by
his method of clear separation—of Abraham Kuenen, who in his
book *Die Profeten en de Profetie onder Israel* (1875), pp. 114 ff.,
gives long lists of seemingly unfulfilled prophecies. But one must
ask, after all, whether the method of listing, as done in so
grandiose a style by Kuenen and in a more reduced manner by
van Ruler (p. 42, note 33), is really appropriate for the matter at
hand. Is it not a deceptive objectivity which in reality does not
exist when one has simply confirmed an opinion which one had
from the beginning regarding the relationship of the Testaments
to each other? For Kuenen this basic presupposition resulted from
his own unshakable faith in the evolution of history. For van
Ruler it is connected with his idea of theocracy, which allows

him to put the Old Testament in first place and above the New Testament.

But the method of mere enumeration in the case of Old Testament prophecies is not adequate. They must rather be grasped inwardly, weighed, and above all related to the whole of the Old Testament. And it is necessary never to lose this total picture against all attempts and possibilities of our thinking in categories, and to assert that the Old Testament is not concerned with principles but with documents of a real history which, however, as a special activity of God in the world are not subject to general laws. It is redemptive history with its own particular nature which we of ourselves do not know, but which we are able to trace cautiously on the basis of the documents. When we say "trace," we refer to rigorous scholarly work which has nothing to do with mere opinions or a free-handed way of thinking-this-to-be-true. This rigor, this subjection of one's self to the matter at hand, is something that one misses in van Ruler.

As we apply this general concept to the specific problems, the variance of the promises appears in a different light. It becomes the sign for the different historical situations of their origin—promise of the possession of the land or the return from the Exile—which nevertheless does not exclude an overarching unity. It is found in the fact that all these promises, each of which may have its historical place, point beyond the historical situation to something that is final or eschatological, i.e., the presence of God among his people.

To the realm of Old Testament promises belong also the offices: the Messiah in his various forms—the Son of Man, the Servant of God. It is true that they are separate from each other in the Old Testament, but that does not give us the right to play off one against the other and to differentiate them from the New Testament. We are concerned with offices amidst the covenant people, with the bearer of redemptive history, and so we may hold to the fact that Jesus claimed them all for himself and that thereby they have come together in the time of fulfillment, a merging most unexpected by the Jews of that time. The New

Testament witness to the claim of Jesus is so absolutely clear that we cannot set it aside in endeavoring to play down in the Messianic concept the warring Messiah as against the Prince of Peace, or perhaps to neglect the one in preference to the other. It is especially in the warring Messiah that the theocratic aspect of hope is anchored, which is so important for van Ruler. It retains its validity in the New Testament and it differs in regard to the Old Testament, not through the content but through the basic truth that Jesus has become its agent.

When van Ruler sees many Old Testament ways of reconciliation, as over against the one in the New Testament, then it is obviously of significance that, as he says, the idea of substitution only emerges finally in the New Testament. This easily arrived at conclusion may claim some facts which lie rather superficially on the surface, but the inner essence of the Bible is opposed to it. In view of Cullmann's book *Christus und die Zeit,* we do not need many words to show how central the idea of substitution is really in the Old Testament from the beginning. This concept finds its climax in Jesus, the Servant of God. Hence it is not the case—as might appear in the way van Ruler formulates the matter—that in the New Testament a truth came to light which up to that time had remained obscure. Israel knew very well what substitution and atonement meant; what it did not yet know was the way of their final realization in Jesus of Nazareth.

Regarding the second point (the human Messiah in the Old Testament, the divine in the New) the facts are related inaccurately and inappropriately for the sake of the contrast. Account is taken only of the nature of the Israelite king and not at the same time of the authoritative position connected with his office. If one takes this into consideration, then one can certainly only say that in the Old and New Testaments the Messiah is divine, there, *per adoptionem,* here, *ex origine.* By the apodictic separation of van Ruler the view of the mystery of the trend of redemptive history is obstructed, especially as it becomes evident in the office of the Messiah: the many adopted functionaries of the old covenant as preparation and *tupoi* in anticipation of the *One* Son.

Concerning the third point we fully agree with van Ruler at first: The New Testament apostolate is not envisaged in the Old Testament. Yet just as fully must we repudiate the negative emphasis which van Ruler gives it to such a degree that he can call Jesus an "emergency measure of God."

In this connection let us hasten to say that while the New Testament apostolate is not envisaged in the Old Testament, the spread of Israel's truth to the nations was nevertheless expected. In this respect the New Testament apostolate has, after all, an Old Testament foundation. The proclamation to the Gentiles as a benefit of the end-time belongs to both Testaments. They only differ in the method of making it actual. In the Old Testament it is seen as part of the final event which comprises salvation and judgment. In the New Testament we find an extension of time during which a period of gospel proclamation is inserted before the judgment and end of the age.[2] How this extension of time should be valued—whether state of emergency or of bliss —the New Testament makes abundantly plain in the words and deeds of Jesus and in the witness of the Apostles: It is a time of grace. It gives a chance to Israel and an offer to the nations in such a way that the Testaments are not separated and the promises of the Old Testament are not nullified. They remain even though their realization takes place in stages.

What that means can be exemplified in the establishment of the new covenant. This has become reality through Jesus' institution; thus it is past in the act of his institution and is present in his existence. It is present in the end-time which the church, equipped with the Holy Ghost, knows as earnest of that which is to come but does not yet know as transformation of nature and men. Jesus has satisfied the law, he has fulfilled it, and for this reason there are not any more works of the law in his church; instead we have "fruits of the Spirit" (Gal. 5:22 ff.). The Holy Spirit can take hold of the nature of man and trans-

---

[2] Cf. F. Flückiger, *Der Ursprung des christlichen Dogmas* (1955), pp. 108 ff.

form it, but he does not thereby become a part of man himself. For this reason the "fruits of the Spirit" cannot be realized without obedience, to which disobedience always stands in contrast. The time which Jeremiah expected with obedience as the only possibility has not yet come. The new covenant, however, which Jesus instituted belongs already to the time of grace when the gospel is proclaimed and not only to the period of its consummation.

10.

THEOCRACY AND SOTERIOLOGY

Comments on A. A. van Ruler's book:
Die christliche Kirche und das Alte Testament
(*The Christian Church and the Old Testament*)

by *Th. C. Vriezen*

translated by James A. Wharton

It is no small task, although one gladly undertaken, to comment upon the recent publication of my esteemed colleague at Utrecht, van Ruler. It is difficult not only because of the subject, but also because of the ideas that are worked out in this book. The author makes it easy for his critic to express his own thoughts in all candor when he begins the foreword with these sentences: "No one will readily suggest that the thoughts elaborated in this essay are the final solution of the problem. I myself, at any rate, would be the last to insist that this is the case." Thus we may count upon at least *one* ear receptive to a few criticisms.

The matter is difficult, if only for the reason that the work is written very briefly, in some respects too briefly. It plunges immediately into the most difficult and profound questions concerning Old Testament theology, without first introducing the reader a bit into the author's own sphere of theological thought and his own presuppositions. It becomes more transparent at every turn, however, that his approach to the Old Testament theological problematic proceeds from his own quite special dogmatic presuppositions. When one works through the book, the impression grows ever stronger that this method of plunging headlong into the problem carries with it not only stimulation but also difficulties.

As early as the second sentence on the first page of the introduction, van Ruler says that in this matter it is the fundamental

theological posture which is decisive for our attitude toward the
Old Testament; a reciprocal relationship obtains between the
two, so that, "On the one hand, the basic theological posture is
normative for our attitude toward the Old Testament, but, on
the other hand, the attitude toward the Old Testament also helps
determine our general theological position." It will become clear
that the first case predominates for van Ruler, most explicitly on
p. 18, where he speaks of the Word of God becoming a book,
and of the inspiration of Scripture in this connection. This dogmatic decision in regard to what he himself calls the "nerve of the
problem of Scripture" determines everything else, because from
this standpoint van Ruler can and must proceed from the Old
Testament as the integral Word of God in a thoroughly inclusive
sense, which in fact he does quite consistently.

This thought is worked out on p. 8, and it is affirmed that the
"central matter of the Old Testament" is decisive for the question
as to how we understand Jesus Christ and his salvation, how we
stand relative to the Christian church and the Apostolate, how
we think about the Kingdom of God, and how we evaluate
earthly life and the total structure of Christian existence.

The question of the proper evaluation of the Old Testament for van Ruler is a problem which should be thought out
anew from the standpoint of systematic theology, because no
form of the Christian church "has had the last word about what
God has in mind with the Old Testament in the Christian
situation, and about what the church itself does and wants to do
with the Old Testament" (p. 9). In the Christian churches many
basic conceptions of the Old Testament are represented (van
Ruler names ten different ones), which nevertheless cannot be
accepted as satisfactory. For this reason the problem should be
posed afresh and rethought from the standpoint of systematic
theology, in view of the results of historical-critical research. At
the end of the book, and at one or two points even earlier, it is
indicated, nevertheless, that the author stands very near certain
solutions proposed by theology in the course of its history. For
example, typological interpretation (which he rejects) returns
again in another form when the Old Testament is seen to provide

illustrations for the message of the gospel; the same holds true for the concept of the preparatory meaning of the Old Testament, when it is acknowledged that in the New Testament many intentions of the Old Testament have passed irrevocably into fulfillment (p. 73). At the same time, there lies in this the tacit recognition of the *heilsgeschichtlichen* understanding of the Old Testament. The distinction which van 'Ruler makes on p. 25 between the idea of progressive revelation (which he opposes) and the idea of a *heilsgeschichtlichen* forward movement of revelation is perhaps indeed too subtle. Thus, in some respects there is a remarkable oscillation of thought in his book which is apparently inherent in the pendulum-like systematic thought of the author.

It is clear from the outset, and as one reads further it becomes increasingly clear, that the issue for the author is the Old Testament as a whole, and that one should not expect from him any subtle investigations of individual Old Testament books and their meaning within the canon. It seems as though this problem does not exist for him at all. Precisely the Old Testament scholars, for whom the book was apparently written primarily, will find this to be a serious omission, because for them the greatest difficulties lie in just these material questions. Is it possible for one to speak at all about the Old Testament (in view of historical-critical research) without touching on this sphere of inquiry? In this regard the book leaves Old Testament scholars "standing out in the cold." The author circumvents just those questions which have occupied them at the deepest level ever since the beginnings of historical-critical research. After the introduction there is no word at all in the book about the results of such research. After making a deep bow in their direction, as it were, van Ruler otherwise passes them by. He is not concerned with historical-critical questions (and therefore with historical-theological questions), but he is concerned with opening a new perspective, a new view of the Old Testament for contemporary theologians—first of all for the Old Testament scholars among them, because he enters energetically into their most recent discussions concerning interpretation—a view which current theology has lost, or rather, which theology in fact has never perceived.

This new perspective consists in a view of the Old Testament rooted in Calvinistic thought and carried out with extreme consistency. First, as if in passing, he establishes the conception of "revelation-become-book" and the inspiration of the Bible (pp. 18 f.), thus securing grounds for his point of departure, presenting the Old Testament in its totality as means of revelation; then he proceeds to the essentials of his argument. This indicates that he is concerned with two matters in the Old Testament: the fact of the theocracy in Israel, and the content of this theocracy; naturally, the two belong inseparably together.

The qualitative substance of the Old Testament is defined more closely in this way: Essentially the Old Testament is not concerned with religion, but "with very concrete, secular things —the possession of land, the gift of posterity, the increase of the people, an 'eternal' monarchy, a community based on righteousness and love. Neither the Israelites nor the authors of the Old Testament nor even God present in the prophetic word and among the people Israel ever goes beyond these concrete, earthly aspects of redemption." It is stated in this way on p. 85: "The quintessence for the Old Testament lies in politics in the broadest sense of the word—the state, social and economic life, culture—in a word, the santification of the earth" (cf. also p. 82). In these earthly things it becomes manifest in Israel what God does and who God is. The material content of the Old Testament, then, is the event of the revelation of the Kingdom of God in Israel, the realization of theocracy in the midst of this people.

From this point of view, preaching must hand on the revelatory witness of the Old Testament (pp. 31 ff.). When this happens in the full sense, "there occurs in the Spirit an incidental repetition of Israel . . . we are made Israel (round about Christ) by the Spirit." If this be the case, then theocracy exists also among us, a theocracy in which "not only the church, but also life and the world, are comprehended, which must be sanctified and Christianized."[1]

While for us theocracy is "perhaps the ultimate prospect," for Israel it exists as "the first *a priori.*" Only from this eschatological, theocratical point of view does preaching become what it ought to be: preaching of the Kingdom; and thus it is not only preaching of the gospel, not only preaching of Christ, but utterly "service of the Word"; as such, it is also "preaching of the law, of the Kingdom, and of the image of God." Thus there is a strong *plus* of the Old Testament Word of revelation over against the witness of the New Testament.

One must acknowledge that theology is being carried on here with passion, imaginativeness, and courage—three elements which are the presuppositions of all true poesy, according to the Hollandic poet Da Costa. This is the voice of one who carries on the theological task only with the most intimate relationship to all of life. For van Ruler, theology is no course of private scientific study, but the vital nerve, the respiratory organ of faith. It is not just later reflection about faith, but is itself a dynamic of faith. Through theology the Word of God and the world are confronted with each other and brought together. The Word of God transposes our life out of death and darkness into the joy of the presence of God, making us citizens of his Kingdom so that we may live in the full sense of the word. The Bible's preaching of the Kingdom is distinctive of this. Theology has to do with the preaching of the Kingdom which holds God and the world in mutual relationship. For this reason van Ruler never tires of speaking about theocracy, pointing to the world as

---

[1] In this connection the relationship of the Roman Catholic Church to the Old Testament is criticized in passing; it is said that Rome, as the eternal Rome, can understand tradition as a stream in which the Scripture or even Christ is continued, and that she consequently forgets the Old Testament more and more. I am afraid van Ruler misunderstands Rome at this point, and that he himself stands nearer to her than he thinks. For is it not so that Rome is able to understand herself as the eternal Rome in the Christian sense precisely because, far from forgetting the Old Testament, she understands herself as a continuation, a repetition of Israel, the new Israel over whom the promises of the old Israel have passed? The difference between van Ruler and Rome, then, is that for van Ruler an *incidental* repetition of Israel occurs through Word and Spirit; cf. what he says on p. 83, that "one touches the kernel of the problem as soon as one sees that all of Christian existence is structured in a radically cultic way, insofar

the goal of God's concern in his revelation for the world. For him, the Lordship of God and the Kingdom of God coincide. The former is not merely the basis for the latter, but both are one in faith. For this reason van Ruler is disposed to be strongly anti-apocalyptic; for this reason he is so enthralled with the Old Testament, because it teaches us properly to evaluate this earth and our life as the sphere of the Kingdom of God. Van Ruler is the passionate revival preacher of the Christian church, who wants to rescue Christianity and theology from its self-imposed "reducing diet" (so-called spiritualization), to give to the church again a genuine message for the world, and to bring it back to its proper apostolic calling, which consists in its rescuing the world from its godforsakenness through the preaching of the Word of God.

The question is, then, whether this theology of theocracy (for this is the best designation[2]) in this form is biblical, or whether perhaps it views certain biblical elements in a false perspective, proceeding from a certain systematic-theological viewpoint, and presents them in a one-sided way.

It is not possible to focus upon all of the questions which the book raises. I shall indicate three serious reservations, which are also related to each other.

1. The first is the evaluation of the Old Testament as the Bible proper (p. 68) in which God has made himself fully known ("all goodness . . . all truth . . . all beauty and the total

---

as it stands in a circle about the great sacrificial act of God on Golgotha, where the means of salvation has become completely the fact of salvation, and *as a result history has become totally cultic.* If this is the case, however, the question as to whether the cultus of the Old Testament is superfluous for the Christian church is hardly legitimate any longer." Are these not precisely the thoughts that lie behind the process of Roman-Catholicizing the church? In the end, van Ruler would lead the Christian church to a new repristinization of Israel, if anything even more consistently than Rome does it. Indeed, he even thinks (p. 19) that the Christianization of culture will only succeed in that degree to which the general cultural awareness is shot through with the basic structure of the Hebrew language and the Old Testament/Israelite manner of thinking. In my view, a basic error in van Ruler's system lies behind these thoughts, in that he does not make a distinction beween the eschatological and the theocratical in the Old Testament —at least not in this essay.

[2] Concerning his theology, cf. K. H. Miskotte, *Naturrecht und Theokratie,* Suppl. to EvTh, 15 (1952), pp. 29 ff.; and A. A. van Ruler, *Theologie des Apostolats,* Evgl. Missionszeitschrift (1954), pp. 1 ff.

saving 'understanding of being' shine forth before us in the
Old Testament"). Even if the Christian church, according to
his view, must take its stand in the New Testament because of
the depth of the love of God revealed to her, she must see and
recognize "the Old Testament, given to us as the canonical Word
of God," as her horizon (p. 53); and only this horizon shows us
the full scope of the revelation of God.

Van Ruler can offer this conception only because (a) he
finds theocracy to be the decisive fact of revelation in the Old
Testament, on the one hand, and (b) he actually hears in the
New Testament, on the other, only the soteriological witness. In
the intended sense, both of these are one-sided, from my viewpoint, and because of this the mutual relationship of the Testaments is wrongly determined. I must raise objections to both
theses.

2. If I may begin with the latter, I have the impression that
van Ruler commits the identical error *vis-à-vis* the New Testament with which he charges Christian theology generally:
namely, that it overspiritualizes the biblical message, reducing
it to a single spiritual denominator. He reads the New Testament very one-sidedly when he finds everything in it concentrated upon the guilt of mankind and the atonement wrought
in Jesus Christ. He thinks that the New Testament is so strongly
concerned with a priestly kingdom that a consequent spiritualizing tendency is unmistakable, one which puts creation in a
precarious position; as a result, he can ask, "What does one do
with the world, actually, from the standpoint of the gospel?"
(p. 48). This question is raised as if the New Testament had or
evinced no comprehension for the glory of the world in the light
of the revelation of God. Was not the eye of Jesus Christ open,
then, to the beauty of the flowers of the field? Did not Paul perceive that the revelation of God in his redemptive deed in Jesus
Christ rescues the whole creation (Rom. 8:19)? Is not Jesus Christ
evaluated at many points in the New Testament as the revelation of the Word which stands creatively at the beginning (John
1; Col. 1:15)? The New Testament is no less theocratically undergirded and no less eschatologically oriented toward the Kingdom

of God than the Old Testament; perhaps one can even say that the New Testament is more intensively, more directly, so undergirded and oriented, even though soteriology be its center. This only makes the tension in the New Testament stronger, so that one cannot conclude that Old Testament and New Testament relate to each other as theocratic versus soteriological preaching. Why is the soteriological concern placed at the center of the New Testament? Why did the redemptive deed of God take the shape of suffering and the form of the cross? Was it not because it had been demonstrated in Israel that theocratic preaching could not save Israel, that Israel could not be transformed into a theocracy without the suffering and sacrificial death of the Servant of God? Theocracy could become a living reality in Israel only through the cross, as in fact it can be realized in any way at all only through the cross. Thus I do not understand how van Ruler thinks it possible to say that from within the New Testament one cannot see in the sacrifice on Golgotha a genuine "confrontation" between God and his people (p. 49). What happens there relates first of all to Israel, even though it also has meaning for world history. Christ is not just any deed of God among other deeds in his history with Israel, but rather the ultimate, the highest, the most profound, *the* deed of God *par excellence* (Matt. 21:33 ff.; Heb. 1) in Israel; as such, however, it has meaning for the whole world. This is so because cosmic significance must be ascribed to revelation in Israel from the very beginning. Therefore in the New Testament, the Spirit, from which van Ruler rightly expects so much that is new, is always bound to faith in Jesus Christ and is active through him. The Lord is the Spirit. Theocracy can take shape, therefore, only from the cross, and only through cross-bearing can it be brought to light. Jesus Christ is the locus of the breaking through of the Kingdom of God in the world. Cross and Resurrection belong inseparably together in the gospel. It is strange that van Ruler hardly mentions the Resurrection, in view of the fact that it affords the decisive solution in the New Testament message.

3. My third and most serious objection must be raised

against the way in which van Ruler understands theocracy in the Old Testament. Is it actually the testimony of the Old Testament that theocracy in Israel is a givenness *a priori* (p. 32)? Can one actually say to Israel from Isaiah 45:14, "God is *in* you" (p. 25)? Must one not read Second Isaiah from the eschatological standpoint? Can one actually maintain the concept of the correlative relationship of God and Israel under a single form (p. 44)? Is not Israel there as the locus of God's breaking through into the world, just as the church is also there for the revelation of the Kingdom of God, in order that the whole world may participate in the redemption of God? Van Ruler would certainly affirm this last point (p. 64).

I find the great shortcoming of the book, at least where it concerns the Old Testament, in the failure to distinguish between the concepts of theocracy and eschatology; rather, the two are used in the same breath as synonyms (pp. 32, 82). I believe it is necessary to reject the confusion of these ideas with respect to Israel. Even if Israel actually had a concept of an *a priori* theocracy, probably as early as the time of the monarchy, perhaps even earlier, and even if this is also surely to be found later in the Old Testament (e.g., in the books of Chronicles); even so, the prophets sharply opposed this complacent assurance of theocracy in Israel, and rejected it decisively. They opposed it with a totally new eschatological preaching of the Kingdom of God, a Kingdom which will be revealed after the terrible wrath of God at the last day. In view of the proclamation of Isaiah 2; 11; Jeremiah 31; or Ezekiel 36, one really cannot assert that they are concerned with totally secular things, although the hope remains this-worldly even in these passages.

In the Old Testament, theocracy stands over against theocracy. I am a little afraid that van Ruler's sketch of Old Testament theocracy leads along the line of the false prophets rather than that of the canonical prophets. According to van Ruler's characterization, the Kingdom of God is too plainly visible in the Old Testament, as if no act of faith at all were necessary in Israel. Beyond this, the Old Testament by no means evinces the uniformity which van Ruler supposes. One cannot receive it and characterize it in such wholesale fashion as is done in his book. It is at this point that the weakness of van Ruler's method appears, by which he reduces the entire Old Testament to a single denominator, overlooking the inner tensions of which it testifies.[3] This method conceals within it the danger of a misrepresentation of the total material. This is true of his sketch of the New Testament as well as of the Old Testament, and injustice is done thereby to both.

The relation of each Testament to the other is more intimate and at the same time more complex than appears in this work. Van Ruler's essay would have gained very much in meaning if it had dealt with the relation between the Testaments a bit less dogmatically and in wholesale fashion, and had gone more into the extremely diverse material of the two collections, taking this more seriously in view of the results of historical-critical research. Unfortunately, the original promise of the work remains unfulfilled. This is lamentable, because on many pages one has the impression that van Ruler has important things to say to the current situation of theology and the church concerning the confrontation of church and world. Van Ruler's passionate longing for a Christian culture in which theocracy takes shape anew is to be acknowledged as a great thought. His deep concern and his total hope are devoted to a visionary faith in the sanctification of the earth. In this is disclosed a longing which the Bible has instilled in him.

The question is, then, whether one can separate reconciliation and sanctification from each other; whether one can separate atonement for sin from theocracy; whether one factually and conceptually can keep earth and sin distinct from each other. In his polemic against the Christian fancy that it is necessary to deny the world in order to follow the Redeemer, van Ruler goes too far when in opposition he calls "sin and reconciliation a secondary problem, protologically and eschatologically" (p. 83), and when he terms Christ an emergency measure of God, an overriding deed of God. At this point an injustice is indeed

---

[3] Cf., e.g., O. Procksch, *Theologie des Alten Testaments*, pp. 592 f., and H. J. Kraus, *Prophetie und Politik*, pp. 76 ff.

done to the Christian faith—the earth as creation cannot be truly loved without the deep confession of the sin which desecrates it, and without knowledge of the grace of God which has broken the power of sin and prepares a new future for the earth. Sanctification without redemption is impossible. There are no secondary and primary elements of life in this regard. Sin is spread like cancer through all normal organs of life and can only be vanquished through a renewal of the inner vital powers of the spirit. This is true for the individual as well as for the whole. As a Christian one cannot speak idealistically about the world as creation without honestly acknowledging sin. This is possible for an idealistic-Jewish theology like Buber's, but not for a biblical theology in the full sense of the word. Therefore the Christian church cannot agree with Buber so unreservedly in his belief in the possibility of the sanctification of the earth. The question is whether Buber is actually right in the view that this faith is congruous with the vision of the God of Israel (p. 85). At any rate, it is an impossible possibility—one which is not open to man (even the man of faith), one which he can only await in faith from the hand of God, for which he can only hope, about which he can only pray, in behalf of which he can only obey God in Christian discipleship.

The Kingdom of God cannot be preached apart from the cross of Christ. It is misleading when van Ruler says repeatedly that the Kingdom of God only revolves about him, but that he is not its content (p. 65). One must add: But it goes forth from him; it comes only from him. The world can be sanctified only through the cross. The Kingdom of God is more than Christ, as the New Testament plainly testifies, as he himself testifies first of all; in this van Ruler is right. But the Kingdom of God never exists for us in a real sense without him. That which was before him was a shadow of the coming Kingdom of God, at best existing in hope, but not in real form (Matt. 11:11 ff.; 13:17). What is revealed about the Kingdom of God in the Old Testament has a twofold form: the form of eschatological expectation and the shadowy image of Israelite institutions. To designate the shadowy and visionary images as a "plus value" (p. 82) over against the one who is called in the New Testament the "bright-ness of *his* glory, and the express image of his person" (Heb. 1:3, K.J.V.) cannot aid or advance a Christian culture.

On the other hand it would be a grave danger if Christian culture should appropriate the stamp of the Old Testament (i.e., institutional) theocracy without the cross. I would not suggest that a *Christianized* form of this institutional theocracy would afford redemption—the impossibility of this was seen in the Middle Ages. But I would say that the church should preach persuasively that God is Lord in this world and will make it new; I would say that the church by its confession leads the world, even in the political and cultural spheres, with the truth and righteousness of the Word of God. She must believe in the hidden theocracy and hope in the Kingdom of God of which she testifies, without desiring to create institutions in order to achieve an external Christianization. Every such Christianization has the danger of repristinization, and would function coercively rather than according to faith.

A still greater danger would be to desire the return of Old Testament institutions and relationships into our world. Would it serve to purify family relationships, for example, if we re-turned to the Old Testament patriarchal structures or even to the Old Testament marriage ethic (as Luther suggested once in a sermon on Genesis 16, using in his application the example of the bigamous marriage of Philip of Hesse)? Neither theo-logically nor out of a desire for the practical achievement of theocracy could one accept the Old Testament as the normative Word of revelation, which "manifests all goodness, beauty and truth, the total right understanding of being."

This review may conclude with the expression of a wish—namely, that evangelical theology might pursue the study of the Bible more as a totality of both Testaments in interrelationship. The necessity as well as the possibility of this comprehensive biblical study emerges especially in this time, when both Testa-ments are being increasingly illuminated in terms of their his-torical background, and when the intertestamental period is becoming better known through new discoveries, with the result that connecting lines in both directions are becoming clear. At the same time it would promote the possibility of a conversation with Judaism, a conversation which the church ought certainly to undertake soon. It is the indisputable contribution of van Ruler's essay that it has made this need clear. He has attacked with courage a high and difficult subject, and in this respect his essay must be called a pioneer work.

11.

IS TYPOLOGICAL EXEGESIS
AN APPROPRIATE METHOD?

by Walther Eichrodt

translated by James Barr

The choice of my theme requires no lengthy justification. Our own time has seen a new awakening of hermeneutical thought and this is a symptom of a profound concern to determine afresh the task of Old Testament exegesis. In this movement a new degree of attention has been given to the exposition of the Old Testament within the New, and also to the later exegesis of the fathers and the Reformers. This material has received careful and critical treatment in well-known works such as L. Goppelt, *Typos* (1939); J. Daniélou, *Sacramentum futuri* (1950); J. Coppens, *Les Harmonies des deux Testaments* (1949); and H. Bornkamm, *Luther und das Alte Testament* (1948). In addition to the dominant exegetical theme of prophecy and fulfillment, it was natural that much consideration should be given to the almost forgotten typological outlook of the New Testament, especially after it had been revived in so striking a way by the exegetes of the dialectical school of theology. Thus in recent years typology has played an important role in the very valuable discussion between Gerhard von Rad and Friedrich Baumgärtel. For the same reason it is also possible that a treatment of typology may provide illustrations for many general hermeneutical questions.

I

For this discussion we should remain at first within the limits which, from the fathers up to the time of Protestant orthodoxy, hermeneutical science has drawn in using "typology" as the designation for a peculiar way of looking at history. These same limits, in more modern times, have been taken as fundamental in such works as that by Goppelt, already mentioned, and Bultmann's essay, "Ursprung und Sinn der Typologie als hermeneutischer Methode," in *Theologische Literaturzeitung* (1950), cols. 47 ff. The so-called *tupoi*, if we follow these limits, are persons, institutions, and events of the Old Testament which are regarded as divinely established models or prerepresentations of corresponding realities in the New Testament salvation history. These latter realities, on the basis of 1 Peter 3:21, are designated "antitypes."

It is not the case, however, that the antitype corresponds to the type in all its properties, so as to form an almost photographic copy of it. On the contrary, the argument envisages only a few analogies, but these of special importance, between the two realities in question. Their other properties can be quite different and need not be considered here.[1] Thus in the parallel of Moses and Christ in 2 Corinthians 3:7 ff., to which we may perhaps add also Hebrews 3:1-6, the concern is not with all possible details of the life and service of Moses, but only with his *diakonia* and *doxa* in the former passage and with his loyalty as leader and mediator of the people of God in the divine *oikonomia* in the second passage.

Emphasis can be given to certain corresponding features also from another side, where the purpose is not to illustrate a likeness but a contrast. An example is the typological correspondence of Adam and Christ in Romans 5:12 ff. Here the comparability of the two is indeed based upon the determinative significance of each for humanity in the period introduced by himself; but this is worked out in detail as a wholly contrasting correspondence, with the sin of Adam and its fruit in guilt and corruption standing opposed to justification through Christ with its fruit in righteousness and life.

But even where the view remains one of analogy rather than

---

[1] As is rightly seen by C. Lockhardt, *Principles of Interpretation*, 2nd ed. (1952), p. 228.

of contrast, a certain element of contrast between type and antitype is always involved, for in the antitype that characteristic
which corresponds to the type "unfolds itself in a fuller and
richer way."[2] This is connected with the fact that the type, like
the entire salvation history of the Old Testament, indicates
only a preliminary stage of the salvation in Christ and cannot
attain to the completeness of the latter. Thus the element of
intensification, even if it is not expressly stated, is always there
in the background.

This connecting of Old Testament and New Testament
events, through pointing to a similarity which links both, has in
itself nothing artificial about it, and does not lose itself in details but always aims toward the center of the establishment of
salvation by God. Thus it is Jesus Christ who provides in the
first place the antitype of the Old Testament types; along with
him we may mention also the apostolic office in 2 Corinthians
3:7 ff.,[3] the sacraments in 1 Corinthians 10:1 ff., and the experience of grace and judgment by the Christians as the people
of the new covenant in 1 Peter 2:5, 9; Revelation 1:6; and 1
Corinthians 10:6. All these cases are not subordinate and insignificant matters, but are central elements in the realization of
salvation.

Correspondingly, the realities of the Old Testament salvation
history which are used as types are by no means called to remembrance as mere facts which, emerging from the normal
stream of history in some ghostly way, here possess an existence
which is unreal and becomes meaningful only when seen from
the angle of the New Testament events. On the contrary, these
are quite concrete things taken from the historical narratives
of the Old Testament, which, precisely because of their real
historical function, appear as valuable testimony to the divine
governance of history. It is not the mere factualness of these
persons, events, and institutions which, by means of some discovered similarity with corresponding New Testament realities,
validates them as types. Rather it is the intercourse of God with

---

2 F. Torm, *Hermeneutik des Neuen Testaments* (1930), p. 223.
3 Goppelt, *op. cit.*, p. 172.

his people, represented, warranted, and actualized by them, that validates them. In other words, their religious and theological significance in the historical revelation of the Old Testament gives to them their significance as divinely established pre-representations of important elements in the salvation manifested in Christ.[4]

It is this peculiarity that differentiates the typological view of Old Testament events in the New Testament clearly from other ways of considering biblical material. It differentiates it, first, from allegory, which has often been lumped together with typology, so that the latter has often had to bear the burden of the former's errors. Yet it is quite impossible to confuse the two if we look at them closely. For typology, the historical value of the text to be interpreted forms the essential presupposition for the use of it. For allegory, on the contrary, this is indifferent or even offensive, and must be pushed to one side to make room for the "spiritual" sense which lies behind. In pursuit of this purpose the earthly objects and persons of which the text speaks are interpreted as spiritual processes and essences with which they have nothing to do if the literal sense is followed. The content of the testimony thus forced upon the text was already fixed and known to the interpreter before he began, and the art of allegorical interpretation consists in the establishment of relations between this content and the text. Thus while the Exodus story depicts Moses as the historical deliverer of Israel, sent by God to lead his people out of slavery into the freedom of the rule of God, allegory describes him as the possessor of knowledge and of the true philosophy, releasing the captured soul from the prison of sensual lust; the destruction of the Egyptian army represents the destruction of the passions. I hardly need to offer more examples, for these facts can be assumed to be widely known.

The whole method obviously involves a consistent depreciation of history, which with its coarse sensible and material processes can have no significance for the provision of salvation.

---

[4] This was already rightly indicated by C. von Orelli, *Die alttestamentliche Weissagung von der Vollendung des Gottesreiches* (1882), p. 45.

On the lines of Platonic philosophy, salvation is seen as something timelessly present and universally attested in the same way for the possessor of knowledge. That this way of considering things is foreign to the historical outlook of both Old and New Testaments is so evident as to require no proof.[5]

Secondly, however, the Old Testament may be considered as a testimony to the will of God, to be valued paraenetically. From this approach typology cannot be differentiated quite so clearly as it can from allegory. In principle indeed there is a clear distinction: Typology is concerned with the reactualization of the Old Testament realities as a prerepresentation of present salvation, while paraenesis values these realities as warning and advising models for the present community. To this one might perhaps add that the relation between type and antitype gives more emphasis to the objective reality, while in instruction and advice attention is concentrated above all upon the subjective attitude of the Old Testament model.

In individual cases, however, it is not always easy to make a decision about the character of an existing practice in the New Testament. Thus Bultmann in the essay mentioned above[6] was probably right in reducing sharply the large area which, according to Goppelt, had been occupied by typological use of the Old Testament. He refused to treat as typology simply any citation of examples from the past as models or illustrations for the present; for example, the depiction in Romans 4 of Abraham as the model for believers. The case of 1 Corinthians 10:1-11 shows, however, how very naturally typology and paraenesis may interlock. On the other hand, Bultmann would prefer to treat the circle of thought involving the new covenant and the new people of God, with the exception of Hebrews 8:6 ff., not as determined by typology but as anchored in the idea of fulfillment.

---

[5] A. G. Hebert in *The Authority of the Old Testament* (1947), pp. 268 ff., tries to reconcile the traditional doctrine of the fourfold sense of Scripture with his own clear preference for the literal sense by making a distinction between the theological and the illustrative uses of the Old Testament and reckoning among the latter those interpretative methods which are scientifically untenable. This solution, however, will hardly suffice to exclude the threat of allegory to sound exegesis, and will always leave the door open to it.

[6] See above, p. 225.

This leads us to our third point, the relation between typology and the interpretation of the Old Testament as prophecy of the fulfillment which is found in the New. There is certainly a very close relation between these two approaches, for each of them sees in the Old Testament the announcement, in a preliminary form and in a time of waiting, of the completion of salvation by God himself. But while in prophecy the messenger of God proclaims the future which has been opened to him and seen by him, a type possesses its significance, pointing into the future, independently of any human medium and purely through its objective factual reality; and in many cases its function is still hidden for contemporary people and is disclosed only when the gaze is turned backward from the New Testament time of salvation. From this point of view one might designate typology as "objectivized prophecy."[7]

If we have outlined the typological approach of the New Testament in its uniqueness, it must now be emphasized that this approach had as yet by no means been developed into a method in any scholastic sense. There is not even a fixed terminology. Paul uses the word *tupos* only twice (Rom. 5:14 and 1 Cor. 10:6) to indicate typologically the prerepresentation of that which is to come. Moreover, in the latter of these two places, as with the adverb *tupikōs* which appears in the same context in 1 Corinthians 10:11, the alternative explanation of a model or example in the moral sense—a sense very frequent in the Pauline letters—could perhaps be maintained. The letter to the Hebrews, in which we have the first case of something approaching a constant typological method, uses the word *tupos* not in the sense of typology proper but as the designation for the heavenly model of the holy tabernacle, and uses *antitupos* in 9:24 for the santuary made with hands, which is also called the *hupodeigma* and *skia* of the heavenly sanctuary (8:5). In so doing the author of Hebrews is following out certain suggestions contained in the Old Testament itself[8] which for their part go

---

[7] It is an underestimate of the importance of this element in typology to call it with Torm "a kind of philosophy of history." His designation "realistic prophecy" (*op. cit.*, p. 227) is better.

[8] Cf. Exod. 25:9, 40; 1 Chron. 28:19.

back to ancient Oriental ideas;[9] but in the New Testament he
stands alone in this. For his typological expositions he is content
with *homoiotēs* (7:15), *parabolē* (9:9; 11:19), or else expresses the
typological relation with a *legetai tauta epi* "this is said about
. . ." (7:13). We are thus still far from a methodical use and development of the type idea. Only with Barnabas and the
Shepherd of Hermas do we have the start of a development of
the typological approach into a method with the help of which
the secrets of the Old Testament can be unveiled, so that types
of Jesus' suffering can be found in such inaccessible realities as
the scapegoat of the Day of Atonement or the ashes of the red
cow. But even among the fathers, and in particular those of the
Alexandrian school, terminology continues to vary uncertainly, as
W. de Boer has made clear.[10]

Nevertheless, the peculiar character of the typological approach can already be clearly recognized in the New Testament
itself. If its outlines still remain variable and if a sharp differen-
tiation of method is not felt to be necessary, this is only part of
the quite unsystematic way in which the New Testament community uses this means, along with others, in order to express
a particular position toward the Old Testament, namely, that
of a dialectical double relation.[11] On the one side, the community, from the new status of salvation, conceives the past
history of salvation as something terminated and brought to
completion. On the other side, like its own Lord, Jesus Christ
himself, the community feels the forces and gifts of this history
of salvation to be so living and so directly active in its own existence that it takes this book right into its own life, completely
avoiding any rational opposition to the law, and, full of joy and
amazement, provides witness in it to its own possession of salvation and thus finds that this possession has been planned and
prepared from long beforehand by the faithfulness of God. Out
of this highly peculiar life-emotion there arise simultaneously

---

[9] Cf. my *Theology of the Old Testament*, I (1961), p. 423.
[10] "Hermeneutic Problems in Early Christian Literature," *Vigiliae Christianae*, I (1947), pp. 150 ff.
[11] Cf. O. Schmitz, "Das Alte Testament im Neuen Testament," in *Wort
und Geist, Festgabe für K. Heim* (1934), p. 66.

both the conscious recognition of limitations for the Old Testament and also the seizing and appropriation of its witness. This follows the line of revelation drawn by the Old Testament itself, and this line permits one to listen in the Old Testament to God's own present Word to his people, and yet also to understand its relation to the Word of God in the New Testament as one of promise and fulfillment.

This dominant idea is used, however, with great freedom as the needs of varying passages require. The fundamental position of the Old Testament as model for the New is not understood as a "systematic principle, methodically applied,"[12] but undergoes manifold transformations; sometimes there is prophecy proper, sometimes a striking picture or a surprising parallel for the life of the community, and in a few cases even a disclosure which has to be interpreted allegorically.[13] But none of the New Testament writers ever thinks of preparing a list of all possible types or of assessing their importance in comparison with other means of illustrating the meaning of the Old Testament for the present time. In this, it is clear, full freedom is left to the Spirit.

II

In what way should modern exegesis relate itself to typology, this peculiar means of expression of one of the New Testament's basic convictions? Can modern exegesis admit it into the circle of its hermeneutical principles, or must it be excluded?

We must say right away that any justification of the use of typology within modern scientific exegesis cannot be simply derived from its use within the New Testament. Nevertheless, the basic conviction of the New Testament, from which this way of thinking proceeds, is our conviction also. The comprehensive view, in which we see how Old and New Testaments belong

---

12 O. Schmitz, *op. cit.*, p. 69.
13 On the difference between a typological exegesis and a typological way of thinking, cf. F. Torm, *Hermeneutik des Neuen Testaments*, p. 225.

in essence together in the community of their revelation of God and in contrast with the rest of religious history, is for us also the presupposition of our work, and from it we come to know the lines which traverse the Old Testament and which have their aim and their point of perspective in Jesus Christ.

It is another question, however, whether in concrete cases we can exhibit such lines in the same way as it was done in the New Testament. There are many arguments, in which the New Testament writers have used Old Testament material, which we cannot make our own, or can make only partially our own. Examples will be found in the citations of Psalms 16 and 110 as David's own words in Acts 2:25 ff. and Mark 12:35 ff. Again, we cannot take over the allegorical interpretations which occur from time to time, for example, the well-known case in Galatians 4:24 ff. with its introductory formula *hatina estin allēgoroumena*. Similarly, and here I agree entirely with the arguments of Coppens, we have to test both individually and collectively the typological interpretations of the Old Testament which we meet in the New, in order to discover whether or not they represent for us an appropriate means of assistance toward understanding the essential correspondence of the Old and New Testaments.

In doing this, a particularly important role will be played by our modern understanding of history, formed by historical criticism, because it hinders us from simply reading the Old Testament in the way in which it was read by Jesus and the New Testament writers. For us the Old Testament history has received in essential points a quite different aspect from that which it could have had for a generation untouched by the historical work of the last two centuries. If this is true of the historical views of the Reformers and the early church, it is certainly not less true of those of the New Testament community. Not that the New Testament's typological view therefore becomes *a priori* impossible for us, but we cannot take it over without confronting it with our understanding of history. In this regard we may note in particular the question of the historical factuality of certain events in the Old Testament.

It is therefore entirely logical that at this point the objections against typological exegesis should begin to appear, and we should reject that exegesis as something representative of an understanding of history which cannot be ours. For this point of view I would like to name in particular two writers who have formulated the decisive questions with special sharpness: Bultmann in his article, already mentioned, in the ThLZ of 1950, and Baumgärtel both in his book *Verheissung* and in his essay on "The Hermeneutical Problem of the Old Testament" (see above, pp. 134-159). In addition I shall cite from time to time certain other scattered essays by Baumgärtel on this subject.

Bultmann's purpose is to show that at the very origin of typology there lies an understanding of time which does not arise from a genuine understanding of history. It is the idea of repetition that dominates typology, and this idea corresponds to the conception of the world process as a cyclic movement, necessarily involving the return or recurrence of similar events. The basis is thus a cosmological theory which has its origin not in Old Testament thought but in ancient Oriental tradition. Although the acceptance and use of this theory in such cases as the doctrine of periods in Daniel or elsewhere in apocalyptic literature may by a fortunate illogicality have suppressed the fresh beginning of the temporal cycle, and thereby have assimilated this foreign material to genuine Old Testament thought, nevertheless, the idea of repetition remains quite opposed to the entire Old Testament way of thinking, oriented to the goal of consummation.

If Bultmann's derivation of typology is correct, one would indeed have to consider the typological approach to the Old Testament as something erroneous from the very beginning and foreign to our historical thinking. One may, however, have serious doubts about the correctness of this derivation. It is not in fact true that the return of the similar is the constitutive idea of typology. On the contrary, as we have argued above, in contrast with the ancient cyclic idea, typology is concerned with the depiction in advance of an eschatological, and therefore an unsurpassable, reality, which stands toward the type in the relation of something much greater or of something anti-thetically opposed. The basic view of history is the same as that involved in the proof through prophecy, in that history is definitely understood as teleologically determined, as salvation history striving toward its end or completion. This view clearly has its origin in the genuine Old Testament understanding of history, which from the experience of divine election and miracle hopes for a similar miracle in future times of neces-sity. Thus typology belongs in principle to prophecy; it is ex-tremely closely connected with the eschatological hope and must be explained from the same fundamental forces as the latter.

This suggestion is confirmed by the fact that even in Old Testament prophecy itself typology is already playing a part.[14] It is Hosea who speaks of a new wilderness period on the model of the first one (2:14 ff.), and this is taken up again by Jere-miah (23:7). But it is Deutero-Isaiah who first gives full force to this theme, setting the deliverance from Exile again and again in parallel with the fundamental act of deliverance by Yahweh in the escape from Egypt, and using the colors of the Exodus story to paint this new picture (Isa. 40:3; 41:17 ff.; 42:16; 43:17; 48:21; 49:10 f.; 52:12; cf. Jer. 31:2 f.). One could indeed probably speak of a "typical" meaning of the Exodus tradition in this case, and the surpassing of the type by the excellence of the antitype is almost always emphasized, especially in Isaiah 43:17 and 52:12. This approach was imitated by many later writers, although in these the Exodus events were often used more as an illustrative example than as a type in the proper sense. It may, for instance, remain uncertain whether the oracle about the new covenant in Jeremiah 31:33 considers the old covenant as a type or not. It can hardly be doubted, however, in face of passages like Isaiah 11:1; Jeremiah 23:5;

---

14 This point has been made independently by E. Jacob, "L'Ancien Testa-ment et la Prédication Chrétienne," *Verbum Caro*, 4 (1950), pp. 153 f.; J. Daniélou, *Sacramentum futuri; Études sur les Origines de la Typologie Biblique* (1950), pp. 257 f.; F. Michaeli agrees with them in his "La 'Typologie' biblique," *Foi et Vie*, 50 (1952), pp. 16 f.

Ezekiel 34:23; 37:24; Isaiah 55:3, 5, that David was considered a type for the coming deliverer-king, who could even be given David's name. The same is true of the high priest and his associates in Zechariah 3:8, of the priests and the descendants of David alike in Zechariah 4:3 ff., of the high priest alone in Zechariah 6:11-13 (MT), and of Moses as the primeval prophet in Deuteronomy 18:15.

As in the New Testament, we find that this typological outlook is not at all developed into a scholastic method. Here again there is no fixed designation for the presaging character of the persons and events, apart from the one passage Zechariah 3:8, where the word *môphēt* comes very close to *tupos*.

Now the general idea in this is that of completion, and this excludes any simple repetition of that which is past. But in cultic experience the thought of repetition plays a part, for in it a salvation set in the past is ever anew awakened to life through the action of the participants in the cult. Let it be admitted that powerful influences from the ancient Oriental conception of life and the world are at work, influences for which the cyclic movement of cosmic process had decisive significance. We cannot go into this problem more closely here. At any rate the repetition of the past, here active, is not an appropriate source from which light can be brought to bear upon the typological prefiguration of consummation, for it is lacking in the element, so decisive and characteristic for typology, of the transcending and surpassing of the past by the consummation.[15]

Thus in the pattern expressed by the formula "primeval time equals ultimate time" (*Urzeit = Endzeit*), which still shows through in many of the prophetic pictures of the time of salvation, there seems still to be a continuing action of the cyclic idea of a regular repetition of the world periods, until the circle begins again with the golden age. But this idea has no longer a decisive part, for there have been added to it, with Yahweh's Lordship over Israel and the nations, new elements which break through the old pattern and alter it at essential points.

---

15 Here I disagree with Bultmann in his work already mentioned.

Friedrich Baumgärtel's objections to the typological view of the Old Testament go deeper than Bultmann's. Unfortunately, I can here discuss his thoughtful work *Verheissung* only from the single aspect of typology, and cannot enter into the many other questions which he has clarified in a very praiseworthy manner.

For Baumgärtel also the opposition of typology to our present historical thinking forms the decisive reason for its rejection. But his objection is not to a contradiction between typology and the understanding of history which we find in the Old Testament and particularly in the prophets. His objection is rather that this understanding of history was taken over, as if it were quite natural to do so, by the New Testament expositors of the Old, and this demonstrates for him that it is impossible for us today to make use of this entire approach. This approach, as he rightly states, goes back to the conception of Israelite history as a history of salvation, the purpose of which was indicated by the predictive words of the prophets and thereby brought into the closest relation with the New Testament history of salvation. But this way of making the Old Testament history into a reality which is meaningful and effective for the Christian of the present day is a way which to him seems impracticable. For the historical facts related in the Old Testament tradition, narrated as God's acts in history and taken up as such in faith by the readers of New Testament times, have been shown through historical-critical research to be a complete distortion of the real state of affairs, and are thereby deprived of their factual nature. "The Old Testament facts are not facts at all, and thus the Old Testament history of salvation is not a history of salvation at all."

Now one should probably say that this wholesale depreciation of the historical tradition of the Old Testament makes the matter rather too easy. Even where critical methods are used to illuminate the material, excellent historical material remains available in adequate quantity at the very turning points of Israelite history, so as to supply real facts as the basis for a history of salvation. Certainly the course of historical events may have been at times somewhat wrongly drawn in details, through a certain schematism (as in the Deuteronomic and Priestly works of history) or through an accentuation of the miraculous element (as we find already in the Elohist); the case of which Baumgärtel thinks in particular is that of the extermination of the Canaanites at the conquest. But though events may have been somewhat misstated, the fact itself remains indisputable, and it is upon this in the first place that the typological use of history relies.

Thus Baumgärtel gives far too little room in his considerations for the fact that the kerygmatic interpretation of historical events which are no longer fully accessible to historical research (as with the stories of the Patriarchal and Mosaic periods) forms a reflection of historical processes in the faith of Israel; the reflection itself has to be valued as a historical fact and to be taken seriously as such. Even where we can no longer grasp the historical event which lies behind the story, with the means of modern scholarship, we nevertheless receive, in the kerygma which grew out of the event, an outworking of the event, and one which provides testimony to its significance.[16] One cannot see why such testimony, which Baumgärtel himself calls "inner facts," should not be used for drawing out the lines of the salvation history.

Conversely, however, one must raise against Baumgärtel himself the objection that he wants to delineate an Israelite history of salvation (and of disaster) as a historical process taking place on a purely empirical level, and one the historical basis of which is in reality not comprehensible. Thus he states, and entirely rightly in my opinion, that the basic divine word of acceptance, "I am the Lord thy God," is the fundamental content of the foundation of the Israelite religion. But how can this fundamental content be demonstrated in the empirical events of the

---

16 Cf. the method so successfully used by M. Buber. Baumgärtel himself can say: "But God acts in external history upon the hearts of men and thus creates inner facts, which are yet facts that can be very well grasped historically in the Old Testament materials. And, seen from the point of view of the gospel, these are the more important facts . . ." (*Verheissung*, p. 123).

history of Israel, if all the concrete assertions about its becoming real in the mighty acts of God—in the Exodus from Egypt, the conquest of Canaan, the establishment of the national state, or the building of the Temple—are only so many misunderstandings of the real will of God, misunderstandings in which God's nature and will are in each case distorted and wrongly interpreted? This is the weapon which Baumgärtel uses against the "naïve" taking over of the Old Testament understanding of history by the New Testament and the church. But this same weapon turns equally against Baumgärtel himself. For if we explain as a misunderstanding the acceptance in faith of the divine self-communication in these historical events, this means nothing else than to declare that the basic word of divine acceptance, which is inseparable from concrete Israelite experience and does not hover in the air like some timeless doctrine, untouched by the destiny of Israel, is only a splendid error and cannot possibly have any normative significance for us. If Israel's faith in deliverance deceives us about every particular revelatory act of God, then the basic promise "I am the Lord thy God," which supposedly stands behind it, can be no more than an imaginary reality, a treacherous and disastrous guide.

But now Baumgärtel adds a very much weightier objection, namely, that the Old Testament understanding of history, which sees divine acts of salvation in Israelite history, cannot be acceptable to us, quite apart from the value of any individual historical narrative, for the reason that it is based upon a conception of salvation quite different from our own. The salvation, the offering of which takes place in God's revelation through history, is in the Old Testament, because it is bound to the this-worldly piety of the Old Testament and to the cultic-national constitution of Israel, quite differently defined from the conceptions of salvation which must be held by the Christian under the guidance of the gospel. "History of salvation" must necessarily have a quite different content in the two situations.[17]

---

[17] Cf. F. Baumgärtel, *Verheissung* (1952), pp. 49 ff.; "Das alttestamentliche Geschehen als heilsgeschichtliches Geschehen," pp. 21 f. (*Geschichte und Altes Testament, Festschrift für A. Alt, Beiträge zur historischen Theologie*, 16, 1953); "The Hermeneutical Problem of the Old Testament," above, pp. 146 f.

Now there is no doubt that in Old Testament piety, being "bound" in the ways Baumgärtel mentions and influenced accordingly, there is in fact, and must be, an emphasis upon the external gifts of salvation quite other than we find in New Testament faith. But one should not overlook the fact that in the Old Testament already the central salvation is the rule of God over Israel and the nations, and that for its sake everything else, including even the existence of the people, can be hazarded. Conversely, in the New Testament the central place in salvation is taken not by the eternal life of glorified individuals in a heavenly Kingdom, an impression which could be read out of the New Testament only by means of an illegitimate spiritualizing of its hope, but by the sovereignty of God upon a renewed earth. But this salvation is communicated at different times under different forms, corresponding to the stage of human knowledge reached and to the task set by God for a particular time. This truth was venerated by Augustine himself as a mystery of divine wisdom, and it should be equally comprehensible to a modern man who thinks in historical terms. Here much more consideration should have been given to the conception, so very common in Lutheran theology, of the condescension of God; for through it it becomes intelligible that even the basic promise of God cannot be set in rigid absoluteness in contrast with all relative promises of earthly good things. Rather it enters into the earthly servant form and uses the earthly and relative salvation as a pledge for the final realization of the completed sovereignty of God.

This thought, however, seems to remove all significance from a third objection of Baumgärtel's. He repeatedly argues that a historical understanding of Old Testament piety is not enough to demonstrate a real theological relevance or "a present sanctifying power from God" for the Christian.[18] Now if along with him we see one of the tasks of exegesis to be the demonstration of the present meaning of the Old Testament for the

---

[18] Baumgärtel, *Verheissung* (1952), pp. 69, 75, 84, 111 ff., 123 ff. "Das alttestamentliche Geschehen als heilsgeschichtliches Geschehen," p. 21. "The Hermeneutical Problem of the Old Testament," above, pp. 142 ff.

Christian church, we shall certainly have to grant that Baumgärtel is right in the inexorable seriousness of this requirement.
Both for the whole area of prophecy and for typology proper
it must be shown that they are a witness of God's action in
history for the realization of salvation in Jesus Christ. If this
were not so, one would have to agree with the criticism that
their use in exegesis is an abstract formalism which could not
create any real connection with the salvation events of the
New Testament.

But it can certainly be demonstrated that these areas have
an inner relatedness to the New Testament faith in salvation.
For prophecy, however, it would take us too far out of our way
to provide this demonstration, and it must be left aside. For
typology Baumgärtel himself admits that it is used in the New
Testament as a re-presentation of the divine action as an action
which took place for us and therefore is directly meaningful for
us. But this possibility is indisputably present also for the use of
the typological outlook today. For typology, as we have defined
it in the stricter sense, emphasizes at central points the continuity and the purposefulness of the divine action. It is not
exhausted by the correspondence of external facts of whatever
kind, but relates itself to the intercourse between God and man
made real through them. In this way it answers an urgent question which agitates Christian faith in relation to the problematic nature of history in general and of Old Testament history
in particular: It points to the realization of salvation through
a history which is molded by the same divine will to fellowship in the Old Testament as in the New Testament communities, and which strives toward a final consummation.[19]
Thus history is lifted out of the sphere of contradictory and
chaotic happening and placed upon the plane of the highest
meaningfulness. But the fact that the salvation was prepared
upon a historical path removes this salvation from any attempt
to spiritualize it, and places it within historical concreteness.

---

[19] "The meaning of the typological outlook is that it opens to us a view of
the unity in God's revelation, and thereby lets us know the lasting significance which every little part of revelation has for the entirety." So F.
Torm, *Hermeneutik des Neuen Testaments* (1930), p. 224.

God's goal of perfection is not a kingdom of spirits, but a new corporality. Finally, typology points to a constancy in God's relations to men, one which adds to the vertical of the divine act of revelation the horizontal of a history of salvation. This history of salvation binds the Old and New Testament communities together through all the changes of time into one people of God, because the continuity of the divine act of love guarantees that they belong together.

In all these points Christian faith must feel itself to be addressed; this does not need to be proved. This is not a rational demonstration, as Baumgärtel thinks, but the believing understanding of the divine molding of history on the basis of an experience, founded upon Christ, of the God who is mighty in history. Thus from our side we must ask Baumgärtel whether his one-sided and all too exclusive emphasis upon the individual Christian with his understanding of existence does not threaten to remove a central element of content in the faith of the New Testament, namely, the consummation of history through the Christ returning in the Kingdom of God, a consummation which stands in an inextricable connection with the divine action in history in the old covenant.

But even if we grant the scholar justification for his pursuit of the typological meaning of the Old Testament, we can still ask whether the evaluation of Old Testament historical facts in this way can belong to the work of exegesis. This question is the concern of Walter Baumgartner in his careful and conscientious study entitled "Die Auslegung des Alten Testaments im Streit der Gegenwart."[20] He declares that the material justifies the Old Testament exegete in looking toward the New Testament, since we naturally see the Old Testament from the side of the New and can, where necessary, complement it from this point of view, using even typological examples where they are in place. But in this he would see a going beyond that which is exegesis in the strict sense of the word, and therefore he would like to describe such exposition as an act which does not arise from the text itself; it is an *applicatio* rather than an *interpretatio*.

---

[20] *Schweizerische Theologische Umschau*, 11 (1941), pp. 17 ff.

Moreover, this position could be strengthened by pointing out that typological interpretation is not in fact concerned with the establishment of the literal sense of a passage, but rather presupposes the literal sense. Thus Daniélou, following St. Thomas Aquinas, states: "Typology is in fact not a meaning of the text, but a meaning of the things. It is a correspondence of the realities of the two Testaments. Thus the text has only a single meaning, the literal, that which was intended by the writer. The realities on their part have a figurative significance which is the object of typology."[21] Thus if one restricts the task of exegesis to the bringing out of that which lies in the text itself, that is to say, the communication of the literal sense of a particular passage with the means of historical and philological criticism, then one will certainly end up in fact with the judgment that typology has no place in it.

Such a restriction of the task of exegesis is, however, hardly tenable. As with any literary work, exposition of the Bible has to go beyond the pure establishment of the literal sense, has to determine the significance of a passage in its wider setting in the history of thought, and has to assess its influence in later times. For the Old Testament this can be done appropriately only if the function of its history as a previous stage of the New Testament history of salvation is taken into consideration. For it is this that differentiates Christian exegesis from Jewish exegesis and from all other kinds of exposition: It believes and recognizes that the Old Testament is determined fundamentally by its directedness toward the New. The task is to make visible this slope toward the New Testament, and typology is one of the factors which serve this purpose.

Now this task certainly presupposes as indispensable a definite position of the scholar, namely, his rootedness in the salvation which has appeared in Christ, or, as Baumgärtel puts it,[22] his being grasped by the Word of God in Christ. Whether or not

---

[21] J. Daniélou in *Dieu vivant*, 16, p. 151, cited after S. Amsler, "Où en est la Typologie de l'Ancien Testament?" in *Études Théologiques et Religieuses*, 27, Nr. 3, *État présent des Études Vétérotestamentaires*, p. 78.
[22] "Ohne Schlüssel vor der Tür des Wortes Gottes?" EvTh, 13 (1953), p. 419.

one should use for this the expression "pre-understanding," coined by Bultmann, at any rate it is only from this point that we approach the right way of posing the questions for the Old Testament text, so that it will disclose its deepest sense or, as Karl Elliger puts it, "its transparence" or "its openness toward the New Testament."[23] In this subjective presupposition of theological research, a subjectivity which is not unknown in other kinds of research work, the exegete is given the "divining-rod," as A. Jepsen has put it in an attractive figure,[24] by which he can discover the peculiar relation of the Old Testament message to that of the New. It is an encouraging sign for the clarification of our present exegetical situation that scholars who in other respects go quite different ways are at one in the recognition of this faith-conditioned presupposition of all theological research. Anyone who, like the author at the Congress of Orientalists and Old Testament scholars at Bonn as late as 1928, has experienced how an attempt to point to this basic determination of theological scholarship has met with almost unbroken incomprehension, must recognize that a hopeful change, and one of wide scope, has taken place.

For now there exists a certain common platform with the supporters of a purely historical exegesis. There is agreement that critical exposition of the Bible does not require being guided or complemented by the addition of anything that is not already contained in the exegetical task as such. The confusing catchwords of pneumatological, Christological, theological, and typologizing exegesis can be allowed to disappear so as to make room for a simply appropriate exegesis, that is, an exegesis which knows of its subjective presupposition in the scholar's decision of faith and one which recognizes the whole compass of its task. Not that it has in its hand a master key to the Word of God, an infallible method by which it could make any text express its meaning. It knows that it is dependent on empowerment through the Spirit, and for this it can only ask. It is not required to profess

---

[23] "Die Bedeutung der Geschichte Israels für die Kirche Jesu Christi," *Für Arbeit und Besinnung*, 2 (1948), pp. 8 f.
[24] "Probleme der Auslegung des Alten Testaments," ZSTh, 23 (1954), p. 385.

ability to preach the gospel out of every word of the Old Testament.[25] But it will use the whole manifold range of assistance
which stands at its disposal, and this includes the typological outlook upon the history of salvation in the Old Testament.

If we see the matter in this way, we can naturally not speak
as if typology had to become the dominating conception in the
area of exegesis. The possibility of using it, as its use in the New
Testament itself shows, is limited. The rules for using it, as S.
Amsler has tried to establish them, hardly go beyond a statement
of the characteristic marks of the phenomenon as a whole, as we
have attempted to develop them.[26] To these rules we might add
one more: A genuine type can never be concerned with mere
external similarities in non-essential points, but deals with an
essential correspondence of central Old Testament facts of history
with fundamental characteristics of the New Testament salvation. Thus every typological correspondence has a part in the
parakalein of the New Testament outlook and puts us within
the field of force of the divine action—a point to which Baumgärtel has correctly given much emphasis.[27]

It is thus open to us to go beyond the New Testament types
and to mention other similar correspondences. In particular Karl
Elliger has used typology in his exegetical works for the elucidation of the Old Testament text.[28] Coppens tries to do the same
thing in his book already cited.[29] But even if these were right in
detail, one would not be able for this reason to make the whole
exposition of the Old Testament into typological exegesis, as von
Rad proposes in his well-known essay "Typological Interpretation of the Old Testament."[30] Unfortunately, we cannot go in
detail into his very important arguments. Basically, however, both
Elliger and von Rad probably mean something rather different

---

[25] In a critic otherwise so sober as Baumgärtel it is surprising to find the
assertion that this requirement, so well known from the dialectical theology,
is a basic duty of all serious exegesis; see "The Hermeneutical Problem
of the Old Testament," above, p. 146.

[26] Cf. Amsler's essay cited above.

[27] "The Hermeneutical Problem of the Old Testament," above, pp. 143 f.

[28] Cf. the latest attempt in this direction in the exposition of the story
of Jacob in Gen. 32:22 ff., in ZThK, 48 (1951), pp. 1 ff.

[29] *Les Harmonies des deux Testaments* (1949), pp. 93 f.

[30] See above, pp. 17 ff.

from typology as I have defined it. They mean the working out of the structural relatedness in the experience of God in the Old and New Testaments, by virtue of which God's action in his community pursues the same goals in each case and illuminates the one covenant through the other. This seems at least to be the idea indicated by von Rad's treatment of Genesis in his commentary. Baumgärtel put this kind of exegesis under the general heading of "the fundamental promise of God"; Jepsen finds this definition too narrow and would prefer to choose as basic theme the Old Testament history as God's history with Israel, directed toward Christ. Probably we need to emphasize still more strongly the decisive significance of the people of God in both Testaments in its vocation to living fellowship with God, and to characterize exegesis as something that proceeds from the analogy of faith or the analogy of communication. However this may be, typology will play only an ancillary part in it, but within this ancillary position will not be unworthy of appropriate exegesis.

12.

THE SCIENTIFIC STUDY OF THE OLD TESTAMENT

by Alfred Jepsen

*translated by John Bright**

No attempt can be made in the pages that follow to deal with the problem of scientific study as such, or even with that of theological science in particular; our only concern will be to consider what relevance the scientific study of the Old Testament really has, and how such a thing is at all possible.[1] You will perhaps ask whether that is altogether a serious question. So I must explain how I happened to arrive at it. The University of Greifswald has celebrated its five-hundredth anniversary, and in the *Festschrift* prepared for the occasion, treatments of the most outstanding figures in the university's history were to be included. Among the theologians the name of Julius Wellhausen was not to be omitted, for Wellhausen was professor of theology at Greifswald from 1872 until 1882, and it was during this interval that he wrote his basic works on the literature and history of Israel: *Die Komposition des Hexateuch;* the fourth edition of Bleek's *Einleitung; Geschichte Israels,* Vol. I (later the *Prolegomena*); and his preliminary sketch of the history of Israel. But this very man, who had given such a decisive impulse to the scientific study of the Old Testament, in 1882 withdrew on his own initiative from the theological faculty and transferred to

---

* I wish to thank Mr. Hans Engler for checking my translation at various points and making a number of helpful suggestions.

[1] Guest lecture, delivered before the theological faculty at Heidelberg on January 25, 1957. The lecture, which had to be drastically abridged, is here given in the form originally intended, but without surrendering the style of oral delivery. As a result of this, an exhaustive discussion of the vast literature, for example with regard to the significance and the interpretation of the Old Testament, could not be carried through. The whole seeks only to review the current debate with regard to the Old Testament at a certain definite point, without attempting in every paragraph to say something new.

Halle as extraordinary professor of Semitic languages. He explained his action as follows: "I became a theologian because I was interested in the scientific treatment of the Bible; it has only gradually dawned upon me that a professor of theology likewise has the practical task of preparing students for service in the Evangelical Church, and that I was not fulfilling this practical task, but rather, in spite of all reserve on my part, was incapacitating my hearers for their office."[2]

With these words Wellhausen placed the "scientific" treatment of the Bible and the practical task of preparing students for service in the Evangelical Church over against one another, and came to the opinion that he was, through his scientific treatment of the Bible, rendering his hearers unfit for their future office. He thus believed that he detected a contradiction between scientific study and practice, or perhaps, to put it more clearly, he came to the opinion that his scientific treatment of the Bible was not theology in the sense of a preparation for the ministerial office. So he felt himself inwardly constrained to leave the theological faculty.

The biographical problem that emerges here must be left to one side.[3] But the material question that this raises surely demands an answer. Is it really true that a scientific treatment of the Bible, by which Wellhausen meant a historical treatment, and theology as an equipment for the ecclesiastical office[4] are mutually exclusive? Wellhausen's predecessors from de Wette, through Vatke, down to Graf and Kuenen, were theologians; his pupils— and that would be the vast majority of theologians—remained theologians. Should one, then, perhaps say that it was Wellhausen alone who was mistaken, or that it was only he who could not lay a bridge between "scientific study" and "practice," as his predecessors and followers were apparently able to do without difficulty?

---

[2] Cf. the full text of the letter in the article "Wellhausen in Greifswald," *Festschrift der Universität Greifswald*, Vol. II (1956), pp. 47 ff.

[3] On this point, see the article cited in note 2.

[4] The relationship of theology and church has not been unambiguously clarified. Cf., for example, the remarks of O. Dibelius, H. Stephan, R. Hermann, J. Schniewind, and others in ThLZ (1947), cols. 157 ff.; also H. Diem, *Theologie als kirchliche Wissenschaft* (1951).

If the gravity of this question was not at once observed in the years that followed, the reason for this lay in the fact that history dominated theology in general. This was the period in which Adolf von Harnack, for example, attempted by means of rigorous historical research to assure the scientific character of theological studies. But the historical treatment of the Old Testament worked even more powerfully than was the case in the other areas of theology toward the isolation of the Old Testament within the theological sciences. Characteristic of the situation in Old Testament studies was Rudolf Kittel's well-known address on the "Zukunft der alttestamentlichen Wissenschaft" ["The Future of Old Testament Studies"], which he delivered in the Old Testament section of the Congress of Orientalists in Leipzig in 1921. Here he stressed precisely the point that the historical approach alone should no longer be allowed to dominate Old Testament studies, but that in the future another question, that of Israel's spirit, would have to occupy the center of attention if Old Testamen science were to remain a theological science, or were again to become such. These sentences which he uttered are characteristic: "I would lay more stress . . . on the working out of the specifically religious content within the Old Testament religion, thus of the very thing that brings our discipline into particularly close relationship to theology." "This assemblage . . . will have special understanding of the connection between our discipline and theology." "We set foot on ground that brings us in closest touch with certain branches of theology."[5] Thus spoke a man who consciously intended to be a theologian. One senses from his words how he was striving to establish Old Testament science as a theological science. But even for him Old Testament science was something independent to begin with, which had first to be brought into connection with theology, and that by a new approach to the problem.

But even though this address met with great approval, its direct effects were not at once apparent. When Hugo Gressmann a few years later wrote concerning the "Aufgaben der alttestamentlichen Forschung" ["The Tasks of Old Testament Re-

---

search"],[6] he scarcely spoke of theology, but rather of the "one goal of Old Testament research," "the historical understanding of the Old Testament," and of the new epoch opened up by Near Eastern studies which would at last place the Old Testament entirely within the context of the ancient Orient.

No attempt will be made here to trace the further development of Old Testament studies in detail.[7] But two tendencies are clearly recognizable. The first of these is the work on the literature and on the history of religion that continues to be carried forward. However critically one may pass judgment upon the scholarly work of Wellhausen, his predecessors and successors, we have not gotten away from the debate with it. Just as little have we gotten away from the "Near Eastern epoch" of Gressmann, especially as the whole sweep of the historical and, above all, the religious life of the ancient Orient has become increasingly clear to us. On the other hand, there has been an ever stronger tendency toward placing the scientific study of the Old Testament within theology and toward the attempt to understand its significance for the faith and the service of the church.

The two tendencies run side by side, to a large degree independently of one another; yet attempts have frequently been made to repudiate both. Is that possible? And if the answer to this question is "yes," how is it possible?

Wellhausen could find no way of crossing over from his scientific (that is to say, historical) approach to the Old Testament to a theological one (that is to say, one that is of service to the church in its ministry). Does this mean that we must dispense with historical research in order to make a theological approach possible? Or is there a legitimate connection—in this case, one that is appropriate to the subject matter—between historical and theological research? Does not any theological approach to the problem in itself mean a perversion of the historical understanding? These are questions which a scientific study of the Old Testament has to clear up in advance.[8]

---

6 Cf. ZAW (1925), pp. 1 ff., when he took over the editorship of ZAW.

7 See now the description of this by Hans-Joachim Kraus, *Geschichte der historisch-kritischen Erforschung des Alten Testaments* (1956).

8 On the general problem, cf. the articles of G. Ebeling, "Die Bedeutung der historisch-kritischen Methode˙ für die protestantische Theologie und

1. The scope and content of any science will be determined by how one conceives of its nature. He who wishes to say what biology or the science of history or of religion should concern itself with must say what he understands under the headings: life, history, religion;[9] and in such a definition a prior decision is often enough involved. Nor is it otherwise in the case of Old Testament science. To be sure, if one takes "Old Testament" seriously as defining the subject matter of this science, the way in which one conceives of it is then relatively simple. For there is no such thing as an "Old Testament" except as a part of the Christian canon. Judaism knows of "the Law, the Prophets, and the Writings," or "the Law and the Tradition," but emphatically not of an "Old Testament."[10] The canon of the Old Testament was fixed (not created!) by the church, if indeed not everywhere in the same way; Old and New Testaments form the Holy Scriptures, the "canon" of the Christian church. Although the notion of canon may be loaded with a great many difficulties for the systematic theologian, the canon as such is a historical phenomenon, an existing fact that has merely to be noted.

And the Old Testament belongs to this canon. There must, therefore, be a science that concerns itself with this part of the Christian canon as such. Old Testament science, consequently, has to do with the study of this part of the Christian canon.

With that, a firm starting point has been won, from which it at once becomes clear that such a science belongs within theology, insofar as the latter has itself to do with the Word of God as witnessed to in the canon of Holy Scripture. Indeed, this science is therewith also given a definite task and a content which is worth reflecting upon afresh.

This starting point is not new. Martin Kähler expressed the same sentiments with all possible emphasis when he wrote:[11]

Kirche," ZThK (1950), pp. 1 ff.; E. Dinkler, "Bibelautorität und Bibelkritik," *ibid.*, pp. 70 ff.

[9] The logical circle involved in all such conceptual definitions need not be discussed here. As regards one particular area, cf. for example, Joachim Wach, *Religionswissenschaft* (1924).

[10] The fact that the name is also used by Jewish scholars does not in principle remove the distinction.

[11] *Wissenschaft von der christlichen Lehre* (2nd ed.), p. 38.

"The church's knowledge of Scripture is not, and cannot be, mere knowledge of Israelite and early Christian literature and history, but must be and remain a science of the canon, that is, of the enduring and ever dynamic historic fact of the Bible. For this reason, it requires the closest possible relationship with the other branches of theology; and this very thing will prevent it from becoming confused with allied, non-theological fields, however freely it may make use of all avenues of learning and all the results of relevant philological and historical research."

But with such a point of departure is not scientific study as a matter of course guided into fixed paths which restrict the freedom of research? Certainly such a scientific study is to be distinguished from an examination of the political and religious history of Israel and its literary remains. This area of inquiry, which has in view the whole of Israelite and Jewish literature and history, also has its place. But even though both areas of inquiry draw in part upon the same sources, a science of the Old Testament has another goal. For it has to do just with the canon of the church, thus with the Scriptures which (along with those of the New Testament) say something to the church concerning God, or which bring the Word of God itself through which the church apprehends the divine revelation. This of course presents a special area of inquiry, yet at the same time, as will become apparent, without prejudicing the freedom of research in any way. It is, to be sure, true that a science of the Old Testament, as a theological science, participates in the presupposition of all theological science, the prior decision of the Christian and the theologian without which no theology is possible, namely, the acceptance of the belief that God speaks through the Word of Scripture. But this belief does not restrict research, but releases it.

If Old Testament science has to do with the canon of the church, then the scope of its sources is clearly defined, at least in principle. What is to be treated is what is canonical and, indeed, canonical in the church. A difficulty arises here in that the Christian churches are not at one in the delineation of canonical Scriptures. To which delineation shall one adhere: that of the Reformed, or the Lutheran, or the Catholic, or, for that matter, the Ethiopian Church? Two possibilities present themselves. The first would be a purely historical delineation. In this case, all writings would have to be treated which are regarded as canonical by any one of the churches, only with a certain gradation:

(a) Writings that are recognized by all churches,
(b) Writings that are recognized by many churches,
(c) Writings that are recognized by a few churches.

This delineation would have the advantage that all books which have enjoyed canonical recognition within the Christian churches would be taken into consideration. Moreover, a necessary presupposition would thereby be provided for the history of the church in which these writings have been more or less widely diffused and regarded as canonical. But it is a question if the other possibility, namely, of delimiting the material, would not be more appropriate. Theology is not—at least it is not at the present—generally Christian, but confessional, in its orientation. Must not a science of the Old Testament, which proposes to be a theological science, be conformable to its church, that is to say, must it not deal with the writings that are recognized by its church? That would provide the Catholic theologian with clearly defined limits, since he is bound by the doctrinal decision of the Council of Trent regarding the scope of the Old Testament. The same would be true of the Reformed theologian, for whom the Masoretic collection is Holy Scripture. The decision would be somewhat more difficult for the Lutheran theologian, since for him, in spite of numerous controversies regarding the Apocrypha, an unambiguous doctrinal decision is lacking. But in Luther's Bible the "Apocrypha" is present and, if not to be as highly regarded as the Holy Scriptures, is nevertheless useful and good to read—which means, no doubt, useful and good for the edification of the community. So the Lutheran theologian ought probably to treat all the writings contained in Luther's Bible and read in his church, but with all emphasis upon the distinction that exists.

If the subject matter and the scope of Old Testament science are stated in this way, then the area of inquiry and the goal of that science have been defined. All science wishes to know what "it" is, how "it" comes or has come into being, and for what purpose "it" exists. A science of the canon of the Old Testament wishes to know what this canon really is—or rather, says—how it came into being as a canon, and for what purpose it is "there" as a canon.

To be sure, these questions cannot be so neatly separated as to be laid alongside of one another, as was just done. The understanding of what is in the canon is dependent upon a knowledge of the age in which and for which it was spoken. We must know history in order rightly to fix the setting of a text and understand it; but we can only comprehend and describe history when we have already rightly understood the sources, that is to say, the texts. Out of a better knowledge of history there grows a better understanding of the texts[12] and, vice versa, out of a better exegesis of the text there grows a more accurate knowledge of history. But the question of the significance of the canon also is not to be severed from the other questions; it is likewise a presupposition as well as a result of interpretation. If, therefore, these questions are taken up seriatim, that is only a makeshift. It must be kept steadily in mind that each area of inquiry fructifies the others.

2. In principle, the first question must of course be: What is really in the canon? How is it to be understood? As long as I do not understand what is said, no fixing of the material in its historical setting, and no objective evaluation of it, is possible. But how is one rightly to understand? Here, too, one must proceed from the fact that the subject matter of this science is the canon, that is to say, the Scripture in which the church knows itself to be "in some way" addressed by God. But it is precisely because of this that a Protestant Old Testament science is bound to listen closely to what is actually said here. Churches for which dogma is fixed through the decisions of ecumenical councils or through the doctrinal authority of the Pope can even permit allegorical interpretations alongside of the verbal.

---

[12] As one example among many, cf. the Babylonian Chronicle and 2 Kings 23:29.

A church that bases itself solely upon Scripture must listen carefully to the Word of Scripture if it does not wish to fall prey to caprice. But that means that a theological interpretation of this kind, which is directed at the Word of God in the canon, does not exclude the so-called "historico-critical interpretation," but includes it. What this last is properly concerned with was long ago formulated with all clarity by Luther, when he said, for example, in his preface to the prophet Isaiah:[13] "Whoever would read the holy prophet Isaiah to advantage, and the better understand him, let him not despise this advice and counsel of mine: First, that he not leap over the title or beginning of this book, from which he can understand in the best way possible how to read. . . . For this same title is to be regarded very much as a commentary and a light upon the entire book. . . . But I do not mean or ask merely that you read and understand the words of the title: Uzziah, Jotham, Ahaz, Hezekiah, kings of Judah, etc. But take to yourself the last book of Kings and the last book of Chronicles, digest the same well, especially the history, discourses, and incidents as they took place under the kings who are named in the title, and so on down to the end of the same books.

"For it is necessary, if one wishes to understand the prophecy, that one know how things stood in the land, how matters were disposed in it; what the mind of the people was, what plans they had with or against their neighbors, friends, and foes; and especially what their attitude was in their land regarding God, the prophet and his word, the worship of God or idolatry. . . . In addition, it would also be well that one should know how the countries were situated with regard to one another, so that the strange, foreign words and names do not prove annoying to read, or create confusion or a hindrance to the understanding. And in order that I may do my simple fellow Germans a service in this regard, I will briefly indicate the territory that lies around Jerusalem and Judah, in which Isaiah lived and preached, in order that they may all the better see where the prophet turned, when he prophesied, whether at midday or midnight, etc."

---

[13] Preface to the Prophet Isaiah of 1528, Niemeyer-Bindseil, VII, pp. 342 ff.

Or more tersely, but perhaps even more impressively, in the Prooemium of the Isaiah lecture of 1527:[14] *"Ad enarrandum prophetam opus est duplici cognicione. Prima Grammatica, et haec potest ut potentissima haberi. Altera magis necessaria, videlicet cognicio historiae. . . . Habita igitur primum grammatica, mox eundum est ad historias, videlicet, quid fecerint reges illi, sub quibus prophetavit Esaias, et haec diligenter perspiciendae ac perscrutandae."*

To be sure, that does not say all that might be said about Luther (see below), but his theological view of the Old Testament included a grammatical and historical clarification as the necessary basis of any right understanding. And, one could scarcely state the demand more clearly than he did when he said that each text is to be explained only in the light of its historical setting, indeed that history is even more necessary than grammar! This extreme way of putting it shows the importance that Luther accorded to a historical interpretation. Over against all attempts to bring historical and theological interpretation into opposition to one another, it cannot be stressed strongly enough that theological interpretation in the Reformation sense includes a grammatical and historical interpretation with all of its consequences. Theological interpretation cannot be something that is added to the purely historical as something foreign, something that elevates it, but rather is what makes the true historical sense apparent.

It is around this last sentence that the current discussion regarding the interpretation of Scripture revolves. That grammatico-historical exegesis is a part of such an interpretation, with all methodological precision and with use of all the helps that are available today, is uncontested and requires in this context no further discussion, provided only that it is recognized that a necessary foundation is gained in that way for a theological understanding. But that is the question: How such a "theo-

---

[14] WA, 31, 2, p. 1. "In order to expound the prophet a twofold knowledge is necessary. First grammar, and this can be esteemed a most potent thing. The other thing is even more necessary, to wit, a knowledge of history. . . . The grammar, therefore, having first been gotten, one is to move straightway to the narratives, to wit, what those kings did under whom Isaiah prophesied, and this is diligently to be examined and scrutinized" [free rendition by the translator].

logical" understanding can be gained without violating or adding
to the historical sense; how such a sense can be regarded as a
historical sense.

"Historical interpretation" as such is not unambiguously defined, for it is possible under widely differing aspects.[15] One can
analyze a literary complex such as 2 Samuel 9-20 from a purely
grammatical point of view, with attention focused upon the
syntactical rules of the Hebrew language. But I can likewise
analyze the unit from a literary point of view, with regard to its
structure, literary forms, and aesthetic beauty. A third possibility would be from the viewpoint of the historian, who must
examine the unit as regards its historical content and its reliability. All three points of view are possible; all three constitute
forms of "historical interpretation." But do these points of view,
and perhaps other similar ones, exhaust the possibilities of
historical interpretation?

Synagogue and church are at one in the belief that with all
these—in themselves possible and correct—points of view not
everything has been said that the unit intends to say. It does not
intend merely to report historical occurrences at the court of
David, though it certainly does that; nor does it intend to be a
masterpiece of ancient Hebrew narrative art, though it certainly
is that; nor does it of all things intend to be a model collection
for the study of Hebrew syntax, even though one can quite
legitimately chop it up for that purpose. For the narrator what
is essential is a statement such as that of 2 Samuel 17:14, which
declares that God plays an active role in all that takes place. Indeed, even a profane historian would concede that this narrator
was strongly influenced by religious convictions, even though he
himself might not take them seriously. Synagogue and church,
however, are agreed that only a theological point of view gathers
in the real concern of this text (and all the others), that is to say,
a point of view that regards these very statements about God as
the essential ones and faces up to them. If the synagogue and the
church see their canons, respectively, in the law, the prophets

---

[15] I take up here what is to me a very important thought of Bultmann's,
ZThK (1950), pp. 47 ff.

and the writings, and in the Old Testament, that is because they live from the faith that these statements about God, in all their concreteness and historical determinativeness, constitute the essential content of Holy Scripture, and that, therefore, only a point of view that takes this essential content seriously does justice to Holy Scripture. A theological point of view, therefore, does not in any way signify a supplementing of the historical sense, but is itself the only true historical sense; that is to say, it is an interpretation that corresponds to the intended sense.

Now with this, to be sure, only a provisional clarification has been arrived at. For what, in particular, is meant by a theological point of view? That the answer is not so easy is evident from the fact that synagogue and church part from one another the moment it becomes a question of defining this theological point of view more precisely. For just as there are in general various points of view, various possible ways of looking at any subject, so there are various theological points of view. The dialogue between church and synagogue is basically a dialogue regarding the right view of Scripture. Judaism, taking its view from the Talmud, sees in the law God's way with Israel and his instruction to her. It seeks, therefore, to apprehend the whole of Scripture in the light of the law, and believes that it has thereby arrived at the right understanding of Scripture.

The church contests this claim of Judaism. When it confesses "the Holy Scripture of the Old and the New Testaments" as the canon of faith, it sees the Old Testament in relationship to the New, and believes that only in the light of the New Testament, not the Talmud, is the Old rightly to be viewed and understood; one can, therefore, do justice to the historical—that is, the intended—sense, only when this relationship between Old Testament and New is seen and recognized. The dialogue with Judaism has long suffered not only from unawareness of the Jewish position, but above all from the want of a clear recognition of the true relationships between the Testaments—and that is to say, from the want of a true interpretation of the Old Testament.

One could set forth a substantial portion of the history of the

church under the heading: divergent understanding of the relationship of the Old Testament to the New. Indeed, every
conceivable shade of opinion has existed, from according the
Old Testament pre-eminence over the New, to asserting the
parity of the two Testaments, on to the subordination, even
the rejection, of the Old. The churches and sects often differ
from one another precisely at this point, a point which is at
times decisive for their whole inner attitude. Even today, almost every possible view is still represented, as van Ruler has
made quite evident in his survey, where he lists ten separate
views of the relationship of Old Testament to New, and that
without being exhaustive.[16]

Lack of agreement at this point has had far-reaching consequences, and a good part of the confessional dissension that
has existed has had its roots here. It is important for the entire
present-day debate regarding the right interpretation of the Old
Testament that this be clearly understood. H. W. Wolff has expressed it most clearly: "When the relationship of the Testaments is thus determined the special approach of Old Testament
hermeneutics is given."[17] Whoever views the relationship of the
Testaments as he does will not be able to avoid drawing the
proper conclusions. The question is not, after all, primarily one

---

16 Cf. Arnold A. van Ruler, *Die christliche Kirche und das Alte Testament*
(1955), pp. 9 ff. Is it accidental that none of the attitudes here adduced
can be viewed as that of Luther? Something essential is surely lacking here,
even though Heinrich Bornkamm's basic work on Luther and the Old Testament is frequently cited.

17 See above, p. 181; cf. also *Die Zeichen der Zeit* (1956), pp. 446-48. It
was only through my lecture in Heidelberg that I became aware of the
article of H. W. Wolff [see above, pp. 160 ff.] which was not previously
available to me; this lays in detail the foundation for his remarks concerning the typological interpretation of the Old Testament, which appeared in
Die Zeichen der Zeit (1956), pp. 446 ff. It is pleasing to see with what seriousness a new attempt is made here to establish the rightness and the
necessity of a typological interpretation of the Old Testament. Since this
is the most recent extended justification of a typological interpretation, a
few words may be permitted with regard to it. There are many statements
in it with which I can at once agree, beginning with the first thesis, which
declares that one may not tailor what the Old Testament has to say according to some preconceived principle, on down to the end, where the
never-to-be-surrendered significance of the Old Testament for the church
is underscored. I am, however, frankly dubious whether H. W. Wolff has
really succeeded in making the meaning and the rightness of typological
interpretation clear.

1. In his clarifying statements (pp. 181 f., n. 74) the concept of typology is
so extended that even Baumgärtel, indeed E. Hirsch himself, could use it

of the method of interpretation, whether allegory or typology
is allowable as proper means of interpretation; the question is
how the relationship of the Testaments is rightly to be viewed—
that is to say, how it is to be viewed in a manner appropriate to
the Testaments themselves. Only from this point can the methodological question of interpretation be posed and handled in a
sensible way. And at this point it becomes very clear that a
science of the Old Testament is only possible as a branch of
theology. As through its labors it itself provides building stones
for theology, that is, for a better understanding of the Word of
God, it stands in dialogue with New Testament science, with
church history and systematics, when it comes to determining
the right relationship of Old Testament and New. And it is at
this point that the unity of theology in the Reformation tradition must become evident, for it is a question of the Scripture,
the Word of God which is the basis of all theology.

Let us summarize what has been said:

A science of the Old Testament has to do with the canon of
the church, or better, with a part of it. If the church associates
the Old Testament with the New, that is because it believes
that the two in some way belong together and thus expound one
another. Old Testament science, as a science of the canon of the
church, must follow up this hint and ask how, from the side of

---

(if I name these two side by side, it is not because they belong especially
close together, but rather in spite of the fact that they have very different
concerns). Even Hirsch could say that the Old Testament needs to be understood in its own peculiar relationship to the New Testament; Hirsch, too,
confronted the question of what the Old Testament text in its historical
meaning signifies for the present-day hearer after the New Testament
kerygma has been placed beside it. So understood, all theological labor with
the Old Testament is concerned with typological interpretation. That is evident even where H. W. Wolff asks the question: What does typology signify
for the interpretation of the Old Testament? (pp. 181 ff.). For the "three
helps" which he mentions (heuristic function, the intentional posing of
questions, theological openness) come into play wherever the question of the
relationship of the Old Testament to the New is raised at all, even though
the answers given may be very different. Under these circumstances would
it not be better once and for all to get rid of this concept, so variously used
and, for that reason, ever and again in need of redefinition? Wolff himself
gets along without it in the first and basic part of his article; to introduce
the concept of typology scarcely gets us any farther (the less so, since the
concept "type" is only very rarely employed in the New Testament with
reference to its relationship to the Old).

2. To indicate the relationship of Old Testament and New, Wolff uses
first of all the words "correspondence" and "analogy," which in my opinion

the New Testament, the right point of view is provided for a full comprehension of what the Old Testament has to say. That presupposes, of course, a clear insight into the relationship between the Testaments.

Only from such an insight does there result the right theological point of view from which a correct historical interpretation is possible.

It would exceed the bounds of these basic considerations if I were now to undertake to review all the viewpoints that are represented today with regard to the right relationship between Old Testament and New; from E. Hirsch on to van Ruler there is far too great a number of them. But this may be allowed as valid: that the theological view that is best in the Reformation sense is the one that is closest to the Scripture; that the interpretation is the most correct that sticks the most unambiguously to the text; that the most appropriate approach is the one that allows the text to speak the most clearly.

In order at least to indicate in what direction the correct point of view may be gained, let us attempt by means of brief theses to suggest approximately how the New Testament looks at the Old.

Two things are to be recognized at once: On the one hand, for the New Testament the Father of Jesus Christ is the God of Israel, the God of the Old Testament; on the other hand, in

---

suggest more unambiguously the way in which he views the relationship. (It may be left open here whether the way by which Wolff arrives at the analogy is really feasible; it is precisely this analogy that the Jew would dispute. We can scarcely get around the historically conditioned context of the Christian canon, and only from there can we proceed to the question whether the Christian church has rightly claimed the Old Testament for itself. Wolff's [certainly correct] historical analysis of the Old Testament alone will scarcely convince the synagogue, since it sees the crucial point otherwise. But since I am in agreement with Wolff that the Old Testament yields its full meaning only in connection with the New, this question may be left to one side.)

Analogy thus means that in the old covenant God discloses himself only in a provisional way, illustratively, in passing, and that a way, shadows, a picture, and a promise are present in it. Wolff thereby recognizes, on the one hand, the complete distinction between old and new, the antithetical element in the progress of the dealings of the living God (ZdZ, p. 447). That would necessarily lead to the conclusion that this old and antithetical element had been superseded by the new. But in that case the Old Testament would be materially and theologically superfluous and would no longer be needed in the canon. Since Wolff does not, and cannot, intend that, he must seek something of enduring validity in a way, shadows, a picture, and a promise. This does not, to be sure, follow directly, but only indirectly by

Christ Jesus something new has taken place, something that is decisively different from what is said in the Old Testament. The first of these involves the conclusion that what the Old Testament has to say remains valid; the second, that a distinction exists between the message of the Old Testament and that of the New. In these juxtaposed statements the difficulty is comprehended; the Old Testament indeed speaks of the one and the same God as the New; it also says something valid, enduringly valid, about this God. But it says something other than the New Testament with its proclamation of Christ—something other, indeed, insofar as it discloses the presupposition under which alone the Word of the cross is to be grasped. "Presupposition" is naturally not intended here in the historical sense, however certain it is that the New Testament can really be explained historically only against the background of the Old Testament and of Judaism (the confrontation with Hellenism is merely a second step, which thus comes only secondarily into question where historical clarification is concerned); rather, "presupposition" is here intended in a material sense, and that in a threefold direction.

1. What kind of God is it whom Jesus called his Father? What kind of men are these whom he called to himself as weary and heavy laden, and to whom he sent his disciples out into all the

---

way of analogy. But if in the New Testament we have goal, embodiment, the thing itself, fulfillment, these expressions would have to suffice ; but then, what is the purpose of analogies which perhaps illustrate, but which can add nothing essential beyond this, as Wolff would have it that they do? For, as he quite correctly sees, without the Old Testament the witness to Christ is handed over to all sorts of errors. But it can only guard from these if it contains a message of its own which belongs unconditionally with that of the New Testament, without being identical with it, and yet which is more than an analogy.

Wolff arrives at this formulation of his because he proceeds from the thesis : We do not have an immediate and unbroken relationship to the words of the Old Testament Scriptures to the degree that we do not live either as Israel or in B.C. (ZdZ, p. 446). From this there follows the conclusion that the Old Testament has (only) an indirect significance for the New Testament people of God. But if the presupposition is really correct, has not the Old Testament been surrendered, since only Israel or humanity B.C. can have a direct relationship to it? What does "direct" mean here? Is it not precisely the belief of the church that it is only she who, through Christ, has the true, direct access to the Old Testament? It seems to me that, here too, a prior theological decision (perhaps one shaped by a Christocentric theology?) has determined the view of both Testaments, a view which after all improperly restricts the validity of the Old Testament. If the Old Testa-

world? The New Testament presupposes as valid that the one God is the Creator who caused the light to shine out of darkness, and from whom all good and perfect gifts come. The Old Testament witnesses to this God as the one God, beside whom there is no other. The New Testament speaks of man who is made in the image of God, and thereby reaches back to statements made in the Old. But the New Testament also knows of the fall of Adam, in which all men sinned, and Paul borrowed from the Old Testament the statement: There is none that is righteous, no, not one. The message of the Old Testament shows what kind of God, what kind of a world and humanity there was, before and without Christ. It witnesses to God's judgment upon the nations, as well as to his forbearance without which mankind would have been lost; it also shows how God held this very world of the nations in his hand, how he guided it and used it for his purposes. God's dealings with the world and with man, and therewith the entire destitute condition of mankind before God—that is the first presupposition of the New Testament.

And the second is that this one God has become manifest in Israel, many times and in manifold ways: many times in the course of a long history, to the whole of which, as well as to its individual parts and climactic points, the New Testament ever

---

ment can guard, and is to guard, the New Testament's witness to Christ from falsification, this is not because the Old Testament has indirect significance for the people of God of the New Testament, but because in the eschatology that is realized in the Christ-event, eyes are opened for the significance of what God, the Father of Jesus Christ, has revealed to the people of God of the old covenant. What that signifies in detail, I have briefly indicated above; it seems to me that greater justice is done thereby to the message of the New Testament as well as to that of the Old, because the unity in divergence (*Einheit in Unterschied*), to use an expression of Friedrich Brunstäd's, has been more appropriately preserved.

To be sure, with all of this the last word has not been said. H. W. Wolff is right when he warns that only an ever more serious absorption in the words of Scripture can lead to greater clarity. At the same time, and for the sake of the scientific study of the Old Testament, a new systematic clarification is needed. It seems to me that precisely at this point theology in the Lutheran tradition has to catch up a bit, even though substantial starts have already been made in that direction. To be noted, among others, are Heinrich Bornkamm, *Luther und das Alte Testament, passim;* the remarks of Arnold Schleiff in the introduction to WA, DB 9, I, pp. xxvii ff.; Schlink, *Theologie der Lutherischen Bekenntnisschriften* (3rd ed., 1948), pp. 187 f.; Rudolf Hermann, *Gottes Wort und Menschenwort in der Bibel* (1956); R. Prenter, "Die systematische Theologie und das Problem der Bibelauslegung" (ThLZ, 81, 1956, cols. 577 ff.); Walther Eichrodt, "Is Typological Exegesis an Appropriate Method?" (See above, pp. 224 ff.)

and again reaches back. In manifold ways through his deeds, God has acted in this history through gracious leading and hard judgment; through the word of the prophets, who accompanied and explained this history by their word, and thus placed it in the light of the divine Word, who brought Israel God's promise and caused the community ever anew to look ahead to the fulfillment of promise, but who also proclaimed to it the divine demands and laid bare its sins. If the New Testament reaches back to this history of God with Israel, that is because in this concrete, actually-having-occurred history, God's dealings were manifest; God so dealt with his people, his prophets, his priests, and kings. And, on the other hand, it is because the answer of the people of God is ever and anew observable here, in faith and unfaith, in trust and hate. In Israel's encounter with its God the whole magnitude of the divine leading is evident, as well as the human answer in all of its manifold quality.

And from these two presuppositions the third follows: The New Testament sees all the glory of the Christ-event, the breaking in of the new aeon, as already intimated in the Old Testament; the need of mankind, which roots in sin, as well as the need for an encounter with God, gave rise to the anticipation of a consummation. It is the content of the New Testament message that in Christ the consummation has broken in, of which the Old Testament had spoken in a promissory way, since all God's dealings with Israel point ultimately to this goal of history, and all revelation of human need and bondage points to a liberation which shall take place then.

So the Old Testament discloses why it is that we need a Saviour; the New Testament announces this Saviour. The Old discloses the goal and the future of the divine dealings; the New announces the beginning of this future. Since this is so, one would perhaps do better not to speak of the Old Testament message of Christ, but rather of its message that leads on to Christ.

2. These may be regarded as the essential aspects under which the New Testament views the Old, and they naturally embrace an abundance of particular relationships. But if these aspects have been correctly seen, the right theological approach

to the problem of interpretation follows inevitably from them.

This would then have to run somewhat as follows: Where and how is there to be found in the canon of the Old Testament the witness to this revelation of God which in such manifold ways leads on to Christ? This question is a very broad one, and yet it places what the New Testament regards as the essential concern at the center. It can even include analogies and types, and it does not exclude prophecy or even allegory. It thus comes to grips with the rightful demand that the principle of interpretation must not do violence to the text, but must prepare for the hearing of what it actually says. It can also claim to be in conformity to the canon insofar as it binds the Old and New Testaments one to the other, without doing violence to either. Moreover, it corresponds to the church's understanding of the canon insofar as the latter presupposes the linkage of the Old Testament to the New.

In all this, however, no violence is done to the message of the Old Testament, for what the interpreter receives from the side of the New Testament is the question, the point of view, not the interpretation itself. Just as one can approach the text with questions of a grammatical, aesthetic, or historical nature without falsifying it as regards its historical sense (to be sure, without exhausting it too), one can also approach it with theological questions framed in the light of the canon. The right question, then, is comparable to a dowsing rod which cannot, to be sure, strike water from every rock like a magic wand, but which can very well call attention to springs of flowing water. It must, then, be shown whether, and to what degree, the Old Testament is better to be understood out of the New than out of the Talmud and, indeed, whether from the Old Testament, when rightly understood, a clear light does not fall upon the New.

This approach to the problem, which is determined from the side of the New Testament, also has a "heuristic function," "promotes the intentional posing of questions," and "is an aid to theological openness"—things that H. W. Wolff claims solely for typology or analogical understanding. All three aspects come into play wherever a positive relationship between Old

Testament and New is recognized, and fructify interpretation.

It may thus be said in conclusion that the interpretation of the Old Testament, being the interpretation of the church's canon, is determined by its connection with the New Testament and by the questions that follow from this. These lead us to find what is there and what is intended in the context of divine history. To that end, we have to listen to the text verse by verse, chapter by chapter, book by book.

3. If Old Testament science has understood the individual writings and teachings of the Old Testament in this way, there next emerges as a second task the question: How did this Old Testament come into being? But for a theological science which has as its concern the hearing of the Word of God, why this second question? Is it not enough to understand? No, and for various reasons:

(a) We cannot withdraw from our times. Inquiry regarding history, regarding the origin and development of human society and culture, determines one side of our epoch, as technology does the other. Science cannot exclude from consideration the monuments of literature which have had such untold influence on the history of Western culture, but rather will seek to understand these also in their origin and development. If theological science does not grapple with this question, then other branches of learning will take it up; and whether it would then receive a better—that is, a more appropriate—answer is far less than certain.

(b) But it is not only for the sake of the general state of science, but for its own sake, that theology must raise this question. What is the nature of the foundation upon which its structure is erected? Is it sufficiently solid to be relied upon? It is precisely the science of the Old Testament that must, as a theological science, raise with all seriousness the critical question of the origin and reliability of the Scriptures.

(c) Moreover, it has already been emphasized above that complete understanding is quite impossible without a grasp of the historical context. A grasp of history is just as much a presupposition of exegesis as a result of it.

(d) Finally, there is a fourth reason, which roots in the peculiar nature of the canon. The canon of the Old Testament in good part relates history, actual history, as the place of divine revelation. The canon of the Old Testament, unlike the Koran for example, does not propose to be the work of a single man; rather, God's revelation is distributed over a long history. The words of the prophets are placed in the reigns of specific kings, indeed are in part precisely fixed to the year and the day. The Old Testament itself thus asserts that it sprang from this same quite specific history. It thus does not propose to be a book of fairy tales or myths, nor yet a system of the philosophy of religion, but rather in good part a witness to a concrete history in which God had spoken. Is that correct? What sort of history is this out of which the canon of the Old Testament supposedly sprang? Are not fairy tales (Märchen) told after all? Are there not many statements that are altogether unbelievable, such as, for example, the statement that there were some two million Israelites in the wilderness, or that 290 years before Abraham's birth a flood had annihilated the whole of mankind? Questions of this sort, which arise out of the canon itself, must be given an answer.

A theology that takes the Old Testament seriously as the canon of the church cannot evade the question of history. This, however, falls into two sub-questions:

(1) What is to be said of the writings of the Old Testament? What do they represent? Works of history? Books of tales? Cult rituals? Or what? And how did all these various sorts of writings actually come into being? At what time? For what purpose? This is the question of the so-called "Introduction to the Old Testament."

(2) What is to be said of the history in which, and out of which, the writings of the canon supposedly arose? Is it possible to write a real history? That is the question of the "History of Israel."

For Old Testament science both questions hang closely together; for it, the writings of the canon are an essential product of the history of Israel. To separate the two complexes of questions is again a sort of makeshift; they belong together, since both in the final analysis have to do with the question of how the writings of the canon are properly to be regarded, how they came into being, i.e., how they are rooted in the history of Israel. They are, for that reason, also mutually dependent upon one another; I can write history only if I have already understood the sources correctly as regards their nature and correctly arranged them in historical order. But such an arrangement is itself possible only if I know the outlines of the history.

4. In the greater part of its writings the canon of the Old Testament proposes to narrate a history, or to repeat historically datable prophetic sayings. To be sure, it is a history of a unique sort: "In the fourth year of Jehoiakim son of Josiah, king of Judah, there came this word to Jeremiah from the Lord" (Jer. 36). The course of human history is important as the time of divine discourse. That is what is distinctive about this history, that in it the acting and speaking of God is reported as the really important thing. But that does not cancel out the fact that this really important thing took place in the course of a history that is quite concrete. This two-sidedness of the history that is reported in the Old Testament is reason for a two-sided view of history.

On the one hand, we have to do with human history as it actually was spun out. If the Old Testament pretends to relate such a human history, history quite in the usual sense of the word, in all of its variety: political, social, economic, literary, and religious—thus, what actually occurred (as opposed to myth and fairy tale)—then this is an assertion that must submit itself to examination.

Such an examination is possible only with the aid of all the tools of historical criticism, such as examination of the sources, arranging them in their historical context, and whatever else the principles of historical science may suggest. No limitations or reservations can be made here; for the demand that the sources of the Old Testament be examined appropriately, in a way corresponding to their distinctive character, is not one that is limited to the Old Testament Scriptures, but one that is valid in the case of all historical sources. The Old Testament itself resists any attempt to protect it from such critical examination; for what the Old Testament has to say depends, on the one hand, on the assertion that in concrete history something has happened, which itself lays bare the ultimate background of history. And, moreover, no criticism has ever succeeded in dissolving the Old Testament into myths and fairy tales.

But even if the actual course of Israel's history is in good part recoverable, does not the undeniable fact still remain that even to a moderate criticism much that is in it has proved to be incorrect? Does not the book of Daniel have a false conception of the order of the kings and their names? And is it not demonstrable that a flood that destroyed the whole of mankind in 2454 B.C. is impossible—to mention only two examples? And is not the entire concern of the Old Testament, so far as it has to do with history, thereby refuted?

A science of the Old Testament may not evade such questions. It must recognize that the Old Testament's depiction of history cannot be maintained at all points (for the fundamental consideration it is a matter of indifference whether such points are many or few; the problem would not be alleviated even if there were only a few points at which critics were obliged to express doubts). But the same distinction both can and must be made here, as is to be made in the case of the world picture. The "world picture" (*Weltbild*) of the Old Testament, and of the ancient Orient generally, is not our own; it is antiquated in many, if not in all, respects. Nevertheless, what is said there regarding the "world view" (*Weltanschauung*), the judgment that the world is God's creation, remains unaffected. It is not the intention of the Old Testament to explain natural science. The relationship between depiction of history (*Geschichtsbild*) and view of history (*Geschichtsanschauung*) is analogous. The Old Testament has a very definite view of history, of the actual history of mankind and of Israel. Its view of this history revolves about the belief that God is the Lord and the guide of just such a concrete history. And that is why so much of this concrete history is related, because in it God's speaking and acting takes place. But this view of history remains valid even though in many, indeed very many, of its details the depiction of history may be in error. For this assertion is an assertion of faith, which can indeed be stated as such, but which cannot be objectified. Moreover, the establishing of individual historical facts does not lead to the establishing of the assertion of faith. If today we must view the incident of the year 701 B.C., when the Assyrian king Sennacherib besieged Jerusalem but could not capture it, as an established historical fact, still that in no way proves that it was Israel's God who saved the city.

To the Old Testament what is essential is the assertion that God is present in man's actual history in all of its concreteness. And that is why history has to be narrated, even when individual occurrences have been displaced in the narrator's memory.

Thus historical criticism, even when—indeed precisely when —it is carried forward with all seriousness, not only cannot at this point do damage to the essential concern of the canon, but instead makes it clear how much historical substance there is in the Old Testament. For it is well recognized today, precisely through drawing upon all possible aids including archaeology and the history of the surrounding world, that Israel for the most part possessed an exceedingly reliable historical tradition, substantial portions of which are preserved in the Old Testament. To be sure, all these historical insights cannot prove the correctness of the theological assertions; but they can show that these assertions stem from a definite history, and one that is in its main features recoverable.

If all this makes it clear that a science of the Old Testament must concern itself with the actual course of history, the question still remains: history of what? What history is the proper subject of investigation? History, like interpretation, has various aspects, and it is not entirely a matter of secondary importance what history I wish to investigate and thus include in my field of vision. I can take my start from the data that is available regarding communal and social life and seek from that point of view to unfold the course of history, or I can place Israel within the context of the power struggle of the day and seek to understand its history from that point of view.[18] Here, too, the question is whether there does not result from an understanding of Old Testament science as a science of the canon a definite angle of vision, which must surely prove to be useful in historical research. The historical problem of the canon, however, is this: From what historically comprehensible entity did it stem? Not from a single person, as did the Gathas of Zarathustra or the Koran of Muhammad, but from a society of a peculiar sort, which understood itself as the people of God, God's community, God's military levy, and which thus saw in its history a divine history. That means that one's view will be directed from the first at the history of Israel as that of a "religious" community.

Naturally, that does not answer the question whether "Israel" had always been that, or whether it only developed into a "community" (*Gemeinde*) out of a "people" (*Volk*). And just because this is uncertain, the view ought not to be directed, as was the case for all too long, only at "the people Israel"; M. Noth was quite right when he entitled his history *Geschichte Israels*, and thereby left it *a priori* open what this entity "Israel" really was. But, in any case, "Israel" was the society within which, through the mouth of the prophets, the Word of God of the Holy Scriptures, which leads on to Christ, was witnessed to and transmitted. The essential concern is with the history of this society. To be sure, this society always existed with some kind of political order, social structure, cultural relationships, and international connections. But as important as all these things indeed are for the history and the origin of the individual writings, and however closely they and much else must be examined, the real goal nevertheless remains the history of those circles and circumstances out of which the "Holy Scriptures" arose. That is the approach that is imposed by the Old Testament, viewed as canonical Scripture; and it remains to be seen whether this is not the only way in which the true nature of this history can be grasped, that is to say, whether this history was not from the beginning, and did not always remain, a "history of religion."

---

[18] See, too, still other ways of approaching the problem, such as that of Max Weber, for example, or even that of S. Passarge.

Most portrayals today begin with Moses as the founder of the community, and end with Ezra or Nehemiah as its reorganizers; but in between there is the "people" (*Volk*). Should not more att·ntion be devoted than there has been in recent years to the "community" (*Gemeinde*) in this intervening period, too? Let it be repeated once again: The method of historical research can only be one, but for a science of the Old Testament the questions posed, the angle of vision, can only derive from the canon, for Old Testament science asks after the history of "God's community," from which the "Holy Scriptures" proceeded.

5. But even when this question is being dealt with, investigation of the history of the Scriptures must go hand in hand with the investigation of that of the community. Hand in hand, because the one line of investigation is dependent upon the other. It was, after all, the greatness of Wellhausen that he related the history of religion and the history of literature to one another in such a way that there resulted from it his picture of the history of Israel. But however close their connection may be to the history of Israel, a special examination of these writings is needed, and here too the correct posing of questions is decisive for an Old Testament science which is a science of the canon.

If the "history of Israel" has to do with the native soil from which historically the "writings" sprang, so now also the question is valid for these "writings" themselves because, and insofar as, they are "Holy Scriptures." Thus the subject matter of this science is not "Israelite-Jewish literature" as such,[19] but only those very books that are recognized as "Holy."

To be sure, even the Holy Scriptures have a side that brings them into the closest relationship to other bodies of literature, especially to the literatures of the surrounding lands. This includes the forms of address, above all of poetry, but also the various literary types. This relationship not only allows, but demands, a treatment of these writings according to the methods of the history of literature in general. These are, for example,

---

[19] Cf. Sellin, *Einleitung in das Alte Testament* (8th ed., 1950), par. 1. It is perhaps better to relate the antithesis to the subject matter of the science —Holy Scripture or Israelite-Jewish literature—and not to method. Even a "history of literature" could be thoroughly "theological."

methods of literary analysis,[20] of fixing a piece in its historical context, or of aesthetic evaluation. As in the case of interpretation all methods of hermeneutics have their use, and as in the case of history all those of historical criticism have theirs, so in the case of literature all the methods of literary criticism again have theirs.

But just as in the case of interpretation it is a matter of posing the right questions for interpretation to aim at, and as in the case of history it is a matter of the right definition of the subject matter, so here too, it must be asked at what a science of the Old Testament should direct its gaze, if it wishes to understand the "Scriptures" as they came into being historically. Four questions are essential here, which may be stated as follows:

(a) What do the Holy Scriptures represent?

(b) How and when did they arise?

(c) How and when were they collected?

(d) How was this collection appropriated by the church?

(a) What do the Holy Scriptures represent? What was it, really, that made them Holy Scriptures? The various literary types are closely related to those of the surrounding world; wherein lies the difference, that these should occupy such a peculiar position? That is the first historical question that must be asked of Scripture.

It must, therefore, be made clear which of the literary types of the surrounding world are seldom or never to be found within the framework of the Old Testament. These are, above all, myths and fairy tales (*Märchen*). If one asks further why it is precisely these types that are not present, something of the peculiar historical character of this collection of writings at once becomes evident. The same is true if one then inquires what sort of narratives come to the fore in place of myths and fairy tales. These are sagas and legends,[21] often fused in a unique way, as well as portrayals of history. And here it is even more clear what constitutes the special quality of the Old Testament writings. They

---

[20] Whether, and to what degree, linguistic evidence is conclusive in such analysis must be tested in individual cases.

[21] The concept is used in the sense of Jolles, *Einfache Formen* (2nd ed., 1956).

intend to relate what happened, and that not only between men, but between God and man, in the course of human history, especially the history of Israel. It is, therefore, a question whether one can make do with the usually recognized literary types, or whether one must not for the matter presently in hand create more precise categories. If saga, for example, is an account of the life of a community based on blood, and if legend is an account of the life of a community of faith, then the Patriarchal narratives offer both conjointly. Neither the one category nor the other is entirely suitable. Or let one recall the discussion regarding the correct understanding of the primeval history: Myth? Primeval history? Primeval saga? However that may be, it is precisely a scientific study, which wishes to discern the unique quality of Holy Scripture, that must guard itself from an all too hasty use of generally recognized categories.

The same thing is true of the other literary types whose connections with the ancient Oriental world are a great deal clearer: e.g., sayings, such as legal decisions, proverbs, and prophetic sayings, as well as songs and Psalms. What made all these literary forms, or the writings that grew from them, Holy Scripture? What is the unique feature? For one thing, certainly this, that they have been given an entirely new stamp by a quite definite experience of God; for another, that these forms and these writings have also to a large degree been set within the divine history and in part receive their meaning from it.[22]

Thus inquiry regarding the "nature" of Scripture is closely connected with the approach of form criticism (*Gattungsforschung*), but leads us more clearly to what is distinctive in Holy Scripture.

(b) How and when did they arise? Here it is even more clear that a purely literary or literary-historical approach to the problem was dangerously wrong, since it could not do justice to the subject matter with which it was concerned. The writers of Holy Scripture were held to be men of letters and editors. That this

[22] Regarding historicizing of this sort, see K. H. Bernhardt's *Das Problem der altorientalischen Königsideologie im Alten Testament* (*Vetus Testamentum*, Suppl. Vol. VIII, Leiden, E. J. Brill, 1961).

did them injustice is widely recognized today, thanks above all
to Gunkel's inquiry regarding the "life situation" (*Sitz im Leben*).
This has proved to be extraordinarily fruitful and has, quite
rightly, been generally adopted. To be sure, it is hardly permissible simply to equate "life situation" with "cultic situation,"
as sometimes seems to be done. But in the present connection,
too, the question must be posed: What is the life situation of the
Holy Scriptures? That is to say, more precisely: When and where
in God's community, Israel, did the Holy Scriptures which are to
be found in the canon of the Old Testament arise out of the
tradition?

This question makes a presupposition: the existence of "God's
community, Israel," and the reality of its history, thus the reality
of a society which understood itself as God's people or God's
community. Here the history of literature builds upon history
itself. But assuming this presupposition—i.e., that the existence
of God's community has been critically verified—one's view is
therewith directed to the question of how, within this community, all the traditions assumed the form that they have in
the Old Testament. With that, there arise all the problems with
which the history of Old Testament literature currently busies
itself, especially the two chief problems: (1) How and when did
the "sacred" tradition arise, how was it transmitted, and how did
it become Holy Scripture? (2) How and why was "profane"
tradition drawn into the sacred and incorporated into Holy
Scripture? To answer these questions a special examination of
each writing and group of writings is presupposed; general answers are not possible, above all, not to the question of when
the transition from oral to written transmission took place.
Precise interpretation and analysis of the writings using all the
means at the disposal of the science of literature is likewise a
presupposition. But attention must remain directed at the real
question: How did the Holy Scriptures, in their unique character,
develop from the sacred traditions of the holy community? That
is the historical question which is to be solved through the means
of historical science or, more precisely, of literary science.

(c) How and when were the Holy Scriptures collected; how

and when did the canon arise? For a science of the Old Testament the decisive question here is: How did the canon of the Old Testament come into being? In connection with this, to be sure, two prior questions must be dealt with: (1) How did there happen to be a fixed collection of Holy Scriptures at all? (2) When and in what way did the Jewish community form and close its canon? Certainly the canon as it was delimited by the Jews exerted an influence on the Christian churches too, some of them even making it explicitly their own canonical norm. But that by no means took place everywhere; so the real question only begins where one usually leaves off, or where one states in a few words that the Christian churches took over the Alexandrian canon or some enlarged collection of Scripture. The history of the Old Testament canon in the Christian church has, so far as I know, never been written, though such a thing would be of decisive significance for a science of the Old Testament. To be sure, one could ask whether the bounds of Old Testament science would not be transgressed thereby, and whether such a "History of the Old Testament Canon in the Christian Church" (thus a companion piece to J. Leipoldt's analogously named work) is not the task of the church historian. But here again it is quite apparent that a science of the Old Testament, as a theological science, cannot and may not be isolated, but can do its work only in close co-operation with all the other disciplines.

(d) How was this collection appropriated by the church? As a fourth theme, Old Testament introduction deals with the history of the text, that is, it provides a survey of the textual tradition (manuscripts and printed versions), as well as of the translations, their origin and their value for textual criticism. Now the significance of textual criticism certainly ought not to be underrated. A science of the canon, in particular, cannot pay too close attention to the text in its attempt to come as near to the original text as possible. And every knowledgeable person knows that at many places it has succeeded with assurance in bettering a corrupt text. But, at the same time, one ought not to overrate the significance of textual criticism for the Old

Testament and for Old Testament science. For at many places where there is corruption, the situation is that, although a glance at the versions may well open up possibilities for a better understanding, real assurance is only seldom forthcoming, with the result that one can scarcely ever base an unambiguous historical or theological statement on an emended passage.

For this reason, another understanding of the history of the text seems to me to be more important for the history of the Old Testament as the history of canonical Scripture. All the copies of the text that have been made, as well as translations of it, were certainly made not in order to hand down literary monuments, but in order that the Word of God contained in it might be heard and passed on. Every such copy, and every such translation, is subject to human fallibility, such as scribal errors of various sorts, or simple misunderstanding. But every copy and translation is at the same time an act of appropriation of, and dialogue with, the Word of God set forth in the text. Many a copyist has ventured emendations because he believed that he understood the text more correctly than his exemplar. Every conscious revision of the original text signifies nothing less than an attempt to present the Word of God to the community in a better way. Just so, every translation, as well as every revision of a translation, is a witness to a living encounter with the Word of God; it is, as has often been emphasized, always at the same time an interpretation of the understanding that has been arrived at. That is true just as much of Jerome with his emphatic adoption of the Rabbinical tradition, as of Luther with his fundamental rejection of that tradition. This dialogue goes on until today, through all the translations and revisions that have been made. Thus the history of the appropriation of the Word of God, which may first be detected in the ancient recensions and translations, also belongs to a science of the Old Testament.

The Holy Scriptures which the church took over and recognized as canonical are the real product of the history of Israel. Old Testament science must in the way just stated concern itself with understanding the historical emergence of the Scriptures, their form—and literary history, their rootage in the historical life of Israel, how they were collected, disseminated, and appropriated. Here, too, the methods of historical criticism are valid, but the approach is determined from the side of the canon.

6. But even with this a science of the Old Testament has not finished. Its concern is not only with the understanding of all the individual statements and writings, not only with discerning their historical rootage; its concern, over and above this, is with the understanding of the Old Testament as a whole. For though the latter consists of many individual writings, it has nevertheless been brought together into the unit which is the canon. By what right? This question is not answered merely by our knowing how the individual writings of this canon sprang from the native soil of the Israelite community as sacred traditions. For however necessary for the sake of the Old Testament itself a sober historico-critical examination of the concrete course of history is, the Old Testament does not propose just to report this history, but along with this something else, namely, to show how this history is to be understood. A science that aims to comprehend the Old Testament as such cannot pass over this side of the matter. The systematic theologian may ask whether such an interpretation of history is at all meaningful or possible; the historian can only state that the Old Testament makes this attempt, and then bend his own efforts to tracing this interpretation of history in its context.

A serious consideration now would be whether such a total view must not be derived from the Old Testament itself and whether any other way of looking at it would not distort the picture. But from the Old Testament itself there could at best be derived a portrayal of the history of religion, based upon historical research, which places each religious statement in its proper historical position. That would still not lead to a total understanding of what the Old Testament intends, for the question still remains open whether the goal of this history is Judaism or Christianity.

But is there not the danger of distortion if only one given point of view is brought to bear upon the Old Testament?

What was said above is true here too: A given question does not carry with it its answer, but it can open the view for certain relationships. Here, again, the theologian who works historically with the Old Testament may not remove it from its context, the context in which it now historically stands as canonical Scripture along with the New Testament. It is only in its connection with the New Testament message that he discovers the "Old Testament," that is to say, the witness to the dealings of God before, and pointing to Christ, which was recognized by the Christian community. Whoever wishes rightly to understand the "Old Testament" historically as a whole may not remove it from this connection. Here, what has likewise already been said above must be especially strongly maintained: the belief of the church that in the Old Testament God's Word leading on to Christ is to be heard must also authenticate itself by yielding a total understanding of the Old Testament that does justice to each individual statement in it.

What does that mean concretely? We confront the task of grasping the essential concern of the Old Testament, in all its manifold writings, as a unity. The church recognized and delimited these writings as its canon because in them, according to the witness of Jesus and the Apostles, the same God speaks and acts who is the Father of our Lord Jesus Christ. And indeed he acted many times in a long history, and spoke in manifold ways through many prophets, up to Christ. Therefore the Apostles, and with them the church, saw the unity of the Old Testament canon in the fact that in it also their God, the one God, is spoken of. And what is said in it remains valid because the Christian gospel presupposes this God, his actions and words, because in the Scriptures of the Old Testament canon we are told what sort of God this really is whom Jesus calls his Father. The New Testament therefore sees the essential concern of the Old in the fact that it bears witness to God's actions and words in the history of Israel, in the course of which he discloses himself as the creating, judging, and redeeming Lord of the world, of man and his history, and thereby leads to Christ. With that, a science of the Old Testament is shown the direction in which it has to pursue its inquiry, namely, after this God who so discloses himself.

This witness does not rest upon abstract propositions, but upon a concrete encounter with God in history. That accords with the fact that the Old Testament itself first of all narrates a history, and that under a double aspect. On the one hand, this history is intended to be viewed as something that really happened; whether and to what degree this judgment is correct, is subject to critical examination of the "History of Israel." On the other hand, however, these same concrete happenings are represented as God's dealings. To be sure, this representation can in no way be objectified; but this does not cancel the fact that, for the history of the Old Testament, this is the real history, for the sake of which alone history is narrated at all. It provides the essential thing, the reality, that is to say, the real operative power in all happenings. God has acted and spoken in this real history: That is the decisive statement. And the community ever and again made new attempts to testify to this true reality of history, from the author of the Court History of David, through the Yahwist, P, and the Deuteronomist, on down to the Chronicler. Always the one goal was in view, to come to grips with him who is the true context of history, the Lord of actual history.

But if the New Testament in its approach to the Old Testament always reaches back to this historical reality as the essential thing, and if the Old Testament to a preponderant degree narrates God's history, should not one regard this assertion about divine history as fundamental when it comes to setting forth the real concern of the Old Testament?

Such an exposition would then have to deal seriatim with the following points:

(a) The presupposition of all history,
(b) The course of all history,
(c) The goal of all history.

It would have to be demonstrated whether or not all statements, even those of the books that are not properly historical, can be fitted into this arrangement.

(a) The Old Testament's portrayal of history begins with statements which are not properly history, but which do indeed indicate the presupposition of all history, when man is first assigned his place in God's creation, and when it is then told how he forfeited that place. It is clear that both statements have their meaning only as the beginning of all history. "Creation" in the Old Testament seldom has importance in its own right; for the most part it indicates the power of God over history. As Creator of the world he is Lord of history; or, still better, vice versa: He alone is the Lord of history, and for that reason he alone is the Creator. Belief in the Creator in the Old Testament has its significance only in connection with the God who is powerful in history.[23] And the same is true of the account of the Fall. Here too, it is not a question of a "Doctrine of Fallen Man," but of the portrayal of man as he sought to take his history into his own hands. Only as a presupposition for the entire portrayal of history that follows do these narratives make sense at this place. Thus even these introductory chapters, and all other statements in the Old Testament regarding Creation and Fall that correspond to them, stand in the closest connection with history, as the presupposition of all history.

(b) Following what the Old Testament has to say regarding the presupposition of all history, what it has to say of the course of history is to be dealt with. Here the essential thing is that mankind and all its peoples, as well as individuals, have always in their history to do with the one God, whether they know it or not.

What does that mean: to have to do in history with the one God? The Old Testament makes that evident in that it narrates first of all a history, beginning with Noah and Abraham and carrying on to the destruction of Jerusalem and the reorganization of the community. This history, quite concretely intended, but interwoven with God's words and deeds, is the one concern of the Old Testament. For this reason, a portrayal of the

---

[23] Cf., for example, von Rad, "Das theologische Problem des alttestament-liche Schöpfungsglaubens" (BZAW, 66, 1936, pp. 138-47), reprinted in *Gesammelte Studien zum Alten Testament* (1958) ; Rolf Rendtorff, "Die theologische Stellung des Schöpfungsglaubens bei Deuterojesaia" (ZThK, 51, p. 3).

essential content of the Old Testament may not pass over this view of history, but must grasp and reproduce its peculiar quality. One has to do here with the view of history, formed out of the experience of faith and the prophetic word, which was, as such, taken over in the New Testament, and which has been operative in the church.

But this whole history is still not merely an end in itself. In the course of this history that so happened and was so understood, God disclosed himself in his actions. And one must comprehend "what sort of God" it really is who reveals himself here. That will scarcely be disclosed in statements about his being, but in statements about his actions. What does God do? That is the real question that arises out of the Old Testament's portrayal of history. So then, the whole sweep of the statements which this portrayal of history provides regarding these actions of God must be brought together here.

These include the statements regarding God's election and deliverance, his promises and commandments, his concern and his help, his judging and redeeming, in short, the whole sweep of the experiences which Israel had with this God. For it is the meaning of this history and of its portrayal that in it the living God himself makes himself known. And even the words of the prophets add almost nothing essentially different; here, too, God's dealings in Israel and in the world of the nations is disclosed. That is, therefore, the second theme in the course of history: Following upon the portrayal of this history of faith is the portrayal of the divine dealings in all their manifold quality.

In addition to this there is a third theme. Not only are God's dealings disclosed in the course of history, but also those of men within this divine history. Every conceivable human attitude toward God is made plain: faith and lack of faith, obedience and disobedience, love and hate, fear and doubt, and even despair. The Psalms and Proverbs have to do with just this answer of men to the divine Word and work which had been experienced in this history. Even such statements as these are not disconnected from history, but sprang directly from the encounter with this one God. From it there grew the Old Testament's view of man which, precisely because it discloses itself in the presence of the living God, is one of the Old Testament's most characteristic teachings.

These, then, are the three major themes that appear in the course of history: (a) the portrayal of a history that is ever more deeply understood as divine history, (b) the portrayal of the divine dealings in this history, (c) the portrayal of man as he is revealed in this history. Through such a portrayal the essential teachings as regards the Old Testament's place in the Christian canon may be grasped from the course of history.

(c) There still remains yet a third major concern: the goal of all history. For the New Testament those statements are likewise essential which point toward a goal and end of history. And there are many of these in the Old Testament. To be sure, there is no "system" of eschatology; nevertheless, there are any number of passages that speak of a new world-period, a new covenant and a new spirit, a new heaven and a new earth, over which the community is to raise a new song. There can be no question of developing from such passages a coherent portrayal of the course of the *eschaton*. But it nevertheless must be made clear that God's dealings in this world, with this humanity, are not meaningless, nor is their meaning exhausted with God's judging and redeeming actions, but that these events press ahead toward a future which is in some way different, in some way new, and that locked up in this future is the fulfillment of history, its meaning and goal.

In such a portrayal of the "message of the Old Testament"[24] (as one would perhaps do better to call it, rather than "theology of the Old Testament") those things must be dealt with that are essential for the canon of the Old Testament. To be sure, many details of the history of Israelite and Jewish religion would be omitted, but scarcely to the damage of the thing with which we are concerned here. For we are concerned here too, and concerned just here in a decisive way, with the question of

---

[24] Cf. Jepsen, "Die Botschaft des Alten Testaments," in *Festschrift für Helmut Schreiner* (1953).

what really makes the Old Testament the Old Testament, i.e., makes it canonical Scripture. But that is God's history with mankind, leading on to Christ, as it is revealed in the history of Israel, the people of God. This history of God presupposes the New Testament as the disclosure of God; the goal of this history has drawn near in Christ.

7. The above may be regarded as a brief outline of the chief problems of the science of the Old Testament, viewed as a science of the Christian canon. It has become evident that no "either-or" exists: either a "scientific" treatment or a "theological" one. Possibly there can be a "scientific" treatment of Israelite and Jewish literature and history which has no relationship to theology. But such a treatment would ignore the "Old Testament" as the church's canon. On the other hand, there can be no serious theological work with the canon of a scientific nature which does not make room for rigorous historical research; but be it noted, make room for it, not exhaust itself in it. For, in the final analysis, all historical work on the Old Testament as canonical Scripture serves the aim of an ever better understanding of the Word of God that leads to Christ.

Have we then disposed of Wellhausen? Certainly not— neither with his character, the greatness and the sincerity of which was respected by everyone who met him,[25] nor, of course, with his work, which continually drives Old Testament science to renewed discussion. Wellhausen saw one side of an Old Testament science but, after all, he no doubt isolated it. This isolation of the science of the Old Testament from the other areas of theology did this science real damage, for which, to be sure, it was not responsible alone. A theology that was shaped by Schleiermacher, Ritschl, and Harnack could accord the Old Testament merely a historical, not a properly theological, significance. Thus it is a good sign for the development of theology that from both sides the attempt is being made to overcome this isolation. The gaze of Old Testament science is more and more directed at the real meaning of the Old Testa-

[25] Cf. Cremer's judgment of him in Part 4 of the article cited in note 2 above.

ment, the theological meaning, in order thus to grasp its significance afresh. But in the other disciplines of theology, too, the material significance of the Old Testament is recognized. New Testament science is learning more and more how to discover the material, and not merely the historical, presuppositions of the Christian message in the Old Testament; it has to describe more clearly than it has heretofore how the New Testament really viewed the Old. Church history pays more attention than heretofore to the significance of the various ways of interpreting the Old Testament in the church, and therewith to the effects of the Old Testament upon the history of the church. Systematic theology, as a result of the whole discussion of the last decades, is more strongly driven than formerly to deal not only with *de usu scripturae,* but particularly with *de usu veteris testamenti,* in which connection, above all, Lutheran theology too is in need of an impulse toward a reconsideration. Finally, that practical theology, and particularly the study of missions, cannot ignore the questions of the Old Testament, requires no lengthy argument. But, in this, it must build on the joint labors of Old Testament and systematic theology.

Only through such a continuing exchange and conversation between the various disciplines of theology can Old Testament science maintain, or win back, its place within theology. For only if the Old Testament is canonical Scripture does it belong in the sphere of Christian theology. But it can only be canonical if God in some way speaks in it. There is, therefore, a legitimate science of the Old Testament only if, even today, God still speaks to the church in the Old Testament.

13.
THE EVALUATION AND
THE AUTHORITY OF
OLD TESTAMENT TEXTS
by Franz Hesse

translated by James A. Wharton

I

In his Psalm lectures, F. Baumgärtel of Erlangen (for whom these remarks are intended as a seventieth birthday greeting) has returned frequently and with relish to the study of Psalm 109. As the fruit of these labors, he produced a brief article some years ago under the title "Psalm 109 in Proclamation."[1] In it, the reader will find hardly a word concerning the positive or negative value of this Psalm; when Baumgärtel speaks of "this prayer of revenge, so very foreign to Christian thought,"[2] this is nevertheless not a judgment of value. This could be said more readily of such turns of phrase as "terrible curse concepts of the Psalmist,"[3] "this Old Testament, unevangelical prayer,"[4] and others. But how reticent such phrases seem by comparison with the characteristic expressions of Rudolf Kittel, who does nothing to conceal his value judgments (or, more accurately, "no-value" judgments): The Psalm "stands under the spell of such strong passion, that our poem has become one of the most questionable imprecatory songs known to the Psalter, marked as it is by repulsive curses shot through with the fiercest vengefulness. . . . The carnal passion which invokes catastrophe, impoverishment, and destruction, not only upon the enemy

---

[1] *Monatsschrift für Pastoraltheologie,* 42 (1953), pp. 244 ff.
[2] *Ibid.,* p. 244.
[3] *Ibid.,* p. 246.
[4] *Ibid.,* p. 253.

himself, one of the godless who is an accuser, but also upon all who belong to him, *cannot* be excused. Let us openly acknowledge the limitation of Old Testament piety, when it is really there, and the shortsightedness of individual believers. Let us only remember that the piety of Israel and the Old Testament is not thereby exhausted, and that, thank God, we can also hear quite different tones there."[5] Gunkel passes a very much briefer but basically even stronger judgment on the Psalm: "A terrible imprecatory Psalm, full of the most shocking maledictions in which a wild fantasy erupts."[6]

At first glance, one intuitively feels moved to second such judgments; there is no doubt that we are a world away from such prayers of revenge. If I judge accurately, however, one can currently detect a tendency toward an essentially more reticent evaluation; people apparently feel a bit uncomfortable before such massive value judgments as those registered by Kittel and Gunkel. Conceivably, this reluctance might be based upon the dogmatically conditioned consideration that such terrible things cannot possibly stand in the Bible, which is after all the Word of God; that, in other words, what *ought* not to be *cannot* be. Insofar as this is the argument we can dismiss it and get on with the business at hand. It seems to me, however, that this is not the only, not even the decisive reason, for the discomfort which we have just described. Perhaps this discomfort partially motivated Hans Schmidt in his Psalms exegesis[7] to give a constructive interpretation,[8] one which does in fact remove every shred of offense, yet one which remains quite unconvincing.

Now the reason for this reluctance which has recently become apparent may not be sought, to be sure, in a discernment that it is fundamentally impermissable to evaluate Old Testament texts. A second argument could operate more persuasively: For an evaluation, a standard of measure is required; such a

[5] *Kommentar zum Alten Testament*, Vol. XIII, 1st and 2nd eds. (1914), p. 396; so also in further editions; cf. 5th and 6th eds. (1929), p. 354.
[6] *Handkommentar zum Alten Testament*, II, 2, 4th ed. (1926), p. 476.
[7] *Handbuch zum Alten Testament*, Vol. I, 15 (1934), *ad loc.*
[8] Artur Weiser follows it in the main; *The Psalms* (1962), pp. 688 ff. (H. J. Kraus also has identified himself most recently as a representative of this interpretation in *Psalmen*, Bibl. Kommentar, XV, 1959, pp. 746 ff.)

standard, however, must be in accord with the material; this means that it may not be borrowed from a totally foreign context. From this standpoint one could object to the above described value judgments that the standards used by the cited Psalm exegetes do not come from the Old Testament but from the Christian ethos; in the last analysis this entails doing violence to this Psalm and its statements, since the Psalmist cannot have known anything about the Christian ethos. If one should argue in this way, however, it would be altogether impossible to compare the ethos of any religion with the New Testament ethos, with that of the Christian faith. But who would want to forbid such a comparison and evaluation? The historian of religions, before whom lies the entire world of religions, will certainly not remain content with pure description in his field; but he will compare and evaluate with a clear conscience, although in so doing he will likewise lay a standard of measure, for instance, upon "primitive" religions of earlier ages which is not derived from them. Indeed, such argumentation would mean ultimately the end of all comparison, of every critique in all areas of life. It cannot be forbidden to judge (and where necessary to condemn) the ethos which emerges from Old Testament texts—among them Psalm 109—from the standpoint of a Christian or humanitarian ethos (or from whatever standpoint of the critic), just as is done in the expressions of Kittel and Gunkel.

The basis of this discomfort in the presence of such devaluating judgments can better be seen in the following necessary observation: These exegetes evince relatively little effort to understand the Psalmist in terms of his presuppositions and his intentions. One has the impression that the evaluation and condemnation have been done all too quickly. The exegetes would have done better, before passing such negative judgments, to have discussed the question: How could the Psalmist have burst out at all with such repulsive imprecations? Are there perhaps certain views or statements in the Old Testament faith and ethos, in Old Testament piety, which not only would open the way for the Psalmist's imprecations but would even make them necessary for him under certain circumstances? In the above cited essay, Baumgärtel has made decisive contributions toward clarifying our understanding of these curses from the standpoint of Old Testament piety, by describing the *locus* of the Psalmist in the structure and history of Old Testament piety.[9] Earlier exegetes were too little concerned about this *locus,* about the basis in faith of the thoughts, intentions, and desires of our Psalmist; therefore their value judgments may strike us as premature.

Even this objection against the negative judgments of Kittel and others, however, is not utterly convincing. Suppose that we understand the supplicant very well from the standpoint of what he believes; suppose, also, that we evaluate his imprecations as the expression of a terrible inner distress, and that from this perspective we would like to recognize them as thoroughly consistent, even though not inwardly necessary. Even so, to understand the Psalmist does not mean to excuse him. The investigation of the background of these imprecations in the history of Old Testament attitudes of faith by no means carries with it a consequent prohibition of every devaluating, condemnatory criticism of them. If for no other reason, this would not follow because even the Old Testament Psalmist is not *compelled* by his experiences to come to the sort of conclusions that we find in Psalm 109; other Psalmists, equally as threatened, did not abandon themselves to such terrible imprecations, but in the main rested content with lamentation because of the antagonist, leaving revenge to their God. But even if the piety and ethos of the Old Testament permitted such imprecations to appear possible, to appear thoroughly consistent—even if not perforce necessary —the fact must obviously remain that they are simply impossible from the standpoint of the New Testament ethos to which we as Christians are obligated. Is it not so, therefore, that we should not only be justified in judging the ethos of our Psalm negatively, but in fact be obligated to do so, however comprehensive our understanding of the *locus* of the Psalmist in the structure and history of Old Testament piety?

---

9 Pp. 248 f. (cf. footnote 1) ; cf. also the article "Die Eigenart der altestamentlichen Frömmigkeit" (1932), which is still unsurpassed in many respects.

II

Regardless of these considerations, we draw back from such an evaluation which is tantamount to condemnation of an Old Testament text. Why is this so?

In my view we are more nearly on the track of the ultimate basis of this reluctance when we have made a clear distinction between evaluation of a text, on the one hand, and an insistence upon its authoritativeness on the other. More precisely stated, a proper evaluation of Old Testament statements is impossible as long as the question of their authoritativeness is not raised and answered. Is Psalm 109, for example, still valid for us? Does it contain a Word of God intended for us which concerns and affects us? This is the most important question, one which must be posed and clarified first of all. In this regard there is no proper clarity among the exegetes mentioned above, and therefore their evaluating judgment is a rather problematical affair to say the least.

A comparative glance at the monetary system, where analogous concepts of "value" and "validity" play a decisive role, may serve to clarify the point that valuation and authoritativeness are not the same thing; further, that nothing binding can be said about "value" as long as the question of validity is not answered—positively. One can talk meaningfully about the value and value relationships of different coins only when the validity of these coins has been established. Now obviously one can confirm the fact that the *Reichspfennig* of our earlier coinage was of less value than a *Reichsmark*. So far as we are concerned, however, this is a purely theoretical observation, one which remains in the realm of the historical, one which in no way affects our present existence. I cannot purchase the least thing either with a *Reichspfennig* or with a *Reichsmark*. It is fruitless for me to note that, once upon a time, a difference of value obtained between the two coins, because they are both invalid. On the other hand, the difference in value between various coins of a *valid* coinage inevitably takes on a high, one could almost say "existential" meaning! Only in the case where the question of validity has been answered positively, then, does the relative value of specific coins have more than a theoretical meaning. At the same time our analogy makes it clear that a distinction between value and validity had better be made. The *Pfennig* of our present coinage is no less valid than the *Deutsche Mark,* but a great difference in value obtains between them.

When we apply this to our subject, it means that observations concerning the value of religious statements remain observations of a purely theoretical nature if we exclude the question of validity. Basically, however, we do not require any analogy from another area of life at all in order to recognize this fact. That should be clear from the following considerations. The evaluation of the content of statements in biblical texts in the way it has been done by the above mentioned scholars is a function of ethics; here the ethical "peaks" are compared with each other and the corresponding judgment is rendered. The ethos of a religion or world view which is not my own, however, has no normative meaning for me. Certainly I can think it over with a degree of benevolent recognition; I can express my misgivings about its lack of "loftiness"; but this all remains in the non-obligatory realm. The negative or positive value of an ethos alien to me does not affect me in my existence. If I raise the question of authoritativeness, on the other hand, there is first of all only the answer "yes" or "no." If I deny the validity of a religious statement, then the supposed positive or negative value of the ethos emerging from this statement no longer applies to me; if I affirm its validity, then the question of value receives an existential point. Now we will see, to be sure, that the evaluation of Old Testament texts which is possible (even obligatory) for us is by no means limited to an evaluation of the ethos, but also, and indeed in the first line, includes an evaluation of statements of faith. Basically it is true for the evaluation of statements of faith, just as for the evaluation of the ethos which proceeds from them, that we cannot make such evaluations before the question of validity has been posed and answered.

If we are reluctant to face the above cited value judgments of a few scholars (and any number of further examples could be adduced), it seems to me that the normative reason for this is the following: These exegetes have, in a sense, taken a second step before taking the first. They have evaluated, they have passed judgment upon the ethos of an Old Testament text without first having expressed themselves responsibly upon the question of authority.

Could it be, on the other hand, that evaluation and the authority question have been confused with each other? Could it be that these scholars believe that the question of authority is answered simultaneously with a judgment of value? This confronts us with an objection lying near at hand: Is it not actually quite obvious that the question of validity is answered negatively by a negative value judgment? A Psalm of the sort that pours forth curses without restraint, testifying to a serious limitation of Old Testament attitudes of faith, obviously does not apply to us! According to all that we have said, however, this is an erroneous conclusion. One cannot and must not decide the question of authority upon the basis of value judgments concerning the ethos of religious statements! The question of authority must be raised *first,* and indeed independently of any attempt at evaluation. Thus the question of whether Psalm 109 is still valid for us is by no means to be decided on the grounds of the positive or negative value of its ethos. We may not answer the question of the validity of any Old Testament text from the standpoint of the alleged value of the statement.

III

According to what we have said, we must answer first of all the question of authority. But just what is meant by what we have called the "authority" or "validity" of Old Testament texts? Specifically, in terms of Psalm 109, what does it mean when we say that this Psalm is still valid for us, or that it is no longer valid for us?

A religious statement is then "valid" for us when it contains a Word of God addressed to us, which involves us, which has us in mind, which affects us.

With this "definition" of validity, of course, we stand before the same dilemma: There is no scientific method by which the validity of a religious statement can be demonstrated. That the Word of the living God addresses me from a certain text, a Word intended for me in my present existence, calling me, judging me, warning, comforting, rescuing—this I can only believe or disbelieve. The assertion that a certain word contains the Word of God and as such is valid for me is not consequently subject to proof. It belongs to those statements of faith, none of which can be proved, but which constitute the presuppositions of all theological reflection and of all further theological statements proceeding from it.

Thus even the statement that the Holy Scriptures of the Old Testament are a witness of the divine Word to us—and that means indeed that the Old Testament is "valid" for us!—cannot be proved; one can only accept or reject it. The question of the authority of Old Testament texts must therefore be answered before theological reflection upon the text begins—more emphatically so before we begin to pass judgment on its value. It is answered in a realm that lies outside the reason and its functions —in the realm of faith. Thus it is a nonderivative decision of faith when we say that in the Old Testament (and Psalm 109 belongs to it) the Word of God is addressed to us, just as it is addressed to us in the New Testament. It cannot be the task of theology to offer grounds for this statement or to reject it because it cannot be proved. We can only affirm that anyone who is not able to join in this statement of faith (the positive answer to the question of the authority of Old Testament texts) simply has a different faith. When I answer this question affirmatively, I make a decision of faith; I can attest it to another, but I cannot demonstrate it to him. In the same way, he cannot persuade me of the rightness of his contrary decision of faith on rational grounds. Here, then, a decision must be made which lies on the same plane with other decisions of faith: e.g., whether I believe that God created me, that Jesus Christ is true man and true God, that he is my Lord, and so on. Of course, I can dispute the right of anyone who cannot join in this my decision of faith (the positive answer to the question of authority) to make any sort of binding statements concerning the value of Old Testament statements. This is so because for anyone who does not acknowledge the authority of the Old Testament for the Christian, the value of its statements of faith and its ethos remains pure theory, beyond any sort of obligation.

We are agreed with Baumgärtel that the question of the authority of the Old Testament for the Christian must be decided positively. This is something that he has stressed tirelessly in the course of his scholarly work[10]; in his essay on Psalm 109, also, there is a passage to this effect: "Nevertheless, Psalm 109 is witness to the Word of God addressed to us, and thus witness to Jesus Christ. This Psalm also . . . must . . . be preachable as the Word of God."[11]

IV

We have said that theology cannot offer grounds for a statement of faith. This does not mean, however, that theology as a science does not have the possibility of explaining statements of faith, of sketching them in, of delineating them over against other sorts of statements; this is precisely its task. "Theology is a function of Christian faith; it is epistemological work carried on within the church. This knowing is not identical with knowing God in Jesus Christ, immediately disclosed in the act of faith, nor is it identical with knowing ourselves or the world. Theology is thought about this knowing; it is reflection—and only as such can it take place in the form of a science. That sort of knowledge immediately disclosed in faith is for every Christian. Theology, on the other hand, presupposes the capacity for reflective thought, and is therefore not every man's cup of tea."[12] Thus it is thor-

---

[10] It is therefore incomprehensible to me that he has had, and still has the reputation among certain theologians (including some with leading functions in the church) of being a last exponent of "liberal" theology, which one generally considers to have been fortunately overcome, at least in the Old Testament field. Apparently judgment has been passed on him rather superficially in this regard.

[11] *Op. cit.*, p. 250.

[12] Paul Althaus, *Die christliche Wahrheit*, Vol. I (1947), p. 7.

oughly legitimate to think through the way in which the Old Testament bears witness to the Word of God. A simple identification is not permissible; we cannot make the formulation: The Old Testament *is* the Word of God, but only: The Word of God comes to us in, with, and under the Old Testament message. From this point we must then ask further, in order to secure a clear answer to the question of authority, how the character of the Old Testament is to be viewed in its property as "vehicle" of this Word of God. In this regard it is always a matter of the Word of God which affects me, not the Word of God addressed to the Israel of the pre-Christian era.

In attempting to describe the relationship of the Old Testament Word to the Word of God more precisely, there is one circumstance that must not be overlooked. We can make parallel statements concerning it: The Old Testament is the history of Israel from its beginning until the turn of the era; we can say about this history that the history of the redemptive activity of God takes place in, with, and under the history of Israel (and indeed in its actual course of events), and that it reaches its goal in Jesus Christ.[13] Just as the Old Testament serves as a vehicle, as it were, for the Word of God, so the history of Israel is a vehicle for that redemptive activity of God which reaches its goal in Jesus Christ. But these two circumstances are neither unrelated to each other nor parallel. The history of the redemptive activity of God, so far as the pre-Christian time is concerned, is seen in the first line as the history of promise, promise subsequently redeemed in Christ. Promise, however, has the character of a Word; accordingly, the redemptive activity of God is manifested, not exclusively, to be sure, but first and foremost in his promising Word. Again, the Old Testament bears witness to this Word of promise, so that the circle is closed and we can formulate thus: In, with, and under the Old Testament Word, witness is borne to the redemptive activity of God which finds its *telos* in Jesus Christ.

At this point a limitation must be made—the circle does not

---

[13] Cf. my article, "Die Erforschung der Geschichte Israels als theologische Aufgabe," *Kerygma und Dogma*, 4 (1958), pp. 1-19.

close quite so seamlessly as might appear from the foregoing. The difficulty lies in the following point: The Old Testament does indeed set out to describe the redemptive activity of God which happens in, with, and under the history of Israel; but the Old Testament witnesses have a conception of the course of this history which does not agree with the actual course, above all in the matter of the early history.[14] But since God's redemptive activity is bound to the actual course of historical events rather than to a history existing only in the conceptuality of Old Testament witnesses (a history which never took place), the Old Testament can bear witness to the redemptive activity of God only in a very conditioned, very fragmented way. Accordingly, that promising Word of God which is bound up with the redemptive activity of God, which accompanies and interprets that activity, cannot be read everywhere and in an unbroken way from the Old Testament.

For this reason also, in my view, the question of the canonicity of the Old Testament is much more difficult to answer than that of the New Testament. For the New Testament we have the clear and convincing investigation of W. G. Kümmel into the "Necessity and Limits of the New Testament Canon"[15]; but our dilemma rests in the fact that we can by no means simply appropriate Kümmel's central thesis about the canonical character of the New Testament writings for the Old Testament. The manifold witness of the New Testament writings for Kümmel has "its normative meaning for all time, not because it is to be found in the canon, but because it stands in a closer relationship, temporally *and* materially, to the historical revelation of Christ. It follows from this that the more unequivocally a New Testament writing (but also, in equal measure, a portion of a New Testament writing) points to the historical revelation of Christ, and the less altered it is by extra-Christian thought or later Christian disputation, the more certainly it may be reckoned to the normative canon. Whatever does not tell of this revelation of Christ and

---

[14] But consider also the substantial deviations of the Deuteronomistic presentation from reality, and even more so those of the Chronicler!

[15] ZThK, 47 (1950), pp. 277-313.

its meaning for believers participates in the normative character of the canon only in a very limited measure, or even not at all."[16] Why can we not appropriate this sentence also for the Old Testament by reading something like "God's redemptive activity until Christ," *"Heilsgeschichte"* or "history of promise," instead of "historical revelation of Christ"? Why can we not say: The more unequivocally an Old Testament writing (but also, in equal measure, a portion of an Old Testament writing) points to the redemptive activity of God until Christ, the more certainly it may be reckoned to the normative canon? This question may be answered in terms of what we have said above: The Old Testament indeed *believes* that it points to God's redemptive activity, even describes it, but the redemptive activity of God attested and described by the Old Testament does not agree with God's actual redemptive activity, as little as the Old Testament conception of the course of Israelite history agrees with its actual course. This may be the reason why our attempts to determine and establish the normative, canonical character of the Old Testament have not produced any satisfactory result. When, e.g., Alfred Jepsen says that for the Christian church we may define "Old Testament" as that which "presses toward Christ,"[17] he has merely stated a "formal principle," and a rather general one at that. This only raises the much more burning question of content—what is it in the Old Testament that presses toward Christ? As long as we do not clearly recognize that the Old Testament bears witness to the redemptive activity of God only in a fragmented way, we readily run the danger of establishing its normative character in a false and short-circuited way; but if we acknowledge this "broken" character of the Old Testament witness, then the proper determination of its normative character is very difficult.

For the same reason also, form critical work in the Old Testament and the task of making its results fruitful are faced with narrower limits theologically than those that obtain for the same kind of work in the New Testament. Certainly the Old Testament

---

[16] *Ibid.*, p. 309.
[17] *Kanon und Text des Alten Testaments*, ThLZ, 74 (1949), cols. 65-74, esp. col. 73.

has witness character, and an Old Testament theology that lays emphasis upon the kerygmatic character of the Old Testament is surely justified, albeit in a conditioned sense. Old Testament and New Testament are one in this, that they testify to a history of redemption; the one testifies to a history of promise, the other testifies to its goal and climax—the Christ-event. For the New Testament, Kümmel again has discovered an appropriate formulation: The normative proclamation of the New Testament "does not consist in a dispassionate, or even in the main simply narrative tradition about Jesus. . . . Rather, the fundamental proclamation of the New Testament consists . . . in the testimony that the man Jesus of Nazareth is Messiah, Son of Man, Son of God, *because* God raised the Crucified One from the dead and 'made him manifest; not to all the people, but to us who were chosen by God as witnesses' (Acts 10:40 f., r.s.v.). The New Testament writings are intended to quicken and strengthen this faith in the reader. Therefore the New Testament canon is not historical communication in its essential intent, but witnessing declaration."[18] Again, the question is raised: Why cannot something analogous be said straightway of the Old Testament? Does not the witness of the Old Testament intend to quicken and strengthen in the reader faith in the deed of God? We must take two things into account here: 1. While in the Old Testament timespan the redemptive activity of God, moving toward Jesus Christ, takes place in, with, and under the course of Israel's history, without there being a single event which is qualitatively inaccessible to historical research, the decisive event of the New Testament redemptive activity of God, the Resurrection of Jesus Christ, cannot be investigated and described with the tools of historical research. There is no earthly event here accessible to research which at the same time can be regarded as "vehicle" of the Resurrection event, in the same way that Israelite-Jewish history, happening in terms of earthly, human laws, is "vehicle" of the redemptive activity of God until Christ. While in the Old Testament, research into the laws governing such history can at

---

[18] *Op. cit.,* p. 295.

least smooth the way for the believing recognition of God's action (obviously it cannot quicken such recognition), historical research cannot do the least thing to prepare the way for faith in the Resurrection of Christ. This faith is absolutely dependent upon the witness of those who received *the* decisive revelation, beyond all historical experience. Therefore the witness character of the New Testament is constitutive for the Christian faith, something that does not hold true without further ado for the Old Testament. 2. Now we return to our theme: The Old Testament attests God's redemptive activity with the aid of conceptions of the course of history which in part are decidedly at variance with the actual course; moreover, the Old Testament witness to God's redemptive activity is a broken one. On the other hand, the witness of the gospel and the Apostles concerning the decisive redemptive deed of God lives from the fact that this deed also happened as they testify; the New Testament evinces a historical picture which is at variance with the actual events only in secondary aspects. Let us make this clear by illustrating with figures which appear in the Bible as prominent objects of God's redemptive activity. The Old Testament sees in Abraham the bearer of the promise and the tried and true man of faith. We cannot accept this witness from the Old Testament without further ado, because we know that this Abraham never existed in this way. The New Testament attests Jesus Christ as the center of the redemptive event. We can believe this witness without reduction because we know about the historical figure of Jesus of Nazareth. That Abraham did not exist as the Old Testament describes him can indeed be a stumbling block for our faith, but one which can be overcome relatively easily by theological reflection; if we had to say the same thing about Jesus, it would be a deathblow to our faith. The Old Testament testimony of faith is radically called in question on many sides by the results of historical research; the New Testament testimony of faith, on the other hand, is hardly touched by such results if we discount the rather marginal mythologoumena. Therefore the witness of the gospel and the Apostles has for us an immediate, inwardly persuasive power, whereas the witness of the faithful in the Old Testament presents a stumbling block at many points because of the fact that its basis, the historical fact which it presupposes, is questionable. Therefore, only the witnessing statements of the New Testament concern us immediately, not those of the Old Testament; because, to summarize once again, the witness of the New Testament is constitutive for us, and at the same time it does not contradict our knowledge of the contemporary events which "carry" the redemptive event; the witness of the Old Testament, on the other hand, does not establish Christian faith, but smooths the way for it, purifies and deepens it; but the Old Testament is subject to the stumbling block that its conceptions quite frequently run counter to the actual event which "carries" the redemptive history that moves toward Christ as its goal.

V

We must now show by another, even more important point, however, how complicated the question of the authority of the Old Testament is. Manifestly the Old Testament is by no means witness, in the first instance, of the words and actions of *God*. When one opens these books he reads in them about the words and deeds of *Yahweh,* and he reads even more about very diverse human responses to the words and deeds of Yahweh. We must pay attention here first of all to the fact that the witness to the redemptive activity of God of which we have spoken hitherto is not identical with the words and deeds of Yahweh, to which, at first glance, the Old Testament testifies. "Yahweh" is by no means solely and exclusively revelation of the living God, but often also mask, disguise. Thus not every word in the Old Testament which bears the formula "thus saith Yahweh" can be called a Word of God, just as little as every account in the Old Testament describing a deed of Yahweh's portrays thereby a deed which belongs to the genuine redemptive activity of God. Many a word of Yahweh in the Old Testament is only supposedly a Word of God; many an account of Yahweh's deeds given by Old Testament witnesses has little or nothing to do with God's decisive deeds toward Israel.

Even more to the point, however, the Old Testament bears witness to human responses to the Word and deeds of God, both to the genuine Word of God and to the supposed word (to the word of "Yahweh"); and again, these responses can be seen as either obedience to the genuine or supposed Word of God, or rejections of it. A large part of the human words of response does not attest the redemptive activity of God, but can run directly counter to it. Not every witness to human listening to the voice of God is a witness of right listening, of obedience; it can also be the witness of a false understanding, a response to a supposed address of God which in reality never went forth; it can be the witness of disobedience. Indeed, we must say it even more pointedly: Every Old Testament answer to the address of God, every later tracing of the ways of God, every description of God's activity in the Old Testament *must* remain inadequate, often also misconceived, even perverted; this is so because the faithful people of the Old Testament live perforce in a revelatory relationship which appears from the New Testament vantage point not only as provisional and obsolete, but as insufficient, even distorted. From the viewpoint of the history of religions, one would say: The Old Testament religion is something qualitatively different from the faith of the New Testament. In the faith of Israel and in Christianity we are confronted with essentially different religions; "the Old Testament is a witness from a religion outside of the gospel and therefore from a religion strange to us. Viewed historically, it has another place than the Christian religion."[19] The theologian sees this circumstance in the history of religions as based upon the fact that the history of a promise which is not yet realized is something essentially different from the history of the redemption of this promise; that the full self-disclosure of God is not yet made in the Yahweh of the Old Testament; rather, that Yahweh can often do more to veil than to reveal the living God, the Father of Jesus Christ. Here we are facing the situation which Paul characterizes by speaking of the veil that hangs before the hearts of those who read the Old

---

[19] So Baumgärtel in his lecture at the Berlin Theologians Conference of January 1954; cf. above, p. 145.

Testament without Christ—"because in Christ it is taken away" (2 Cor. 3:12-16). Quite apart from the fact that it ought so to be, according to God's inscrutable counsel, that Israel remain under the promise yet unrealized, not yet honored with the full self-disclosure of God, we must also see this: that man can easily control a promise when redemption is still outstanding; he can set as the goal of this promise, as the divine *telos* of history, that which corresponds to his own dreams, wishes, and conceptions. This was in fact the case in Israel of old, which had indeed received the promise that God desired to be its God, but which did not yet know the valid redemption of this promise, the Saviour of the world. Rather, Israel constructed its own conceptions of how God's salvation must be accomplished. The man who has been renewed by Christ knows, however, how the redemption of the promise really appeared; therefore, he can only see the thoughts of Old Testament people about the realization of salvation for what they frequently are: human errors, even human faithlessness, and therewith, human guilt.

This statement must be secured, however, against two possible misunderstandings: 1. It is not as if only a part of the Old Testament witnesses had fallen victim to such error, while to others it was given to be authentic witnesses of an unbroken divine revelation. Thus we cannot begin to distinguish within the Old Testament between words and portions which bear a fully valid witness to the Word of God and those which do not do justice to the revelation of God, indeed, which veil it directly. "With the *entire* Old Testament we are in the realm not of the evangelical, but of the Israelite *nomos*. . . . Everywhere in the Old Testament the God relationship is understood under presuppositions different from those of the New Testament; therefore, the Old Testament is simply not in a position to speak of the new creature in Christ as the New Testament does."[20] Each and every human statement within Israel stands under this omen; it has to do with God who is not yet fully revealed, and therefore it is basically not secured against erroneous conceptions of the will

---

[20] Baumgärtel, *Psalm 109 in der Verkündigung*, pp. 245 f.

and purpose of this God. This insecurity holds equally as true for the classical prophets as for the Chronicler; for the author of the 103rd as well as the 109th Psalm, although self-evidently differences are at work here which must not be overlooked, differences which must yet be discussed. 2. This error (even guilt) of the Old Testament witnesses *vis-à-vis* the divine revelation does not happen outside the will of God, and surely not against it. God has ordained that those whom he addressed should have answered in just this way, and not otherwise. Of course, this does not make truth out of their error, nor does it justify the guilty. God so ordered the course of history that there is a history of condemnation in the midst of the *Heilsgeschichte;* so that alongside the witness of truth there have also appeared erring, even lying witnesses, whose error and lying are not immediately perceptible because their witness often enough purports to be genuine response to the address of God. In and alongside the history of redemption, God has permitted a history of the hardening of hearts to take place; his redemptive activity toward Israel leads not only to the Crucified One, but also to those who crucified him. Because God's *Heilsgeschichte* bears this puzzling double aspect (indeed, from this standpoint the term *"Heilsgeschichte"* again is shown to be rather questionable; we retain it, nevertheless, because the cross, toward which the "hardening" activity of God among the Jews moves, does ultimately mean salvation for us); because God effects unfaith and disobedience in order to prepare thereby the cross-event, thus realizing salvation; therefore, we must expect to meet traces of this "hardening" activity on every hand in the Old Testament. At the same time there emerges from these considerations the insight that God is nevertheless totally present, even in the erring human word of the Old Testament, even in the witness of disobedience and obduracy which we find in the Old Testament. For even to those words which are recognizable as erroneous and guilt-laden, God binds a certain purpose for us which must yet be discussed. Even the Old Testament answer of men to an address of God (genuine or supposed) is full of the Word of God, because God has effected and directed this answer, just as it is, for the sake of the execution of his *Heilsgeschichte* to which this human answer also belongs. In every word of man written and spoken within the history of Israel, God is there. God is at work in everything which is done, thought, spoken, and written down in this history as the "bearer" of the *Heilsgeschichte;* even in that which is ethically question- able, even in that which is human (all too human), even in the so-called "sub-Christian" aspects, God's voice is there. In, with, and under all that belongs in the history of Israel, above all, the structure and history of its piety (and even Psalm 109, this im- precatory prayer, is part of this!), this history of the promise of God takes place, a history which also includes the erring reaction of men which runs counter to the redemptive will of God. Paul's discussion in Romans 9-11 shows that this view of things is not unbiblical, however risky it may seem at first glance. According to this passage, the history of Israel's hardening of heart is not somehow to be dissociated from the *Heilsgeschichte;* it is not to be seen only as a calling in question or endangering of this his- tory of redemption; rather the *Heilsgeschichte* comprehends also Israel's hardening of heart, because this belongs in God's plan of redemption, proclaimed through the gospel and the apostolic message. This may be incomprehensible to reason; faith, how- ever, knows the truth of this enormous, shattering circumstance, which confronts us with the majesty of the *deus absconditus.*

Thus the Old Testament bears witness to a "dialectic" re- demptive activity of God, in which a history of the hardening of hearts, in accord with the will of God and culminating in the enemies of Christ, takes place together with a history of redemp- tion culminating in Christ. The two lines confront each other in the cross of Christ. Now each one of the many known and un- known people whose voices we hear in the Old Testament must also be a witness, each in his own way, for the line of obduracy; not only in such a way that he knows of the hardening of Israel's heart and describes it, but above all, in such a way that he him- self in some way participates in this history of not understanding the true purpose of God—sometimes, indeed, also in a history of not wanting to understand it. He does this as an Old Testament man before whose heart a veil hangs, because he does not yet

know of Christ, according to the above cited words of Paul. But
as soon as we have called the Old Testament the witness of a
"dialectic" redemptive activity, we must immediately add that
the Old Testament itself is not recognizable as this sort of witness unless the eye is opened for it through the kerygma of the
New Testament. For example, Isaiah not only scores the obduracy of his people; he not only feels that the hardening of
Israel's heart is precisely his task; but he himself participates in
this line of obduracy in his proclamation (surely against his
intent), in that he depicts before the eyes of his people a Messianic age of salvation for the immediate future, which did not
correspond to the will of God; or in that he sees salvation as so
closely bound to Zion. We come to understand only from the
New Testament standpoint that throughout such prophetic
proclamation there is not only God's instruction, but also human
thought concerning the way of God with his people.

We have said that in all of this the Word of God is there.
Even the human thoughts which God has not acknowledged, even
the erroneous, even the guilt-laden misunderstanding and distortion of the actual will of God—all of this is witness of the
Word of God which also involves us, precisely us, only us. *This*
witness of the Word of God was indeed not yet recognizable for
Israel; not until the New Testament was this vista opened. Just
as the total history of Israel, as the history of redemption/con-
demnation, bears witness to the gracious and to the heart-harden-
ing activity of God, to the history of promise and to the action of
the inscrutable God who does not allow his people to recognize
the Saviour of the world, so the entire Old Testament, including
its human aspects, bears witness to the Word of God for us.
Every page of this book would say to us: Here you confront the
living God and his history which began long ago with Israel and
which he carries forward to its goal in Christ.

VI

Now by what we have just said we have apparently described
a Word of God from the Old Testament which comes to us. It is

a Word which indeed throws light on all sorts of occurrences, but one which in no way speaks to our present existence or lays claim upon it. We do learn (and even that only with the aid of the interpretation which the New Testament gives to this witness!) how God acted in the remote past, in the era before the coming of Jesus Christ; we do learn in what way he prepared his salvation and led his people toward it. But the question nevertheless lies near at hand: What does all of this mean to us? Is not our interest in these events only a purely historical one? Surely there can be no talk of an "existential" meaning in the Old Testament so interpreted. This witness can touch us in our existence at best only in the way any other testimony of a past history also does, about which we know that it partially determined and shaped the present event, whether directly or indirectly. Can this witness be of such great importance, however, that Christianity must retain the Old Testament on its account?[21]

This objection would be valid if the temporal category were adequate to determine the essence of the history of the activity of God, but this is simply not the case. Of course, we can divide the history of God's redemptive activity temporally into a pre-Christian era attested by the Old Testament and the temporally consecutive era which begins with what is attested in the New Testament and reaches its goal in the ultimate coming of the Kingdom of God. But this still does not describe adequately the essence of this history; one must immediately add that these two temporal stages correspond to two modes of human existence sharply distinguished from each other by a decisive event. The dividing line of the *"Heilsgeschichte"* is the full self-disclosure of

---

21 The same question is raised by O. Cullmann (*Christ and Time,* tr. Filson, 1949), p. 132, and, above all, on p. 226, and an attempt to answer it is made. The answer of Cullmann appears inadequate to me, however, for reasons which cannot be further elaborated here. This is shown in the fact that with his interpretation our participation in the redemptive meaning of the pre-Christian era of the *Heilsgeschichte* cannot be made understandable; cf. the section pp. 226-230. I would like to retain the term *"Heilsgeschichte"* with Cullmann, in spite of the partially valid objection to Cullmann's work expressed by R. Bultmann (ThLZ, 73, 1948, cols. 659 ff.). I do not see otherwise how we could affirm any theological relevance of the Old Testament. What Bultmann has said on this question in his essay "The Significance of Jewish Old Testament Tradition for the Christian West" (*Essays Philosophical and Theological,* 1955) seems insufficient to me.

God in Christ. It divides "Old Testament" time of promise from the "New Testament" time of salvation. Certainly the same event is the dividing line between Old Testament and New Testament man; at least one can say that before this event which has broken into the midst of our time, the existence of New Testament man is unthinkable. Now, however, we can say with equal justice that the dividing line between pre-Christian and Christian man is the personal appropriation of God's offer of salvation which is made in Christ, or, in other words, faith. Here we have moved from a temporal into an "existential" category. Temporal and existential dividing lines, however, do not stand alongside each other without mutual relationship. The Christ-event is to the course of the *Heilsgeschichte* what faith is to the man confronted by the salvation of God. The pre-Christian period of God's redemptive activity, in which the man addressed by God is yet moving toward the goal of Christ, corresponds to the man who has not yet laid hold of the salvation offered him in Christ, exactly as the Christian/post-Christian *Heilsgeschichte* corresponds to the man who believes. In the promise of God to his people that he desires to be its God, an offer was made to Israel. The Israel of that time could hear this offer, could accept or reject it, thereby deciding ultimately for or against Christ. In the same way, I, to whom the salvation of God is offered, can accept it or reject it and therefore also decide for or against Christ. We can say, accordingly, that the "Old Testament" man in the existential sense is the man indeed addressed by God, but not yet participating in full salvation—the man called to faith, but not yet in the full sense believing (according to Paul, man under promise and under law, Gal. 3); the "New Testament" man is the one who has spoken his "yes" to the full self-disclosure of God in Christ. The "Old Testament" man is the man still underway to God's salvation; the "New Testament" man is the man who has already laid hold upon it because God has laid hold upon him.

At this point it is valid to reflect that in the life of the Christian man there is no moment of grasping the salvation offered him in Christ which serves as an unambiguous dividing line between two modes of existence clearly distinguishable from each other in point of time. The Christian, *simul justus simul peccator,* always still remains an "Old Testament" man, before whom lies the appropriation of salvation. He can also go the wrong way in the daily situations of decision in which he is placed, rejecting the offer of salvation through unfaith and disobedience. Because there is no temporal dividing line between the two modes of existence, and because we are indeed always still underway as those who are called to salvation, as New Testament men we are always relapsing, becoming Old Testament men who act as if the full salvation of God had not yet appeared at all, or as if we could take possession of this salvation in a high-handed way. We are also still "Old Testament" men in our existence in that we are still underway toward the unbroken realization of complete salvation; "Thy Kingdom come" is also truly our prayer even yet. Thus the mode of existence of the "Old Testament" man is an inescapable possibility for us at every moment, and in part also a danger, quite regardless of the fact that the Old Testament time lies almost two millennia behind us.

Here we have reached the point at which it becomes clear that the Word of God from the Old Testament by no means proposes merely to inform us about the way in which God acted in the time before the full realization of his salvation; in the first line it proposes to call us and affect us at the point where we step back and out of our existence as "New Testament" men (as believers, and thus as those who belong to the new era) into the mode of existence of "Old Testament" men, which indeed ought to be abrogated for us. Baumgärtel has specifically and tirelessly stressed this "existential" side of the Word of God from the Old Testament—indeed so strongly that, because of it, the "temporal" line of the history of God's redemptive activity almost appears to be forgotten.[22] Let us note here, above all, the discussion in the book *Verheissung,* especially part IV E, pp. 64-68.

---

[22] For a criticism of Baumgärtel's position which in my view is called for at this point, cf. my essay cited in footnote 13, above all, part IV.

VII

Thus the Word of God from the Old Testament claims authority over us, because we also are still underway toward salvation. At the same time, however, the Word of God attested in the Old Testament also has authority for us as a warning no longer to remain "Old Testament" men in the existential sense just described, but to become what we are—children of the New Testament. The entire Word of God which lays claim upon us from the Old Testament demands authority also at the point where it lets us perceive the "line of obduracy"; also at the place where Old Testament man misunderstands the address of his God or refuses to hearken to it; also at the place where he seeks high-handedly to take possession of the promised salvation. This Old Testament Word of God claims authority because and insofar as it leads us to walk toward the promised salvation; it claims authority because and insofar as it warns us against going the way of error and disobedience of Old Testament man, about which the Old Testament bears such a manifold witness.

Here, however, we stand precisely at the point where evaluation of the Old Testament must be brought alongside the assertion of its authority. It is perhaps not superfluous to stress the fact that this evaluation appears considerably different from that which is carried on in the New Testament. We must also evaluate among New Testament statements, because not everything that the New Testament says agrees perfectly with the apostolic witness to Christ.[23] Here within the Old Testament, however, we must make judgments of value because an Old Testament statement does not make clear from the outset whether it contains an instructive or a warning Word of God; whether it is a statement which moves toward salvation or the statement of one fallen victim to hardness of heart.

Let us recall once again what was said in part V: In the Old Testament we discover the word of Yahweh from the lips of men who purport to have heard it. In this word of Yahweh, the Word

---

[23] For this, cf. Werner Georg Kümmel, *op. cit.*, pp. 310 f.

of the living God can reveal his redemptive purpose with Old Testament men; it can lead, as a Word of promise, toward the full self-disclosure of God. However, the word of Yahweh can also be a direct veiling of God's redemptive activity; it can be understood as a word which is a part of the history of obduracy, according to the will of God. Confronted with a word of Yahweh recounted for us in the Old Testament, we know from what has been said above that the authority of this word for us stands firm at all events. But we must now make an evaluation; that is, we must ask whether it was a word of salvation for Israel or a word which induced hardness of heart. In order to answer this evaluative question we require a standard of measurement; but only the New Testament kerygma of the fullness of time in Christ affords us this standard.

Let us illustrate this with the example of Jeremiah and Hananiah (Jer. 28),[24] which Gottfried Quell adduced in his masterful presentation of the weighty problem of the false prophets. Hananiah proclaimed that Yahweh would break the yoke of the king of Babylon. At first Jeremiah was not in a position to say anything to the contrary; not until some time later did he have a word of Yahweh at his disposal: Yahweh will make not only Judah, but in fact the entire cosmos, subject to Nebuchadnezzar. The word of Yahweh against the word of Yahweh—and only one can correspond to the true will of God! Who is right? We usually answer, Jeremiah. He is then the true prophet, Hananiah the false. But why is this so? Is it because Jeremiah's prophecy came true, or, more than this, because within a short time his death threat against Hananiah was fulfilled? Is it because Jeremiah prophesied condemnation and Hananiah salvation,[25] or because Jeremiah became a Scripture prophet and Hananiah did not? We shall not master this difficult problem with such obvious arguments. We can only give the final answer from the viewpoint of the goal of the *Heilsgeschichte;* only from this viewpoint can we make the evaluation: Jeremiah is the prophet who proclaims the

---

[24] *Wahre und falsche Propheten* (1952), above all, pp. 43 ff.

[25] Jeremiah himself proposes this sort of canon, according to which the burden of proof as to whether one is a true prophet lies with the prophet of salvation, Jer. 28:7-9.

will of God because he summons the people to repentance, because he clearly exposes their entanglement in guilt for what it
is, and because he proclaims unmistakably that God leaves no sin
unpunished. In his own way he showed that man as sinner, or
even God's people as a sinful people, is delivered up irrevocably
to the wrath of God according to his holy will. Hananiah, on the
other hand, contributed to the hardening of Israel's heart with
his proclamation in which he knew salvation as something guaranteed to the people of God regardless of its moral condition (and
a quite earthly, political salvation at that). How should people
who see their God in such a light ever come to recognize that
they require a plenipotentiary of God to redeem them from god-
lessness and guilt? Thus we also have to evaluate words in the
Old Testament which claim to be words of Yahweh, but we can
only do this from the standpoint of the New Testament, which
gives us the standard of measure. In other words, the problem of
false prophecy is not to be solved by the use of standards taken
from the Old Testament.[26] Our evaluation goes yet one step
further, however, in that it says, *"tua res agitur!"*—you, as a man
who always takes the wrath of God so lightly, certain that salvation is somehow guaranteed to you, let the Word of God through
Jeremiah tell you how terrible it is to be delivered up to this
wrath, how everyone who sins is delivered up inevitably to this
wrath. Therefore take refuge in the place where alone the wrath
of God is overcome, where God himself has overcome it—in the
cross of Christ! Moreover, by the word of Yahweh through
Hananiah, be warned against the madness (which so easily befalls
you as an "Old Testament" man) that the offer of God to be
your God guarantees salvation to you regardless of your moral
condition (a salvation probably also conceived as coming in the
earthly sphere of this world). The New Testament says to you
that this is a madness leading to destruction; this Yahweh word
of the false prophet could only have effected hardening of heart,
and if you do not let it serve you as a warning, it will also lead
you toward destruction. In no case, then, could we understand

---

[26] The best example of this is Quell's book (cited above), with its renunciation of any solution.

such a Yahweh word, patently belonging to the "history of obduracy," as a demand upon us to be obedient to it as to the Word of God; we are summoned to evaluation, recognizing that a Word of God comes to us in this passage because and insofar as we are always still Old Testament men—a Word which warns us against following this Yahweh word.

In the Old Testament we find human witnesses which are response to the word of Yahweh. We find testimonies of obedience to the word of Yahweh, but also examples of disobedience. Yet even in the case of witnesses of obedience it is still not established that we may understand them as proper responses to the address of the living God, because, as we have just seen, God is not simply to be identified with Yahweh. Even among the witnesses of Old Testament men which obviously say "yes" to Yahweh's word, activity, and operation, there can be words which do not correspond to the true will of God; even they can be part of the history of the hardening of hearts. When we encounter a human response to the word of Yahweh in the Old Testament, then, the authority of the word stands firm at all events, even there. But we must evaluate; we must ask whether it was a right response to the redemptive will of God toward Israel or not. Indeed, we must reckon with all sorts of intermediate stages; even a response which is proper in itself can be burdened, nevertheless, by the fact that the man who makes it is an "Old Testament" man—i.e., not yet a witness of the full self-disclosure of God.[27] Again, we require the standard measure which, here also, only the kerygma of the New Testament witness can give us.

Let us take another example at this point, one which will bring us back at the same time to our point of departure. In Psalm 109, as well as in Psalm 90, response is made to Yahweh's action toward men. Both Psalmists have experienced something of that depth of human existence into which God casts even his own. In their "reaction" to this, both are thoroughly Old Testament men in their witness; in Psalm 90 as well as in Psalm 109, binding elements of Old Testament faith can be demonstrated,

---

[27] Above all, we must take this into account for Old Testament witnesses which seem so "near" to us, such as Psalms 51, 103, etc.

and yet the responses are completely different in each case. From
the standpoint of the presuppositions of Old Testament piety we
can make both responses understandable. Now, however, it is
in order to go one step further and make an evaluation. Which
response is the more authentic affirmation of the will of God?
Which corresponds more to the response which the witness of
the full self-disclosure of God suggests to us? Here we must judge
that the author of the 90th Psalm—relatively speaking—has discovered the response more nearly corresponding to the New
Testament; in many respects we can make it thoroughly our own
response to the hand of God which leads into suffering. On the
other hand, we must evaluate the answer of Psalm 109 as one
which runs counter to the true will of God; we cannot repeat it
as our own. Also in this case we are asked by the Word of God
to us in both Psalms, insofar as we are still Old Testament men,
"What is the quality of your response?"

At this point it also becomes clear that this evaluation of Old
Testament texts of which we are speaking by no means belongs
only in the realm of ethics. The task of such evaluation is un-
avoidably laid upon us as Christians who must hear the Word of
God from the Old Testament; but the point is not (at least not
in the first instance) to test the ethos which issues from a statement, nor is it to render judgment as to whether a statement already has the ethical "sublimity" of the Christian ethos, or
whether it must be called "sub-Christian" or "unchristian." The
point of the sort of evaluation we intend is something much more
important; it is the proper appropriation of the Word of God
which wants to strike home to us from the Old Testament. Is the
text in question a witness to Christ in the immediate sense (more
exactly, is it history of promise which finds in Christ its goal), or
is it to be understood as such in an antithetical sense? Is it the
exhortation to hearken, to respond to the address of God just as
Old Testament man did, the exhortation to perceive and follow
the word of Yahweh as the call of the living God? Or is it warning
against a way which leads toward hardness of heart and reproba-
tion? This evaluation of Old Testament statements, then, is anything but tedious theological trifling; it is the only method by

which we can make the Old Testament witness hearable for us, who are always still Old Testament men, and by which we may hearken to it, to the end that we can move in a proper way toward salvation and be transformed from Old Testament to New Testament men.

14.

REDEMPTIVE EVENT
AND HISTORY[1]

by Wolfhart Pannenberg

translated by Shirley Guthrie

History is the most comprehensive horizon of Christian theology. All theological questions and answers are meaningful only within the framework of the history which God has with humanity and through humanity with his whole creation—the history moving toward a future still hidden from the world but already revealed in Jesus Christ. This presupposition of Christian theology must be defended today within theology itself on two sides: on the one side, against Bultmann and Gogarten's existential theology which dissolves history into the historicity of existence; on the other side, against the thesis, developed by Martin Kähler in the tradition of redemptive history, that the real content of faith is suprahistorical. This assumption of a suprahistorical kernel of history, which was actually present already in Hofmann's delimitation of a theology of redemptive history (*Heilsgeschichte*) over against ordinary history (*Historie*), and which still lives today especially in the form of Barth's interpretation of the Incarnation as "pre-history" (*Urgeschichte*), necessarily depreciates real history just as does the reduction of history to historicity. Both theological positions, that of pure historicity and that of the suprahistorical ground of faith, have

---

[1] The following discussion is a slightly revised lecture given in Wuppertal on January 5, 1959, at a meeting of teachers from the theological schools of Bethel and Wuppertal. Especially in the first part, it deals with a theme on which a theological circle originally from Heidelberg has worked regularly for seven years. Although I am responsible for the following considerations, many of them could not be expressed as they are without my continuing conversations with M. Elze, K. Koch, R. Rendtorff, D. Rössler, and U. Wilckens. The conclusion of the first section, which is printed here, has been shortened.

a common extra-theological motive. Their common starting point is to be seen in the fact that critical-historical investigation as the scientific verification of events did not seem to leave any more room for redemptive events. Therefore the theology of redemptive history fled into a harbor supposedly safe from the critical-historical flood tide, the harbor of a suprahistory—or with Barth, of pre-history. For the same reason the theology of existence withdrew from the meaningless and godless course of "objective" history to the experience of the significance of history in the "historicity" of the individual. The historical character of redemptive event must therefore be asserted today in discussion with the theology of existence, with the theology of redemptive history, and with the methodological principles of critical-historical investigation.

I. The Accessibility of Reality as History Through the Biblical Revelation of God

1. It is commonly recognized in contemporary research that Israel occupies a singular position in the history of religion because of its historical consciousness. The people of the ancient Orient also recognized, of course, what we call today "historical event." They even developed a historiography; its significance and basic concepts have recently been pointed out.[2] But they could not find any meaning in that which incessantly changes as such. Human life seemed to be meaningful only insofar as it

---

[2] Mircea Eliade, in his work *Der Mythos der ewigen Wiederkehr* (1953) [Translator's note: Page numbers are from the English translation, *The Myth of the Eternal Return*, 1954.], has comprehensively shown the uniqueness of Israel's historical understanding of reality. The description above follows his exposition. The fact of this uniqueness has been emphasized by Ed. Meyers, *Geschichte des Altertums*, 2, 2³ (1953), p. 285, and in Old Testament investigation by G. von Rad and W. Eichrodt, ThZ, 4 (1948), pp. 321 ff. H. Gese has recently not so much disputed as more clearly defined it in his "Geschichtliches Denken im Alten Orient und im Alten Testament," ZThK (1958), pp. 127 ff. Gese sees the uniqueness of Israel's consciousness of history not simply in the fact that it holds fast to historical occurrences; nor in the fact that these occurrences are understood according to a particular scheme (the sequence of good and bad times, or the connection between act and consequence); but rather in the fact that history moves from God's promise to a goal (p. 141), and that the covenant of God is consequently not an archetypal pre-temporal event but a "historical process" (p. 142). Precisely the last peculiarity shows how for Israel the historical process as such

participated in a pre-temporal divine event which was reported by myth and to which men remained in contact through the cult insofar as in the cult the myth was realized. Man saves himself from the threat of the constant change of history in the security of the changeless mythical primal reality which is reflected in the circular course of earthly history. By way of contrast, Israel is distinguished by the fact that it experienced the reality of its God not in the shadows of a mythical primitive history, but more and more decisively in historical change itself.

The disclosure of history in Israel appears to have different roots than those Mircea Eliade holds responsible. Eliade connects Israel's discovery of a meaning of history with prophetic proclamation: The prophets threatened historical catastrophes as God's punishment for the transgression of the people, and history gained meaning and coherence when these announcements were fulfilled in the historical destiny of Israel (pp. 149 ff.). But Eliade's arguments do not touch the real basis of the Israelitic consciousness of history. It cannot originate with the prophets' proclamation of judgment because the beginnings of Israelitic historical writing, which can be recognized as the characteristic understanding of history for Israel, reach back into the time of David and Solomon.

The presuppositions of the historical consciousness in Israel lie in its concept of God. The reality of God for Israel is not exhausted by his being the origin of the world, that is, of normal, ever self-repeating processes and events. Therefore this God can

---

becomes the vehicle of meaning, whereas the concept of a pre-temporal covenant of God (p. 130) or of an ideal order leaves as the meaning of the sequence of time only that which corresponds to the extrahistorical original, so that history as such has no meaning at all (pp. 134 f.). The facts to which Gese calls attention to this extent agree completely with the basic view of Eliade (*op. cit.*, pp. 141 ff.), although the details of Eliade's more phenomenologically than historically oriented description may need examination. It is today generally acknowledged that the conceptions of history outside Israel were caught in a cyclical understanding of time. This view cannot be refuted simply by pointing out that no mythological circular conceptions are to be found in the historiographic documents of the ancient Orient (Gese, *op. cit.*, p. 127). The historiographic schemes could still have an inner connection with such myths, especially if a fundamental motif of the cyclical understanding of time is participation in archetypal events and relationships which Gese, in agreement with Eliade (pp. 85 ff., 90 ff., and other places), has pointed out in the historiographical schemes of the ancient Orient.

break into the course of his creation and initiate new events in it in an unpredictable way.[3] The certainty that God again and again performs new acts, that he is a "living God," forms the basis for Israel's understanding of reality as a linear history moving toward a goal. But we have not yet thereby described the structure of this history itself.

Within the reality characterized by the constantly creative work of God, history arises because God makes promises and fulfills these promises. History is event so suspended in tension between promise and fulfillment that through the promise it is irreversibly pointed toward the goal of future fulfillment.

This structure is pregnantly expressed, for instance, in Deuteronomy 7:8 ff.:

> . . . it is because the LORD loves you, and is keeping the oath which he swore to your fathers, that the LORD has brought you out with a mighty hand, and redeemed you from the house of bondage, from the hand of Pharoah king of Egypt. Know therefore that the LORD your God is God, the faithful God who keeps covenant and steadfast love with those who love him and keep his commandments to a thousand generations . . . (R.S.V.).

The goal here of Yahweh's action in history is that he be known —revelation. His action comes from his love, begins with his vow, and aims at the goal that Yahweh will be revealed in his action as he fulfills his vow.[4]

What is here compressed into an especially deep and signifi-

---

[3] It is characteristic of Greek thought that the nature of the gods is exhausted in the function of grounding the normal order of reality. Behind their normal working there is no suspected "hidden form" which needs special revelation (cf. W. F. Otto, *Theophania*, 1956, p. 29; B. Snell, *Die Entdeckung des Geistes*, 1955, pp. 45 ff.). On the other hand, it is characteristic not only of Yahweh but of the gods of the ancient Orient generally that such a "hidden form" of the god behind his normal working is presupposed (H. Schrade, *Der verborgene Gott*, 1949, pp. 128 ff.; H. Kees, *Der Götterglaube in Alten Ägypten*, 1941, p. 346). Is this not the reason for the fact that the ancient Oriental gods intervene very arbitrarily in history and can work also in an extraordinary way to bring about conditionally a change from a time of happiness to a time of distress (Gese, *op. cit.*, p. 133)? Despite their similarity, the gods are different from the "living God" of Israel in that even in their conditional working they are bound to a higher order (*ibid.*).

[4] On the basis of 1 Kings 20:13, 28, and especially the sayings of Ezekiel, W. Zimmerli has established the probability that the formula ". . . that you

cant formulation is expressive of the structure of the Israelitic consciousness of history in general. The tension between promise and fulfillment makes history. The development of the Israelitic writing of history is distinguished by the fact that the horizon of this historical consciousness becomes ever wider, the length of time spanned by promise and fulfillment ever more extensive.

The first developed concept of history of this kind in Israel[5] is the account of the succession to David's throne (2 Sam. 7—1 Kings 2). It begins with the promise to David through Nathan the prophet, the assurance of the continuation of the Davidic dynasty. Everything connected with what is reported here faces the question of who will be the successor to the throne. How will the promise be fulfilled? It often seems that the promise will be frustrated. Finally the fulfillment comes with Solomon's coronation.

In a much greater framework the Yahwistic history certainly shows a similar structure. After the introductory statement of the pre-history, Genesis 12 opens with the promise to Abraham. The J document ends in the book of Joshua with the fulfillment of the promise through Israel's reclaiming the land.

In the Deuteronomic source the promise-fulfillment structure appears in a somewhat different form. Promise alone controls the course of history in the account of the succession to the throne and with the Yahwist. This brings all the more impressively into the open the errors of the men involved: *Dei providentia, hominum confusione.* The D document, on the other hand, attaches a qualification to the promise—the qualification of the fulfillment of the law. Along with the promise, the law comes to be the power which determines the course of history. Here we may see the influence of the prophetic proclamation of judgment. With the qualification of the promise by the law, the author of the D source explains why history has worked out negatively. Because of the ever growing guilt of the people, Israel must lose its

---

may know that I am the Lord" points back to a form of prophetic speech (W. Zimmerli, "Das Wort des göttlichen Selbsterweises," *Mélanges Bibliques rédiges à l'honneur d'André Robert,* 1957, pp. 154-164).

[5] The following discussion depends on G. von Rad, "Theologische Geschichtsschreibung in Alten Testament," ThZ, 4 (1948), pp. 161 ff.; and *Theology of the Old Testament* (1962), pp. 334 ff.

monarchy and the land which God had promised and given it. Only on the periphery here does the question perhaps remain —whether God nevertheless will cause his promises to triumph. With the law, therefore, the ever growing sin of the people comes to be a power which determines history alongside the promise.

After the genealogies of the Chronicles had already begun history with Adam, Jewish apocalypticism completed the extension of history so that it covered the whole course of the world from Creation to the end.[6] This extension of the concept of history has two important presuppositions: (1) The fulfillment was no longer (as was still the case with prophets) expected within history and therefore seen as a goal which could be superseded, but it was expected at the end of the whole of world history; (2) as already was the case in the D document, the promise is bound to the law. But for apocalypticism the law is not effective only from the time of its historical proclamation; it is an eternal law which is the unchangeable ground of all world history. An eternal election precedes the course of history. The communication of the law through Moses is the saving gift which in the future judgment guarantees to the elect salvation through the promises connected with the fulfillment of the law. Jewish apocalypticism may be distinguished from Parsiism precisely by its connection with the scheme of promise and fulfillment.

Thus Israel not only discovered history as a particular sphere of reality; it finally drew the whole of creation into history. History is reality in its totality.

In light of the Israelitic historical writings, it is amazing that Collingwood in his *The Idea of History* (Oxford, 1946) asserts that the quasi-historical elements in the Old Testament are not essentially different from the views of other ancient Oriental literature.[7] According to Collingwood, it was not Israel but the

---

[6] Cf. D. Rössler, *Gesetz und Geschichte im Spätjudentum* (Heidelberg Dissertation, 1957, printed in 1959 by Verlag d. Ev. Erziehungsvereins, Neukirchen). For a different position see M. Noth, "Das Geschichtsverständnis der atl. Apokalyptik" (1954), *Ges. Studien z. AT* (1957), pp. 248 ff., esp. 260, 264 ff., 271 ff.

[7] Collingwood emphasizes only that the "theocratic" element shows not a particularistic but a universalistic tendency (p. 17). Orientalists have also rejected his description of the ancient Oriental historiography (cf. the literature cited by Gese, *op. cit.*, p. 128, n. 2).

Greek Herodotus who discovered history (p. 17). This judgment shows that he has something in mind quite different from history in the sense of an understanding of the reality of all existence distinguished by certain characteristics. Collingwood means by history the methodical determination of past events—not *Geschichte* but precisely *Historie*. When I distinguish between history as *Geschichte* and as *Historie,* I understand by *Historie,* as H. Diem puts it, "not the history which happened as such" with its own peculiar structure of reality, "but the *historein* of this history" in the sense of the "becoming-acquainted-with and bringing-into-experience and reporting on that which is experienced."[8] Herodotus became the father of history by critically determining the military activities of his time through questioning eyewitnesses so that he was able to make an informed judgment about what actually happened. His express intention, as the autobiographer of his generation, was to create a literary monument to his time.[9] In comparison with other Greek thinkers, Herodotus thereby founded a new methodical way of reporting on past events, but not a new understanding of reality. In this sense Karl Löwith has emphasized that until Polybius Greek historical writing remains completely on the ground of the cyclical understanding of time.[10] The Greek urge toward the unchangeable betrays also in its philosophical form a connection with the way of life of all religions which seek salvation from the "terrors" of historical change in an imitative participation in the archetypical. And the intention of Herodotus not to let the deeds of men be lost with time (I, 1) suggests comparison with the belief of the ancient Egyptians that mortal man may live on in a monument and thus outlast death. In any case, we see in Herodotus anything but an interest in historical change as such.

2. Judaism and the New Testament also hold fast to the reality of history discovered by Israel. In *Geschichte und Eschatologie* (1958)—[Translator's note: Quotations are taken from *The Presence of Eternity*]—Bultmann argues against this. He sees

---

[8] H. Diem, *Der irdische Jesus und der Christus des Glaubens* (1957), pp. 9 f.

[9] Collingwood, *The Idea of History* (1946), pp. 25 f.

[10] K. Löwith, *Meaning in History* (1949), p. 17.

a close connection between apocalypticism and dualistic Persian eschatology (pp. 26 ff.) and makes a sharp contrast between apocalypticism and the Old Testament understanding of history. Eschatology is said to contradict the Old Testament concept of God: The dualism of the doctrine of aeons contradicts the Old Testament doctrine of creation; moreover, in the Old Testament God is thought of as the Ruler not of world history but of the history of Israel (p. 28). Neither of these arguments of Bultmann's is convincing. The concept of aeons in apocalypticism[11] did not displace faith in creation, but rather the law of God controlled the course of history. Already in the prophets God as the Ruler of history is not limited to Israel. Indeed, the pre-history of J places Israel among the peoples of the world. Eschatology is not new in apocalypticism, but only the fact that instead of the inner-historical eschatology of the prophets there is now an eschatology of the end of history. In any case, we cannot accept Bultmann's assertion that "now . . . history is understood from the point of view of eschatology, which is a decisive change from the Old Testament conception" (p. 29). On the contrary, we must say that the historical consciousness of Israel was always eschatologically oriented insofar as, on the basis of the promise and beyond all historically experienced fulfillments, Israel expected further fulfillment. It is significant that Bultmann does not consider the connection between the apocalyptic picture of history and the Old Testament scheme of promise-fulfillment. On the basis of this connection, he could have understood the end of history as the goal of fulfillment belonging to history, whereas he maintains that "The end is not the completion of history but its breaking-off . . ." (p. 30), and that apocalypticism means a "dehistorization" of history (p. 35).

It seems to me that the eschatology of the New Testament stands in contradiction to the structure of the historical consciousness of Israel just as little as does that of apocalyptic eschatology. Bultmann's judgment that in the New Testament "history is swallowed up by eschatology" (p. 37) is closely connected with

---

[11] On the following, see D. Rössler, *op. cit.*

his concept of Jewish apocalypticism, the profound influence of which he himself emphasizes (except in the Gospel of John). It is true that in contrast with apocalypticism, Jesus made expectancy of future salvation depend no longer on relation to the law but on relation to his person.[12] But otherwise the apocalyptic scheme of history is maintained. The anticipation of the eschatological decision in the decision with reference to the person of Jesus does not mean the elimination of the futurity of the end. Yet, without destroying this futurity, Jesus is the anticipated end and not the middle of history.[12a] We shall see what consequences the presence of the yet outstanding eschaton in Jesus Christ has for the understanding of history.

Bultmann asserts, "Paul has interpreted the apocalyptic view of history on the basis of his anthropology" (p. 41). "But although the history of the nation and the world has lost interest for Paul, he brings to light another phenomenon, the historicity of man . . ." (p. 43). The "historicity of man" means that ". . . he gains his essence in his decisions" (p. 44). This understanding of Pauline theology as anthropology is characteristic also of Bultmann's *Theology of the New Testament*. G. Bornkamm has protested and convincingly argued that Paul is not concerned only with a new self-understanding but with "a new history and existence," in which I am taken up into the history of Christ.[13] Beyond this it must be emphasized that Paul also held fast to the continuity between the salvation event which happened in Christ and the history of Israel. Bultmann obviously does not know what

---

[12] Bultmann, *Theology of the New Testament*, I (1951), pp. 7 ff. Also, according to Ph. Vielhauer ("Gottesreich und Menschensohn in der Verkündigung Jesu," *Festschrift G. Dehn*, 1957, pp. 51 ff., esp. pp. 77 ff.), this is a permanent characteristic of Jesus' total proclamation, although Vielhauer does not believe the sayings about the Son of Man (also in Mark 8:38) are authentic. This peculiarity of Jesus' message would be even more sharply clear if H. E. Tödt (*Hoheits-und Niedrigkeitsvorstellungen in den synoptischen Menschensohnsprüchen*, Heidelberg Dissertation, 1957) is right against Vielhauer that the Son of Man sayings (especially in Mark 8:38) are genuine. My description of the relation of the message of Jesus to the apocalyptic scheme of history follows D. Rössler.

[12a] Cf. R. Bultmann, ThLZ (1948), pp. 659 ff., in contrast to Cullman's conception.

[13] G. Bornkamm, "Mythos und Evangelium," ThEx, NF, 26, p. 25. Joh. Körner's assertion that Bultmann himself wants to say "nothing other" than this (*Eschatologie und Geschichte*, 1957, p. 124) is refuted by Bultmann's own discussion in *History and Eschatology: The Presence of Eternity* (1957), pp. 43 ff.

to do with the main document of this continuity, Romans 9-11. He thinks only that the question of the fulfillment of the promises to Israel creates a "difficulty" for Paul (p. 42). But why then is Paul in Galatians 3:15 ff. so decisively interested in the fact that the faithful are the heirs of the promise to Abraham? The promise-fulfillment structure remains constitutive also for Paul. This is shown precisely in Romans 9-11 where Paul, without dealing with its details, discusses, so to speak, the general structure of God's redemptive history only to show how the Gentiles are introduced into the redemptive history whose goal is the salvation of Israel (Rom. 11:11 ff.).

Bultmann's crowning witness for the dehistorization of history by eschatology is John (pp. 47 ff.), with his renunciation of "apocalyptic eschatology" (p. 47). It is well known that Bultmann comes to this understanding of the Gospel of John by excluding expressions which sound apocalyptic on literary-historical grounds.[14] In case these literary-critical operations should prove valid, one must nevertheless agree with the theological judgment of the "early church" that in Christian theology the renunciation of the goal of history is intolerable. But even apart from these considerations, the Gospel of John thinks of Jesus as the fulfillment of the Old Testament witnesses when it calls them witnesses to the Son (John 5:39).

3. It is of great theological significance that the confession of Israel and that of the community of the new covenant consistently hold fast to the one history of God which binds them together. The connection between the Old and New Testaments is made understandable only by the consciousness of the one history which binds together the eschatological community of Jesus Christ and ancient Israel by means of the bracket of promise and fulfillment. Jesus is the revelation of God only in light of the Old Testament promises. When one takes the title "Christ" together with "Son of Man" and "Lord," he must conclude with van Ruler: "Speaking from a Christian point of view, everything stands and falls with the Messiahship of Jesus. And one can decide

---

[14] Cf. R. Bultmann, *Das Evangelium des Johannes* (1952), p. 196 (on John 5:28 f.) ; p. 162 (on John 6:40, 54).

about this Messiahship only when the question is raised and
answered whether Jesus really does the works of God. But one can
know what the works of God are only on the basis of the Old
Testament."[15] However, we must also admit with van Ruler that
the "subject matter" of the Old Testament received its "foundation" only in Jesus Christ (p. 71) insofar as in him the promises
of the Old Testament are fulfilled—in an unexpected way, of
course. But the basis for all further Christological statements
about Jesus of Nazareth is formed by the dependence of the meaning of Jesus on the fact that his way is understood in the framework of the history of God with Israel attested by the Old Testament. This dependence must not be degraded to a secondary
interpretative statement of a Christology which begins with a
doctrine of the Incarnation, much less of a Christology which
with Schleiermacher begins with the fact of the Christian community. On the contrary, the meaning of Jesus on the basis of his
connection with Israel's history of promise is the only foundation on which the doctrine of the Incarnation is to be judged.
We must understand also the New Testament proofs from prophecy in terms of the fundamental meaning of this history for the
recognition of Jesus Christ. It will not do, as it happened again
and again in the case of Schleiermacher and still happens with
Baumgärtel,[16] to dismiss the New Testament arguments from
prophecy as nothing but an apologetic against the Jews, relevant
only to the New Testament period. The use of prophecy as proof
is the sharpest expression of the connection between the meaning
of Jesus and the history of God with Israel to which the Old
Testament witnesses—even though our present historical consciousness cannot uncritically develop the connection in this
form.

One gains the impression from the present discussion of the
theological hermeneutics of the Old Testament that the theories
we have mentioned about the connection between the Old and
New Testaments very often do not do adequate justice to history

---

[15] A. A. van Ruler, *Die christliche Kirche und das Alte Testament* (1955),
p. 70.
[16] Fr. Baumgärtel, *Verheissung* (1952), pp. 75 ff. Cf. Schleiermacher,
The Christian Faith, par. 12, 2.

as the unity which holds the old and new covenants together. This is true when the connection is grounded on other phenomena than the process of the history of promise. I shall attempt to indicate what I mean by this with respect to Bultmann, Baumgärtel, and the advocacy of a typological exegesis of the Old Testament.

It is the merit of Bultmann's essay "Prophecy and Fulfillment"[17] that it seeks the connection between the Old and New Testaments in the factual course of Israel's history. But Bultmann determines this connection in such a way that Old Testament history is a history of failure. According to him, this history has a promissory character precisely because in the failure of the hopes centered around the covenant concept, in the failure of the rule of God and his people, it becomes clear that "the situation of the justified man arises only on the basis of this miscarriage" (p. 75 above). In answer to this position, Zimmerli has rightly asked whether for the New Testament the hopes and history of Israel are "really only shattered." "Is there not fulfillment here even in the midst of the shattering?"[18] Zimmerli sees clearly that the concept of shattering or failure becomes the means by which Bultmann is able "to elevate the Christ-message purely out of history in existential interpretation." Zimmerli's question whether the concept of a pure brokenness of the history of Israel must not lead to an unhistorical conception of the Christ-event, to a "new Christ-myth" (p. 120), carries much weight. Of course he does not dispute the fact that the New Testament fulfillment of the Old Testament promises does indeed mean a shattering of the original expectations. But he points out that the prophets themselves bear witness to the freedom of Yahweh to "legitimately interpret his promise through his fulfillment, and the interpretation can be full of surprises even for the prophet himself" (p. 107). The fact that Bultmann finds no continuity with the New Testament is certainly connected with the fact that he does not begin with the promises and their structure which for

---

[17] "Prophecy and Fulfillment" first published in 1949, reprinted in *Glauben und Verstehen*, II (1952), pp. 162-186. See pp. 50 ff. above.
[18] W. Zimmerli, "Promise and Fulfillment." See pp. 89 ff. above.

Israel were the foundation of history, and therefore does not understand the events of the history of Israel in their significance as change, as God's "interpretation" of the content of the promises—promises which thus endure precisely in change.

Baumgärtel cannot follow Bultmann's thesis of a total failure.[19] He assumes an enduring "basic promise," the content of which is said to be the promise "I am the Lord thy God." Instead of seeking the significant, revelatory history precisely in the transformation of the content of prophecy, he completely abandons the proof from prophecy as unacceptable to our historical consciousness. Beyond this Baumgärtel sees the meaning of the Old Testament only in the fact that its frustrated "salvation-disaster history" exemplifies the way of man under the law and as such is still relevant also for us. Here Baumgärtel comes close to Bultmann's view of the failure of Israel's history and like Bultmann relates it, in dependence on the Lutheran doctrine of the law, to the way of salvation of the individual. It is clear that the history of Israel has no positive theological significance when it is split up into an illustration of the way of the law, on the one hand, and a general basic promise, on the other. Baumgärtel therefore maintains characteristically that the historicity of Jesus Christ is grounded not on the Old Testament but on the Incarnation (p. 113). One sees how the historicity of Jesus Christ falls when the history of Israel falls.[20] Von Rad attacks the unhistorical concept of a "basic promise" which makes invisible any positive theological significance of the history of Israel. He characterizes the separation of such a general basic promise from particular historically realized promises and prophecies as a "presumptuous encroachment."[21]

The advocacy of a typological exegesis of the Old Testament is based on a concern to find in the Old and New Testaments not only a common "doctrine" or "spiritual content," but to "regain reference to the facts attested in the New Testament"; that is, to discover the connection between the Testaments in the historical

---

[19] Fr. Baumgärtel, *Verheissung* (1952).
[20] A. A. van Ruler, *op. cit.*, pp. 79 ff.
[21] G. von Rad, "Verheissung," EvTh, 13 (1953), pp. 406-413, 410.

process itself.[22] Therefore one looks in the "history worked by God's Word" to the places where "the Christ-event of the New Testament is prefigured" (p. 31). But it seems that this emphasis on typological prefiguration as that which really connects the Testaments tends rather to undermine the important intention of discovering the connection between them in historical facts. Not that the existence of such analogies is to be contested. Of course we do find analogies between the acts of God, and also in the behavior of men in response to the historically acting God. Thus, for instance, in Romans 4 Paul can describe the meaning of faith with the example of Abraham. But it is doubtful whether in such analogies, or in those of Hebrews, we see the real unity of the Old and New Testaments. Do we not thereby lose the connection again in a finally unhistorical, purely structural similarity of the Old Testament type to its New Testament counterpart? It is true that the typological analogy begins with a relationship which takes place in history. This is reflected in the way the New Testament counterpart goes beyond its Old Testament prefiguration. But for the typological consideration does not the course of history which unites type and counterpart emphasize the distinction between them, while the connection is discovered in their structural correspondence?[23] But then, it is difficult to see why the Old Testament types should still be relevant for Christians after the New Testament prototype itself has appeared. So long as the connection between the Christ event and the Old Testament is sought primarily in structural agreements, the primary realization in Christ necessarily depreciates the shadowy

---

[22] G. von Rad, "Typological Interpretation of the Old Testament," pp. 17 ff. above.

[23] H. W. Wolff, "The Hermeneutics of the Old Testament" (pp. 160 ff. above), emphasizes that history is the foundation of typological connections. The analogy is "supported by the historical relation" (pp. 180 f.). This is expressed, however, as the "historical distinction" in the analogy between the old and new covenants (p. 180). But the historical relation may not be understood only as historical distinction. Precisely the connection between the old and new covenants consists not only and not primarily in the structural analogy, but also and above all in the temporal, historical continuity of that which is not comparable structurally. Doubtless much would be gained and many a hesitation overcome if the historical relation, also in the sense of the historically demonstrable connection between the changing contents of the promise in the process of their change, were emphasized as that which bears and limits the analogous agreements and guards against wild analogizing (cf. W. Eichrodt, pp. 224 ff. above).

preliminary representation in Old Testament history. The Old Testament then becomes only a copious picture book—not only of the history of faith,[24] to be sure, but above all of the Christ-event. Those who advocate typological exegesis would doubtless not intend that the Old Testament should be no longer constitutive for the meaning of the Christ-event but only serve as an illustration of it. Von Rad expressly emphasizes: ". . . for our knowledge of Christ is incomplete without the witness of the Old Testament. Christ is given to us only through the double witness of the choir of those who await and those who remember."[25] Nevertheless, the conceptual means of the typological analogy is not adequate to express the qualification of the Christ-event by Old Testament history, since in any case nothing is added to the more perfect of the two compared realities (or more exactly, relations) by the analogy with its prefiguration. It is another question whether the typological trains of thought in the New Testament do not mean more than is expressed by the conceptual means of the typological analogy. One would have to investigate the extent to which in the New Testament typologies the theological emphasis falls precisely on the anti-typical element of the Christ-event, especially as it is clear in Hebrews. The relationship between the anti-typical as such and the Old Testament types—a relationship which can hardly be understood to imply only a difference of degree[26]—is a very important theological problem.[27] This relationship will be understandable only as a temporal continuity, not as a purely structural correspondence. It is based on the fact that the promises of God were fulfilled in a different way

---

[24] Von Rad, p. 27 above, thus describes the view of Althaus (*Die christliche Wahrheit*, I, pp. 229-240). This description may be extended to characterize also Bultmann, and to some extent Baumgärtel.

[25] G. von Rad, p. 39 above. Cf. H. W. Wolff, *op. cit.*

[26] Thus F. Torm, *Hermeneutik des Neuen Testaments* (1930), p. 223; and L. Goppelt, *Typos* (1939), p. 244. But Paul's "how much more" (Rom. 5:17, for instance) expresses precisely the incomparability of Christ and Adam —the point at which there is not simply a higher degree within a common quality, but at which the analogous relationship of the typological parallels is broken. Cf. G. Bornkamm, "Das Ende des Gesetzes," *Paulusstudien*, I (1952), pp. 86 ff.

[27] Here we meet the difficulty designated by the concept "prophecy." Prophecy must be distinguished from typological analogy (as Baumgärtel in opposition to Goppelt has emphasized in *Verheissung*, p. 71, n. 63), but at the same time the former can be connected with the latter (i.e., 1 Cor. 10:4).

from that in which they were understood by those who first received them, but in such a way that the promises themselves hold
good in the change of their content. The new covenant belongs
together with the old because of this historical unity, seen in the
continuity of the promises in the change of their content. Only
from this point of view does the Old Testament remain an independent basis also for the Christian faith—just because the
promise must go before the fulfillment if the fulfillment is to be
different from the promise. W. Zimmerli has to date worked most
decisively in this direction.[28] Certainly on this foundation one
can then establish all kinds of typological connections and structural agreements. But they can never be understood as that which
constitutes the connection between the Old and New Testaments.
This connection is constituted by the one history which includes
both Testaments, the history which is itself grounded in the unity
of the God who works here as well as there and remains true to
his promises.

4. The critique of an anti-historical interpretation of New
Testament eschatology in the second section above has consequences for the evaluation of the Christian theology of history in
its relation to the New Testament. The theology of history now
appears in principle at least as the legitimate heir of the biblical
understanding of reality. This point must be made with reference
to the two philosophers who have been especially concerned with
this problem, Karl Löwith and Wilhelm Kamlah.

Since Löwith depends exegetically not on Bultmann but on
Cullmann, he does not speak of an opposition between eschatology and history, but between the salvation event and history.
"Considered in the light of faith, worldly occurrences before and
after Christ form no continuous sequence of meaningful events,
but only the external framework of redemptive history."[29] The
anti-historical result is nevertheless similar to that of Bultmann's
thought. Löwith speaks of a "modern overrating of history" as
the "consequence of our alienation from the natural theology of
antiquity and from the supernatural theology of Christianity"

---

[28] See pp. 89 ff. above.
[29] K. Löwith, *Meaning in History* (1949), p. 184.

(p. 176). He does not understand that redemptive history is not a suprahistory, but because of its universal tendency essentially includes all events. For him Augustine's theology of history is already on a wrong track, although it considers world history only as a "fragmentary reflection of its suprahistorical substance" (p. 166).

Kamlah, who appropriates the Bultmannian school's interpretation of early Christian eschatology, makes an even sharper judgment: "According to the original proclamation, Jewish history was in no way continued but rather broken off by Christ."[30] But already in the writings of Theophilus of Antioch "the turn of the aeons has become the turn of a Christian-historical world process" (*ibid.*). Kamlah considers this development to be an inevitable withdrawal from early Christian beginnings. In this respect he differs from Bultmann: The abolition of the "system of law" in Jesus' proclamation cannot be realized "as soon as and so long as history continues" (p. 25). Thus the delay of the *parousia* must lead to a new turning to the historical. The breach presupposed here by Kamlah does not exist, however, if one maintains the historical horizon of the New Testament itself as the basic presupposition of the early Christian proclamation.

On this basis, it is also not necessary to think so simply as Löwith that a philosophy of world history in the West is a deviation from its origin in the Jewish-Christian understanding of history. Löwith has pointed out very impressively that Western philosophy of history in its whole development, even in its deterioration, lives from its Christian origin. The deterioration takes place, however, not in the concept of world history as such, but only in the fact that since the Enlightenment, since Vico and Voltaire, man has been exalted to the place of God as the one who bears history.

5. Biblical faith is not only the temporary, accidental presupposition of the Western consciousness of historical reality, but the origin to which this consciousness remains essentially bound.

When man—first of all in the form of mankind—becomes the

---

[30] W. Kamlah, *Christentum und Geschichtlichkeit* (1951), pp. 111 f.

center which bears history, this function must finally fall to the individual man as soon as the insight prevails that man exists concretely only as the individual. But when the individual man be:omes the point of reference for history, then the unity of history is necessarily dissolved into a multiplicity of aspects of the past. Historicism's relativistic dissolution of the unity of history, therefore, was the consequence of the anthropocentric turn of the philosophy of history. The next step along this road could only be the atrophy of the historical consciousness and historical (or at least universal historical) interest generally.[31] With the historical dissolution of the unity of history came automatically the evaporation of the uniqueness of historical reality—including the historicity of man—over against natural reality. Collingwood emphasizes that the interest of the historian rests on presuppositions of faith which have their deepest root in Christianity. In Christianity there is in fact an interest in the past which cannot be surrendered, because it contains the promise which will be fulfilled in the future. Historical experience of reality is preserved only in the biblical understanding of history, in the biblical faith in the promise. With the loss of this origin the experience of reality as history threatens to disappear today.[32]

For Dilthey the relativization of all historical phenomena and traditions means at the same time the opportunity for the pure development of the historicity of man. The historicity of human freedom in all its creative origin and peculiar significance becomes visible for the first time when the comprehensive world views and systems, including the philosophies of history, lose their claim to authority. "The last step to the liberation of man is the historical consciousness of the finiteness of every historical appearance and every human or social condition, of the relativ-

---

[31] Is something like this beginning to happen with the orientation of historical interest today around the problem of the present? Cf. R. Wittram, *Das Interesse an der Geschichte* (1958), pp. 7 f.

[32] Though without consistent clarity, already Nietzsche attempted to turn back from historical thinking to the ancient conception of nature. Cf. K. Löwith, *Nietzsches Philosophie der ewigen Wiederkehr des Gleichen* (1956), pp. 113 ff. Löwith himself, following Nietzsche, seems to strive to turn away from history to "natural" thinking (cf. Löwith, *Meaning in History* (1949), Appendix II.

ity of every sort of faith."[33] The later Dilthey expected as the consequence of this liberation the development of a unitary culture of humanity made possible by the relativization of all particular pasts and traditions.[34] In a peculiar transformation of Dilthey's thought, Heidegger also achieved the historicity of existence by going behind the "vulgar" understanding of history. ". . . because factual existence breaks up, decaying, into the anxious, it understands its history first of all in a world-historical way."[35] Heidegger's concept of the experience of anxiety and being-unto-death achieves something analogous to the historical relativization of world historical content:[36] the liberation of man to his real historicity in existential freedom.

It is understandable that this philosophical position could be appropriated by Christian theology as in Bultmann. The eschatological proclamation also liberates man from the world, from the powers, from the shells of tradition. One cannot deny that there is a certain similarity between these philosophical ideas and the Christian faith. Dilthey himself was aware of the fact that the historicity of man was discovered by Christianity.[37]

There is of course a limitation to this similarity to the Christian faith. Heidegger agrees with Dilthey that the origin of all history is to be sought in the historicity of man: "Existence does have its 'history' and can have it because historicity constitutes the being of this existing one."[38] It must be asked, however, whether historicity rather is not grounded in the experience of reality as history, just as it is made accessible in the history of promise of God with Israel pointing toward the anticipated fulfillment in Jesus Christ. Dilthey's insight that Christianity discovered historicity certainly points most obviously in this direction, and not to the idea that history is grounded in historicity. If the latter were true, that would mean that "Christianity" itself

---

33 W. Dilthey, *Gesammelte Schriften*, VII, p. 290; cf. VIII, p. 223. See also the excellent characterization in E. Fülling, *Geschichte als Offenbarung* (1956), pp. 36-61.

34 W. Dilthey, *op. cit.*, VIII, p. 167. Cf. Fülling, *op. cit.*, p. 55.

35 M. Heidegger, *Being and Time* (1962), pp. 440 f.

36 *Ibid.*, pp. 390 f., 382 ff.

37 Cf. Fülling, *op. cit.*, pp. 57 f.

38 Heidegger, *op. cit.*, p. 434.

is understood as the expression of the "historical" freedom of man which itself gives form to his life. But if the historicity of man has its origin in the Jewish-Christian faith, and therefore is bound to the experience of reality as history, then it will hardly survive for very long the destruction of the understanding of reality as historical process. The emancipation of historicity from history, the reversal of the relationship between the two so that history is grounded in the historicity of man[39]—this seems to be the end of the way which began when modern man made man instead of God the one who bears history.[40] When the historicity of man is set up in opposition to the continuity of the course of history, the last possible step is taken along the way which leads to the loss of the experience of history as well as that of historicity.

Bultmann[41] and Ernst Fuchs[42] summarize the criticism of the theology of history with the formula that Christ is the end of history. In Christ the eschaton has already appeared. Therefore it seems that history, at least in the sense of a universal historical process, is finished. Christ is the end of history: That means that for the man who believes in Christ the problem of universal history no longer exists. Now we have already seen that the universal historical framework of apocalypticism remains completely valid for the proclamation of Jesus and the New Testament witnesses. From Bultmann's point of view this must appear as a compromise or as an anachronistic holdover. Bultmann is of course correct in saying that for the whole New Testament the eschatological decision takes place already now in encounter with Jesus or the proclamation of him so that the end of history is already here. But this end is provisionally only anticipated within history. What it means that in the person of Jesus the end of history is already anticipated can itself be understood only within the apocalyptic concept of history. Thus the historical

---

[39] So also John Körner, *Eschatologie und Geschichte* (1957), pp. 111 f.

[40] Gerh. Krüger, *Die Geschichte im Denken der Gegenwart* (1947), pp. 14 ff., has excitingly described the "historicity" of existential philosophy as the expression of the anthropocentric character of modern thought.

[41] R. Bultmann, "History of Salvation and History" in *Existence and Faith* (1960), pp. 227 ff.; "Prophecy and Fulfillment," pp. 71 f. above; *History and Eschatology: The Presence of Eternity* (1957), pp. 40 ff.

[42] E. Fuchs, "Christus das Ende der Geschichte," EvTh, 8 (1948/49), pp. 447-461, esp. pp. 454 ff.

framework remains intact. History is by no means abolished. On the contrary, an understanding of history as a whole is made possible for the first time because the end of history is already present.

The misunderstanding that the anticipated appearance of the end of history in the person of Jesus of Nazareth does away with history seems to have risen from making a false parallel to Paul's statement about Christ as the end of the law (Rom. 10:4). But this parallel is not convincing. Law and history are not comparable for Paul. He is concerned with the question of whether the law or the promise controls history (Rom. 4; Gal. 3). History remains the framework of Paul's questioning and within this framework he asks in opposition to apocalypticism whether it is not the promise rather than the law which plays the decisive role in history. He grants that the law is a controlling factor only in a particular period of history—the period which reaches its end with the coming of Christ.

We have said that the anticipated coming of the end of history in the midst of history, far from doing away with history, actually forms the basis from which history as a whole becomes understandable. This does not make possible, however, an oversight over the drama of world history as from a stage box. Second Corinthians 5:7 applies here: "We walk by faith and not by sight" (R.S.V.). Jesus Christ, the end of history, is not available to us as the principle of a "Christologically" grounded total view of world history. Christ's Resurrection, the daybreak of the eschaton, is for our understanding a light which blinds as Paul was blinded on the Damascus road. Even the New Testament witnesses, however powerfully they attempted to express as clearly as possible the reality of this event, could only stammer of it, each in his own way, all of them together in a right contradictory way. Also our participation in this event, the hope of our own resurrection, is still hidden under the experience of the cross. No one can make the eschaton into a key to calculate the course of history, because it is present to us in such a mysterious, overpowering, incomprehensible way. We know only that everything earthly must pass through the cross. The coming of the end of time has broken through all conceptions of the promise of God; indeed, in the event of the Resurrection, it has broken through everything we can conceive of. Therefore we are made receptive to the command of Jesus not to calculate the end (Luke 17:21, 23 ff.). The Father alone knows the hour (Matt. 24:36). Thus the freedom of the pure futurity of God is preserved, and thereby also the independence of man, from supposed laws of the course of history.

Does this mean, then, that a theology of history is after all impossible? Not at all. It is one thing to renounce from the very beginning every universal conception of history. It is something quite different if the total view of reality as history which moves from promise to fullfillment is broken open as it were from within. This happens first of all through the unexpected way in which God fulfills his promise, but then through the fact that this fulfillment, the end of history in Jesus Christ, has provisionally already come—and yet precisely thereby is deprived of all comprehension. We can say what such an outbreak of the incomprehensibility of the eschaton in history means only in the framework of a universal historical understanding of the reality in which this outbreak occurs, just because through it the universal historical scheme itself is forced open. Also the sending and history of the eschatological community in the world can be understood only from this point of view.

15.

THE UNDERSTANDING
OF HISTORY IN THE
OLD TESTAMENT PROPHETS[1]
by Hans Walter Wolff

translated by Keith R. Crim

It is an alarming sign of our time that interest in history has become discredited.

To be sure, there is among us interest in past existence as a unique accomplishment of life. Also we are concerned in individual cases with the continuous pre-history of present relationships and tasks, as, for instance, in a problem in a scientific speciality. But who is still fired with an interest in universal history so as to inquire, after the manner of Friedrich Schiller's plan in his inaugural address in Jena, "Beginning with the latest state of the world back to the origin of things"?

However, wherever a passion for universal history is alive today, as in the Marxist historical science, questions concerning the present and the future dominate the field in such a manner that interest in past happenings exists only in as far as it refers to our own present and future. All attention is directed to the laws of evolution. Thus interest in past events, as simply things that happened, is extinguished, and with it the passion for research into the variants in analogies, for the individual and the contingent event.

Thus it is not surprising that among the great mass of our contemporaries interest in history is pushed into the background by interest in natural law and its application in technology. In this no one even dreams that by the schism between conscious-

---

[1] Inaugural address in Mainz, January 28, 1960.

ness of history and natural science *the* danger to life in our age arises, for indeed self-knowledge and responsibility are not to be separated from attention to history.

Therefore it is necessary that we inquire into the origins of the interest in the totality of past history as an elementary need of life. We must here assume as a result of research that these origins are to be sought in the Old Testament.[2] The Old Testament understanding of history received its particular expression in the prophecy of the 8th to the 6th centuries. Today we shall inquire into the distinctiveness of the prophetic understanding of history and its continuing significance.

I

1. The uniqueness of the prophetic understanding of history can be comprehended only in the light of the specific starting point of its message. The thought of the prophets is produced by a future event which they are to proclaim. Amos recognizes that "The end has come upon my people Israel" (8:2, R.S.V.). In visionary and auditory experiences, Yahweh, the God of Israel, commissioned those who spoke for him to proclaim the future event. This word of the future evoked prophetic thought and speech about the past and the present of those who heard it. Thus the prophetic knowledge of history must first of all be understood as *knowledge of history from the point of view of the future.* How then does the future appear in prophecy?

(a) In prophecy the future appears throughout as the future of Yahweh, of the God of Israel himself. Yahweh appears personally before Israel in the superior Assyrian troops of Tiglath-Pileser III. "For I will be like a lion to Ephraim, and like a young lion to the house of Judah. I, even I, will rend and go away, I

---

2 Eduard Meyer, *Geschichte des Altertums*, II, 2³ (1953), p. 285; Karl Löwith, *The Meaning of History* (1949), pp. 18 f.; Mircea Eliade, *The Myth of the Eternal Return* (1954), pp. 160 ff.; Gerhard von Rad, *Der Anfang der Geschichtsschreibung im alten Israel* (1944), Ges. Studien z. AT (1958), pp. 148 ff.; Alfred Jepsen, *Die Quellen des Königebuchs* (1953), pp. 106 ff.; Hartmut Gese, "Geschichtliches Denken im Alten Orient und im Alten Testament," ZThK, 55 (1958), pp. 127 ff.; Wolfhart Pannenberg, "Redemptive Event and History," *vid. supra*, pp. 316 ff.

will carry off, and none shall rescue" (Hos. 5:14, R.S.V.). As
author of the future he is the absolute Lord of history. The appropriate expression for history in the prophetic books is, therefore, "the work of Yahweh." Isaiah uses it in this sense first of
the future (5:19), in parallel to the "counsel of Yahweh" (28:29),
but then by analogy, in the same manner of the past (28:21;
5:12), and of the whole course of history, which is called "all
his (i.e., Yahweh's) work" (10:12). Significantly, the emphasis
lies here again on the future, "When the Lord has finished all
his work on Mount Zion and on Jerusalem he will punish the
arrogant boasting of the king of Assyria and his haughty pride"
(R.S.V.). History is the whole work of the God who is coming.

(b) The future of God is anticipated in the prophetic word.
"Surely the Lord GOD does nothing, without revealing his secret
to his servants the prophets" (Amos 3:7, R.S.V.). Consequently, a
revealing of coming history takes place in the prophetic word.
In this it must be noted that the Hebrew *dābār* denotes word as
well as event; in this it can only be compared to our word "history," which we use for that which is spoken (recounted history)
and for that which occurred (experienced history). Compare
Jeremiah 1:12, "For I am watching over my *dābār* to perform
it"; and Ezekiel 12:25, 28, "the *dābār* which I speak will be performed," on which cf. Zimmerli, BK, XIII, pp. 274 f., 277. History is imparted to the prophet in the word. According to Amos,
there is no future which does not appear beforehand in the
prophetic word.[3]

What follows from this? Since the future appears first in the
historical event of the prophetic word, history is understood here

---

[3] Cf. Reinhold Schneider, "There is no catastrophe, unless it be preceded
by a misunderstood prophet" (*Pfeiler im Strom*, 1958, p. 55). That the
word of the prophet anticipates history is particularly clear in the symbolic
actions of the prophets. See H. W. Wolff, *Hosea*, BK, XIV, p. 72.
   It is primarily in this light that the fact of the formation of tradition in
prophecy must be seen. As a herald of history the word first awakens a waiting for history (Isa. 8:17). The word which has gone forth and the facts
which occur must be compared. If they do not correspond to one another,
then one must wait under the "hidden face of God" while the word is carefully preserved for coming history (Isa. 8:16), "as a witness for ever" Isa.
30:8. Thus in prophecy the formation of tradition results from this objective
necessity. And so, for the preservation of the prophetic words we are not
"indebted, as in all history of tradition, to a chain of innumerable accidents"
(Eduard Meyer, *op. cit.*, p. 286) but above all to its peculiar nature, namely,

as a dialogue of Yahweh with Israel. This can be clarified by further observations. Amos saw that already in the past all kinds of catastrophes had broken in on Israel: crop failures, plagues, earthquakes—in which, in the providence of Yahweh, his call to repentance went forth. Amos had to proclaim as Yahweh's word of accusation, "Yet you did not return to me" (Amos 4:6 ff., R.S.V.). The nature of history as dialogue is shown quite directly in that Yahweh's word for the future very often confronts the voice of the contemporaries in a quotation. "But you said, 'No! We will speed upon horses,' therefore you shall speed away; and, 'We will ride upon swift steeds,' therefore your pursuers shall be swift" (Isa. 30:16, R.S.V.).[4] In a great number of prophetic words, future history appears as Yahweh's judgment and its proclamation by the prophet as a court trial with occasionally a lively exchange of interrogation and defense, of accusation and pronouncement of sentence.[5] In this way first of all, in the prophetic word the character of history as conversation is disclosed.

By these observations a misunderstanding of history as the "work of Yahweh" is avoided, namely, in reference to the function of man in history. He is certainly not the antagonist of God, nor yet the proper subject of history, but neither is he a simple object; he is to be understood as a partner in conversation with the God who creates history.

---

that it is a word directed toward a future in history. This observation must be considered in the comparison of Old Testament prophecy with prophetic phenomena in the ancient East. See EvTh, 15 (1955), p. 450.

Even the roots of the Old Testament *canon* must be understood in terms of such a comparison of the prophetic word which went forth, and the events which occurred. These roots are to be sought in the period of the Exile as prophetic words of judgment which had been fulfilled (Deut. 18:22; Jer. 28:9). The word of outsiders and opposers becomes canonical and at the same time determines what part of the literature of the pre-exilic period is to be handed on and what not. "Evaluation and revaluation took place in the burning light of the divine judgment" (Th. C. Vriezen, *Theologie des Alten Testaments in Grundzügen*, n.d., pp. 39 f.). So the correspondence of prophetic word and the course of history contributed greatly to the formation of tradition and of the canon. In relation to the course of tradition itself, cf. Antonius H. J. Gunneweg, "Mündliche und schriftliche Tradition der vorexilischen Prophetenbücher als Problem der Neueren Prophetenforschung," FRLANT, 73 (1959).

4 Cf. H. W. Wolff, *Das Zitat im Prophetenspruch*, EvTh Beih., 4 (1937).

5 Cf. Isa. 3:13-15; Hos. 4:1-4; Mic. 6:1 ff.; Jer. 2:5-13; also Hans Jochen Boecker, *Redeformen des israelitischen Rechtslebens*, Diss. Bonn (1959).

(c) The future of God appears in the prophetic word mainly as a historical future, not as an end of history. It is comparable to past occurrences. A catastrophe will come over Ahaz that is comparable to the revolt of the ten tribes in the days of Rehoboam (Isa. 7:17). A further future will follow the day that is coming. Assyria and Babylon are announced as Yahweh's implements of judgment against Israel "until the time of his own land comes" (Jer. 27:6 f., R.S.V.; Isa. 10:12 f.). In the manifold character of the future actions of God, an intention can be recognized. "I will return again to my place, until they 'are laid waste' and seek my face. When they are in distress they will seek me" (Hos. 5:15[6]; cf. 3:4 f.; 2:16 f.). Thus the prophet recognizes, with the future, the finality of history.[7]

This decisive disclosure of the *finality*[8] of history has been already anticipated in the correspondence of prophetic word and history. It later becomes explicit in the transmission of the words of Jeremiah. That is, it is repeatedly stressed in the book of Jeremiah that the proclamation and transmission of the words of judgment took place with the aim that they should be heard, and awaken the spirit of repentance so that the threatened judgment might not occur (Jer. 25:3 ff.; 26:2 f.; 36:2 f.; Jonah 3:8 ff.). The prophetic word is not here primarily directed toward its fulfillment in history, but is an instrument of history that is intended to bring about the conversion of those who hear it, and therewith the non-fulfillment of what was threatened. It shows in extreme clarity the character of history as dialogue, but at the same time its stirring finality.

---

[6] On the problem of the text, see H. W. Wolff, BK, XIV (1957), pp. 147 f.

[7] There is an "alien work" of God in history (Isa. 28:21b) that is related to his major work in a systematic way. Yahweh varies the methods and tools of his actions in history, as, in the life of the farmer, processes and tools vary with the respective seasons and fruits. This does not occur arbitrarily but in wisdom, in a freedom that corresponds to his saving plan. "He is wonderful in counsel, and excellent in wisdom" (Isa. 28:23-29, R.S.V.).

Thus far we have consciously avoided the catchword "eschatology." In this connection the reader should compare the recent works of Alfred Jepsen, RGG, 3rd ed., II, pp. 655 ff., and Richard Hentschke, "Gesetz und Eschatologie in der Verkündigung der Propheten," ZEE (1960), p. 47. The prophetic proclamation of God's future is to be termed eschatological in the sense that the previous history of God with Israel reaches its end, an end in history, which corresponds to the beginning in history. The sharpest threats express it as follows: Hosea, in the negation of the formula for the establish-

Thus we hold as our first conclusion: *For the prophets, history is the goal-directed conversation of the Lord of the future with Israel.*

2. We inquire further, how the Old Testament prophets came to consider the whole course of history as seen from the announced future. To be sure, the decisive stimulus to prophetic thought is given by the prophecies that were to be announced. But the prophetic thought which resulted from this, and consequently the bulk of the oracles, does not deal with the future, but with the present and the past of the hearers. Phenomena from the whole course of history can appear in the prophetic word, for the God who is proclaimed as the Coming One is no other than he who has already dealt with Israel in past history and has spoken to it, and to whom the present Israel is therefore responsible. In this constancy of God the *unity of history* is established for the prophets. How is this second step of understanding arrived at?

(a) The future is always placed in relation to the observable course of history.

First of all, the many prophetic threats of judgment show by the accompanying accusations that the future is grounded in the present.[9] In this way, as elsewhere in the ancient Orient, a direct connection can be shown to exist between an action and its results. "Because you have plundered many nations, all the remnant of the peoples shall plunder you" (Hab. 2:8, R.S.V.). "Ephraim shall stumble in his guilt" (Hos. 5:5, R.S.V.). Here history appears above all as the consequence of human actions, as

---

ment of the covenant, "For you are not my people and I am not your God" (1:9, R.S.V.) ; Amos, in the threat to drive the nation out of the land (4:3 ; 5:27; 6:7), which canceled the gift of the land in the early days (2:9 f.) ; Isaiah, for example, in the return to the old holy war, in which Yahweh now fights against Israel instead of for her (28:21). In this end in history, history as such does not come to its end. Prophecy knows eschatology also in the other meaning, that there is to be beyond the end of the old salvation history a basically new meeting with God in the midst of judgment, with new divine ordinances.

8 The concept of finality is used in this paper to denote the purposive quality of God's historical actions as it appears in the witness given within concrete circumstances. It is not therefore to be interpreted in the sense of a teleological view of history which excludes contingency.

9 Cf. H. W. Wolff, "Die Begründung der prophetischen Heils- und Unheilssprüche," ZAW, 52 (1934), pp. 1 ff.

if man were the subject of history. Prophecy takes up this view,[10] which, as the experience of wisdom, was widespread in the ancient Orient, in order to make clear the strict relations between events. It was, however, thoroughly permeated with the certainty that it is Yahweh who established the relationships. Thus Hosea proclaimed, "And I will requite them their doings" (4:9).[11]

In this way, man's deeds *can* return to him in the future, but it is not necessary that they do so. Causal thought became a secondary key to understanding, but not the absolutely dominant one. Yahweh is free. The words of promise appear always without any word of their being grounded in prior human conduct.[12] But even the connection between threat of punishment and the ground for punishment is not necessarily of itself definite. Rather, under the God to whom Israel has long been responsible, factors are regarded as guilt, which are related not to the future, but to prior acts of God and to the still valid covenant relationship. Thus the whole sweep of life can be observed, from the luxury of Samaria and Jerusalem to the misery of the widow; from the practice of rendering judgment to the priestly dereliction of office; from trade treaties with Assyria to war coalitions against Babylon.[13] In this manner the depth of history is disclosed; Hosea brings to light the revolution of Jehu of a hundred years before (1:4), many references are made to the time of David (Amos 9:11; Isa. 29:1), or to the beginnings of the monarchy (Hos. 9:15; 13:10 f.), to the period of the judges (Isa. 9:3). The Exodus from Egypt and the possession of the land appear again and again (Jer. 2:5 ff.; Amos 2:9 ff.; Hos. 2:10; 11:1 ff.), as does the time in the desert (Amos 5:25, etc.). Hosea can even trace the deceitful spirit of Israel back to Jacob in the patriarchal period (12:3 ff.). As history under God, what has happened is not really

[10] H. Gese, *op. cit.*, pp. 135 ff.

[11] For a critical development of the ideas by Klaus Koch, ZThK, 52 (1955), pp. 1 ff. Cf. Friedrich Horst, EvTh, 16 (1956), pp. 72 ff., and H. Gese, "Lehre und Wirklichkeit in der alten Weisheit" (1958), pp. 45 ff.

[12] Cf. the exact presentation of R. Hentschke, *op. cit.*, pp. 50 ff.

[13] Prophecy does not distinguish "a sacred history" from "the profane as different in meaning" as Karl Jaspers erroneously assumes for Christian faith (*Von Ursprung und Ziel der Geschichte*, 1955, p. 14). Neither Luther nor Melanchthon separated ecclesiastical and profane history. Cf. Reinhard Wittram, *Das Interesse an der Geschichte* (1958), p. 137.

past, but a continuing fact. The unity of history in all areas and periods is contained in the constancy of the God of Israel.

Thus the course of history does not derive its continuity from man nor from an arbitrary, unchangeable divine will, but from the obligatory, continual, free conversation of God with Israel. In this way the structure of the conversation becomes even clearer. It has the continuity of an unbreakable covenant of life. Therefore Hosea can compare it to the story of love between a man and a maid (2:4-22), or to the struggles of a father with a son who is hard to raise (11:1 ff.; cf. Isa. 1:2 f.). For all its obligatory continuity the conversation retains the freedom of a partnership. Obedience occurs (Jer. 2:1 ff.; Hos. 10:11) as well as the revolt of man (Jer. 1:16; 2:5; Hos. 9:10), God's righteous punishment as well as God's mercy (Hos. 11:8 f.). Thus continuity can be concealed in the concrete course of history by crass discontinuity; only through the prophetic word is it revealed and brought to light.

In such free, continuous conversation, reality is first disclosed as history. Now reality no longer mirrors mythical, cosmic events in such a way that all interest attaches to the cyclical return of things that are finally unalterable, nor to the synthetic world order of the context of an action and its result. Rather now it is the unforeseen fact which attracts interest, the change in history, the new in the irreversible progress of events. And yet—this must not be overlooked—history can be understood as a unity because of the constancy of God.

(b) The future is brought into relation to the historical beginning. The continuity of history is fully understood only when we see that in the prophetic eschatology an analogy to the beginnings of Israel's history occupies the foreground. The historical end defined by the prophets leads to a new beginning that corresponds to the historical beginning. It is truly a second word. In Hosea the threatened return to the wilderness contributes to the new, alluring conversation of God, who is Israel's constant lover despite all disappointments; he will then renew his gift of the civilized land to the faithless wife, and Israel will hear the echo of love, "as in the days of her youth, and as in the day when she came up out of the land of Egypt" (Hos. 2:15, K.J.V.). Jeremiah (31:31-34) leads us a step further. In the coming days the new covenant will enter history. It will be the same as the old, in that all initiative proceeds from Yahweh, that its goal is Israel's freedom and its document a covenant agreement. But to the things that are the same, something new is added; no further external teaching of the law need take place, but each will know the will of his God in the new, intensive oneness of the people with their God; finally, the new covenant will be unbreakable because Yahweh will forgive guilt. So to the nuclei of the old and new covenants a new coefficient is added which means intensification and completion. Together with the faithfulness of God, his free, goal-directed will is recognized. This specific analogical relationship which is to be observed here and often elsewhere in the prophetic writings, and which presupposes historical continuity and shows therein intensification or fulfillment of specific and fundamental (typical) facts of history, we call typology.[14]

The relation of tension between beginning and goal can become such that it is possible to speak of discontinuity. This can be so strongly expressed that Second Isaiah can proclaim to the generation in exile that has lived through the judgment, "Remember not the former things, nor consider the things of old.

---

[14] The Old Testament relationships which are so designated are of at least the same relevance for biblical hermeneutics as the Pauline typology (cf. especially E. Fuchs, *Hermeneutik*, 1954, pp. 200 f.). If it is true "That the *comprehendere* starts from the Scripture and not from the exegete" (G. Ebeling, ZThK, 48, 1951, p. 175), then it becomes of even greater importance to us how understanding occurs in the Scripture itself. We are faced with the task of clarifying typology as a hermeneutic aid. As a supplement to and a further development of what was said above (pp. 160 ff.) I would like to present the following points:

1. The relation of prophetic eschatology to the themes of the salvation history as sketched above has been confirmed for me by the correctness of the criticism of W. Pannenberg (see above, pp. 326 ff.). Typology, in the prophetic writings as in the writings of Paul, presupposes the continuity of God's actions in history. The contents of the proclamations vary with the various relationships, but they stand nonetheless in a discoverable historical context. Because that variation and this context are to be seen in terms of the freedom and faithfulness of God, we remain free to see the correspondences as well as the differences and the contrasts.

2. In this way it becomes clear that typology, as it confronts us today, goes hand in hand with historical interpretation. In our theological and hermeneutic considerations we have paid too little attention to the meaning which typology gains in the present-day science of history, which has recognized the limits of the one-sided, individualized approach of historicism. Cf. Theodor Schieder, *Der Typus in der Geschichtswissenschaft*, Studium gen-

Behold, I am doing a new thing . . . I will make a way in the wilderness and rivers in the desert" (Isa. 43:18-19, R.S.V.). He is moved by the incomparable nature of that which is coming— the new, which will eclipse not only the terrible time of judgment that has come upon their smug piety, but the old salvation history as well. And yet it is precisely in Second Isaiah that it is always recognizable in the presentation of the new that the earlier salvation history is being called to mind (48:20-22; 52:11 f.; 55:12 f.). Indeed, even the days of Noah are mentioned in 54:7-10, "For this is like the days of Noah to me: as I swore that the waters of Noah should no more go over the earth, so I have sworn that I will not be angry with you and will not rebuke you . . . and my covenant of peace shall not be removed" (R.S.V.). The God of Israel ultimately remains true to himself and to his people. He remains the free God, free also not to be circumscribed by human defiance (Hos. 11:9). To this extent, the continuity of history, which holds together all actual discontinuities, is not postulated on the basis of the oneness and constancy of the Lord of history, but makes itself known in the correspondence of beginning and end.

So we hold as a second conclusion: *Prophecy can perceive history to be a continuous unity because it recognizes in the coming actions of God the beginnings of the salvation history.*

---

erale, 5 (1952), pp. 228-234. He refers to Jacob Burckhardt and his concern "to seek to pursue the repetitive, the constant, the typical in history" (p. 229) ; he warns against "cryptotypes which enter in, where we are not conscious of the question concerning the true comparative types," and (p. 231) he distinguishes by way of clarification, structural, progressive, and form types (pp. 232-234). Cf. also R. Wittram, *op. cit.*, Ch. IV, "Vergleich, Analogie, Typus," especially pp. 54-58. The stimulus given by J. Burckhardt has so far been worked out most fruitfully in the history of art ; after that the question of historical types has especially promoted the disciplines of the history of constitutional law and jurisprudence. Basically no field of history is exempt from it. In that we have recently introduced it into biblical hermeneutics—where it found in prophecy and in the Pauline writings a use that was spiritual-historically, and also methodologically different, but nonetheless comparable, and, above all, relevant—we must carefully inquire into the "various fundamentals of historical occurrences," into the "astounding phenomena" in the chaos of events (Wittram, *op. cit.*, p. 57). Therefore we by no means are inquiring into the "suprahistorical," but into the "limited number of patterns in history" (*op. cit.*, p. 58).

3. Without this question concerning what is typical in the texts of the Old and New Testaments we will scarcely be able to find the narrow way between historical fragmentation and the leveling out of history through individualized investigation and an existential dissolving of history in his-

3. The uniqueness of the prophetic understanding of history is not exhausted in the recognition of the finality and the continuity of history. Necessarily a view of universal history emerges.

(a) Already for Amos, reality as history is fully comprehended only when it is seen in the context of the history of the nations. He warns against misunderstanding Yahweh's dealings in the history of salvation as a sacral history without analogy: " 'Are you not like the Ethiopians to me, O people of Israel?' says the LORD. 'Did I not bring up Israel from the land of Egypt, and the Philistines from Caphtor and the Syrians from Kir?' " (9:7; R.S.V.). Beside the God of Israel there is no one else who initiates history in the world of the nations. Israel is distinguished only by the continuous address of Yahweh. This particular history, however, is inseparably intertwined with world history. Just as the superstate Egypt and the peoples of Palestine had to be mentioned immediately at the beginning of God's dealings with Israel, so in his new dealings Assyria comes into the view of the prophets in the eighth century, Babylon in the seventh and sixth centuries, the Persians in the middle of the sixth century—and all of them are instruments of Yahweh's actions in history (Isa. 10; Jer. 27; Isa. 45). In the framework of Yahweh's salvation history for Israel they have their role to play as instruments of his judgments,

---

toricity (cf., e.g., C. H. Ratschow, *Der angefochtene Glaube*, pp. 150 ff., pp. 162 f.). By inquiring into the typical we overcome the non-obligatory comparison of partial phenomena, the capitulation before the "omnipotence of analogy" (Troeltsch). At the same time, in the light of this question, we will now be able, if at all, to evaluate the relevance of that which is always meaningful. In the present state of research we must particularly inquire into the typological building of traditions, into the typological structure of faith or exhortation, into the typological ways of speaking of God, into the typological relation of correspondence between word and event. However, above all, the types of testimonies of God's mighty deeds in history, which are the ground of faith, are to be recognized anew in the Old and New Testaments and in comparison with the surrounding world.

In this, typology helps to distinguish the variable from the constant, yet without making the constant absolute or the variants relative. Modern typology must no longer be permitted to succumb to a naïve objectification. In that it adopts as its own a recognition of existential interpretation. But, faith in Jesus of Nazareth finds its basis as the final Word of God in history because the types of the two Testaments help interpret each other and together stand in contrast to that which is typical in the surrounding world. God's dealings in Israel and in Jesus of Nazareth are witnessed to and known, and through them we are challenged to proclaim God's acts for ourselves and for our world, not in a way that is objectively of universal validity, nor, on the other hand, subjective and optional, but as a valid aid for each of the corresponding types of the kerygma for each corresponding hour.

and then as objects of his judgment because of their *hybris* against Israel (Isa. 10:12 ff.).[15] In the breakup and decline of the great empires, Yahweh shows that he is Lord of world history. World history, too, is understood in its continuity and finality from the point of view of salvation history.

In Jeremiah an entirely different motive for interest in world history appears. In the legal proceedings in 2:10 f., where Israel is accused of apostasy from Yahweh, we read, "For cross to the coasts of Cyprus and see, or send to Kedar and examine with care; see if there has been such a thing. Has a nation changed its gods, even though they are no gods? But my people have changed their glory for that which does not profit" (R.S.V.). It should be noted with what zeal the prophet urges, as it were, research expeditions and study of source materials in the general history of religion. "See, send, examine, see!" He challenges them to compare Israel with the nations of the West as well as with those of the East in order to bring to light the singular nature of Israel's apostasy from her God. Thus in the midst of the crisis of salvation history ethnological interest appears because Israel's unique nature comes to light only in the framework of the history of the nations.[16]

Finally, however, prophecy sees that Yahweh is also carrying out his purpose in the Gentile world in an effectual manner, and in particular this is true in Ezekiel, where his special intention for Israel becomes a historical reality. "And the nations shall know that I am the Lord, when I shall be sanctified in you before their eyes" (Ezek. 36:23; cf. 36; 21:4, on which see Zimmerli, BK, XIII, p. 466, and Isaiah 40:5; 43:8-13). Previously Isaiah had already seen that in the end all nations would flow together to Zion and there receive the instruction and law of the God of Israel (Isa. 2:2-5). Thus in the end, because of the uniqueness of God, the lines of the history of the nations and of Israel come together in a historical goal.

---

15 Cf. A. Alt, "Die Deutung der Weltgeschichte im Alten Testament," ZThK, 56 (1959), pp. 134 ff.

16 The way in which a mandate for research in world history is present in the passage Deut. 4:32-35 should be noted. It inquires back into the beginnings of human history and includes the whole extent of the world of the nations. The sources of interest in world history in the Old Testament are in need of a new historical and theological investigation.

(b) In a final expansion, the universal interest of the prophets reaches out over the history of the nations into the history of nature. Second Isaiah recalled to mind the waters which were subdued in the days of Noah. Amos showed how drought, locusts, blight of grain, plagues, and earthquakes were intended to effect the return of Israel to the covenant demands of God (4:6 ff.). Since the God of Israel, as the Lord who has at his disposal the ordered course of nature, is the sole one who causes even such natural catastrophes, these actions of his also are to be understood in relation to his continuous and goal-directed conversation with men. He who rejects this connection must prepare to stand naked before his God. In a different manner Hosea shows in a breath-taking sequence that Israel's faulty consciousness of history has consequences that are cosmic in scope. If there is lacking in the land that knowledge of God which is possible in Israel, then the first result of all is a destruction of community life. But in the constantly increasing use of force even life on earth itself is threatened. The destroying fire that man in his incompetence for community has let loose brings death to the plant and animal world and even to the fish of the sea (4:1-3). On the other side, Second Isaiah can anticipate that even the wilderness plant life will exchange its thorns and thistles for cypresses and myrtles when Yahweh leads his people out into freedom (55:13). Unanticipated natural catastrophes as well as unanticipated fruitfulness share in God's history with the nations. Here it is plain that the prophetic understanding of total reality as a continuous, conclusive historical context necessarily moves toward universal history.

We hold as a third conclusion: *In prophecy interest in universal history is aroused because the coming God of Israel is recognized as the sole Lord of all reality.*[17]

---

[17] The roots of the prophetic view of history which has been developed here are to be found neither in prophecy itself nor in the world of Israel's environment. They lie in the old Israelite's traditions.

1. The prophetic view of the unity and continuity of history presupposes the exclusive nature of the Yahweh faith as it is manifest from the beginning, particularly in the Sinai tradition. Yahweh's jealousy forbids in unsurpassable strictness the worship of other gods. This basic presupposition underlies even the oldest historical sketch in the salvation history Credo (Deut. 6:21 ff.; 26:5 ff.).

2. This confession of the early saving deeds of Yahweh in the Exodus from

Finally, in this connection two things must be underscored. First, that such interest in history is, as it were, a by-product of the prophetic proclamation of the coming God. Because the speaking and acting of the God of Israel is related exclusively to ascertainable, this-worldly occurrences, total reality is included on the basis of the prophetic theology as history in the sense developed here.

Second, it must be said that nowhere in the prophets is a plan presented for history. All their zeal is directed to assault each contemporary situation from the point of view of the coming God. It is in this zeal that they proclaim that no hearer can understand their God if he does not at the same time understand reality as history determined by him and directed to him, as his conversation, first with Israel, but finally drawing in the whole world of the nations. Intimation is always of more value in prophecy than a clear statement.

II

It is not possible for us here to follow the working out of the prophetic understanding of history.[18] But we would yet like to ask whether our relation to history, which has become problematic, must not share the fate of cut flowers because we can no

---

Egypt and the occupation of the land of Canaan shows, from the first, contacts with world history. The God of Israel has shown his strong hand in dealing with the might of Egypt as well as with the previous inhabitants of Canaan. The presuppositions of the prophetic view of the universality of history are contained in such primitive confessions of Israel, not only in respect to the still limited role played by the history of the nations in the history of salvation, but also in reference to the certainty that natural events are included, as for example, the east wind at the Red Sea (Exod. 14:21).

3. Already in the ancient Credo there are intimations of the goal-directed nature of history. Yahweh's actions do not really take place in the course of the natural year, but they are an irreversible sequence in the free field of history. So the two basic facts of salvation history are from the first united toward a goal: "He brought us out from there, that he might bring us in, to give us the land which he swore to give to our fathers" (Deut. 6:23; cf. Lev. 25:38). Thus there are at least hints of the finality of the prophetic understanding of history in the early traditions.

On the basis of these suppositions it was possible for the true writing of history to begin long before the time of the great prophets. Cf. G. v. Rad, *Ges. Studien zum AT* (1958), pp. 152 ff.

18 The first fruit of the prophetic understanding of history lies in the so-called Deuteronomic history. Cf. M. Noth, *Überlieferungsgeschichtliche Studien* (1943), pp. 1-110. It exists in its time and in its environment as a singular document of genuine history writing within world literature. This is so in several respects.

longer draw nourishment from the roots of the prophetic understanding of history which we have sought to recognize. I shall
inquire in three directions.

1. How is the concept of a *unity* of history possible for us? It
presupposes that the contingent (that which is always more or
less a surprising occurrence) and the coherence of history have
the same origin.[19] Otherwise, our historical understanding would
be dissolved into episodes, or at best into cultural cycles. Or, on
the other hand, through imminent regularities which appear to
be discernable, the contingent events are in danger of not being
recognized. Then free research into total reality is endangered.
The certainty that in the reality of the world the conversation of
God with Israel, and through Israel with humanity, takes place
and that to this extent reality is not to be understood as unified,
goal-directed history, is basic to the origin of historical thought
in the prophetic writings. It is saying too little to say that either
God or even man is the subject of history.[20] Contingent happenings are rooted in the freedom of God's conversation with man;
the continuity of all history, however, is rooted in the supreme,
inclusive faithfulness of God. That is a prophetic certainty. It is
in accord with this that our generation must attempt anew to
conceive of the unity of history in our own thought forms. Otherwise, it faces the dilemma either of honorably renouncing[21] an

---

1. In its will and capability for following the whole history of Israel for
some seven centuries from the time of Moses to the time of the author in
the Babylonian Exile.

2. In its conscientiousness in dealing with the literary sources that had
been handed down and were now collected and edited, and in its respect for
what actually happened (cf. M. Noth, *op. cit.*, p. 108).

3. In the compactness of its conception, which with all respect for the
traditions and individual facts grasps such an extensive history as a unity
and presents the continuity of this history in a convincing manner.

This unitary concept is possible because the author, in the details and in
the total picture, recognized the correspondence of the proclaimed Word of
God and the actual happenings. The whole history, including the period
of the monarchy, is comprehended in the words of Moses in Deuteronomy.
(Cf. the conditions attached to the promise of Nathan in 1 Kings 2:3 f.
to 2 Kings 23:2 ff.)

The goal of this history is not to make the present intelligible to the reader
as God's judgment, much less to explain it as the final termination of salvation history. If this were the goal it would be impossible to understand why
again and again times of apostasy, of judgment, and of the continuation of
the salvation history are presented according to the new ordinances of
Yahweh (cf. especially Judg. 2:11-22; 1 Sam. 12:6-25). Rather, we can
discern the intention of bringing the contemporary generation to return to

understanding of the unity of all of history, or, on the other hand, with postulated laws of evolution or other world views which are always founded in only a *portion* of reality, of endangering the freedom of research into the *total* of actual events.

2. But how is the *recognition* of the unity of contingent happenings possible? Reinhard Wittram says in this connection:[22] "If the question of the beginning of world history is not decisive, then the end of world history is by no means an object of historical science, but the quest for it is decisive for our comprehension of history." What then? A contemporary says, "Since we cannot conceive of the end, in our world views we have obstinately held fast to the moment."[23]

For prophecy, as we saw, recognition of the continuity and finality of history was possible only because the Word of God for Israel was for them an unsought-for, even feared, but yet decisive event. In this Word future history broke into their present in a recognizable way. Basically this future Word corresponded with the actual events of past history in all areas of reality. Thus it provided the basis for an approach to the possibility of recognizing the finality of all of history. But only an approach!

For us to be able to carry this out, the end of history must be

---

the Word of God, which had been long since proclaimed and was now substantiated through history. At all decisive turning points of the course of history this intention is apparent. In this connection it is to be noted in addition to the passages already mentioned that the main catchword "repent" occurs over and over again in 1 Sam. 7:3; 2 Kings 17:13; 23:25, above all, in direct address to the exilic generation in 1 Kings 8:46 ff.; Deut. 30:1-10; 4:30 f. The dovetailing of Deuteronomy with the Deuteronomic history in the introductory and concluding sections of Deuteronomy must be subjected to a new literary-critical investigation, especially for chapters 4 and 30, in consideration of the concern of the historical work for proclamation.

In the presence of the recognized continuity and the proclaimed intention of God's dealings in history, universality moves into the background, if the connection of the history of Israel with that of the neighboring nations is left out of account. The universal goal of God's dealings with Israel is indicated only once in passing (1 Kings 8:41-43; cf. 9:7-9). From the theological starting point, however, it comes to the astonishing proclamation of a program of research in universal history, as mentioned above in note 16, in Deut. 4:32-35.

[19] Cf. W. Pannenberg, KuD, 5 (1959), pp. 280 ff.

[20] Thus, for example, R. Bultmann, *History and Eschatology: The Presence of Eternity* (1957), p. 143, *passim.*

[21] For Bultmann's consequences, *op. cit.*, p. 154 f.

[22] *Op. cit.*, p. 135.

[23] R. Hülsenbeck, "Der halbe Mensch," FAZ, 20, 1 (1960).

recognizable, that is, not only future history, but also the
novisimum extremum. Primitive Christianity asserted that according to the prior prophetic word, the final Word of God was
given when Jesus of Nazareth appeared in history.[24] It was a
certainty of early Christianity that in his words and deeds, in his
death, and decisively in the Resurrection of the Crucified One
from the dead, the end of history, if not "anticipated," was nonetheless made discernible; indeed it had been entered upon, in
that this was the end of God's conversation with man. Thus
according to the Christian confession, in Jesus of Nazareth the
end of history has become an object of research in the midst of
history.

The early Christian recognition of Jesus of Nazareth as the
final Word of God is indissolubly connected with the recognition of his historical connection with the Old Testament salvation history. We theologians are confronted in our generation, in
view of the sundering of disciplines in the generation of our
teachers,[25] with the great task of grasping first of all the theology
of the Old and New Testaments in a new, historical-critically
oriented hermeneutic consideration in terms of the historical
distance of each Testament from the other, but also in their continuity and analogy. Our Old Testament theology would be false
if alongside the historical distance from the New Testament we
ignored the aids to understanding which are supplied in the New
Testament analogies and the New Testament completion of
God's history with Israel. In the same way, our New Testament
theology is largely only half true, because it fails to recognize the

---

[24] The historic connection between the prophetic and the early Christian
kerygma cannot be understood without the connecting link of Apocalyptic.
The relationship of the latter to history is often underestimated. (See Dietrich
Rössler, *Gesetz und Geschichte in der spätjüdischen Apocalyptik*, Heidelberg
Dissertation, 1959, VLG.d.Ev. Erziehungsvereins, Neukirchen.) The relationship here is to be sought in the fact that the God of Israel is more and more
spoken of as the hidden one (Isa. 29:14; Jer. 15:18; Isa. 45:15) and at the
same time with increasing emphasis as the coming one. Jesus himself understood his message "as the last Word of God before the end" (H. Conzelmann,
RGG, 3rd ed., II, p. 668).

[25] R. Bultmann has kept us back from conversation with the Old Testament science of the last thirty years. As W. Zimmerli has set forth above,
pp. 89 ff., Bultmann's essay "Prophecy and Fulfillment" (see above, pp. 50
ff.) is an example of what untenable scientific consequences this leads to.
Cf. also, above all, G. v. Rad, *Theologie des Alten Testaments*, Vol. II.

historical bonds that tie it to the Old Testament. These bonds must essentially be much more decisive than those which tie it to contemporary Judaism and Hellenism. So we must work toward a new outline of historically oriented *biblical* theology, which the coming generation must then recognize as its task.

For in biblical theology the scientific presuppositions are present which make possible the recognition of the unity and goal-directed nature of all of history, provided that the eschaton of all history, which is implied in the Old Testament and to which witness is borne in the New Testament, has in principle become subject to historical investigation in the history of Jesus of Nazareth. It is not that belief in God supplements reason in the recognition of reality, but that it rather liberates it for an objective view of data which are historically comparable to each other. At the same time, unbelief runs the risk of partially distorting this view and thus becoming semi-realism.[26]

On the whole, our generation is threatened from the left by a refusal to recognize the unity of history, from the right by the postulate of a goal of history at the expense of total reality, and above all, by the exclusion of the history of Israel and of Jesus of Nazareth from the exploration of total reality. This generation, therefore, is vigorously asked whether it will expand the historical research limitlessly and whether it can recognize the goal of history and with it the unity in the singular phenomena of prophecy and of Jesus of Nazareth, without which *human* existence is not really possible.

3. But have we not learned that God is not to be seen in the process of world history? Have we not just learned, as Christians or as nihilists, to reduce history to the authenticity of existence?[27]

---

[26] Cf. the important references of W. Pannenberg, *op. cit.*, pp. 276 f., to Luther's discussion of the evidence of Scripture in *De servo arbitrio* (WA, 18, pp. 607 ff., etc.).

[27] Historicity as "responsibility for the heritage of history in respect to the future" (Bultmann, *History and Echatology: The Presence of Eternity*, 1957, p. 143); cf. F. Gogarten, *Der Mensch zwischen Gott und Welt* (1956), pp. 388 ff.; and, fundamentally, M. Heidegger, *Being and Time* (1962), § 74 (The Ordinary Understanding of History and Dasein's Historizing) and § 75 (Dasein's Historicality and World-History), e.g., pp. 442 f.; "Real historicity understands history as the reoccurrence of the possible, and realizes therefore that a possibility reoccurs only when by fate existence is momentarily open for it in its predetermined repetition."

Have we not fortunately dissolved the totality of history into existential accomplishments?

Due to the renunciation in principle of universal history we are obliged to abandon critical comparison and with it the question of truth. Therefore the necessary and inevitable step of existential philosophy and existential theology must not remain the final step. After philosophy, through the impulse given it by Kierkegaard, took the commanding position, theology is now called upon to lay anew its weight of biblical theology on the scales.[28] Can our generation then hold fast to the separation of the existential accomplishments from universal history at a time when world history first begins to take place as an empirical unity?[29] The pupil of Huizinga, Theodor J. G. Locher, professor of general history in Leiden, stated in a lecture in Mainz in 1952, "Our age is now faced with the mighty task of giving its historical background to the *one world,* which we must bring to realization amidst all its diversity or perish."[30] I believe that we are faced with the question in all its acuteness of how we intend to make the one world a reality and exist in it today if we cut ourselves off from the roots of our historical thought. Prophecy, which repeatedly addresses its hearers, does not thereby succumb to a pointilism, which is at present our greatest danger. It addresses men in an irreversible and unrepeatable context of events, in which God's conversation with the hearer takes place. In this the objects of our natural science are just as much involved as the dealings of human polities. Interest in universal history stands and falls, as we saw, with the certainty that the address of the Lord of all history is heard in the midst of history.

Wherever scientific research no longer deliberately cuts itself off from the biblical origin of our understanding of history, but remains open to total reality, it experiences how the source of a new passion of the academic disciplines for one another springs forth, just as certainly as the university cannot be separated in its

---

[28] While we are canonizing Kierkegaard's necessary contradiction of Hegel, we have already been attacked from the opposite direction.

[29] Cf. H. Heimpel, "Der Versuch, mit der Vergangenheit zu leben," FAZ, 25, 3 (1959).

[30] Quoted by R. Wittram, *op. cit.,* p. 128.

origin from a confession of the Lord of all history. In 1789, Schiller could say in his already quoted inaugural address in Jena, "The Christian religion has so manifold a part in the present form of the world, that its appearance is the most important fact of world history. But neither in the time in which it appeared, nor in the nation in whose midst it arose, is there a satisfactory basis for explaining its appearance." To be sure, this basis can be found only in the Lord of all history, to whom the prophets bore witness and whom the New Testament presupposes. Schiller already saw clearly the threatened separation of our sciences. He said, "Where the hireling (he who separates his scientific specialty from all others) divides, the philosophic spirit unites." Can the philosophic mind manage to do this unless its interest draws a sustenance and strength from the roots of our historical thinking?

At the outset we said it was an alarming sign of our time that interest in history has become discredited. Can we expect anything else from our contemporaries who are oriented in terms of natural science and technology, as long as anything less is looked for in history than the address of the Lord of the whole of reality, anything less than the exhortation and the appeal of the Lord of the future?

BIBLIOGRAPHY
Selected from the Literature on Old Testament Hermeneutics Appearing in Recent Years

Amsler, Samuel, *L'Ancien Testament dans l'Église*. Neuchâtel: Delachaux & Niestlé, 1960.

————, "Où en est la Typologie de l'AT," *Études Théol. et Rel.*, 1952, Jg. 27, 3.

————, "Prophétie et Typologie," RThPh, 3, 1953, pp. 139-148.

Auvray, P., *et al.*, *L'Ancien Testament et les chrétiens*, Paris, 1951.

Baumgärtel, F., "Erwägungen zur Darstellung der Theologie des AT," ThLZ, 1951, cols. 257 ff.

————, *Verheissung. Zur Frage des evangel. Verständnisses des ATs.* Gütersloh: C. Bertelsmann, 1952.

————, "Das alttestamentliche Geschehen als heilsgeschichtliches Geschehen" in *Geschichte und AT, Festchr. A. Alt* (Beitr. z. histor. Theol. 16), 1953, pp. 13 ff.

————, "Ohne Schlüssel vor der Tür des Wortes Gottes?", EvTh, 13, 1953, pp. 413-421.

————, "Der 109. Psalm in der Verkündigung," *Mon. schr. f. Pastor. theol.*, 42, 1953, pp. 244-253.

————, "Der Dissensus im Verständnis des ATs," EvTh, 14, 1954, pp. 298-313.

Baumgartner, W., "Die Auslegung des ATs im Streit der Gegenwart," *Schweiz ThU*, 11, 1941.

Bea, A., S. J., "'Religionswissenschaftliche' oder 'theologische' Exegese?", *Biblica*, 40, 1959, pp. 322-341.

Bernhardt, K.-H., *Die gattungsgeschichtl. Forschung am AT als exegetische Methode.* Berlin: Evangelischer Verlag, 1959.

Blackman, E. C., *Biblical Interpretation.* Philadelphia: The Westminster Press, 1957.

de Boer, W., "Hermeneutic Problems in Early Christian Literature," *Vigiliae Christianae*, I, 1947, pp. 150 ff.

Boisset, J., *et al.*, *Le Problème Biblique dans le Protestantisme.* Paris: Presses Universitaires de France, 1955.

Bonhoeffer, D., *Prisoner for God.* New York: Macmillan, 1958. British edition: *Letters and Papers from Prison*, SCM Press.

Bornkamm, H., *Luther und das Alte Testament.* Tübingen: Mohr, 1948.

Buber, M., *The Prophetic Faith* (Torchbook 73). New York: Harper & Brothers, 1960.

357

————, *Das Kommende I. Königtum Gottes.* Berlin: Scholocken Verlag, 1956, 3rd ed.

Bultmann, R., "Ursprung und Sinn der Typologie als hermeneutischer Methode," ThLZ, 1950, cols. 205-212.

————, "The Significance of Jewish Old Testament Tradition for the Christian West," *Essays Philosophical and Theological.* London: SCM Press, 1955.

Cazelles, H., "Instaurare omnia in Christo (Eph. 1, 10)," *Biblica,* 40, 1959, pp. 342 ff.

Childs, B. S., "Prophecy and Fulfillment," *Interpretation,* Vol. XII, No. 3, July, 1958, pp. 259 ff.

Coppens, J., *Les Harmonies des deux Testaments.* Tournai-Paris: Casterman, 1949.

————, *Vom Christlichen Verständnis des Alten Testaments.* Bruges-Paris: Desclee de Brouwer, 1952.

Daniélou, J., *Sacramentum futuri, Études sur les Origenes de la Typologie Biblique,* I, Paris, 1950.

Diem, H., *Grundfragen. der bibl. Hermeneutik* (ThEx h. NF 24). München: Chr. Kaiser Verlag, 1950.

————, "Die Einheit der Schrift," EvTh, 13, 1953, pp. 384-405.

————, "Jesus, der Christus des ATs," EvTh, 14, 1954, pp. 437-448.

————, "Die Schriftauslegung als der Ort des dogmatischen Denkens," EvTh, 15, 1955, pp. 49-65.

Dinkler, E., "Bibelautorität und Bibelkritik," ZThK, 47, 1950, pp. 70-93.

Dodd, C. H., *According to the Scriptures: The Substructure of New Testament Theology.* London: James Nisbet & Co., 1952.

Ebeling, G., "Die Bedeutung der historisch-kritischen Methode für die protestant. Theol. und Kirche," ZThK, 1950, pp. 1-46.

————, "Die Anfänge von Luthers Hermeneutik," ZThK, 1951, pp. 172-230.

————, "The Meaning of 'Biblical Theology,'" JThSt, 6, 1955, pp. 210-255.

————, "Wort Gottes und Hermeneutik," ZThK, 1959, pp. 224-251.

Eichholz, G., "Der Ansatz K. Barths in der Hermeneutik," in *Antwort, Festschrift für K. Barth.* Zollikon-Zürich: Evangelischer Verlag, 1956.

Eichrodt, W., *Theology of the Old Testament.* Philadelphia: The Westminster Press, 1961. British edition: SCM Press.

Elliger, K., "Die Bedeutung der Geschichte Israels für die Kirche Jesu Christi," *Für Arbeit und Besinnung,* II, 1948, pp. 1 ff.

————, "Der Jakobskampf am Jabbok, Gen. 32:22 ff. als hermeneutisches Problem," ZThK, 1951, pp. 1-31.

Ferré, N. F. S., "Notes by a Theologian on Biblical Hermeneutics," JBL, 78, 1959, pp. 105-114.

Filson, F. V., "Method in Studying Biblical History," JBL, 69, 1950, pp. 1-18.

Fohrer, G., "Die zeitliche und überzeitliche Bedeutung des AT," EvTh, 9, 1949/50, pp. 447-460.

————, *Messiasfrage und Bibelverständnis.* Tübingen: Mohr, 1957.

Gogarten, F., *Der Mensch zwischen Gott und Welt.* Stuggart: Friedrich Vorwerk Verlag, 1956.

Goppelt, Leonard, *Typos: Die Typologische Deutung des Alten Testament im Neuen.* Güterssloh: C. Bertelsmann, 1939.

Grass, H., "Grundsätze katholischer Bibelauslegung," ThLZ, 1952, cols. 487 ff.

Gross, H., "Zum Problem Verheissung und Erfüllung," *Bibl. Zeitschr.*, 1959, pp. 3-18.

Hebert, A. G., *The Throne of David*. London: Faber & Faber, 1948.

————, *The Authority of the Old Testament*. London: Faber & Faber, 1947.

Hermann, R., *Gotteswort und Menschenwort in der Bibel*. Berlin: Evangelischer Verlag, 1956.

————, "Offenbarung, Wort und Texte," EvTh, 19, 1959, pp. 99 ff.

Hertzberg, H. W., "Ist Exegese theologisch möglich?", *Für Arbeit und Bessin.*, V, 11.

Hesse, F., "Die Erforschung der Geschichte Israels als theol. Afgabe," KuD, 4, 1958, pp. 1-19.

————, "Das AT in der gegenwärt. Dogmatik," ZSTh, 1960, pp. 1-44.

The Interpreter's Bible, Vol. I: "The History of the Interpretation of the Bible," I, R. M. Grant; II, J. T. McNeill; III, S. Terrien; pp. 106 ff. New York: Abingdon Press, 1951.

Interpretation, Vol. XV, 1961 (all four numbers on Old Testament interpretation).

————, Vol. V, April and July, 1951.

Irwin, W. A., "The Interpretation of the OT," ZAW, 1950, pp. 1-10.

Jacob, E., "L'AT et la Prédication Chrétienne," *Verbum Caro*, IV, 1950.

Jepsen, A., "Probleme der Auslegung des ATs," ZSTh, 23, 1954, pp. 373-386.

Kamlah, W., *Christentum und Geschichtlichkeit*. 1951, 2nd ed. (Chap. 1: "Die Überwindung der christl.-jüdischen Geschichtlichkeit").

Knight, G. A. F., *A Christian Theology of the Old Testament*. Richmond: John Knox Press, 1959. British edition: SCM Press.

Köhler, L., "Christus im Alten und Neuen Testament," ThZ, 9, 1953, pp. 248-259.

Kraeling, E. G., *The Old Testament Since the Reformation*. London: Lutterworth Press, 1955.

Kraus, H.-J., "Freude an Gottes Gesetz," EvTh, 11, 1951/52, pp. 337-351.

————, "Gespräch mit M. Buber," EvTh, 12, 1952/53, pp. 59-77.

————, "Das Problem der Heilsgeschichte in der 'Kirchl. Dogmatik'" in *Antwort, Festschrift für K. Barth*. Zollikon-Zürich: Evangelischer Verlag, 1956, pp. 69-83.

Kümmel, W. G., *Promise and Fulfilment* (Studies in Biblical Theology 23). London: SCM Press, 1957.

Lampe, G. W. H. and K. T. Woollcombe, *Essays on Typology* (Studies in Biblical Theology 22). London: SCM Press, 1957.

Lerch, D., "Zur Frage nach dem Verstehen der Schrift," ZThK, 1952, pp. 351-367.

Lys, D., *A la Recherche d'une Méthode pour l'Exégèse de l'AT* (Études théol. et relig. XXX, 3). Montpellier, 1950.

Maass, F., "Von den Ursprüngen der rabbin. Schriftauslegung," ZThK, 1955, pp. 129 ff.

McCasland, S. V., "The Unity of the Scriptures," JBL, 73, 1954, pp. 1-10.

McKenzie, J. L., "Problems of Hermeneutics in Roman Catholic Exegesis," JBL, 77, 1958, pp. 197-204.

Michaeli, F., *L'Ancien Testament et l'Église chrétienne d'aujourd'hui*. Neuchâtel-Paris: Delachaux & Niestlé, 1957.

————, *La 'Typologie' Biblique* (Foi et Vie 50). 1952.

Michel, O., *Das AT im NT* (Bahnauer Hefte 5, n.d.).

Miskotte, K. H., *Als de goden zwijgen. Over de zin van het OT*. Amsterdam: Utgevesmaatschappij Holland, 1956.

————, *Zur biblischen Hermeneutik*, ThSt, 55, 1959.

Mowinckel, S., *The Old Testament as Word of God*. New York: Abingdon Press, 1959. British edition: Blackwell.

Muilenburg, J., "Preface to Hermeneutics," JBL, 77, 1958, pp. 18-26.

Prenter, R., "Die systematische Theologie und das Problem der Bibelauslegung," ThLZ, 1956, cols. 577 ff.

Preuss, Ch., "The Contemporary Relevance of Von Hofmann's Hermeneutical Principles," *Interpretation*, 1950, pp. 311 ff.

Rad, G. v., *Genesis* (Old Testament Library). Philadelphia: The Westminster Press, 1961. British edition: SCM Press.

————, "Verheissung," EvTh, 13, 1953, pp. 406-413.

————, *Theology of the Old Testament*. Vol. I, New York: Scribner's, 1962; Bd. II, 1960, München, Kaiser. British edition: Oliver and Boyd.

Rendtorff, R., "Zur neueren Auslegung des ATs," VuF, 1956/57, pp. 142-151.

————, "Hermeneutik des ATs als Frage nach der Geschichte," ZThK, 57, 1960, pp. 27 ff.

Rowley, H. H., *The Unity of the Bible*. London: Kingsgate Press, 1953.

Ruler, A. v., *Die christliche Kirche und das AT* (BEvTh 23). München: Chr. Kaiser, 1955.

Rylaarsdam, J. C., "The Problem of Faith and History in Biblical Interpretation," JBL, 77, 1958, pp. 26-32.

Schelkle, K. H., "Heilige Schrift und Wort Gottes," *Theol. Quartalsschr.*, 1958, pp. 257-274.

————, "Von alter und neuer Auslegung," *Bibl. Zschr.*, 1957, pp. 161-176.

Schildenberger, J., *Vom Geheimnis des Gotteswortes*. 1950.

————, "Vollsinn und typischer Sinn im AT," *Bibel und Liturgie*, 24, 1956/57.

Schlink, E., "Gesetz und Paraklese," in *Antwort, Festschrift für K. Barth*. Zollikon-Zürich: Evangelischer Verlag, 1956, pp. 323-335.

Schnackenburg, R., "Der Weg der katholischen Exegese," *Bibl. Zschr.*, NF 2, 1958, pp. 161-176.

Schmid, J., "Die alttestamentl. Zitate bei Paulus und die Theorie vom sensus plenior," *Bibl. Zschr.*, NF 3, 1959, pp. 161-173.

Schweitzer, W., "Das Problem der bibl. Hermeneutik in der gegenwärt. Theologie," ThLZ, 1950, cols. 467-478. (Contains a survey of Hermeneutics in both the Old Testament and the New Testament up to 1950 and lists books published after 1938 and articles appearing after 1945. The survey may be used in connection with the present bibliography as a further look into the past.)

Sick, H. J., "Der heilsgeschichtl. Bezug der Jabbok-Perikope," EvTh, 14, 1954, pp. 466 ff.

Stendhal, K., "Implications of Form-Criticism and Tradition-Criticism for Biblical Interpretation," JBL, 77, 1958, pp. 33-38.

Smart, James D., *The Interpretation of Scripture*. Philadelphia: The Westminster Press, 1961. British edition: SCM Press.

Sutcliff, E. F., "The Plenary Sense as a Principle of Interpretation," *Biblica*,
1953, pp. 333 ff.

de Vaux, Roland, "A propos de l'théologie biblique," ZAW, 1956, pp. 225 ff.

Vergegenwärtigung, Aufsätze zur Auslegung des ATs. Berlin: Evangelischer
Verlag, 1955.

Vischer, Wilhelm, *Die Bedeutung des Alten Testaments für das christlichen
Leben* (ThSt 3), 2nd ed., 1947.

————, *The Witness of the Old Testament to Christ*. London: Lutterworth
Press, 1949.

Vriezen, Th. C., "Theokratie und Soteriologie," EvTh, 1956, pp. 395 ff.

————, *An Outline of Old Testament Theology*. Oxford: Blackwells, 1955.

Westermann, C., *Verkündigung des Kommenden. Predigten alttestamentlicher Texte*. Münich: Chr. Kaiser Verlag, 1958.

Wildberger, H., "Auf dem Wege zu einer biblischen Theologie. Erwägungen
zur Hermeneutik des ATs," EvTh, 19, 1959, pp. 70-90.

Wolf, H. H., *Die Einheit des Bundes. Das Verhältnis von Altem und Neuem
Testament bei Calvin*. Neukirchen Kreis Moers: Verlag der Buchhandlung des Erziehungsvereins, 1958.

Wolff, H. W., *Jesaja 53 im Urchristentum*. 1952, 3rd ed.

————, "Der grosse Jesreeltag," EvTh, 12, 1952/53, pp. 78-104.

————, "Erwägungen zur typolog. Auslegung des ATs," ZdZ, 10, 1956, pp.
446 ff.

————, *Die Bibel—Gottes Wort oder Menschenwort?* Dargestellt am Buch
Jona und am Apostolat des Paulus nach 2. Kor. 4. Mit J. Moltmann
u.R. Bohren. Kreis Moers: Verlag der Buchhandlung des Erziehungsvereins, 1959.

Wood, James D., *The Interpretation of the Bible: A Historical Introduction*.
London: Duckworth Press, 1958.

Wright, G. E., *God Who Acts* (Studies in Biblical Theology 8). London:
SCM Press, 1952.

————, "Archaeology and OT-Studies," JBL, 77, 1958, pp. 39-51.

————, "Interpreting the Old Testament," *Theology Today*, 1946-47, pp.
190 ff.

Zimmerli, W., *Das AT als Anrede* (BEvTh 24). München: Chr. Kaiser Verlag,
1956.

————, "Das Gesetz im AT," ThLZ, 1960, cols. 481 ff.

ORIGINAL TITLES AND SOURCES

1. GERHARD VON RAD, Das Alte Testament ist ein Geschichtsbuch
   ("Typologische Auslegung des Alten Testaments," *Evangelische The-ologie*, 12, Jahrgang, 1952/53, pp. 17-33. Chr. Kaiser Verlag, München; and *Interpretation*, July 1961.)
2. CLAUS WESTERMANN, Zur Auslegung des Alten Testaments (Geschicht-liche Einleitung)
   (Shortened version of the first part of "Zur Auslegung des Alten Testaments," *Vergegenwärtigung*, 1955, pp. 88-100. Evangelische Ver-lagsanstalt, Berlin.)
3. RUDOLF BULTMANN, Weissagung und Erfüllung
   (*Glauben und Verstehen*, 2. Band, 1952, pp. 162-186. J. C. B. Mohr [Paul Siebeck], Tübingen.)
4. MARTIN NOTH, Die Vergegenwärtigung des Alten Testaments in der Verkündigung
   (*Evangelische Theologie*, 12, Jahrgang, 1952/53, pp. 6-17; and *Interpretation*, Jan. 1961.)
5. WALTHER ZIMMERLI, Verheissung und Erfüllung
   (*Evangelische Theologie*, 12, Jahrgang, 1952/53, pp. 34-59; and *Interpretation*, April 1961.)
6. CLAUS WESTERMANN, Bemerkungen zu den Thesen Bultmanns und Baum-gärtels
   (Shortened version of the second part of "Zur Auslegung des Alten Testaments," *Vergegenwärtigung*, 1955, pp. 101-116.)
7. FRIEDRICH BAUMGÄRTEL, Das hermeneutische Problem des Alten Testa-ments
   (*Theologische Literaturzeitung*, 79, Jahrgang, 1954, cols. 199-212. Evangelische Verlagsanstalt, Berlin.)
8. HANS WALTER WOLFF, Zur Hermeneutik des Alten Testaments
   (*Evangelische Theologie*, 16, Jahrgang, 1956, pp. 337-370; and *Interpretation*, Oct. 1961.)
9. JOHANN JAKOB STAMM, Jesus Christus und das Alte Testament
   (*Evangelische Theologie*, 16, Jahrgang, 1956, pp. 387-395.)
10. TH. C. VRIEZEN, Theokratie und Soteriologie
    (*Evangelische Theologie*, 16, Jahrgang, 1956, pp. 395-404.)
11. WALTHER EICHRODT, Ist die typologische Exegese sachgemässe Exegese?
    (*Vetus Testamentum*, Supplement IV, 1957, pp. 161-180.)
12. ALFRED JEPSEN, Wissenschaft vom Alten Testament
    (Shortened version of pamphlet 1 in the series "Aufsätze und Vor-träge zur Theologie und Religionswissenschaft." Hrsg. Erdmann Schott und Hans Urner, 1958. Evangelische Verlagsanstalt, Berlin.)
13. FRANZ HESSE, Zur Frage der Wertung und der Geltung alttestamentlicher Texte

(*Festschrift zum 70. Geburtstag von Professor Friedrich Baumgärtel.*
Erlanger Forschungen, Reihe A, Band 10, 1959, pp. 74-96. Universi-
tätsbung Erlangen e. V.)

14. WOLFHART PANNENBERG, Heilsgeschehen und Geschichte
(Shortened version of the first part of "Heilsgeschehen und Geschichte,"
Kerygma und Dogma, 1959, pp. 218-237. Vandenhoeck & Ruprecht,
Göttingen.)

15. HANS WALTER WOLFF, Das Geschichtsverständnis der alttestamentlichen
Prophetie
(Evangelische Theologie, 20, Jahrgang, 1960, pp. 218-235.)

INDEX OF PASSAGES CITED

I. *Old Testament References*

365

II. *New Testament References*

9:9	52, 54	3:24	74	8:5	63, 229
10:1 ff.	226	3:27 f.	63	8:6 ff.	228
10:1-4	52	4:24 f.	188	8:8-11	52
10:1-11	228	4:24 ff.	232	8:8-12	62
10:4	328	5:6	63	9:9	230
10:5-7	52	5:22 ff.	209	9:12	114
10:6	180, 226, 229	6:2	175	9:24	180, 229
10:11	50, 180, 229	6:15	63, 72	10:1	63, 180
10:15	78	6:16	114, 172	10:5-7	54
10:18	72			10:10	114
11:25	176	EPHESIANS		10:16 f.	62
12:12	63	3:6	129, 130	11	86
12:12 ff.	179	5:23	181	11:19	230
14:21	54			12:18	35
15:23-28	67	PHILIPPIANS		12:18 ff.	179
15:27	52, 54	3:3	63, 72	12:26	54
16:22	114	3:12	115	13:12 f.	62
		3:12 f.	114		
2 CORINTHIANS				JAMES	
1:20	113, 128, 181	COLOSSIANS		1:1	72, 173
2:14-16	67	1:15	217	5:10 f.	86
2:16	193	2:11	63		
3:16-18	62	2:16 ff.	179	1 PETER	
3:7 ff.	38, 225, 226	2:17	180	2:5, 9	226
3:12 ff.	182	3:11	63	2:10	174
3:12-16	301			3:21	181
4:7 ff.	63	HEBREWS		4:8 ff.	179
5:7	114, 334	1	218	4:17	193
6:2	67	1:1	36, 88, 120		
8 f.	179	1:3	222	1 JOHN	
9:12	178	2:6-8	54	5:4	68
10:3	67	3:1-6	225	5:12	175
		4	179		
GALATIANS		6:6	193	REVELATION	
2	179	7:13	230	1:6	226
3	183, 189, 306, 334	7:15	230	7:4 ff.	173
3:15 ff.	323	7:23 ff.	175	21:12-14	173
3:22 f.	74	7:27	114	22:20	114

III. References to the Pseudepigrapha

ASSUMPTION OF MOSES		SYRIAC APOCALYPSE	
10:1	65	OF BARUCH	
		21:23, 25	65

IV. References to Early Christian Writings

BARNABUS		1 CLEMENT	
9:8	55	17:7	55

INDEX OF AUTHORS